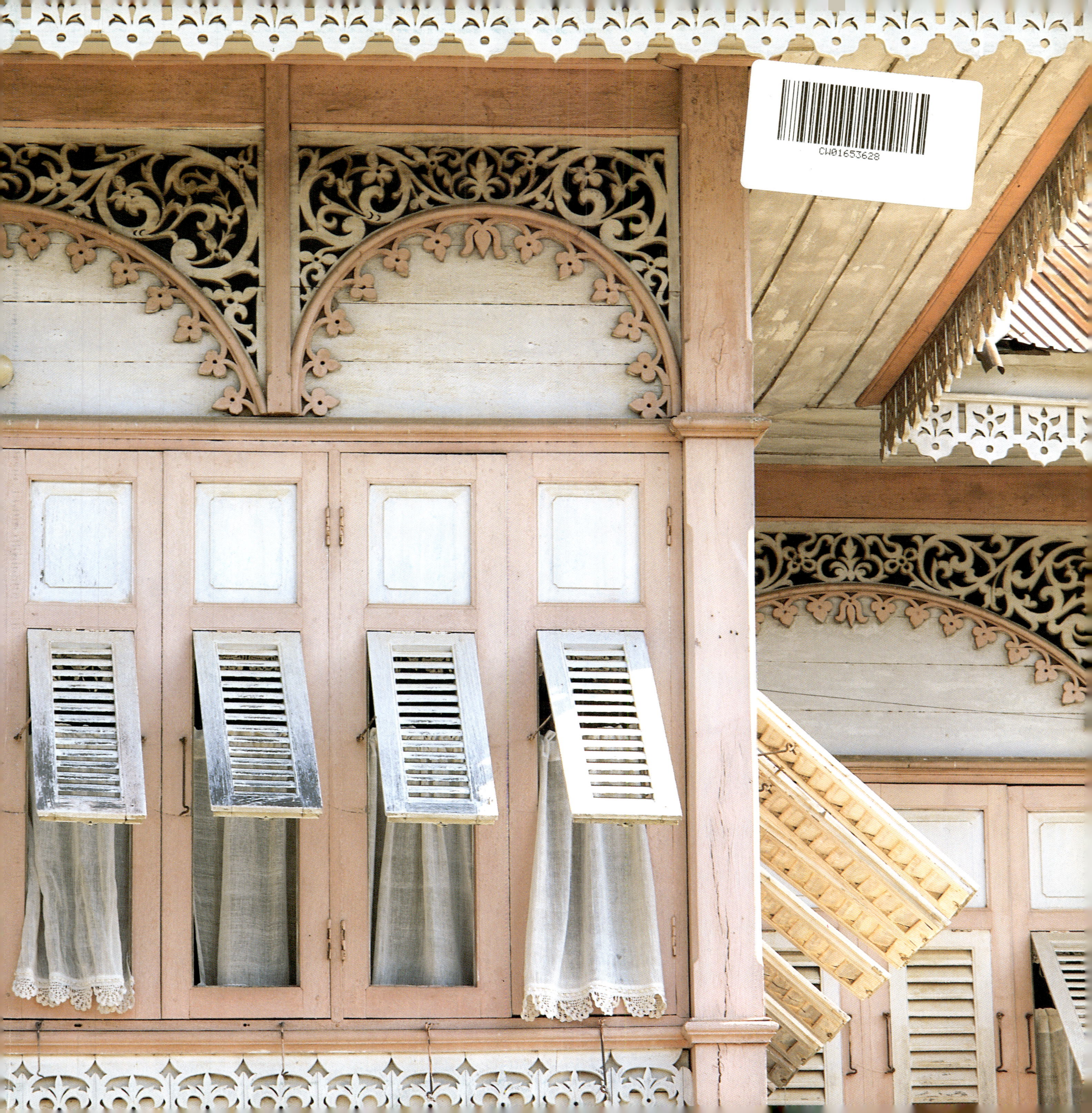

HERITAGE HOMES OF THAILAND

Third Printing 1999
ISBN: 974 8298 34 5

Published by The Siam Society Under Royal Patronage
131 Soi Asoke, Sukhumvit 21, Bangkok 10110, Thailand
Tel: (662) 661-6470-7; Fax: (662) 258-3491
E-mail: siams@telecom.scb.co.th
www.siam-society.org

Distributed in Thailand by Asia Books Co., Ltd.
5 Sukhumvit Road, Soi 61
P.O. Box 40, Bangkok 10110, Thailand
Tel: (662) 714-0740-2, ext 221-223
Fax: (662) 391-2277, 381-1621
E-mail: asiabook@ksc.th.com

Produced by Monsoon Editions
245/3 Sukhumvit 21, Bangkok 10110, Thailand
Tel & Fax: (662) 258-7184
E-mail: pimpa@loxinfo.co.th

Originally sponsored by Amway (Thailand) Ltd.
Research by Vimala Siripongse
Printed by Sirivatana Interprint Pcl.
Color separation by One Hundred Co., Ltd.

This entire book has been printed on paper from Advance Agro
and 100% of the pulp used has originated from tree farms,
thus preserving our natural forests.

Cover jacket photo : *Interior of Devavesm Palace, built during the reign of King Rama VI.*
Back jacket : *Classically-inspired columns and Palladian window in a hallway of Bangkhunprom Palace.*
Inside cover : *Louvered shutters of Vongburi House in Phrae.*
Pages 2-3 : *Interior of Chateau William on Klong Mon in Bangkok.*
Page 4 : *Upstairs of the Gingerbread House, located in the heart of Bangkok.*
Page 6 : *Fountain in the garden of Bangkhunprom Palace.*
Page 8 : *Stairhall of Devavesm Palace.*

HERITAGE HOMES of Thailand

THE SIAM SOCIETY
Under Royal Patronage

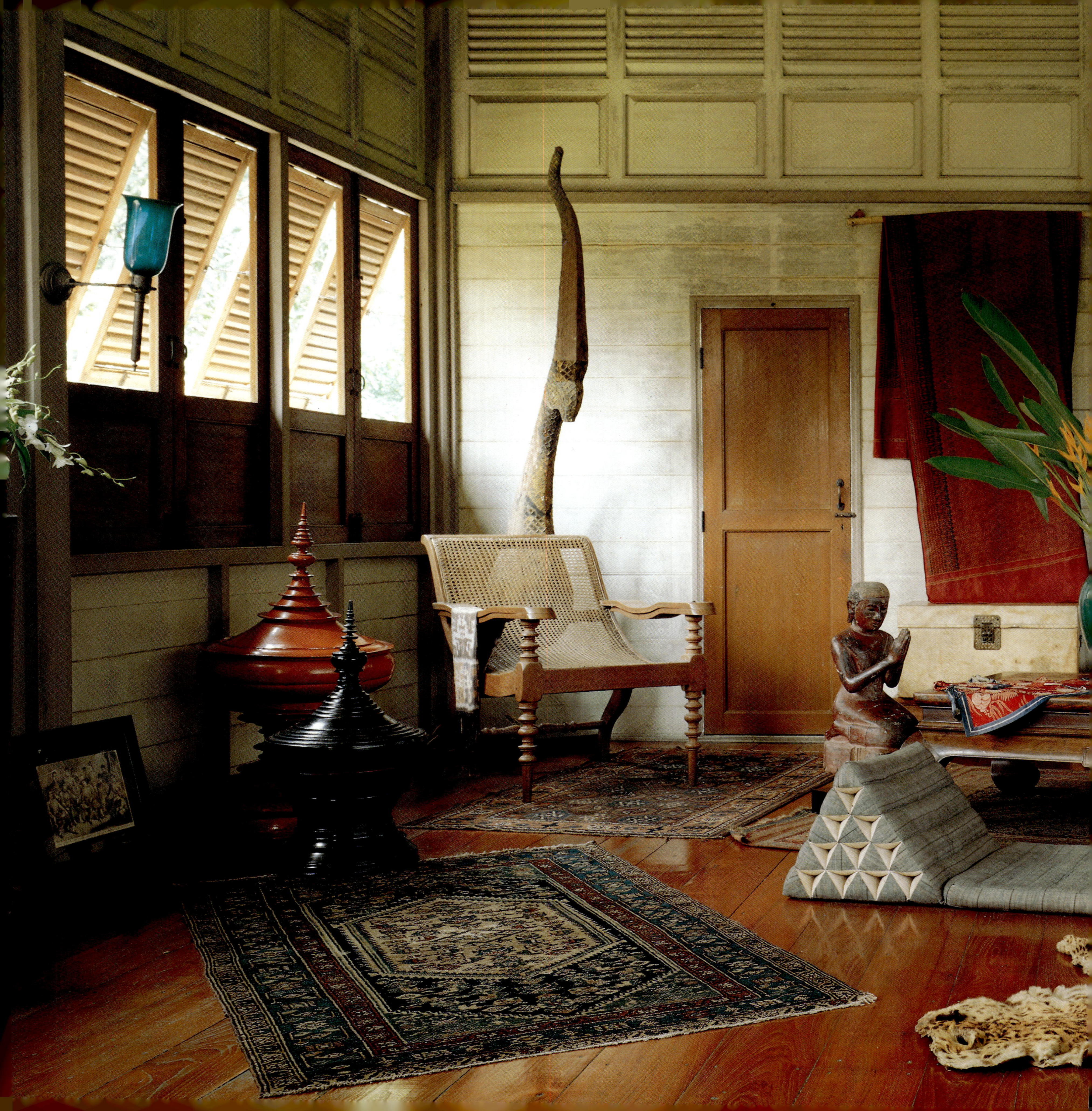

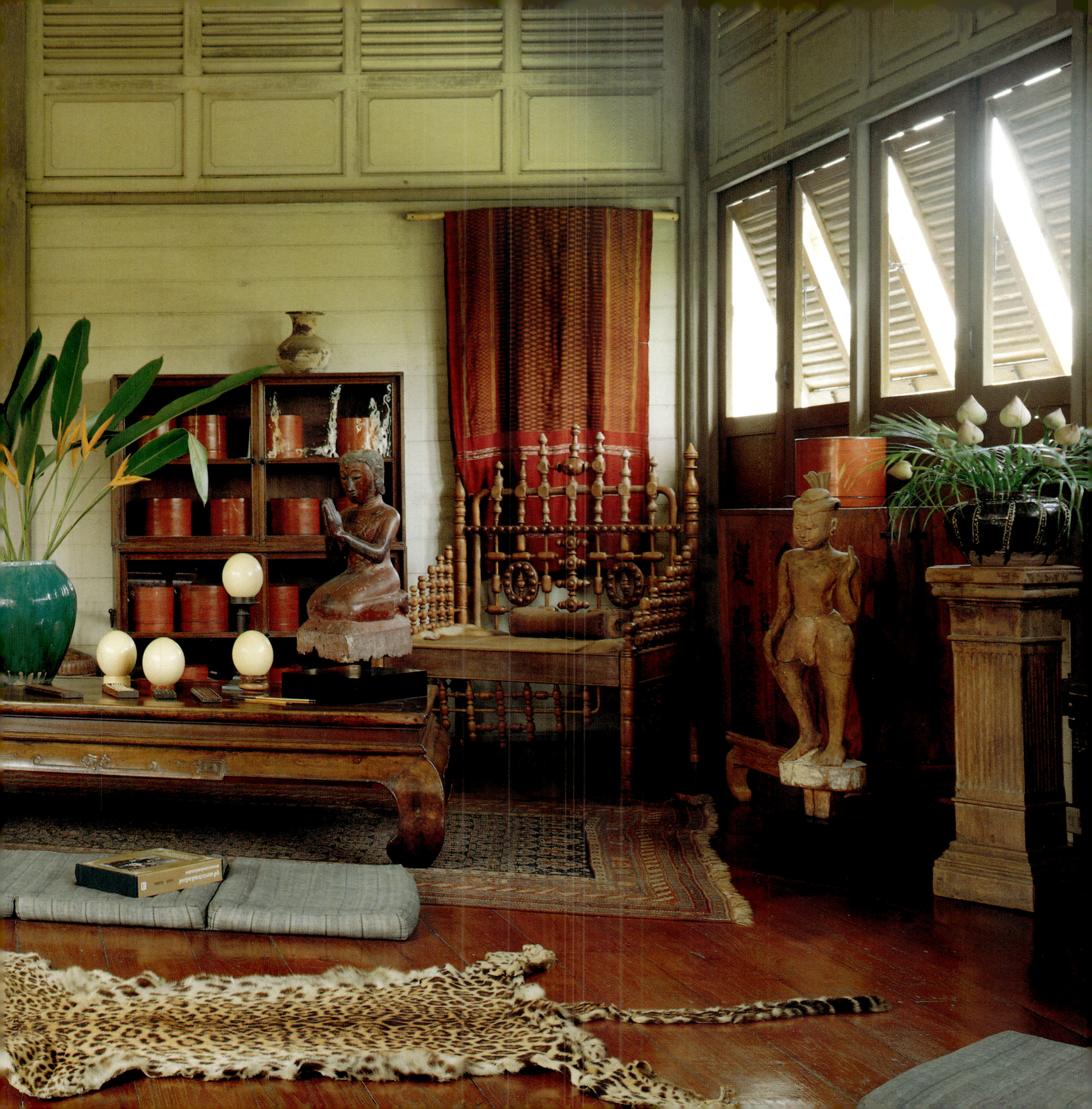

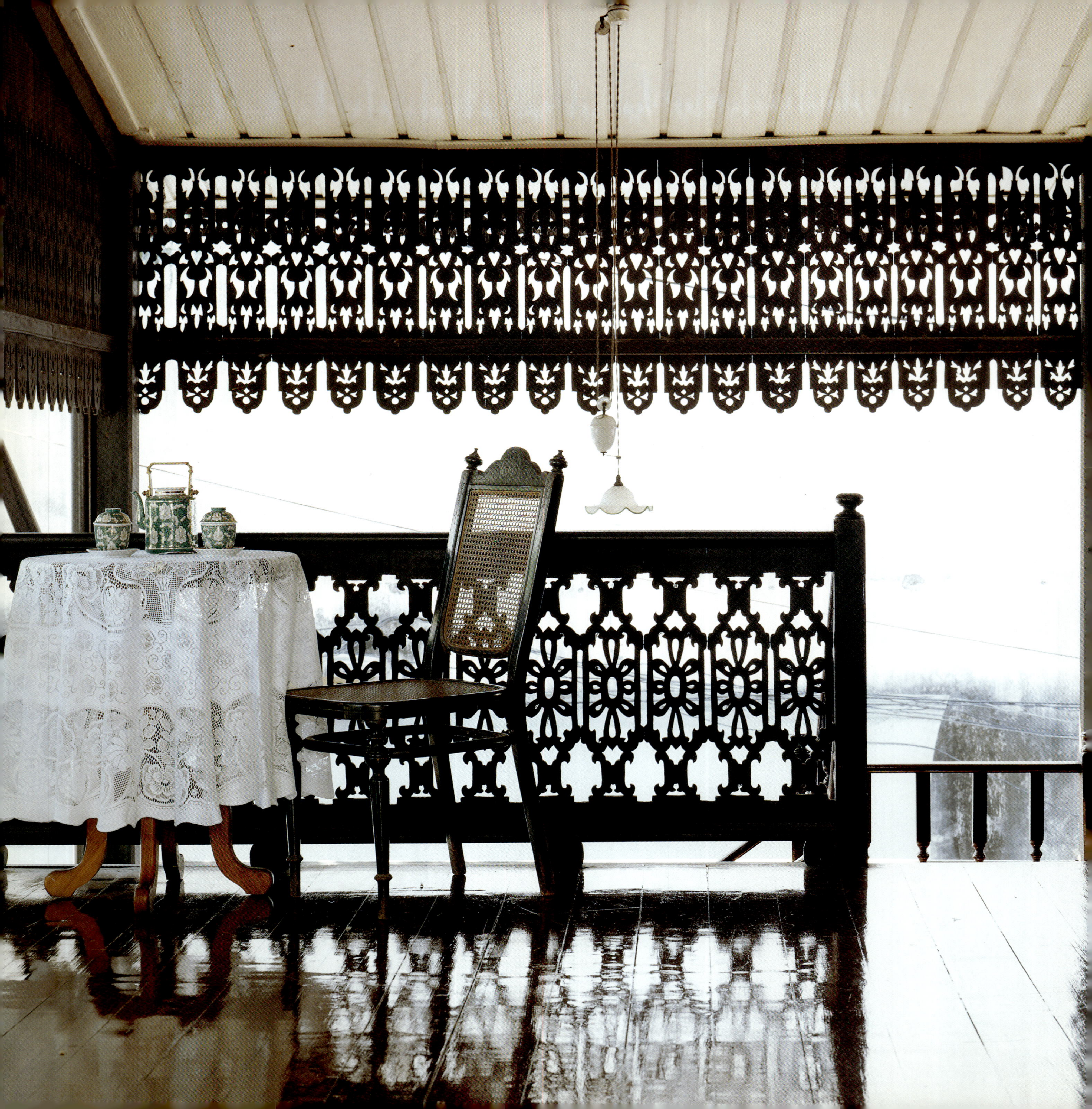

THE SIAM SOCIETY
Under Royal Patronage

Heritage Homes of Thailand

Photographed by **Ping Amranand** • Written by **William Warren**

ASIA BOOKS

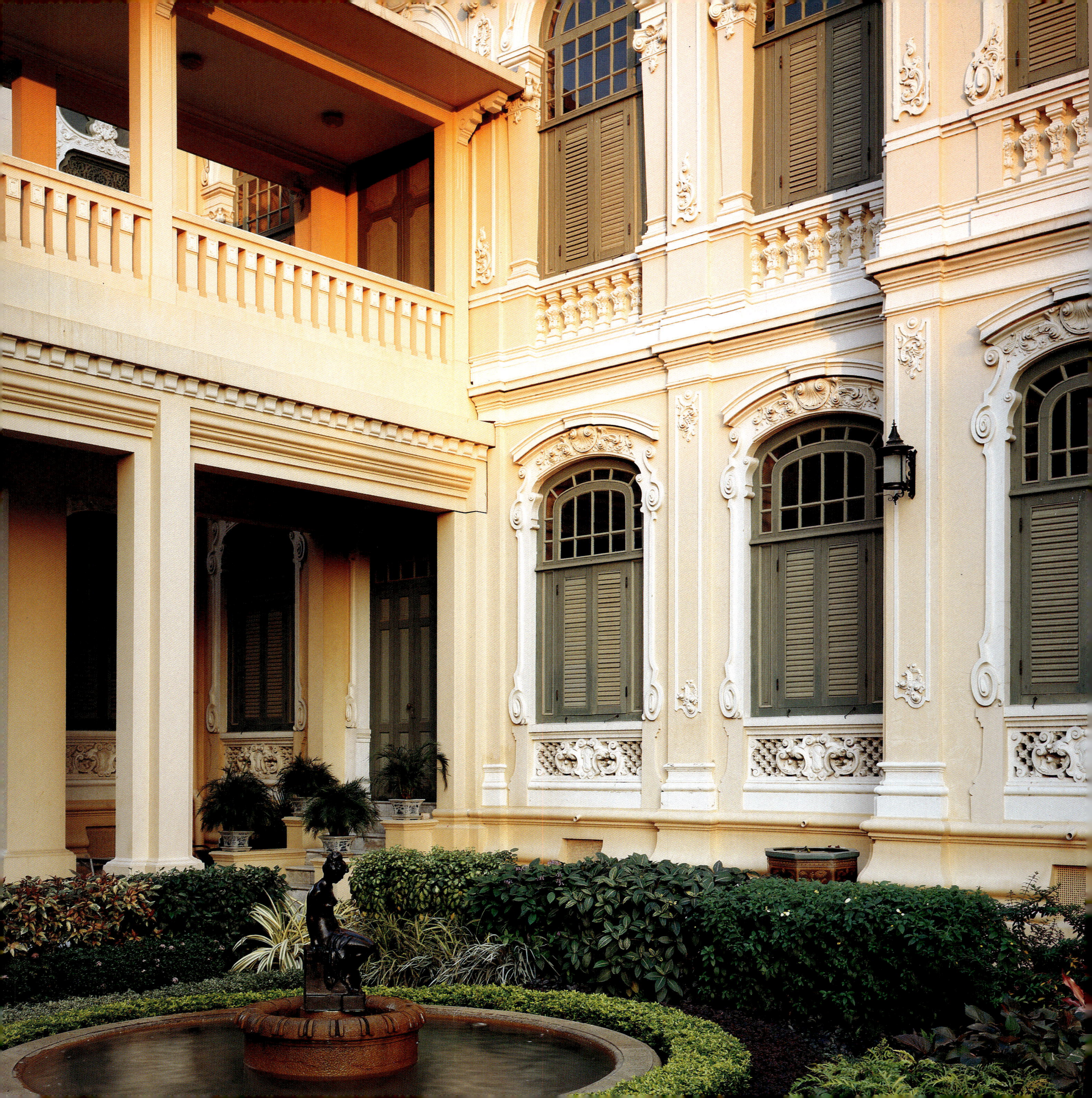

Contents

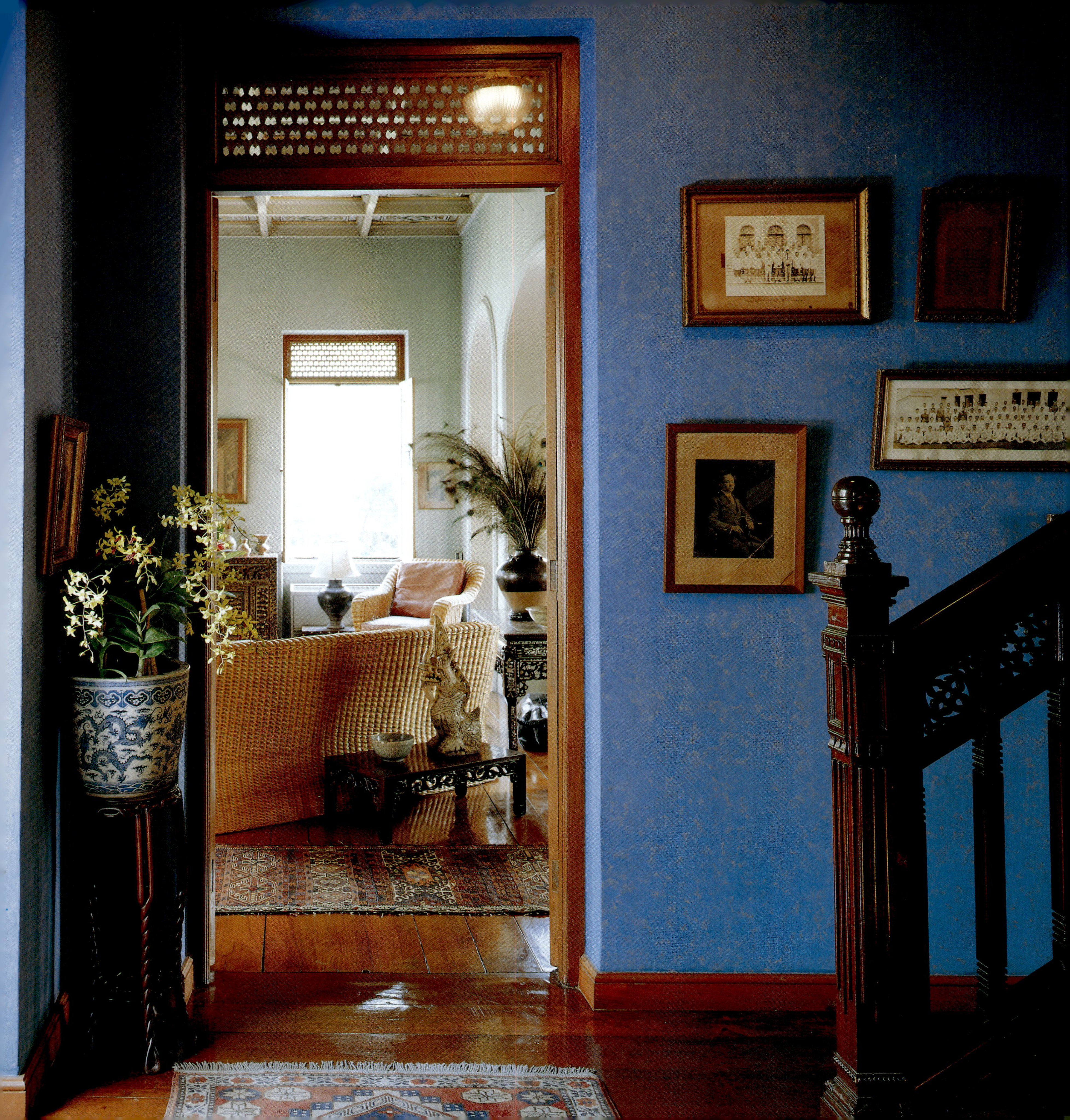

Foreword

Dedication To
Her Royal Highness Princess Galyani Vadhana
Krom Luang Naradhiwas Rajanagarindra

The Heritage Homes of Thailand program was inaugurated by The Siam Society on the occasion of the Sixth Cycle Birthday Anniversary of Her Royal Highness Princess Galyani Vadhana Krom Luang Naradhiwas Rajanagarindra.

It is my privilege to dedicate this book, which forms a part of that program, to Her Royal Highness. Her generous interest and guidance is a constant source of inspiration to all those engaged in the conservation of Thailand's historical and cultural heritage.

At no time in our nation's history has Thailand's architectural heritage been under as great a threat as it is today. The initiative taken by The Siam Society to promote the conservation of the country's secular architectural heritage is admirable. Even more heartening is that the Society recognizes that these ambitious goals cannot be achieved through the sole undertakings of any single person or any individual organization, however committed or active they may be. The collective effort of the public and private sectors, as well as of dedicated professionals is essential if important parts of our national heritage are to survive the pressures of rapid economic development.

I would like to take this opportunity to call on every individual to play their part in this effort, as well as encourage the public and private sectors to extend their organizational skills and numerous other resources for the accomplishment of this important mission.

P. Krairiksh

Dr. Piriya Krairiksh
Chairman of the Board of Trustees
'The Heritage Homes of Thailand'

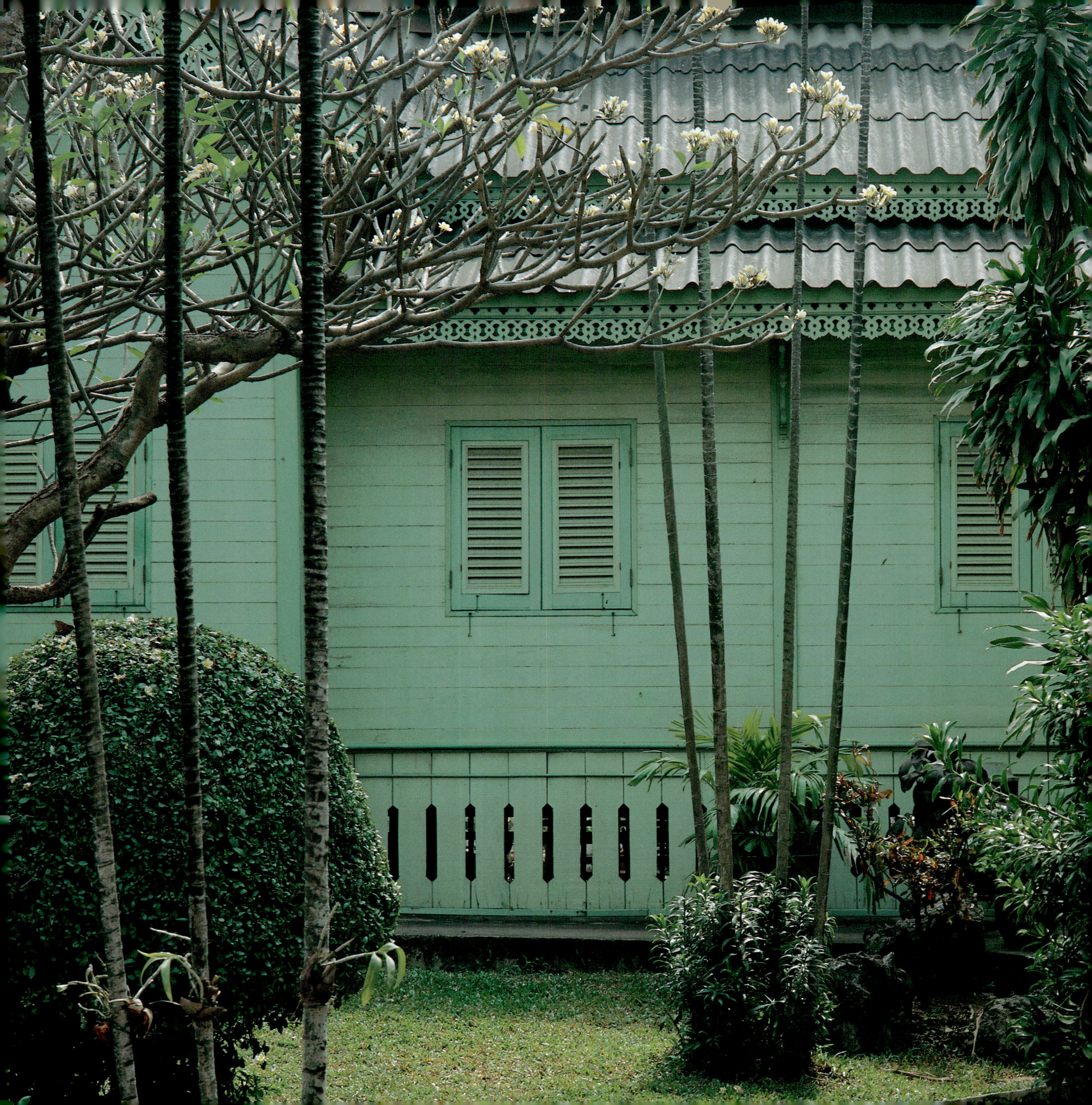

Introduction

An Endangered Heritage

In 1852, seventeen years after he took up residence in Bangkok, the American missionary Dr. Dan Beach Bradley decided to build his dream house. He had suffered considerably in previous residences. The first, which he and his wife shared with another couple, was a rough, barn-like structure on a plot of low, swampy land, within audible distance of the main Chinese market ("well-located for coming in contact with the people," Bradley noted tartly, "but a miserable place for the settlement of [missionary] families"). Later he moved across the Chao Phraya River to another house near the present Santa Cruz Cathedral, a district then mostly inhabited by Portuguese and other Europeans. This was not much of an improvement, however; made of wood, it was thatched with attap leaves and had only two rooms above a low basement floor, as well as a narrow verandah on the front.

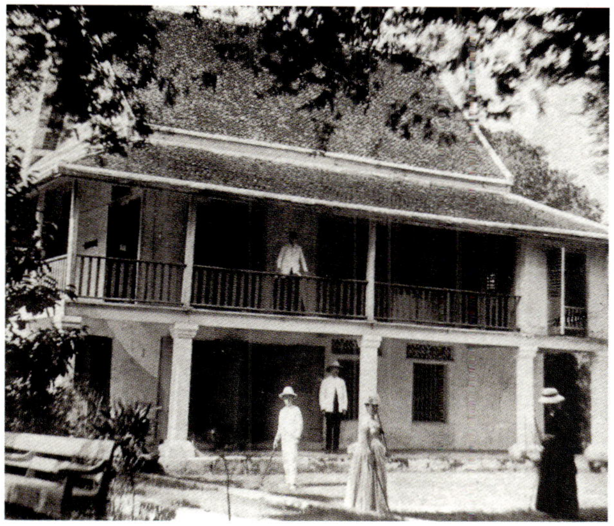

One feature particularly annoyed the doctor. "The two doors leading into the bedroom and verandah had, in accord with the best style of those ancient times, each a threshold ten or twelve inches high, which warned us perpetually to take heed to our steps and continually demanded of us extraordinary efforts to pass over them. They were practically toll gates, taking strength from us incessantly. Oh what a source of weariness they were to the delicate unacclimated housewife! It makes me weary even to think of them."

Such raised thresholds were, of course, a feature of traditional Thai-style houses, providing architectural support for the prefabricated method of their construction; but Dr. Bradley was determined not to have them if he ever got to build a house of his own. He wanted something light and airy, easy of access, with plenty of room—something, indeed, very similar to the charming missionary dwellings he had stayed in on a stop in Singapore en route to Siam, which in turn were inspired by the classic bungalows built by the British throughout their tropical empire.

His opportunity came when he was given royal permission to settle on the right bank of Klong Bang Luang, now known as Klong Bangkok Yai. Here he put up two large houses, each two stories tall with tiled roofs. Spacious verandahs extended all around them, the doors went down to the floor, and "the upper part of the window shutters were made of a coarse kind of Venetian blinds, the first thing of the kind ever made in Siam."

Bradley's house survived for a surprisingly long time after his death in 1873 and that of his second wife in 1893. His daughter Irene continued to live there for nearly fifty years, sharing it with two broods of dogs—one upstairs and one down—who never came into contact. In 1941, the year she died, the Thai government asked for the property to be returned but she refused, saying that it had been given to the family by King Mongkut (Rama IV). Actually, there was no title deed and the land did in fact belong to the government. No one knew this until after her

Above : *Dr. Bradley's house in the late 19th century.*
Left : *Wooden house in Royal Navy compound (c. 1903) adjacent to the site where the Bradley home once stood and formerly used as hospital for naval students.*

Below : *King Taksin's Palace in the Royal Navy compound, built in the 18th century when Thonburi was the capital.*

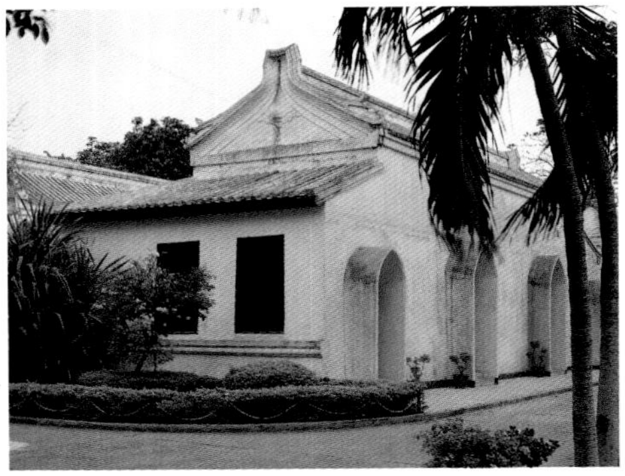

death, however, when the house (and presumably the dogs) became a part of the Royal Thai Navy headquarters.

Forgotten by the city, the building remained behind the thick walls of the compound for several more decades. Eventually, however, by which time it was no doubt showing its age, it was torn down and replaced by a nondescript modern cooperative store for workers in the compound.

Why should we regret the passing of the Bradley home? Not solely because of the architectural novelties that so pleased its builder. Others in the same general bungalow style can still be found elsewhere in Bangkok, especially in the older sections near the river, though in steadily dwindling numbers. But an additional quality did indeed make it special and worth preserving and that was the aura of history that clung to those cool verandahs and pioneering Venetian blinds. While Bradley, like most of his fellow missionaries, enjoyed very limited success at making Christian converts, he nevertheless looms as a major figure in the Thai past, credited with the introduction of modern surgery, vaccination against smallpox, and the printing press, as well as the first newspaper, to which his friend King Mongkut often contributed articles. By providing a visible link with this remarkable man and his achievements, the house formed an important part of Thailand's heritage, and its destruction thus assumes much greater significance, especially when viewed as part of a continuing process that threatens countless others.

Buddhist temples and a few royal buildings appear to be relatively safe, at least for the time being, but these are exceptions; increasingly in recent years, countless residences (including some originally built by royalty) of architectural and historic value have disappeared, most of them without stirring any sort of protest. A drive along Bangkok's Sathorn Road offers compelling evidence of the process at work. Even twenty years ago this was one of the city's most attractive streets, shaded by mango and mahogany trees and lined with elegant mansions built in the early years of the century. Nearly all are now gone and the rest are under imminent threat. The same is true not only in other parts of the capital but elsewhere in Thailand as well.

The historic homes that still exist mostly owe their survival not so much to any real appreciation of their cultural value but rather to geography and relative land values. Bangkok, for example, was originally centered on areas close to the Chao Phraya River—Rattanakosin Island, Chinatown, and, somewhat later, the Dusit District where King Chulalongkorn (Rama V) sought to emulate the broad avenues and parks of European capitals. When the city embarked on its rapid expansion after the Second World War, new centers rose far from the river and far, too, from the spacious residences of the past. Often neglected and faded by heat and rain, sometimes concealed behind a grim wall of non-descript row shops, a few still sheltered descendants of the families who had built them, while others were turned to commercial uses but nevertheless retained their essential character. Developers, so far at least, have not really been tempted; the big profits still lie elsewhere in the newer suburbs, where there is plenty of room for shopping centers and high-rises; even Dr. Bradley's house, secluded within the Navy compound—indeed, only a short distance from the Chinese-style palace where King Taksin resided during Thonburi's brief period as capital—might have survived if it had been tucked away in a less useful place.

The same has been true outside the capital. Chiang Mai and Lampang

Below : *The controversial Chinese Chamber of Commerce on Sathorn Road, threatened with demolition.*

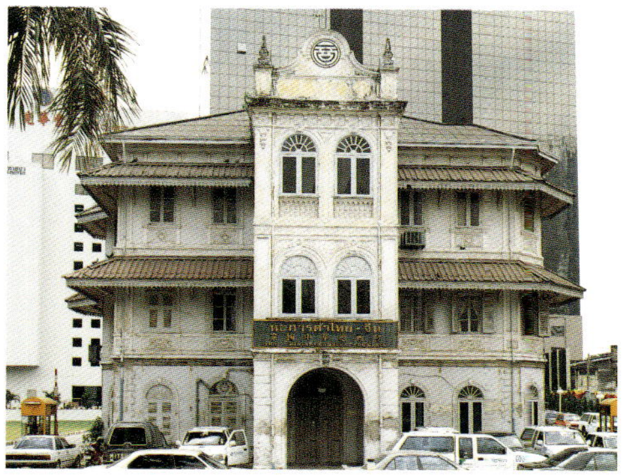

were small towns even a decade or so ago, Hua Hin merely a quiet resort favored by aristocratic families, Phuket a prosperous but remote island mainly known for its tin mining. Not until the advent of mass tourism and the consequent rise in land values did the old residences in these places face a real threat to their continued existence.

There are, of course, highly practical arguments against the preservation of such buildings, and most of them were expressed during a debate in 1995 over whether or not to tear down one being used by the Chinese Chamber of Commerce on lower Sathorn. Graceful as the old structure was, it was in such a state of disrepair that large sums would have to be spent on restoration. Even worse, in the opinion of some, it blocked the view of the very expensive modern high-rise that loomed behind it on the valuable piece of property. Finally, or so one of the owners was quoted as saying, it was not 'Thai' but rather Western in style and so of no architectural value—a curious point that, if applied generally, could justify the destruction of nearly every royal palace built since the middle of the 19th century.

Whether voiced or not, these are the arguments that have led to the destruction of countless other buildings. The only valid response is that the old houses, whatever their condition, reflect various periods in Thailand's past; they should be preserved, not merely because of architectural or historical distinction, but because, once lost, they can never be replaced.

Other countries, of course, have faced the same problem and met it in varying ways. In some, like England and France, the value of such buildings has long been recognized by both the government and the public and thus they are protected by strict laws, not merely from destruction but from drastic alterations; special funds, either official or from business firms, are available to help offset the high cost of their maintenance. Elsewhere, as in the United States and Singapore, awareness came late—very late in the case of Singapore—but not too late to save many historic structures. In a few places, Hong Kong for example, the past has been almost entirely obliterated in the name of progress—all one sees is the present, impressive in its way to be sure but lacking any sense of contrast and evolution.

"Throughout Asia, which culturally tends to prefer the new, preservation of old houses generally has low priority," Donald Smith has written in the National Geographic. "Most Asian countries preserve major sites such as palaces, shrines, and temples, where hordes of tourists come to catch glimpses of the opulent lifestyles of the wealthy, the powerful, and the holy...But many of the structures where ordinary people lived and worked have disappeared, victims of wrecking balls."

In Thailand, there are some suggestions of a change in attitude. A number of the houses in this book have been not only preserved but lovingly restored by their owners; they have become a source of pride, even when they might have provided large sums of money. Some, like King Taksin's Palace, have been recognized as historic structures and transformed into museums that will continue to attract future generations. Official and private organizations like the Fine Arts Department and the Association of Siamese Architects are playing a more effective role in educating the public on the importance of such buildings and working for their preservation.

Only if such efforts continue and increase can this valuable part of our endangered cultural heritage be saved.

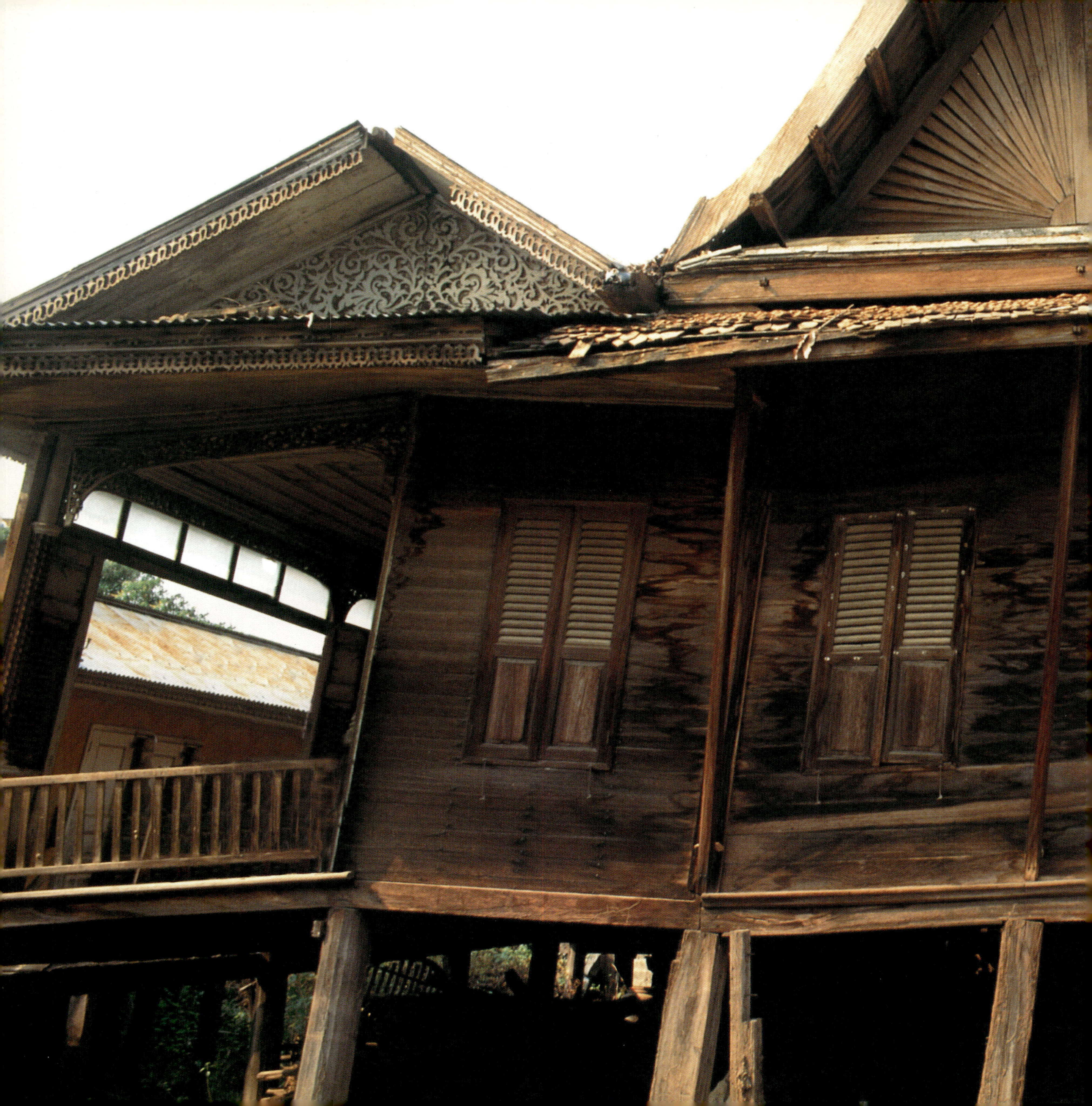

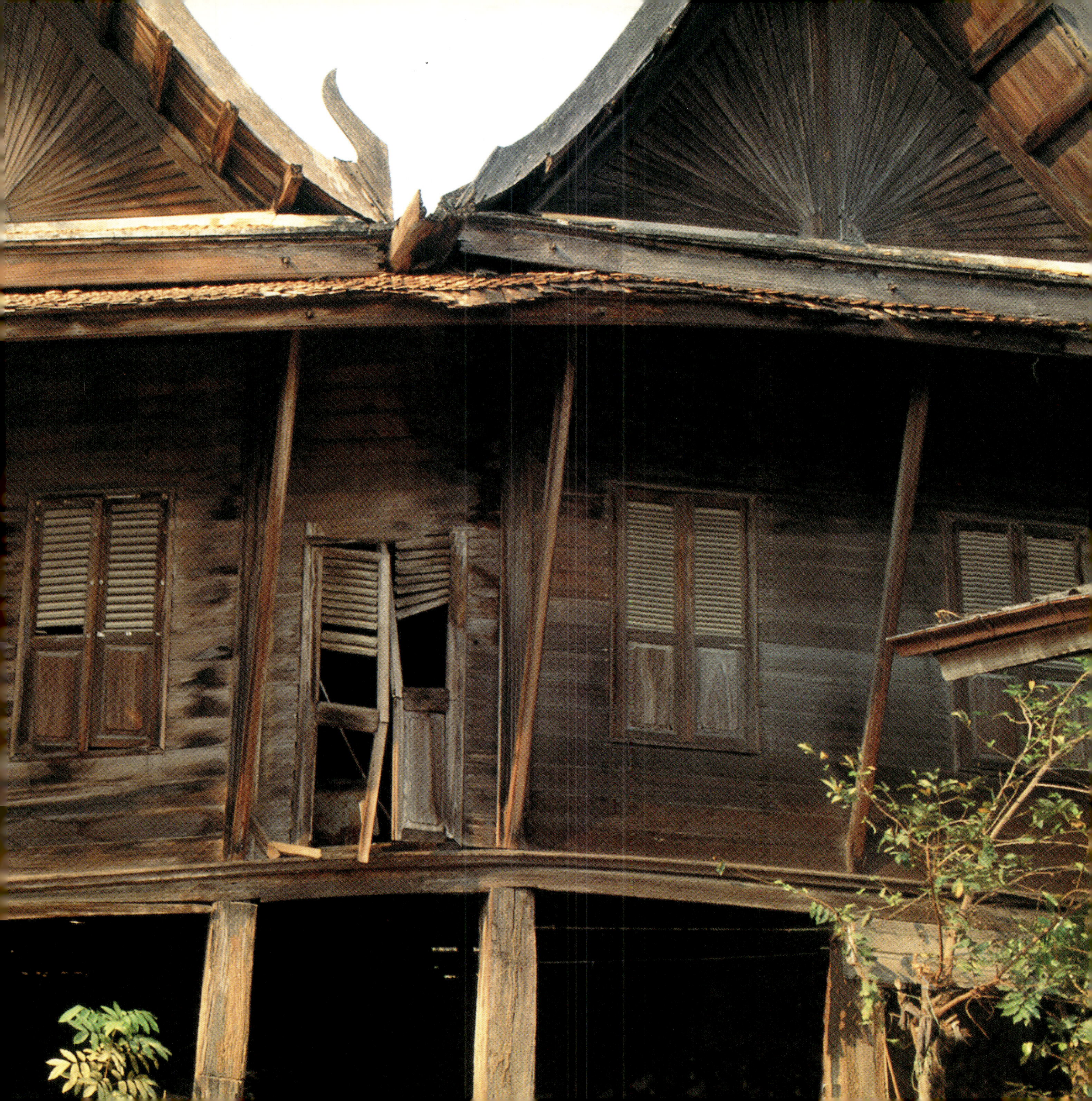

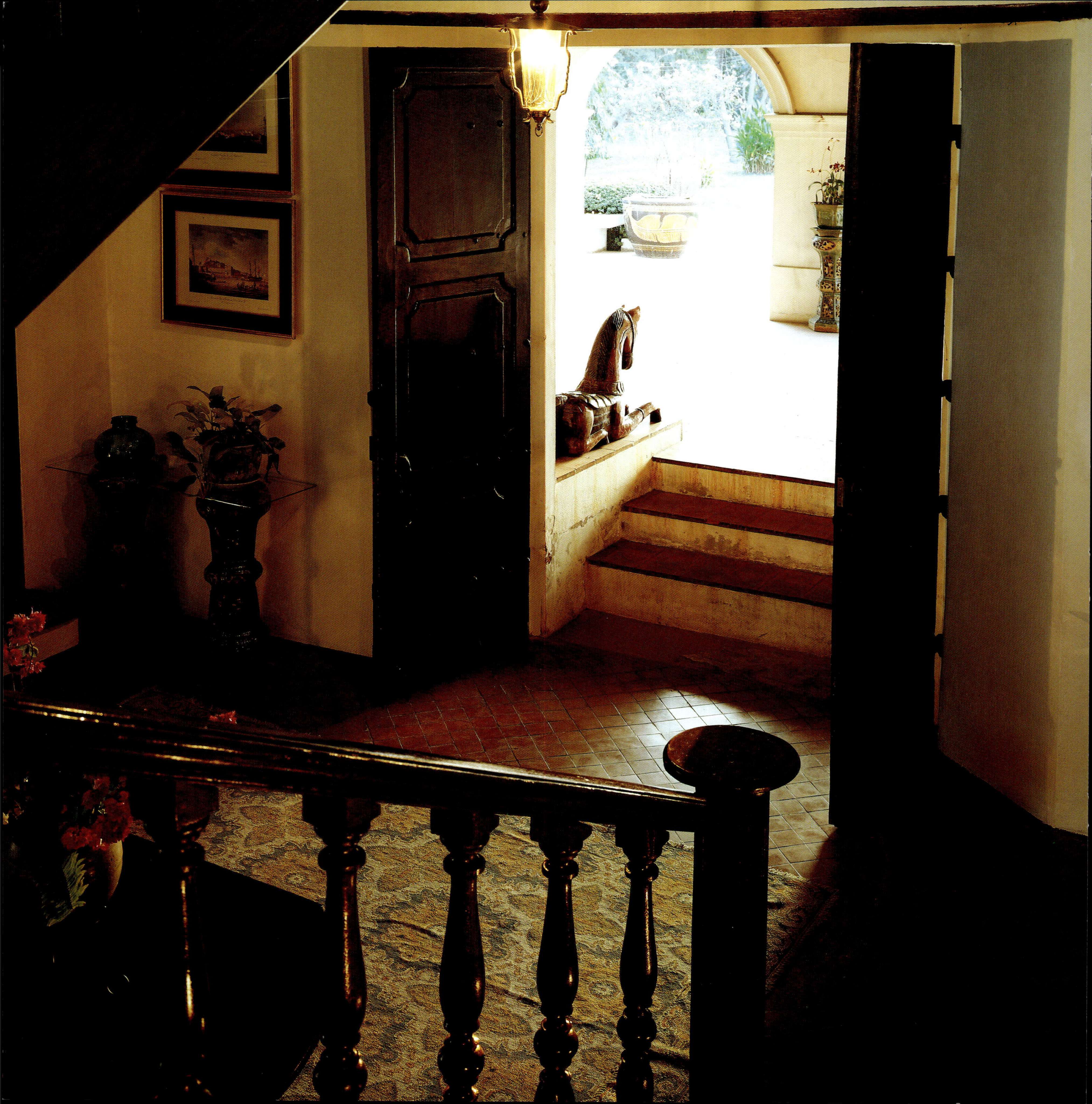

Bangkok & Environs

Established as the capital in 1782, Bangkok remained for the next fifty-odd years a predominantly Thai city. The Grand Palace enclosure and several of the Buddhist temples were conscious recreations of similar buildings in the old capital of Ayutthaya, from which many of the materials used in their construction came, while ordinary people lived mostly in plain wood or bamboo houses outside the city walls, often in floating structures anchored two or three rows deep along the banks of the Chao Phraya River.

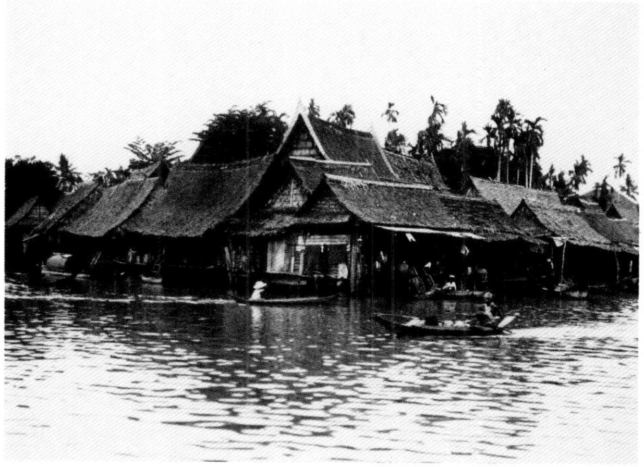

Other architectural influences began to appear significantly during the reign of King Rama III (1824 - 51), when trade with China became a major force in the economy. Increasing numbers of Chinese came to live and work in the capital, and Chinese styles were popular not only in houses for the more successful of these immigrants but also in temples and within the royal palace compound. The first Westerners also took up residence at the time. One of them, Robert Hunter, built a substantial brick residence on the west bank, reputedly the first European-style house in Bangkok, which was soon followed by others such as the Portuguese Consulate in its present east bank location.

Western concepts, both social and architectural, grew stronger during the next reign. Sir John Bowring, who came in 1855, describes a private meeting with King Rama IV in a house "fitted up, for the most part, in European style" and Alexander Griswold, one of Rama IV's biographers, says the King had a preference for "cool stuccoed buildings of one story, ridge-roofed and colonnaded, whose aspect recalls in simpler form the glories of the late Greek Revival in South Carolina and Louisiana." Bangkok's first roads were built at this time, and with them came shophouses similar to those of Singapore.

Such Western-style buildings, both commercial and residential, proliferated under the next two rulers. The Chakri Maha Prasat, built by King Rama V (r. 1868 - 1910) in the Grand Palace, was designed by an English architect as a wholly European building; only when it was nearly complete were three Thai-style spires added to harmonize with the surrounding traditional structures. Outside the palace the preference was for commodious wooden bungalows or for more substantial residences of brick and mortar, often designed by one of the Western architects who had set up business in the city. The river and canals ceased to be the major means of communication, land deeds were issued for the demarcation of property, and, increasingly, houses were built to face roads rather than waterways.

Similar tastes were apparent in outlying areas. Bang Pa-In, where King Rama V had a summer palace, displayed an eclectic mixture that ranged from Renaissance to Neo-Gothic. King Rama VI (r. 1910 - 25), who built the present Government House in a style inspired by Venetian palaces, was also responsible for several European-style palaces near Nakhon Pathom.

This period of intensive construction came to an end in the 1930s, by which time there were few traditional Thai buildings left in Bangkok. A new period, even more active and threatening to older structures, was launched in the 1950s, with results that we still see rising everywhere around us.

Left : *Stairhall of the Portuguese Embassy on the Chao Phraya River.*
Above : *Early Rattanakosin houses built along the river.*
Preceding pages : *An old Thai-style house in Tak Province.*

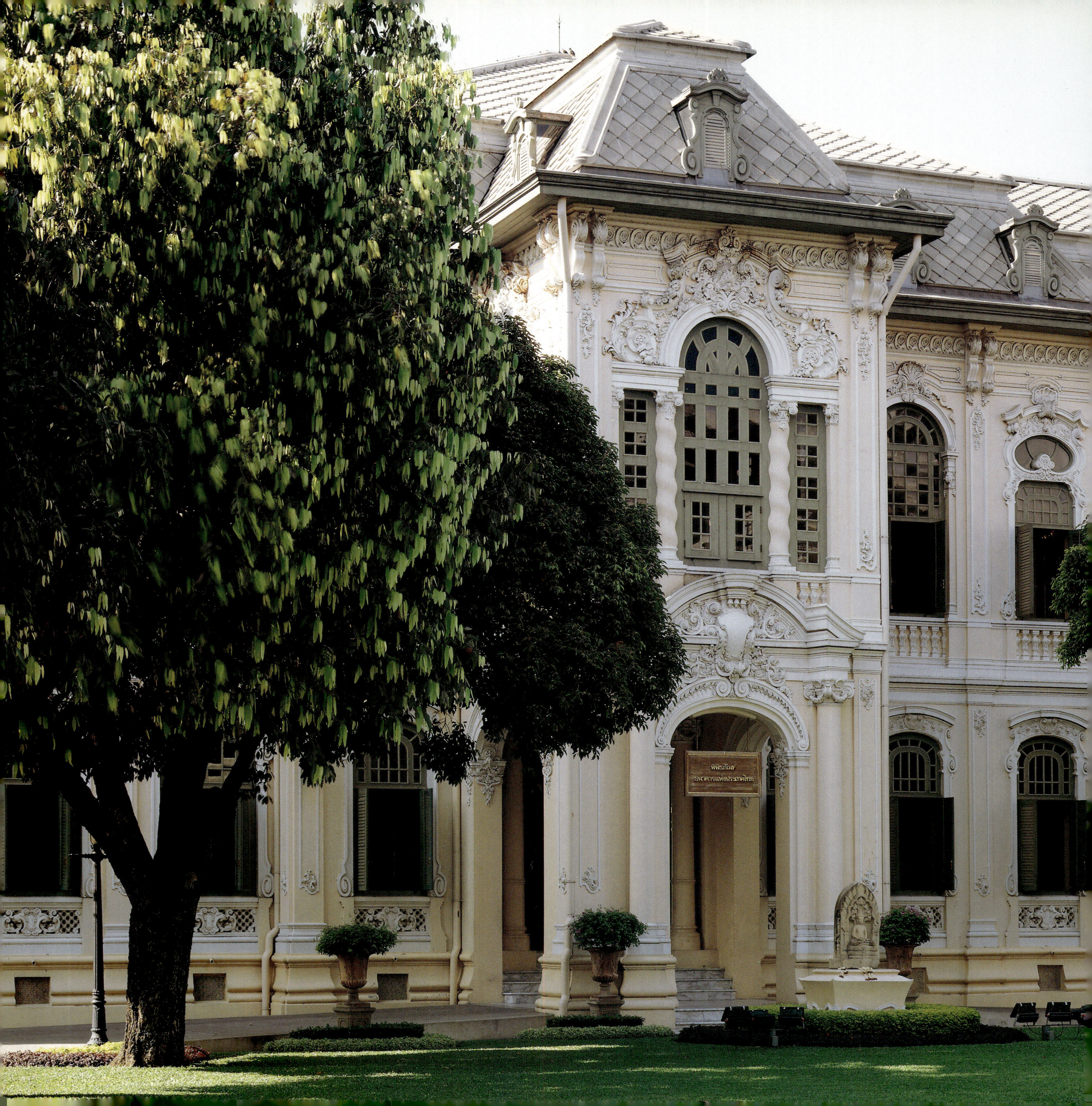
พิพิธภัณฑ์
ธนาคารแห่งประเทศไทย

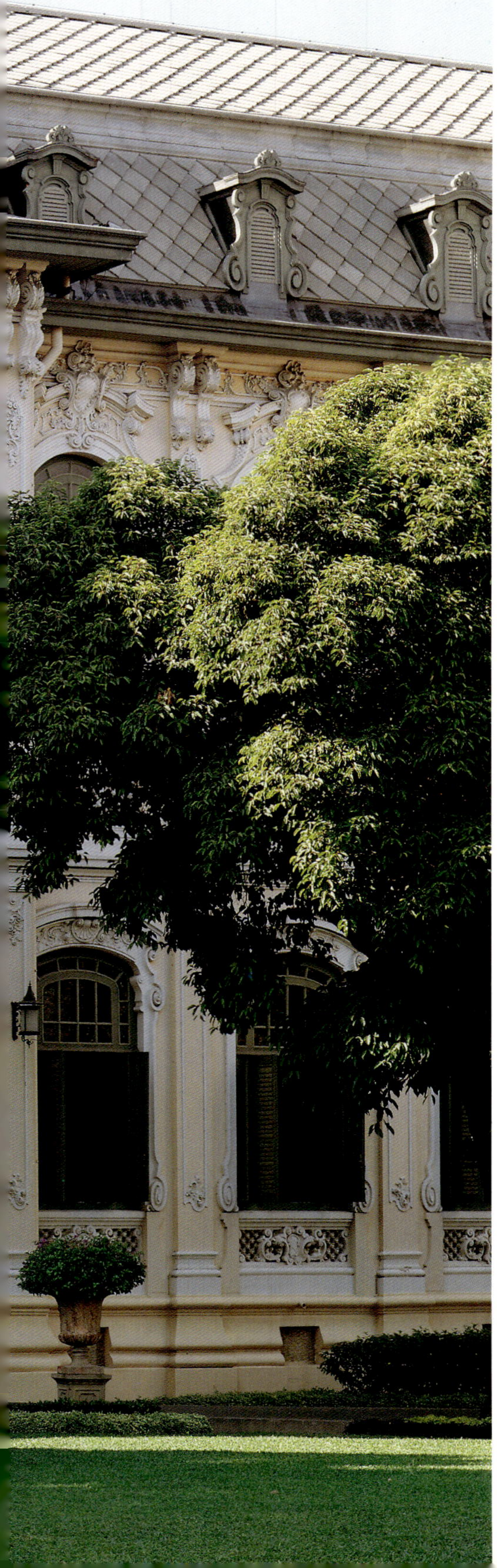

Bangkhunprom Palace

Born in 1881, Prince Paribatra Sukhumbhand was the only son of Queen Sukumala and King Chulalongkorn. He was sent abroad to be educated under the guidance of Emperor William II in Germany where, in addition to a taste for Western music, he acquired an admiration for Renaissance architecture. On his return to Thailand in 1903, he held a number of increasingly high positions in the military and eventually became the President of the Supreme Council of advisors to his half-brother, King Prajadhipok. He was holding this position in 1932 when a coup d'etat brought the absolute monarchy to an end; Prince Paribatra was forced to leave the country and went into exile in Java, never to return. "Thus," wrote Prince Chula Chakrabongse in his history of the Chakri Dynasty, "passed from Thai history this intelligent and sympathetic figure whose home was one of the centers of the arts of Siam and the Western world."

The home mentioned above was Bangkhunprom Palace, a splendid structure on the bank of the Chao Phraya River which was built shortly before the end of King Chulalongkorn's reign. Prince Paribatra selected Karl Dohring, a German architect, to design the palace, which displays a blend of Renaissance, Baroque, Rococo, and Art Nouveau architectural styles—all of which were becoming popular in Thailand at the time as a result of the growing passion for Western culture, especially among the foreign-educated aristocracy.

The extensive compound contains a number of buildings, the most prominent being the Tamnak Yai and the Tamnak Somdej. The Tamnak Yai, or main building, is situated parallel to the river in a north-south direction and consists of a central section flanked by two wings; it has ornate stucco and wood decorations, Palladian windows, classic columns, and a magnificent marble staircase in the central hall. The smaller Tamnak Somdej, constructed later, reflects the growing popularity of Art Nouveau and has elegant bas-relief patterns, pastel colors, and a fresco by Carlo Rigoli, one of the Italian artists who painted the murals in the dome of the Ananta Samakhom Throne Hall.

The palace served as Prince Paribatra's residence for some 30 years, during which it was a popular gathering place for artists as well as government officials and visiting dignitaries. After his exile it was taken over by the government and was used for a variety of purposes until it became the headquarters of the Bank of Thailand in 1945.

In the early 1990s, the Bank commissioned a complete renovation of the palace, incorporating a museum of Thai currency and also ensuring that the historic buildings would remain as part of the country's architectural and cultural heritage.

Left : *Facade of the Tamnak Yai, or main building, of Bangkhunprom Palace, designed by the German architect Karl Dohring in a blend of Renaissance, Baroque, Rococo, and Art Nouveau styles.*

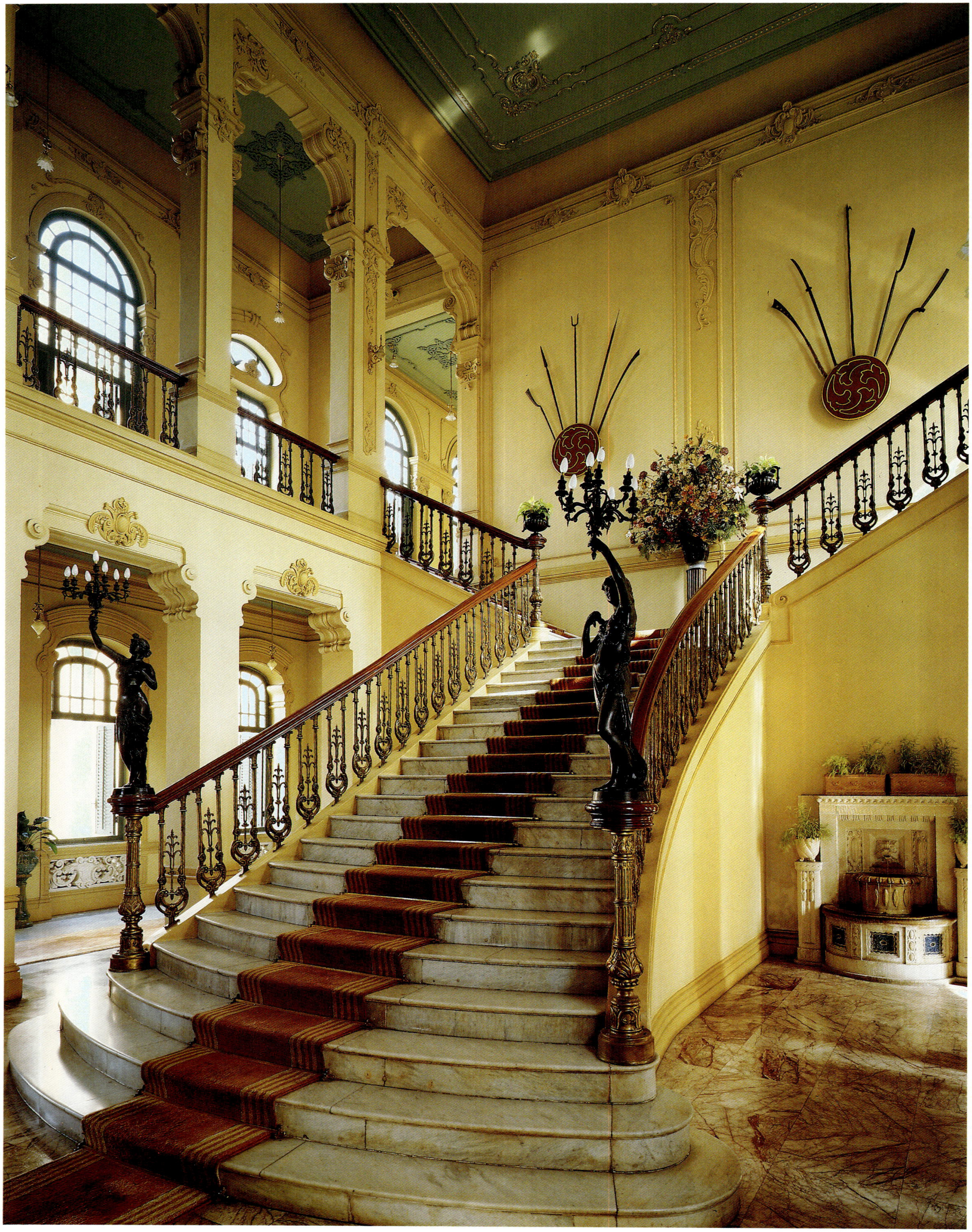

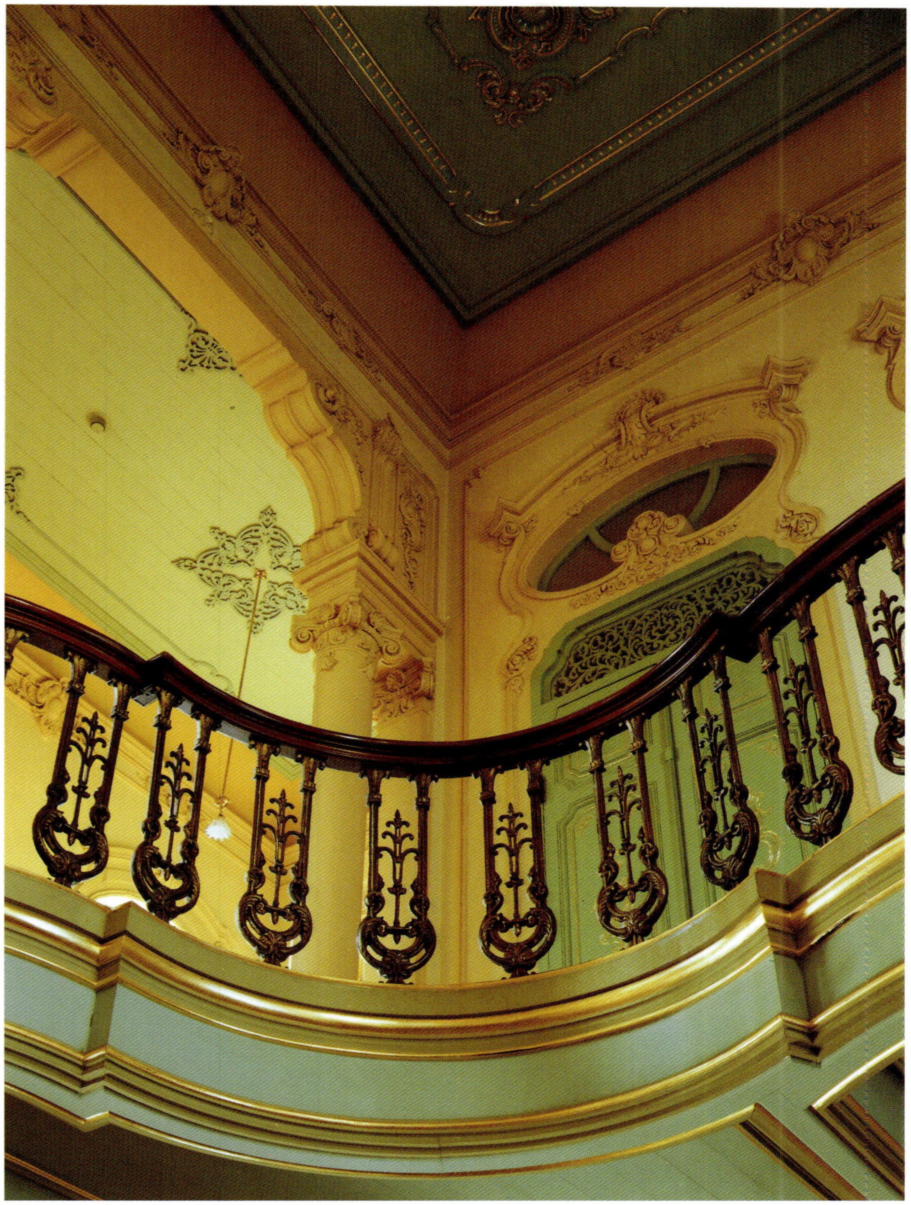

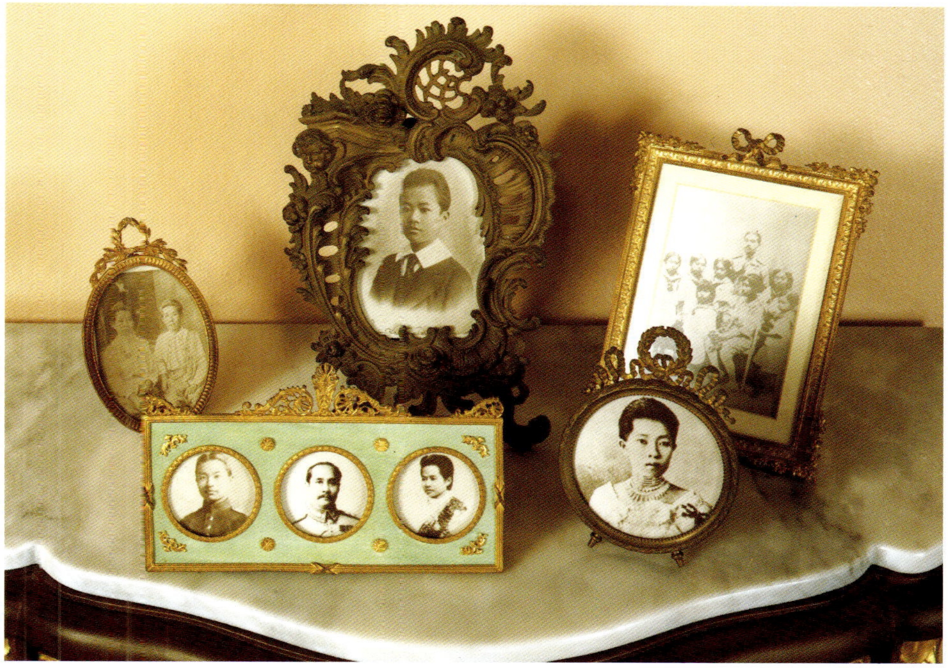

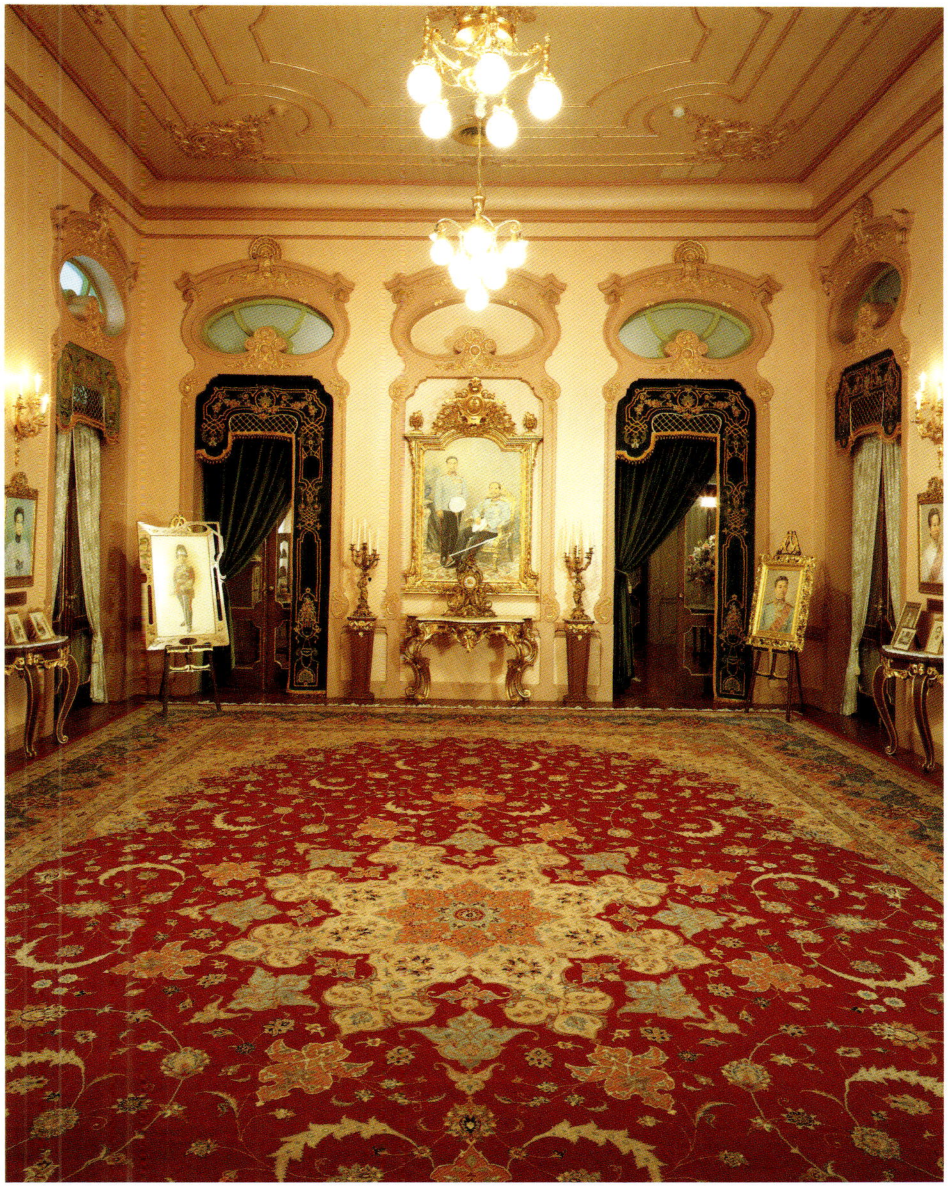

Left : *The splendid marble staircase in the Tamnak Yai, showing the Western-style decorations of the main hall.*
Above : *Hallway of the Tamnak Yai, with bas-relief decorations and an ornate banister rail.*
Right : *The Pink Room in the Tamnak Yai, as restored by the Bank of Thailand during a complete renovation in the early 1990s.*
Above right : *A display of old photographs; Prince Paribatra Sukhumbhand is shown in the carved frame at the rear, while in front the Prince is on the left and King Chulalongkorn in the middle. H.S.H. Prasongasom is in the round frame on the right.*

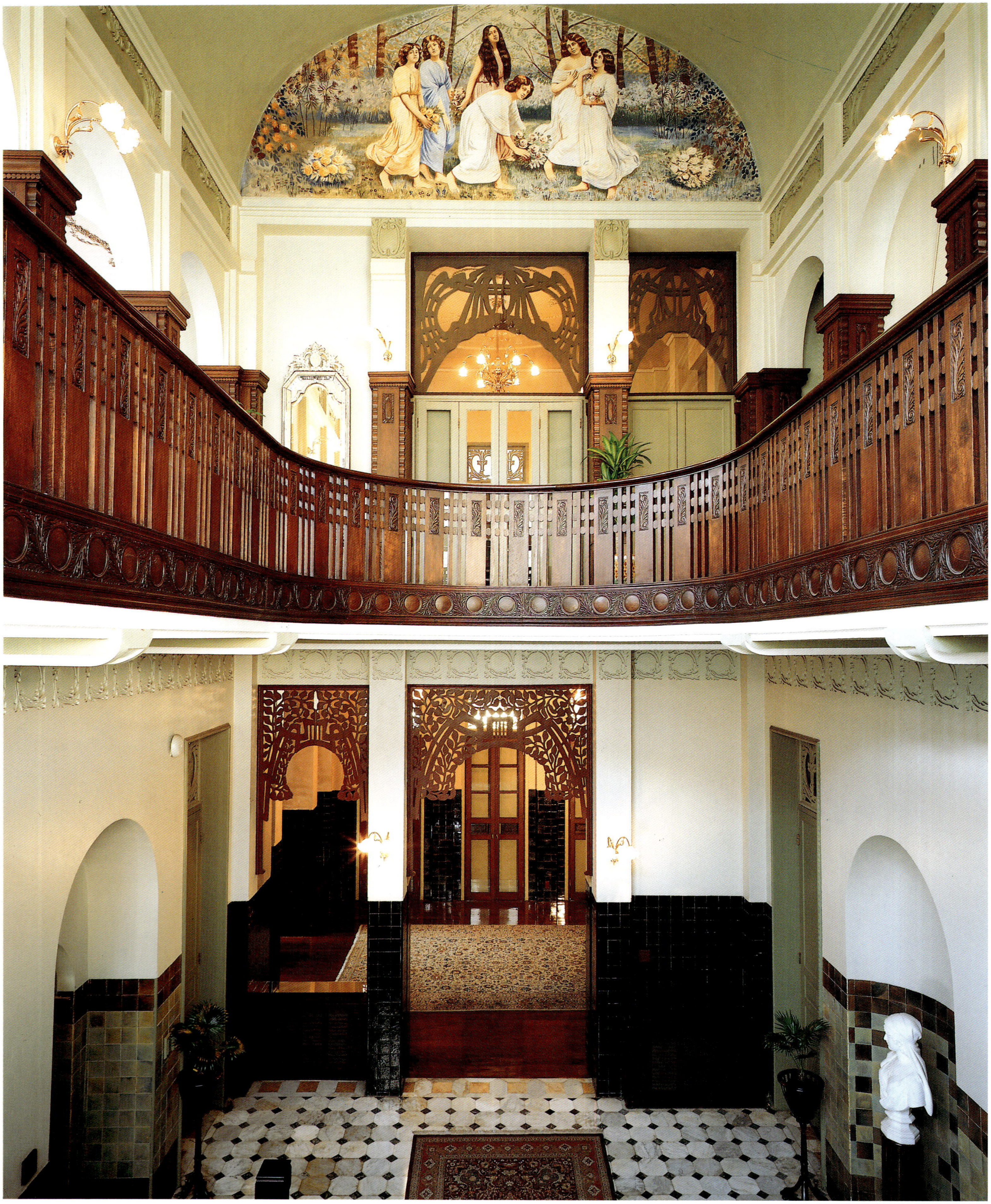

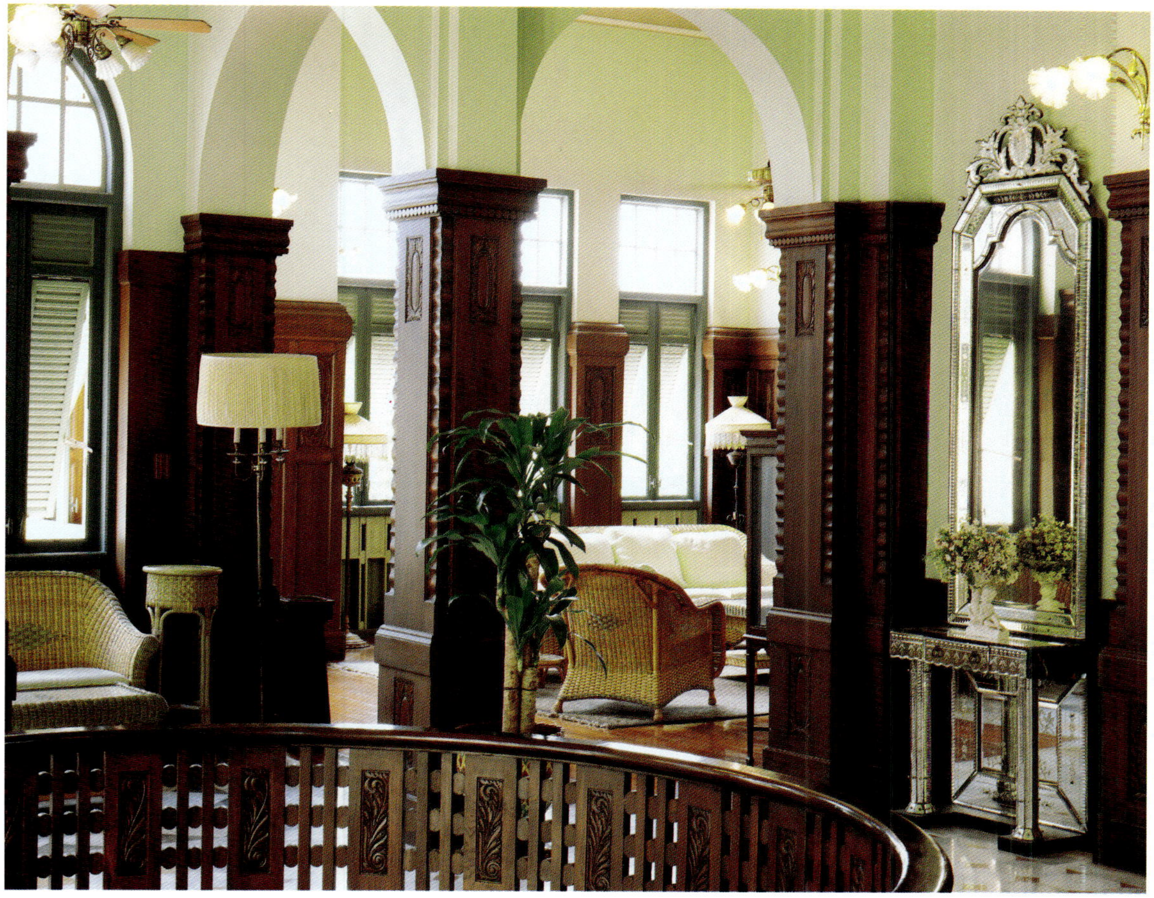

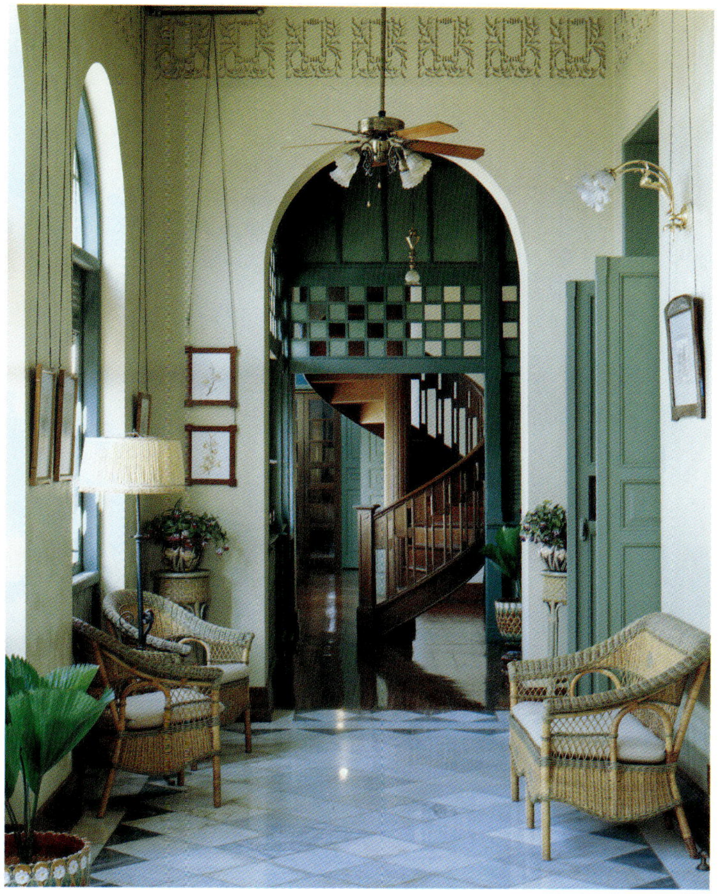

Left : *Stairhall of the Tamnak Somdej, decorated in Art Nouveau style; the fresco on the second floor, uncovered during the restoration work, was done by the Italian artist Carlo Rigoli.*
Above : *Upper part of the stairhall of the Tamnak Somdej; at the rear is a verandah.*
Above right : *A marble-floored verandah in the Tamnak Somdej; behind can be seen an elegant spiral staircase.*
Right : *The Tamnak Somdej, smaller of the two main buildings in the Bangkhunprom Palace compound, constructed somewhat later than the Tamnak Yai.*

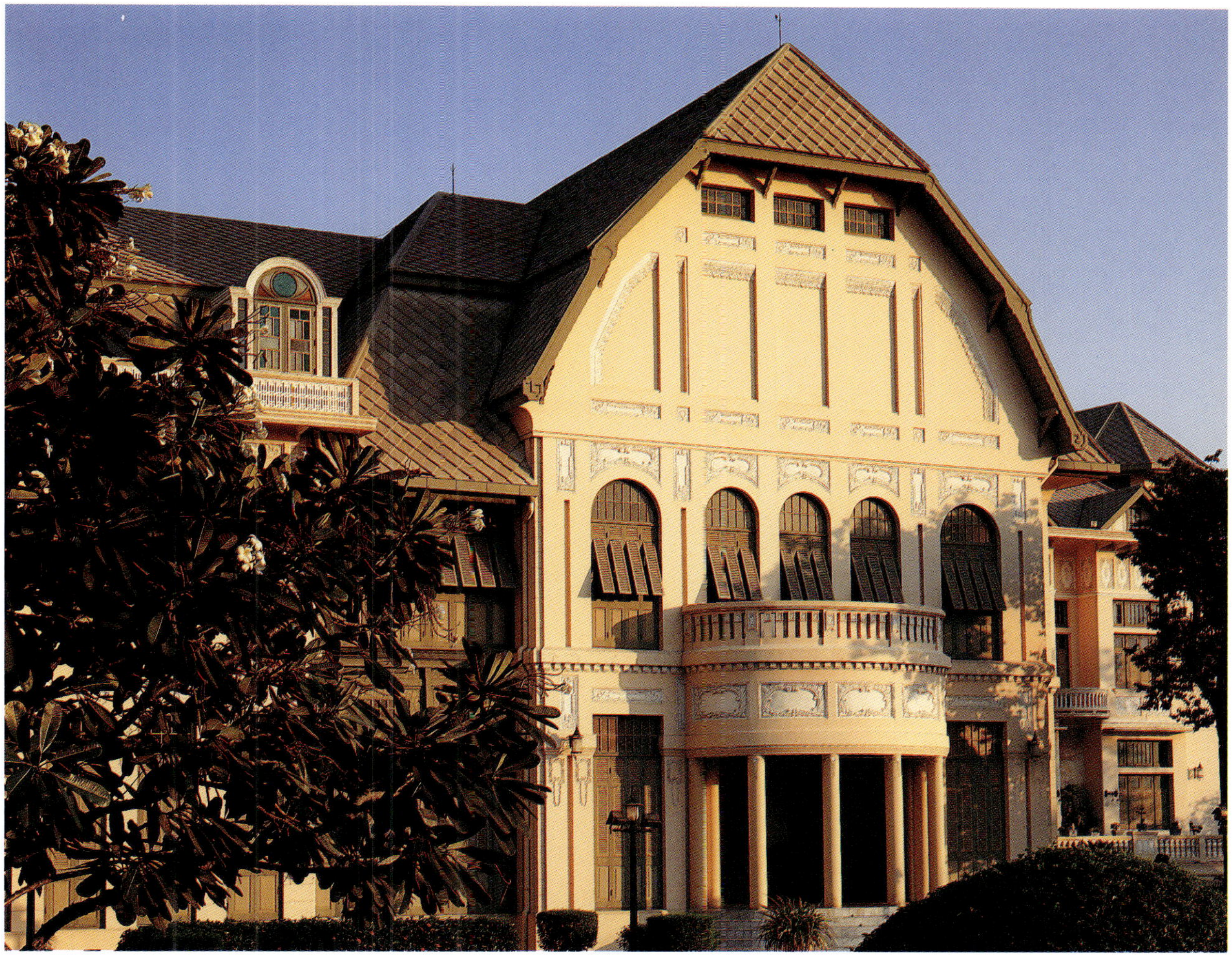

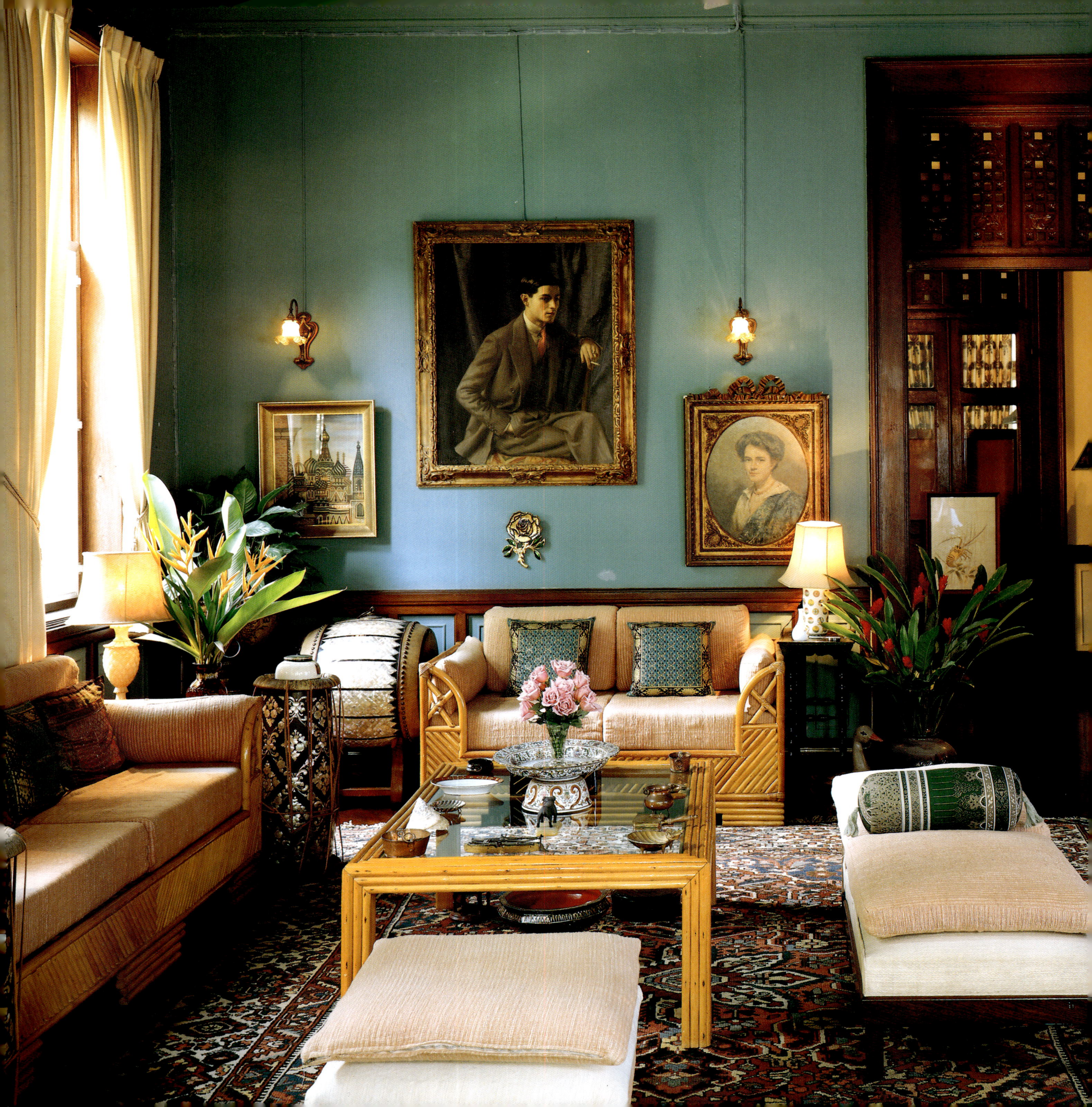

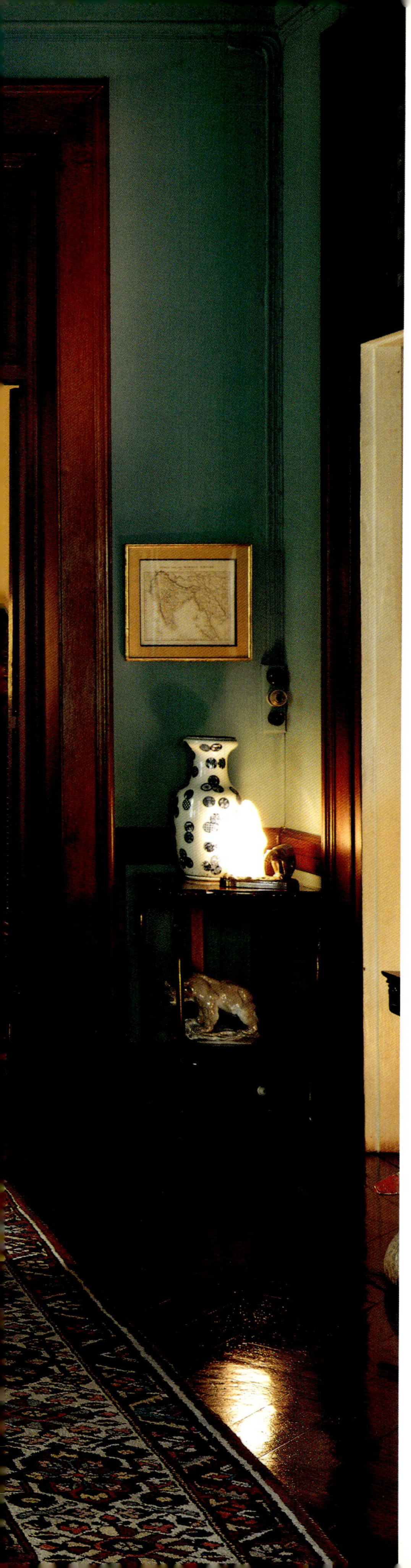

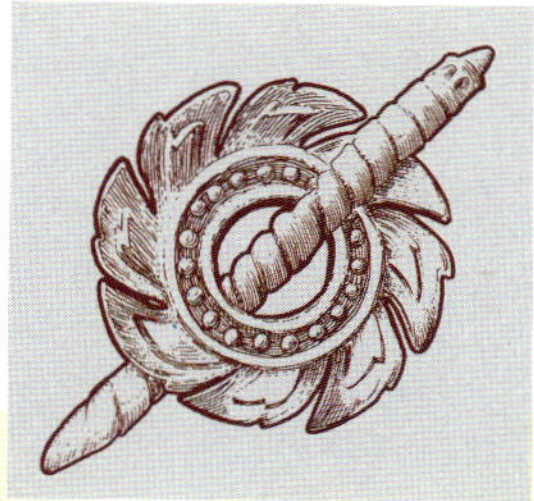

Chakrabongse House

Prince Chakrabongse of Phitsanulok, as he came to be known, was a son of King Chulalongkorn and Queen Saowabha Phongsri and, according to most accounts, a particular favorite of both. He was sent abroad to study, first briefly to England and then, in 1898, to Russia, where Emperor Nicholas II had offered to guide his education. It was in St. Petersburg, in the spring of 1905, that he met and fell in love with a Russian girl named Ekaterina Ivanova Desnitskaya, also called Katya. Without telling either the King or the Emperor, the couple eloped and were married in Constantinople; they then proceeded to Singapore, where Katya remained while Prince Chakrabongse continued on to Bangkok to break the news to his father.

In the event, gossip and rumor did the job for him. Both the King and the Queen were furious. The King never received his daughter-in-law during the four years that remained of his life, though Queen Saowabha eventually relented and became close, especially after the birth of Prince Chula Chakrabongse in 1908. Following the death of King Chulalongkorn in 1910, the new King Vajiravudh officially recognized Katya and also invested her with a royal order.

The couple's principal residence was Paruskavan Palace, designed by an Italian architect and set in a spacious garden. They later decided to construct a simpler, smaller villa on the bank of the Chao Phraya River at Ta Tien, just across from the soaring towers of Wat Arun, the Temple of Dawn; this they planned to use when they went boating on the river or for changing before going to ceremonies at the Grand Palace just upstream. (On a trip to the Gulf of Thailand, they also discovered a small village called Hua Hin and there built another house, thus starting the vogue for what became Thailand's first seaside resort.)

Sadly, despite the obstacles overcome, the marriage proved unsuccessful in the end. They separated and, in 1919, divorced; Prince Chakrabongse died the following year, while Katya moved first to China and eventually to Paris, where she died in 1960.

Paruskavan Palace is now a government office, its former elegance gone along with the gardens planted by Katya. Chakrabongse House, however, has been carefully preserved and remains a prominent riverside sight with its tall tower surrounded by a "widow's walk". It now serves as a Bangkok residence for their granddaughter M.R. Narisa.

Left : *Living room of Chakrabongse House; the portrait in the center is of Prince Chula Chakrabongse, while on the right is one of his mother, Mom Katerin (Katya) .*

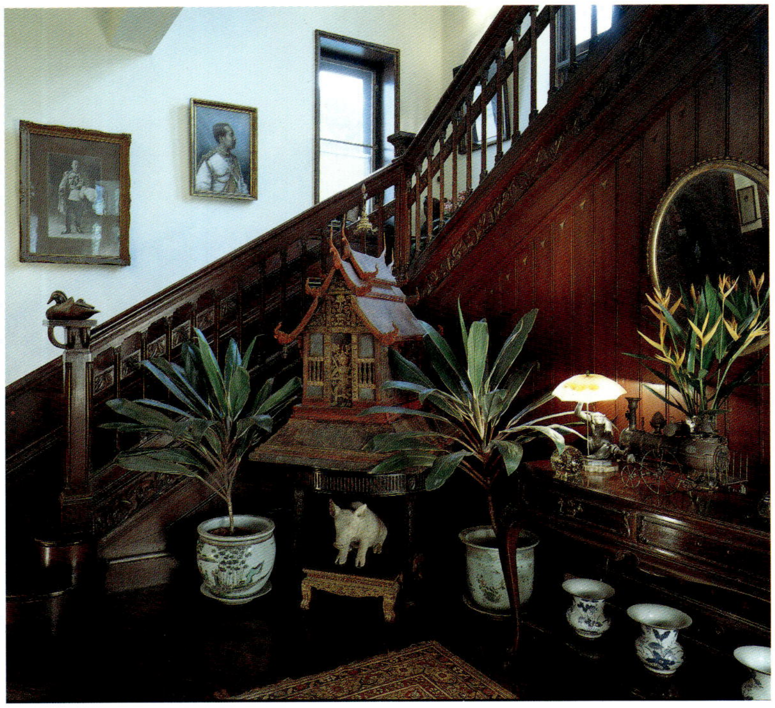

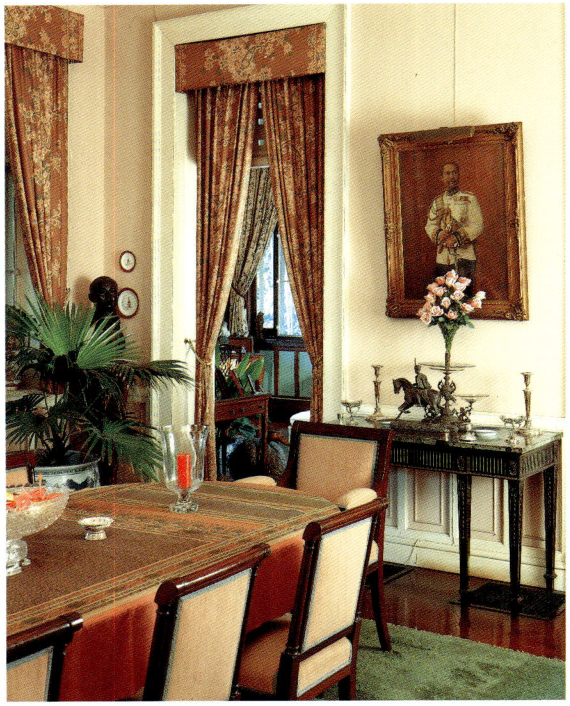

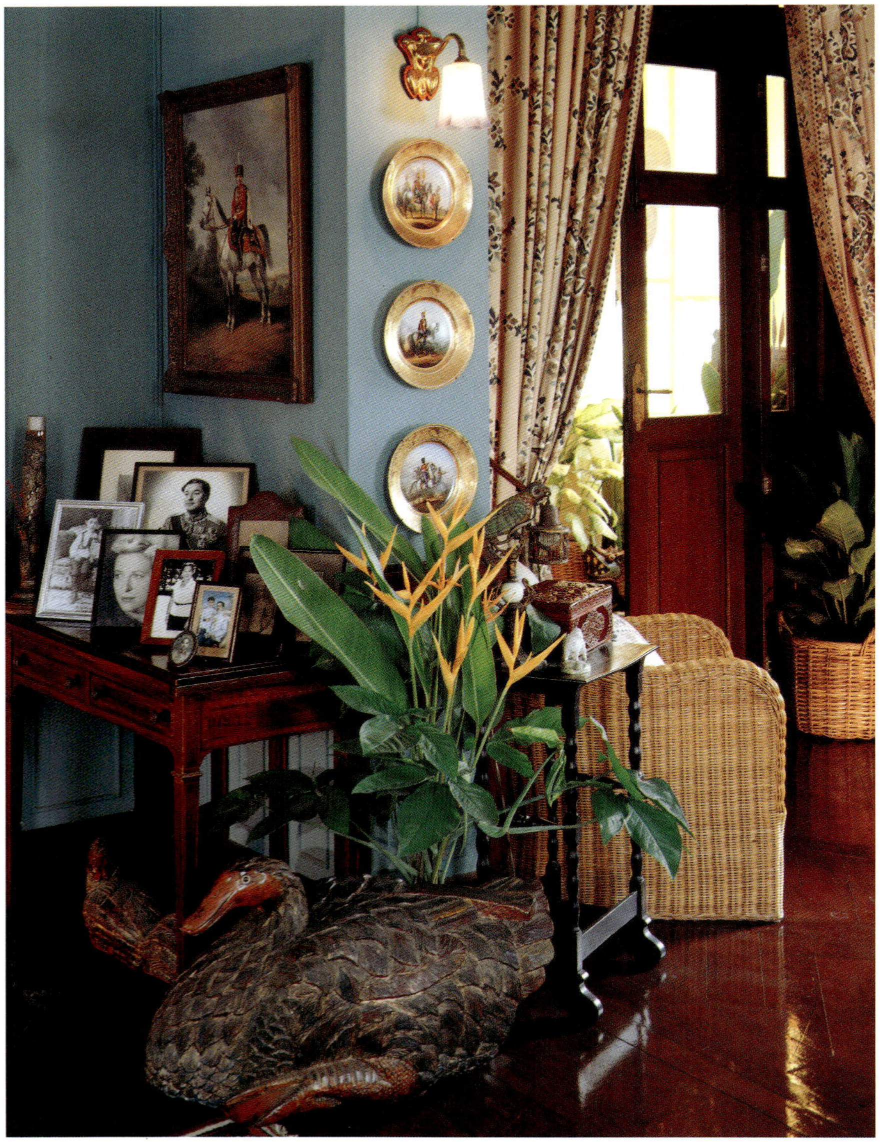

Right : *The dining room, showing carved air vents above the doorways.*
Below left : *Family photographs are displayed on a table in the living room.*
Above left : *Staircase of house, with family portraits on the wall.*
Above : *Dining room, with portrait of King Rama V by the Italian artist Carlo Rigoli.*

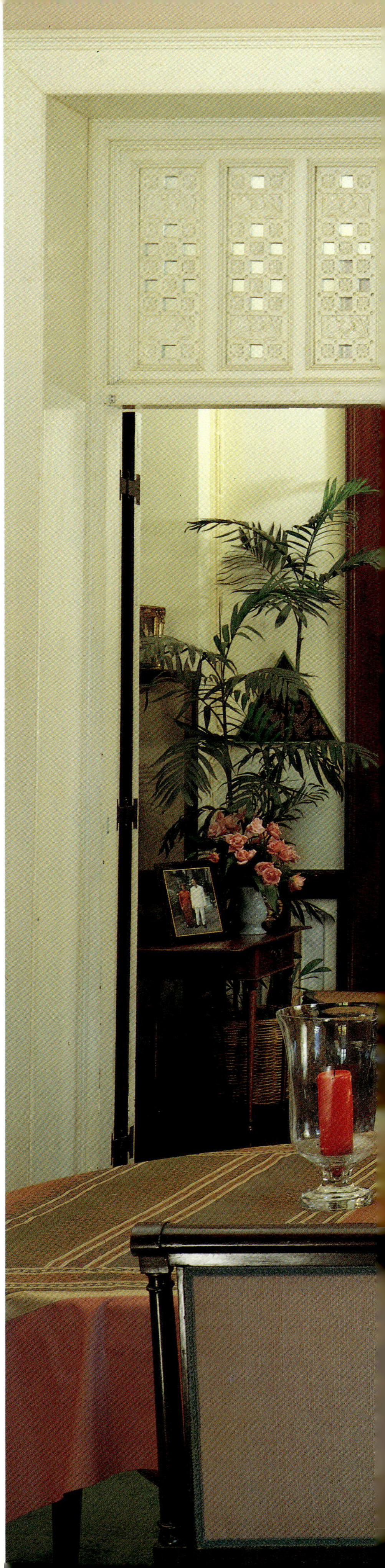

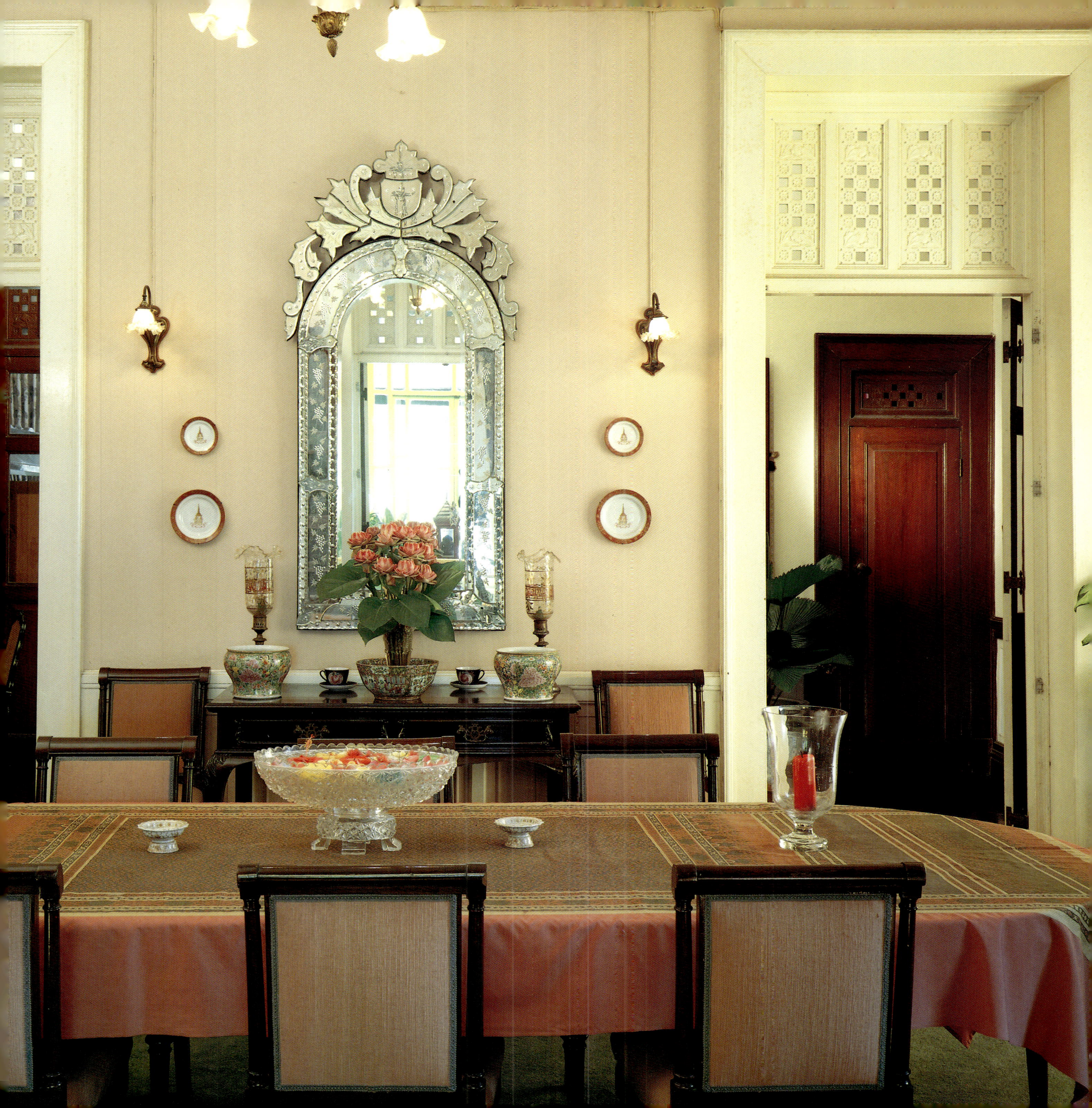

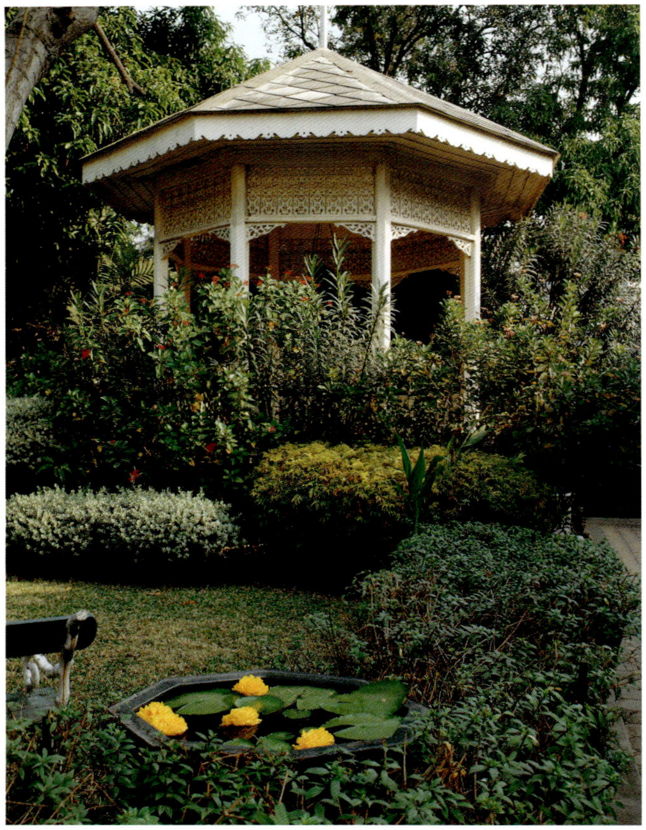

Right : *Front view of house; the tower is surrounded by a widow's walk.*
Bottom : *View of the garden; a Khmer-style statue adorns a formal pool.*
Left : *A garden pavilion; built by a Russian carpenter, this was originally at the family home at Hua Hin and moved to the present site.*
Below : *View from house of Wat Arun across the Chao Phraya River.*

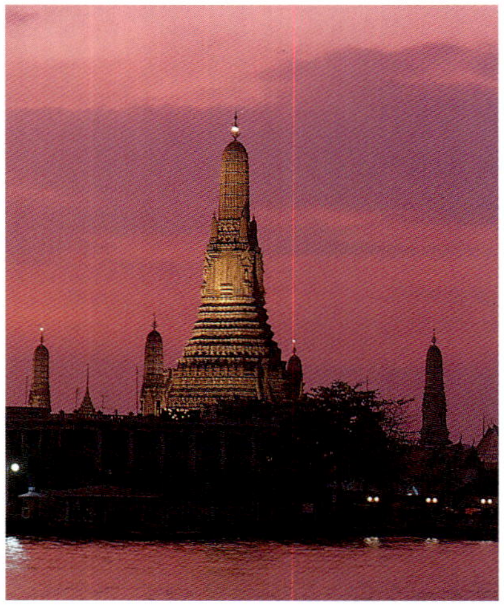

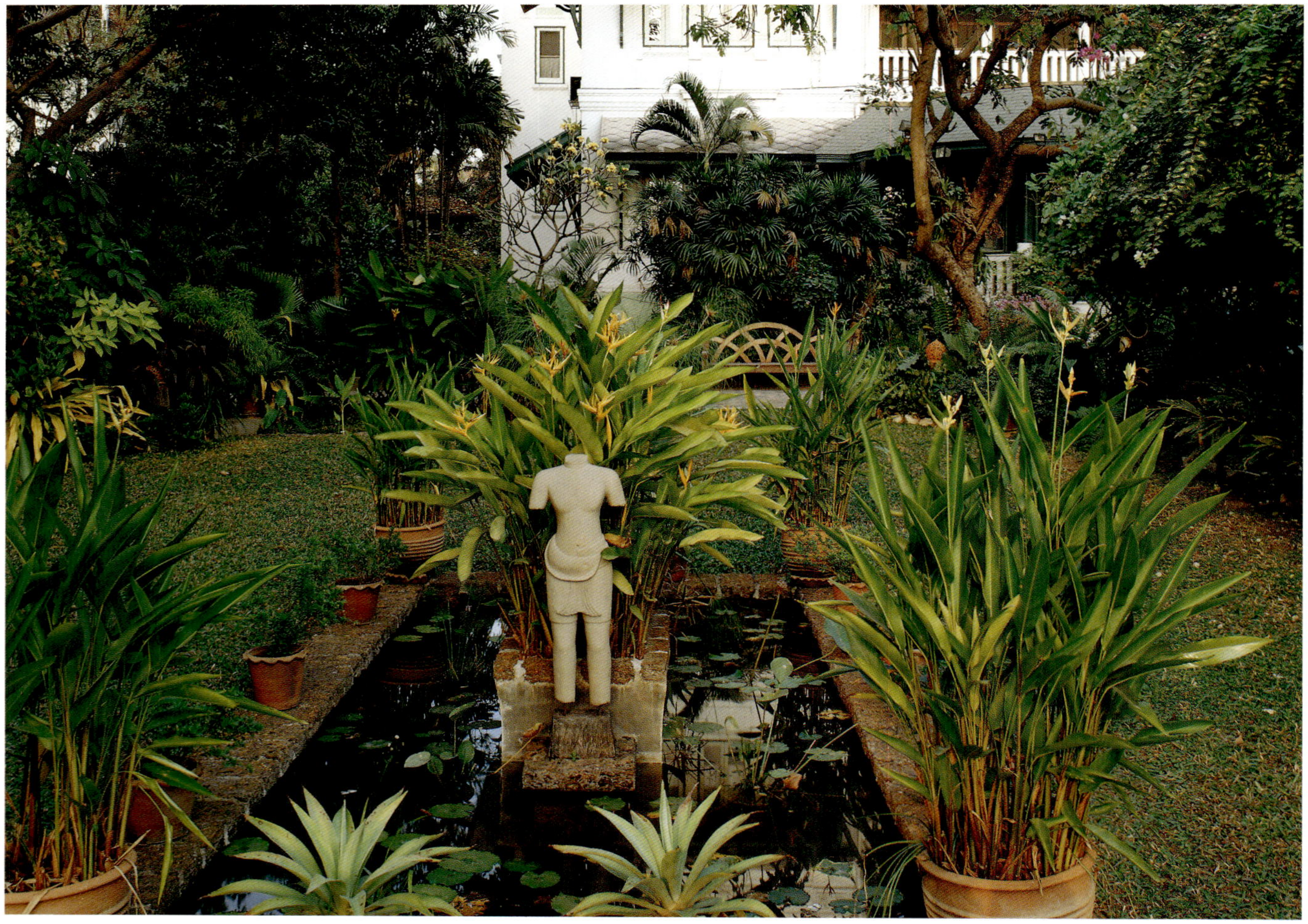

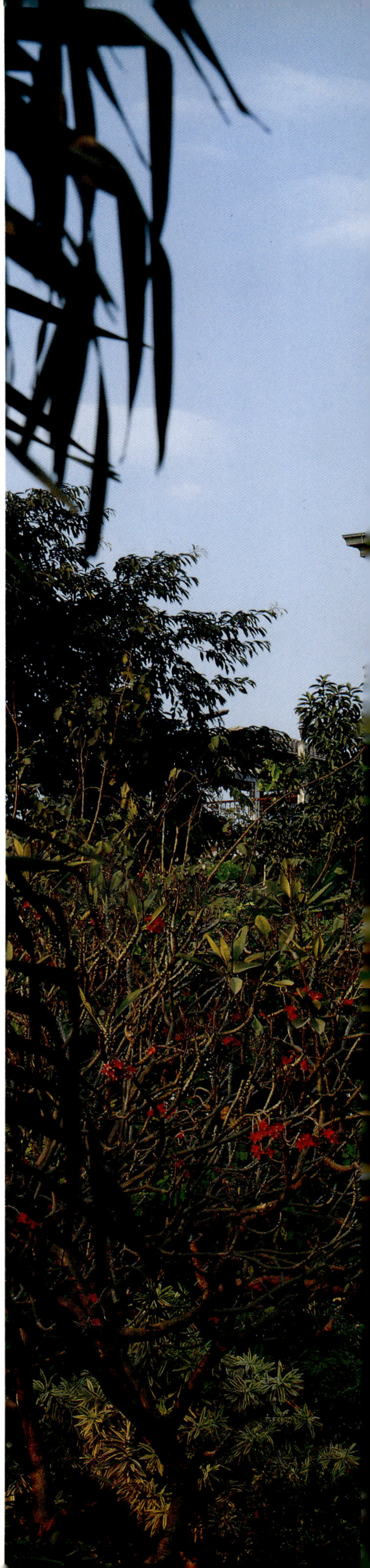

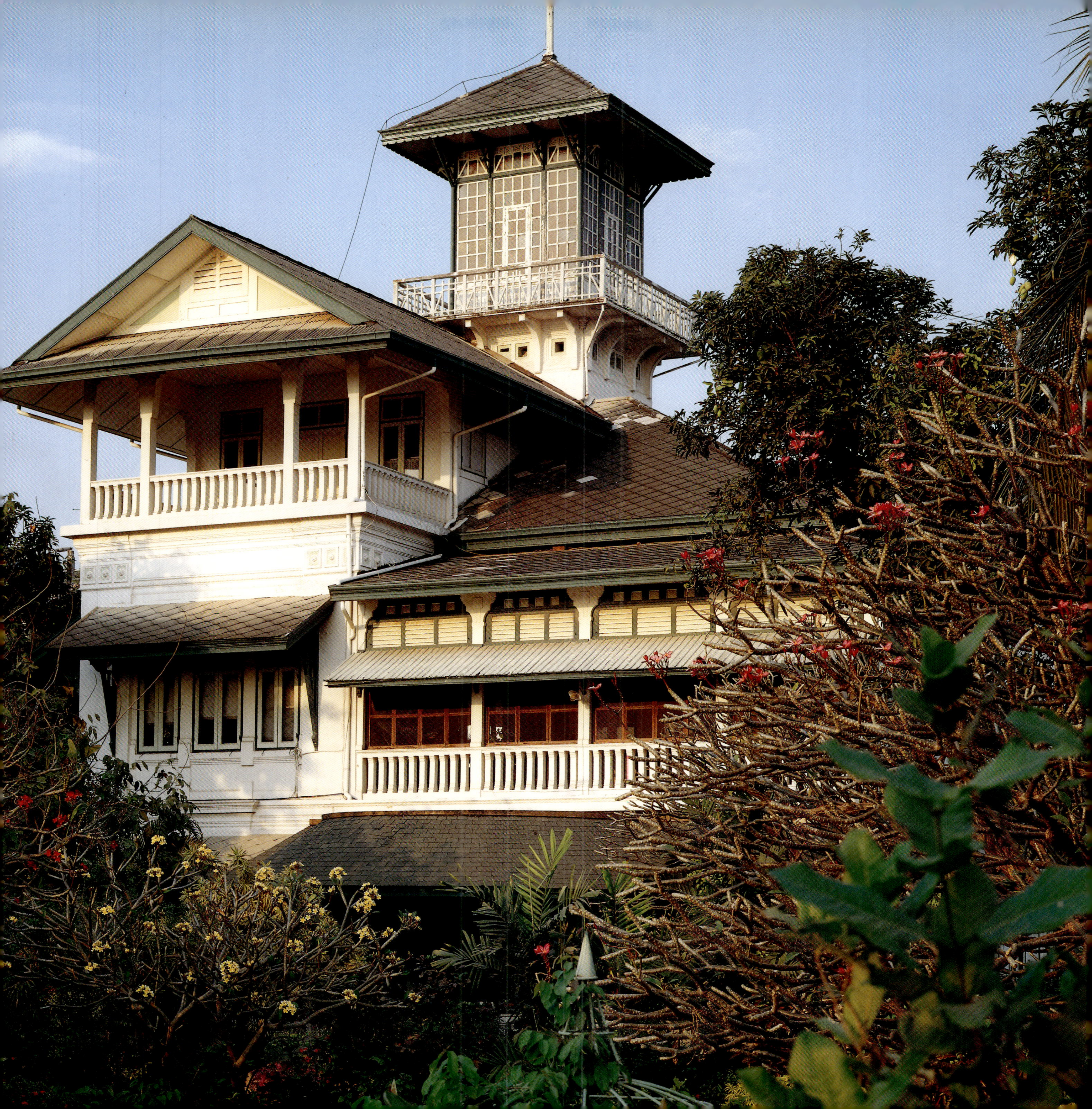

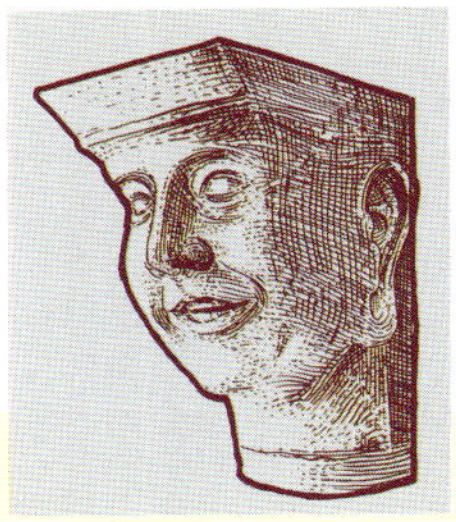

American Embassy Residences

"One day we were driven to the residence of the Prince Regent, along a bumpy dirt side street. The road was called Witayu, or Wireless Road, because of the location of a naval wireless station at one end of it. During the rainy season the road became a muddy mess and was almost impassable. But there, set far back, with an avenue of magnificent dark spreading Rain Trees leading to it, we saw a sprawling sagging house, painted chocolate brown, shutters hanging precariously; indeed, the whole house listed to one side. The extensive garden surrounding the house was crammed with rusted war junk, remnants of jeeps, trucks, gun carriages and tanks left there by Japanese troops."

Thus Edwin F. Stanton, the new American ambassador, described the discovery of his future residence in 1946, soon after his arrival in Thailand. The house he saw had been built in 1914 by Horatio Victor Baily, a British engineer who became a founder of the Siam Motor Works and a purveyor of silver to both King Rama V and King Rama VI; the latter conferred on him the Thai name and rank of Phra Padibat Rajaprasong. After Baily's death in 1920, the house was administered by his solicitors until 1926, when it was bought by the Ministry of Finance. His family, however, had already moved out, and it served as the Belgian legation from 1922 to 1927.

The Belgian Minister, Baron de Villenfagne de Sorinnes, noted that the house was "without doubt one of the most beautiful in all of Bangkok. The entire living area is raised one story above the ground, thus making it cooler...The building, carefully planned down to the last detail, together with the garden make a truly elegant legation."

In 1927, the property was transferred to the Ministry of Foreign Affairs and the house became the residence of Raymond B. Stevens, American advisor to the ministry. It was then used by his successor until the outbreak of World War II, when it was taken over by Japanese forces and reduced to the sad condition in which Ambassador Stanton and his wife Josie found it.

With the help of the Ministry of Foreign Affairs, the Stantons gradually restored the house and garden and it has since been the ambassadorial residence. As Dr. Sam Westgate has written, "the architecture of the house is not unique, combining as it does both European and tropical features especially favored by the British of that period...The basic structure is that of the traditional tropical wooden house on stilts built with a skeletal construction in which the roof and floor are supported entirely by the frame and pillars. The walls serve to protect the interior from the sun and rain but they do not bear any weight."

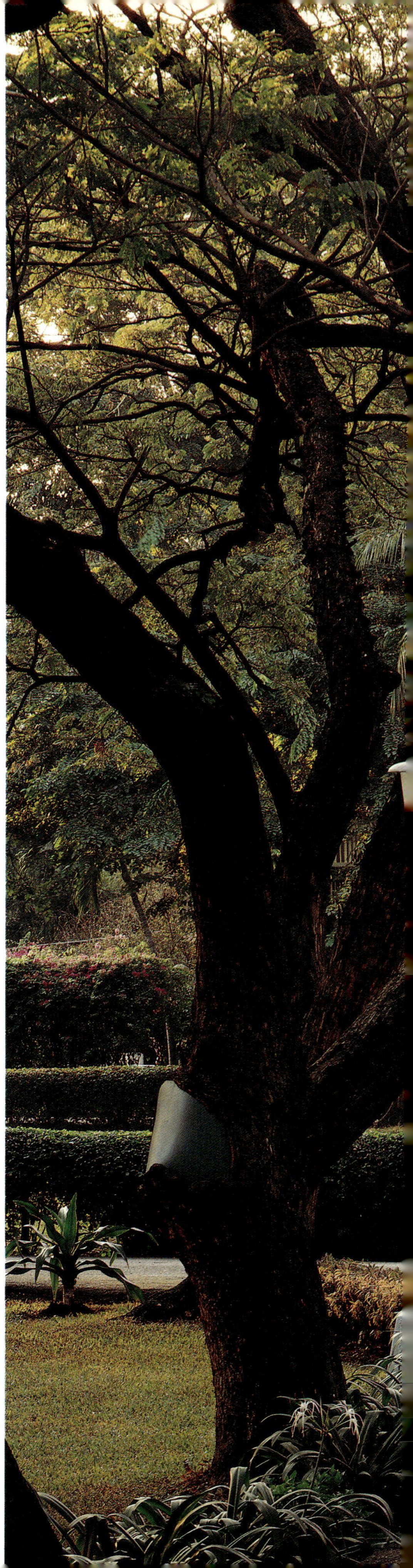

Right : *Facade of the American Embassy Residence, approached by a drive lined with venerable Rain Trees.*

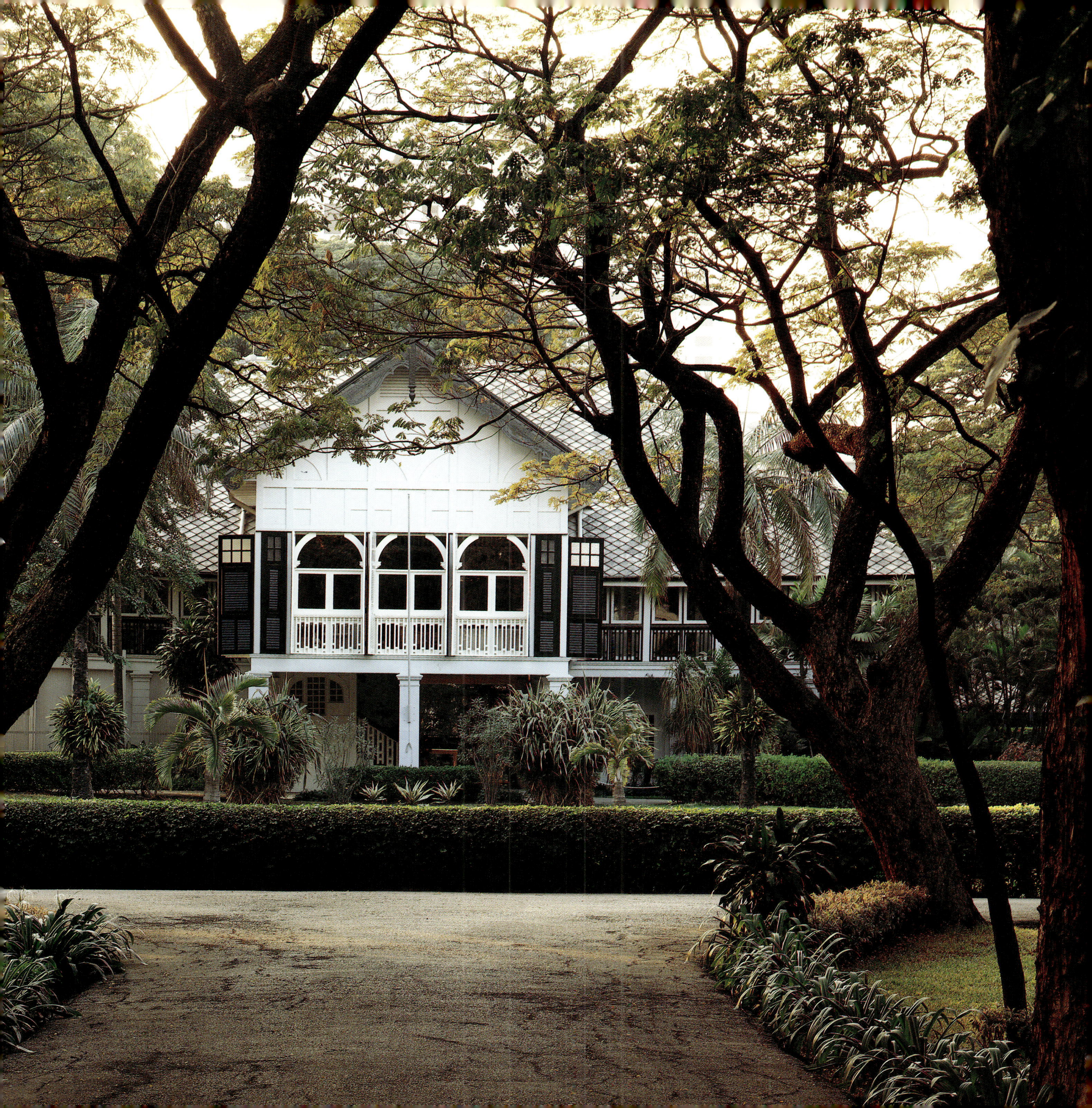

The house was designed to permit as much air circulation as possible, with high ceilings, latticework grills at the top of the teak walls, an open gallery surrounding the living quarters, and a large verandah at the front over the driveway. Both the gallery and the verandah have now been enclosed and such modern comforts as central air conditioning and a swimming pool have been added; a separate guest house was built on the property in 1954.

Another group of notable houses used by U.S. Embassy personnel is located on Rajdamri Road across from the Royal Bangkok Sports Club. Designed by Phya Burutratana Rajapallop by order of King Rama VI, these were constructed for rental to foreigners with the proceeds going to the Royal Pages School, later Vajiravudh College.

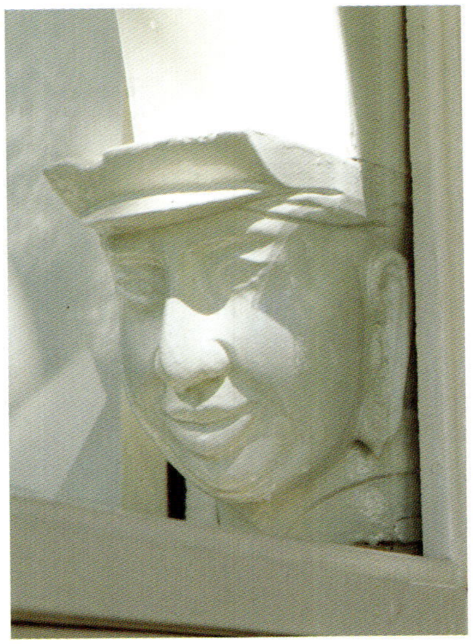

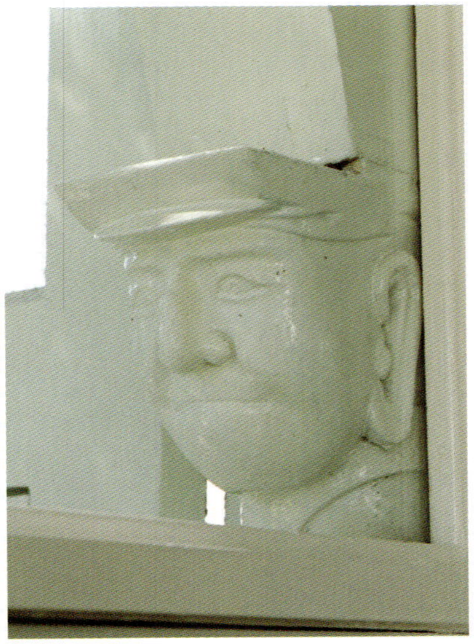

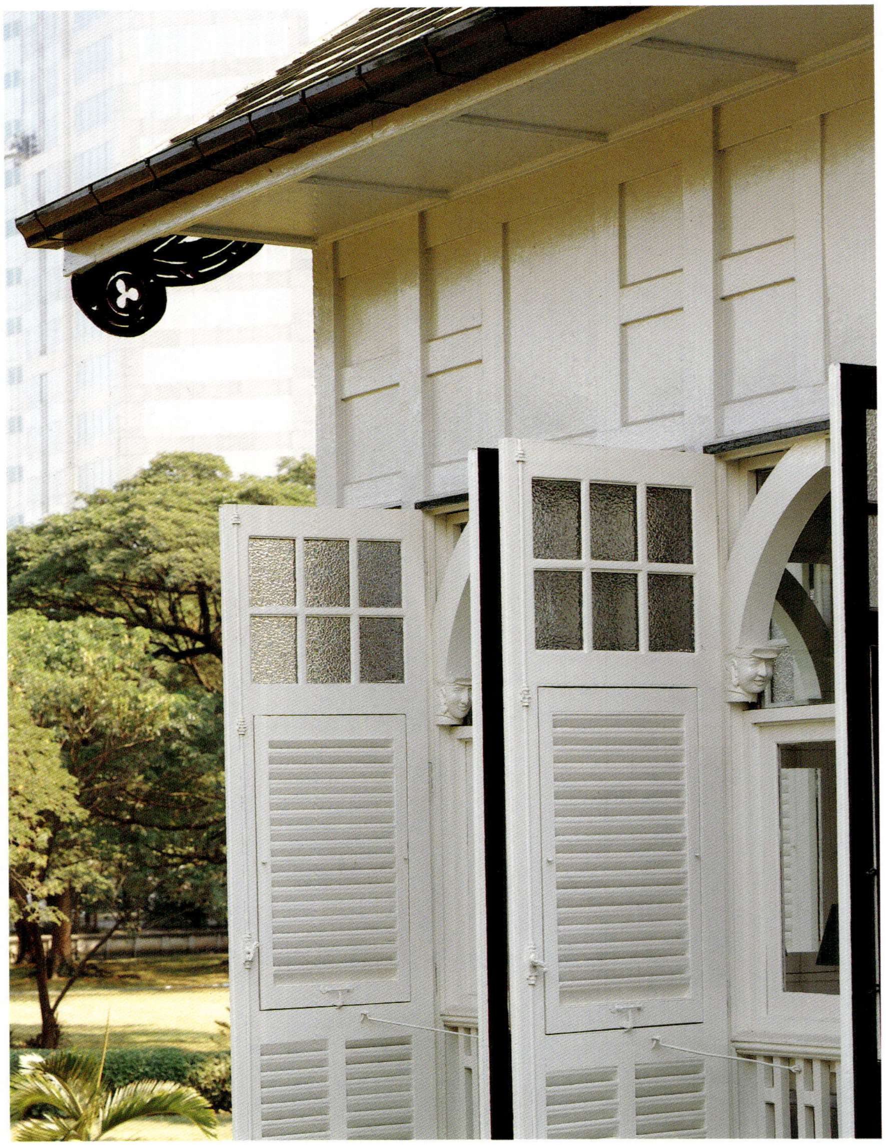

Right : *Louvered shutters on the upper floor, a feature of many similar houses built at this time; whimsical faces adorn the curved brackets at the top of the windows.*
Below : *Entrance to the Residence; the upper floor was originally an open verandah but has now been air-conditioned and served as part of the living room.*

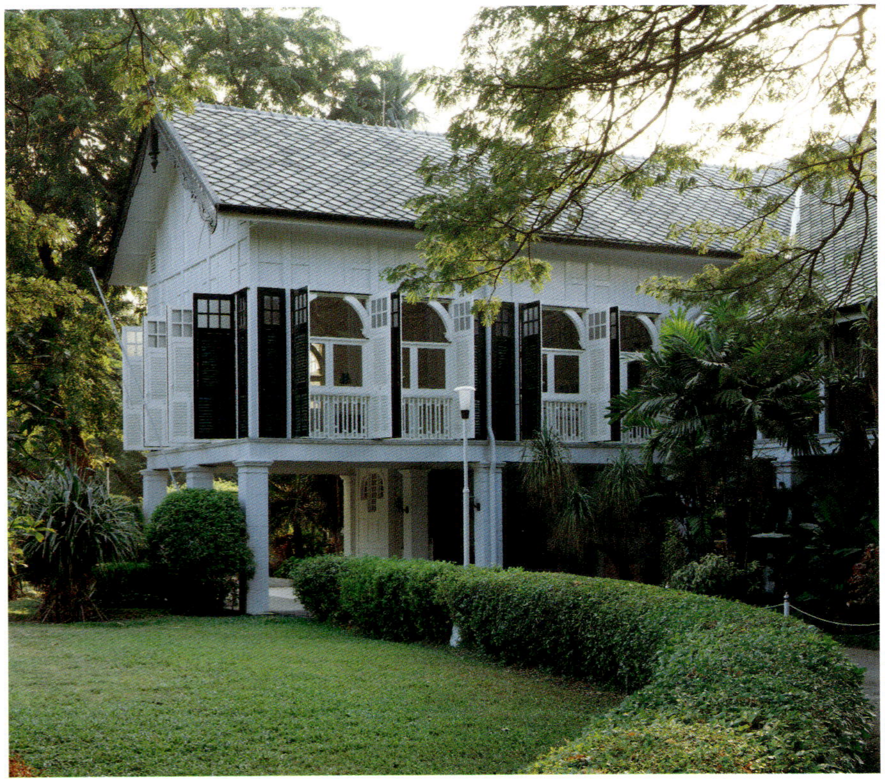

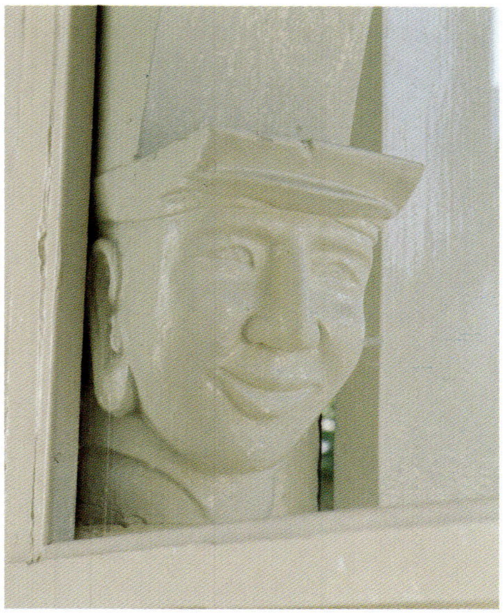

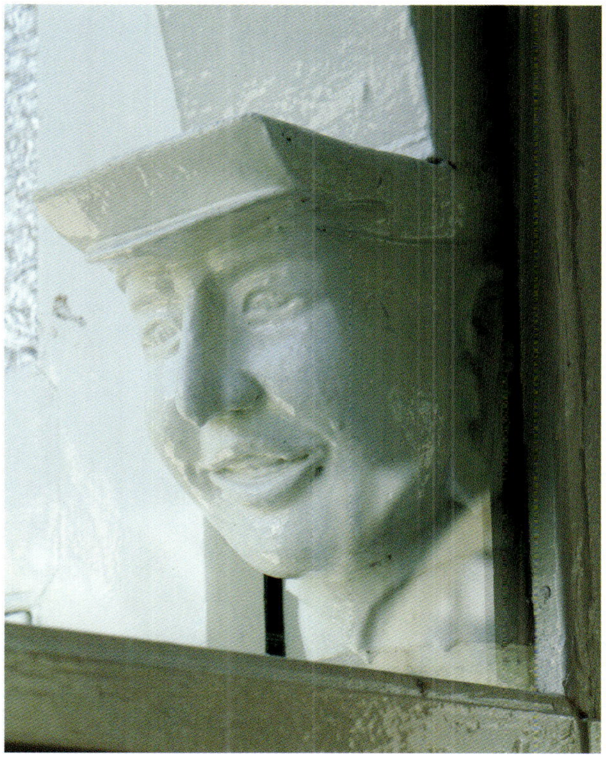

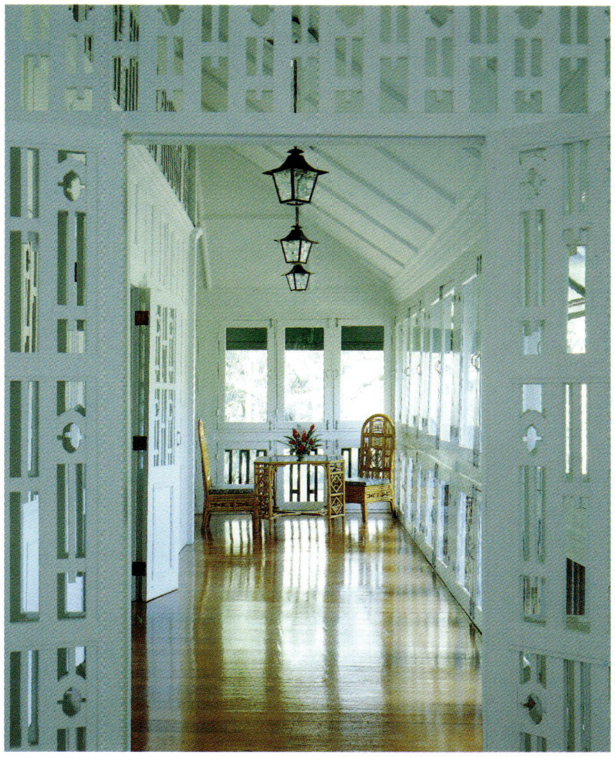

Above : *Some of the faces that decorate the upper part of the living room windows, displaying a variety of expressions.*
Top right : *Upstairs hallway leading to the residential quarters, formerly an open verandah but now enclosed.*
Right : *The main living room on the second floor, now air-conditioned; the latticework grills above allowed air circulation in the original residence.*

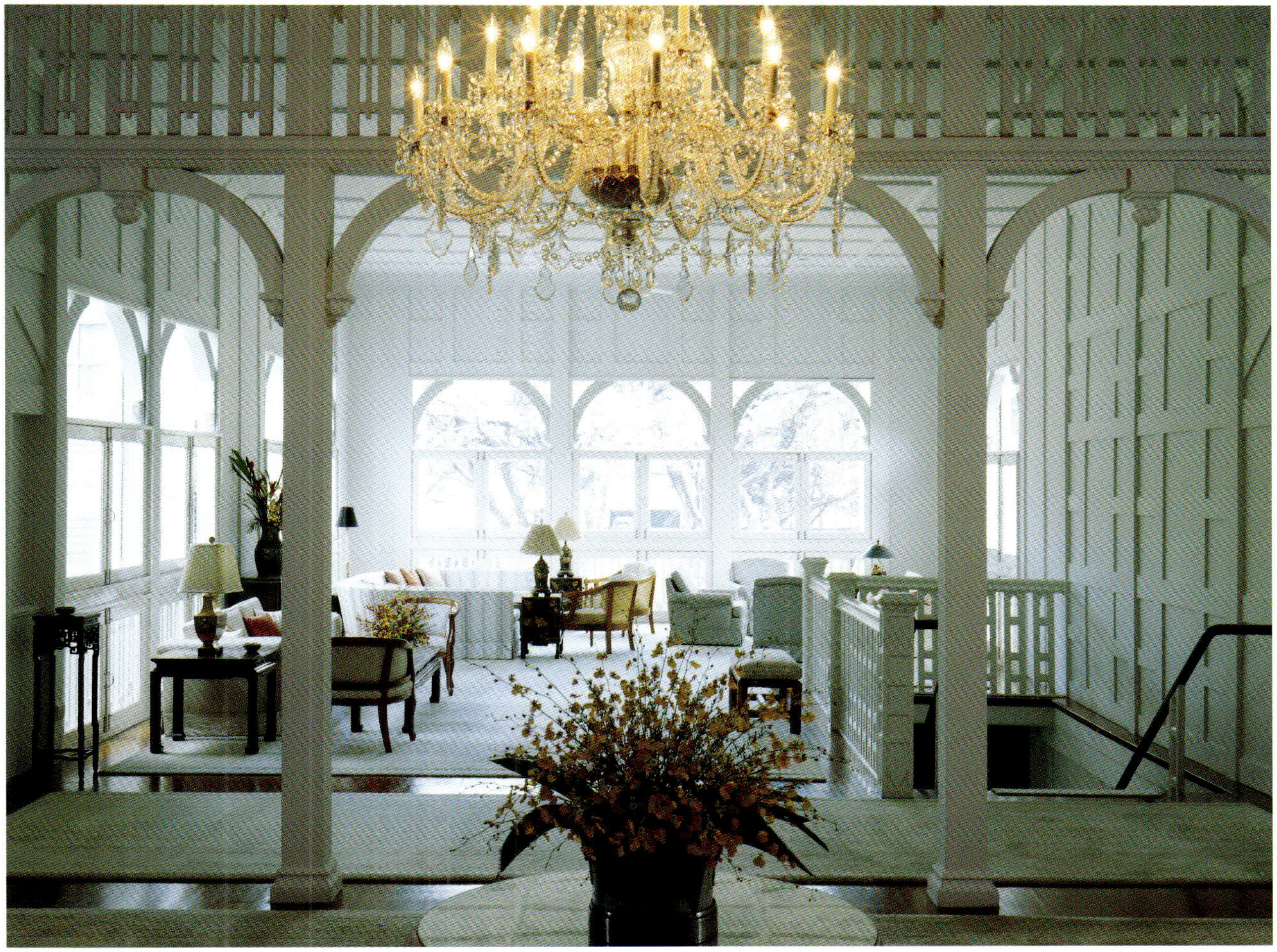

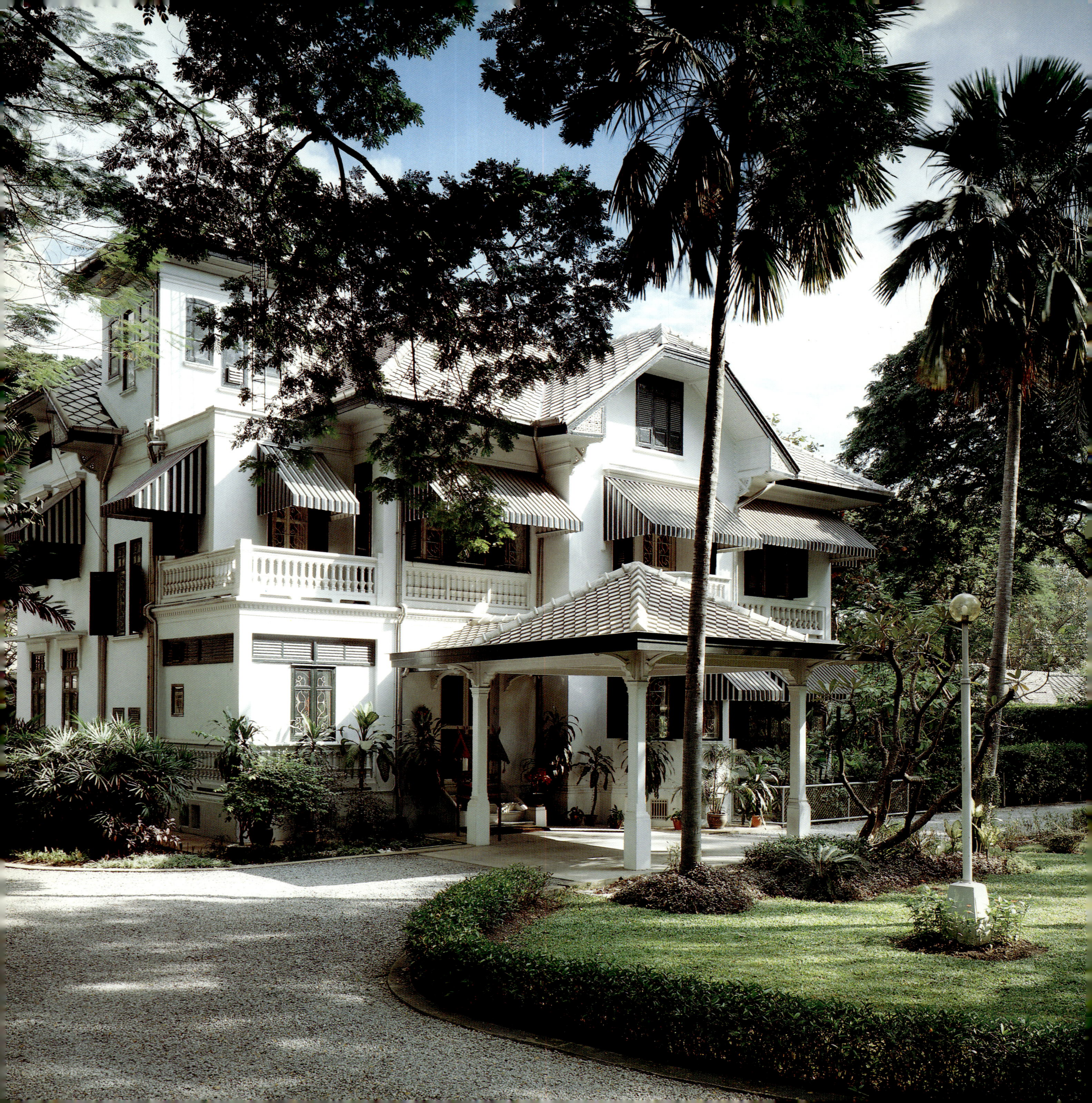

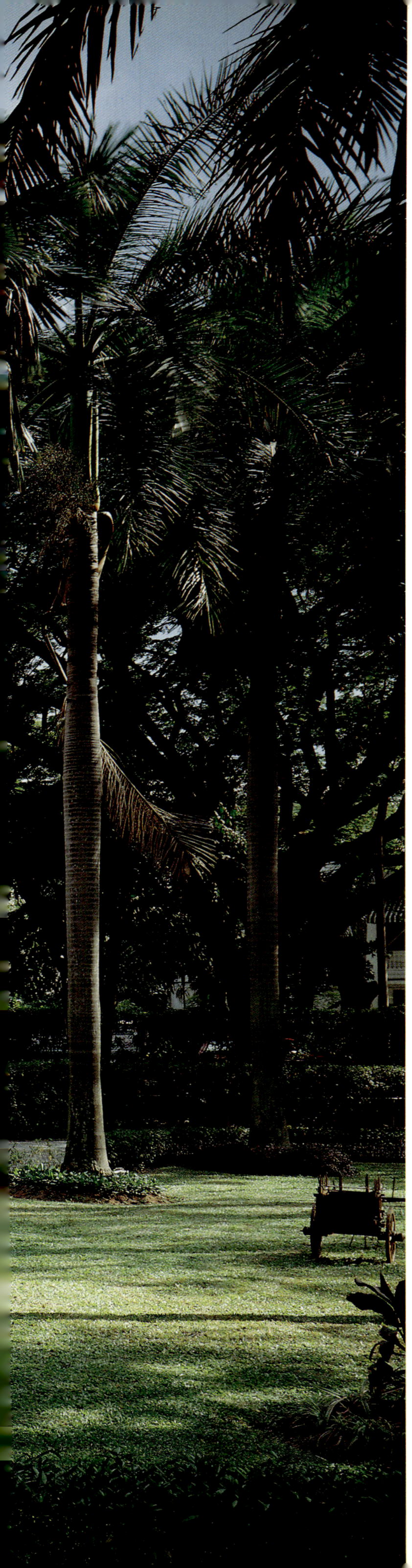

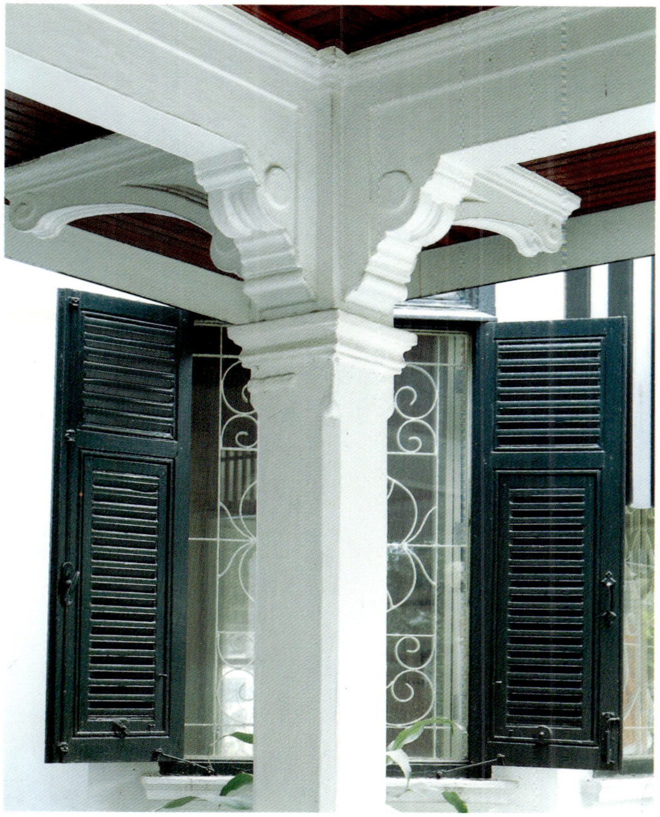

Opposite page : *Victorian in inspiration, the house of the Deputy Chief of Mission on Rajdamri Road was given to the American Embassy just after the Second World War.*
Left : *One of the columns supporting the entrance pavilion; the house was built during the reign of King Rama VI.*
Below : *Living room, decorated with objects acquired during service in a number of Asian countries.*

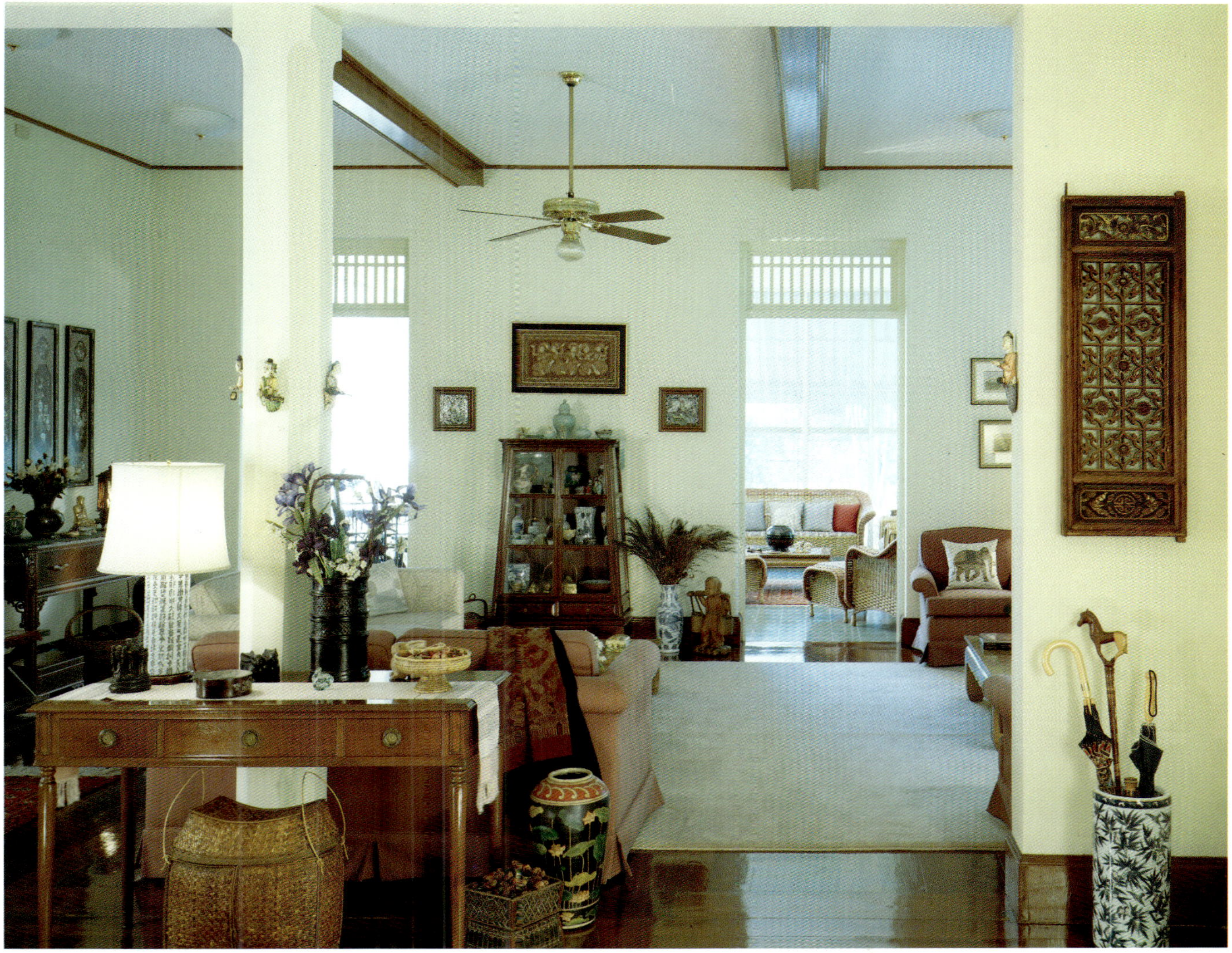

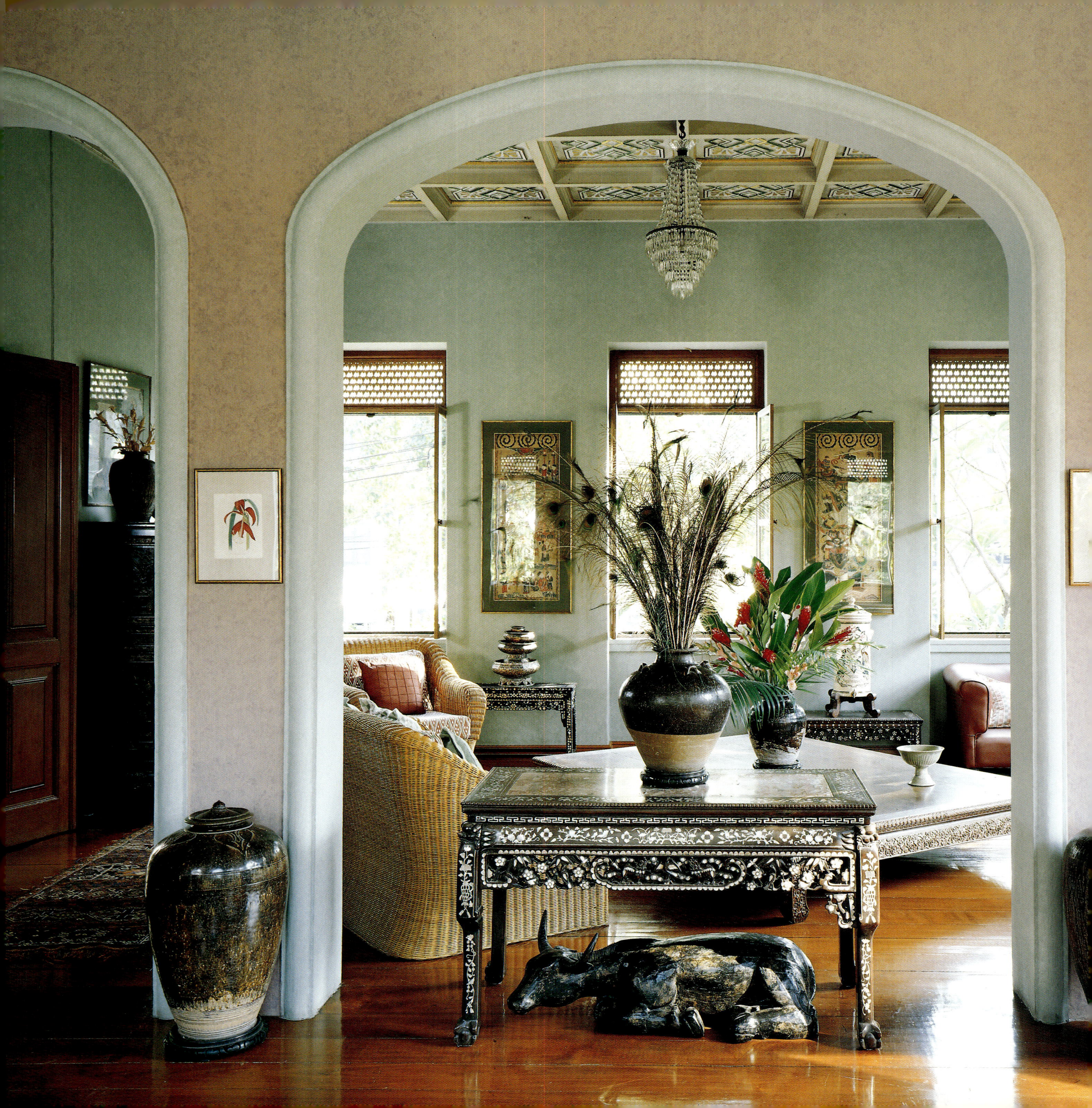

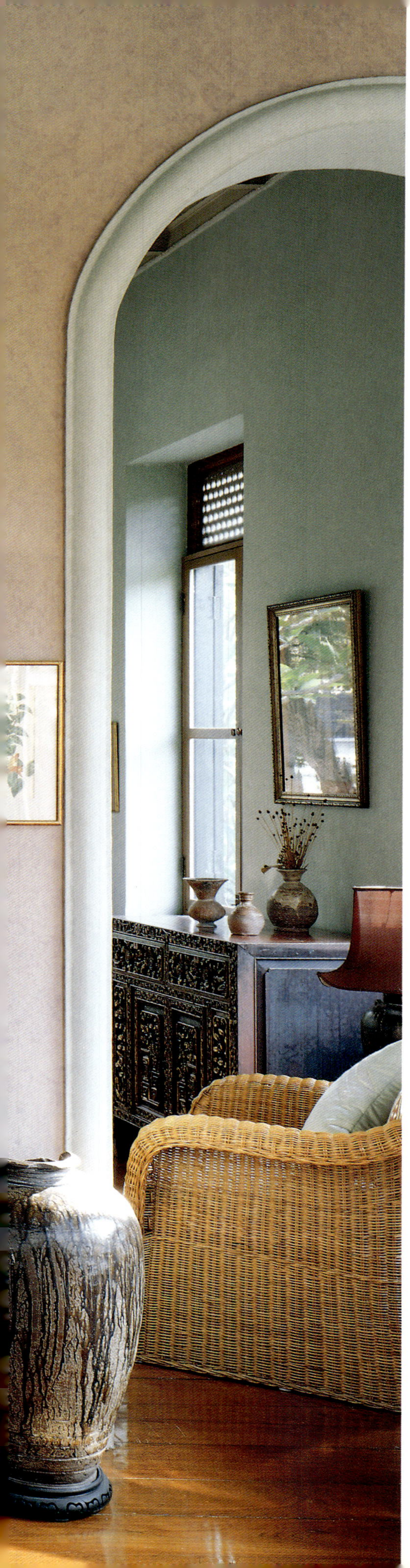

Devavesm Palace

Devavesm Palace was built during the reign of King Rama VI for H.R.H. Prince Devawongse Varopakarn, head of the Devakul family. An elder brother of Queen Saowabha Phongsri. Prince Devawongse served as Minister of Foreign Affairs for 38 years under both King Rama V and King Rama VI. He formerly lived at Saphan Than Palace, but when that area became too crowded King Rama VI and the Queen Mother built the new palace for him on Samsen Road, between two others built for Prince Paribatra to the south and Krom Phra Chandhaburi to the north, the land having already been granted by King Rama V for the prince to use after his retirement.

E.G. Gollo, an Italian engineer who came to Thailand in 1900 and helped supervise construction of the Ananta Samakhom Throne Hall, served as architect on the new palace. When the residence was completed in 1918, the name "Devavesm Palace" was bestowed by King Rama VI.

The palace actually consisted of several buildings, which after Prince Devawongse's death in 1923 were divided among his children. This particular building, by then in a state of considerable disrepair, was sold by the Devakul family and eventually acquired by Phya Vidura Dharmabinet during the Second World War. A few years later, he bought one of the other buildings opposite.

Phya Vidura, a Privy Councilor under Rama VI and Rama VII and later elected a Member of Parliament from Uthai Thani, restored the palace, repairing the fine Roman-style stucco work and installing crystal chandeliers from Europe, and used it to entertain friends and foreign diplomats. A noted orchid enthusiast, he was reputed to have the best collection of Catleyas in Thailand at the time and was fond of giving the finest ones to the wives of his ambassadorial guests at dinner parties. His son, the future Ambassador Prok Amranand, lived there during his time as a student at Thammasat University and, later, after his return from studies abroad for a short time.

Over the years, somewhat confusingly, both Wang Krom Phra Chandhaburi (home of the Kitiyakara family) and Wang Devavesm became known as Wang Deves, no doubt because both are located in the Deves district and perhaps also, in the latter case, because of a similarity of names.

Dr. Piyasvasti and Khun Anik Amranand currently occupy this palace building, a three-story structure with louvered shutters, two wings, and handsome stucco decorations. Thanks to their care and restorations, this elegant relic of Bangkok's past continues to be a part of its very different present.

Left : *Interior of Devavesm Palace; originally two separate rooms, these were opened to make twin sitting rooms by Phya Vidura Dharmabinet, the current owner's grandfather.*

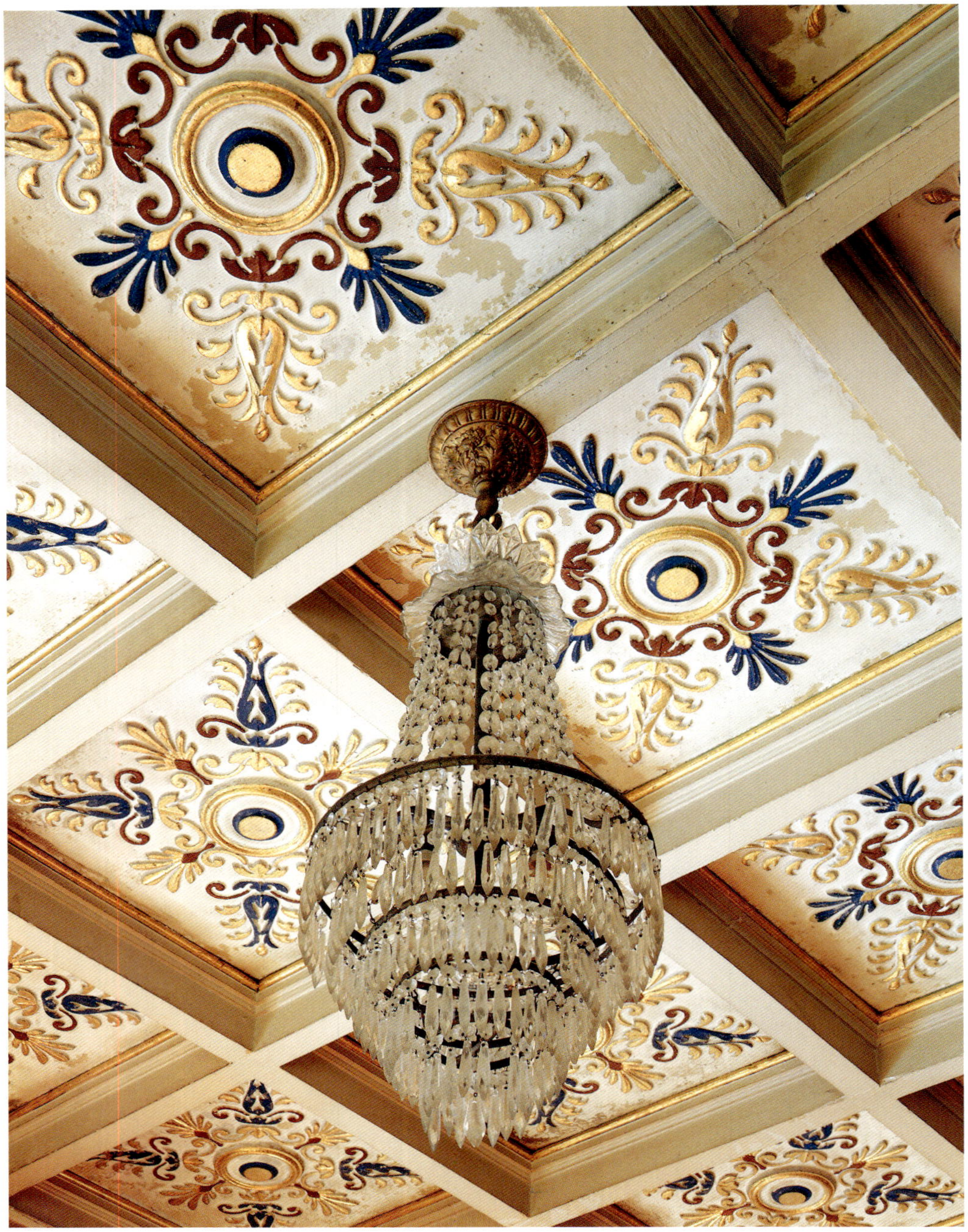

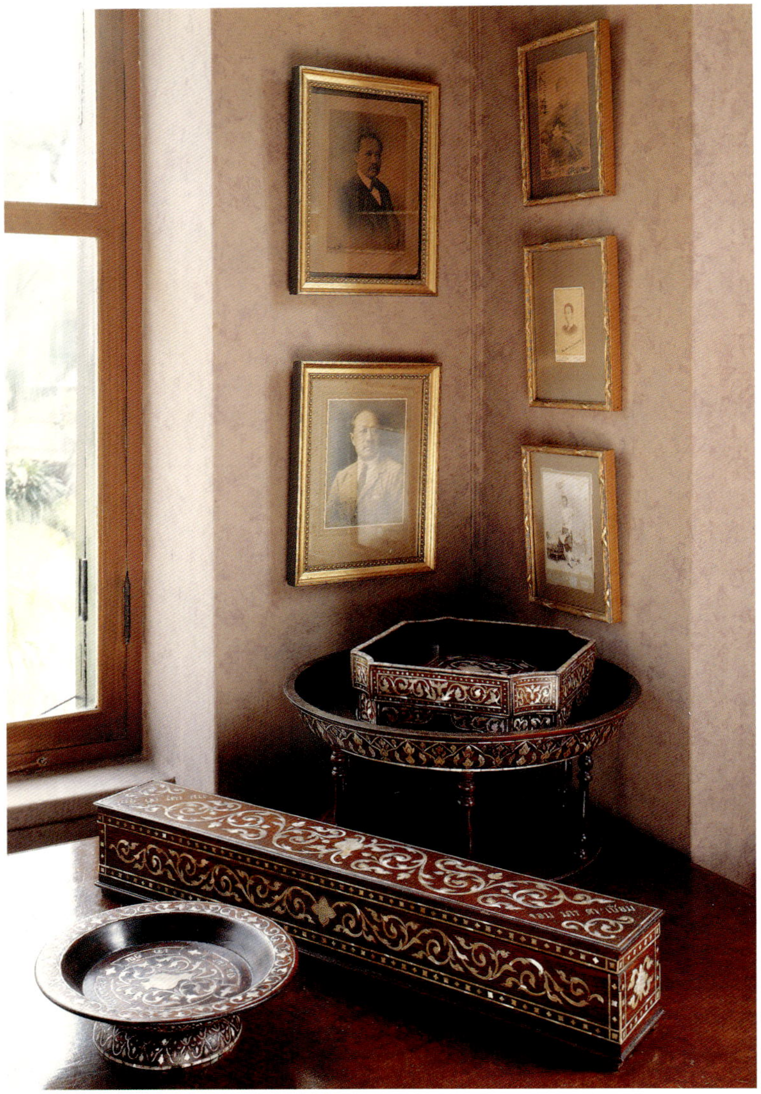

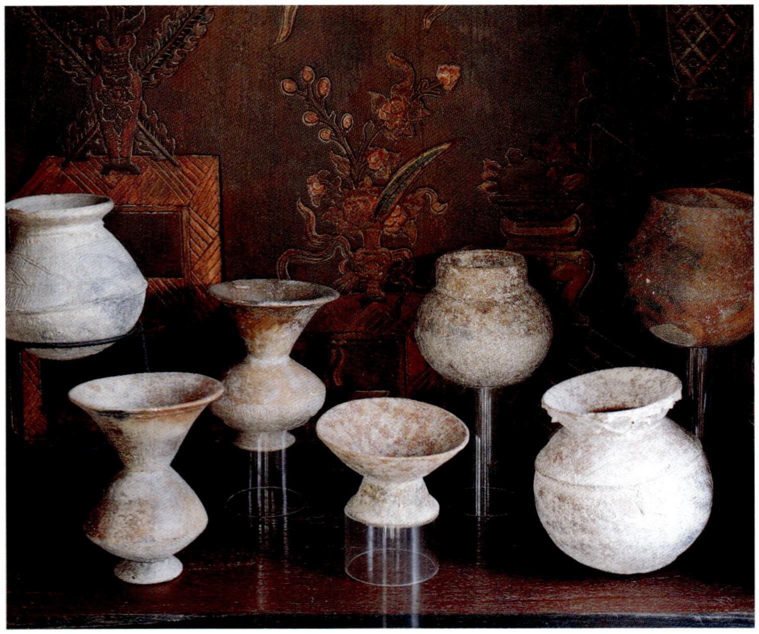

Above : *Detail of ceiling stucco decorations; the crystal chandelier came from Europe.*
Above left : *Items decorated with mother-of-pearl inlaid designs.*
Left : *Prehistoric pottery in a Chinese display cabinet.*
Opposite page : *Sitting area; the carved gable on the wall is from northern Thailand.*

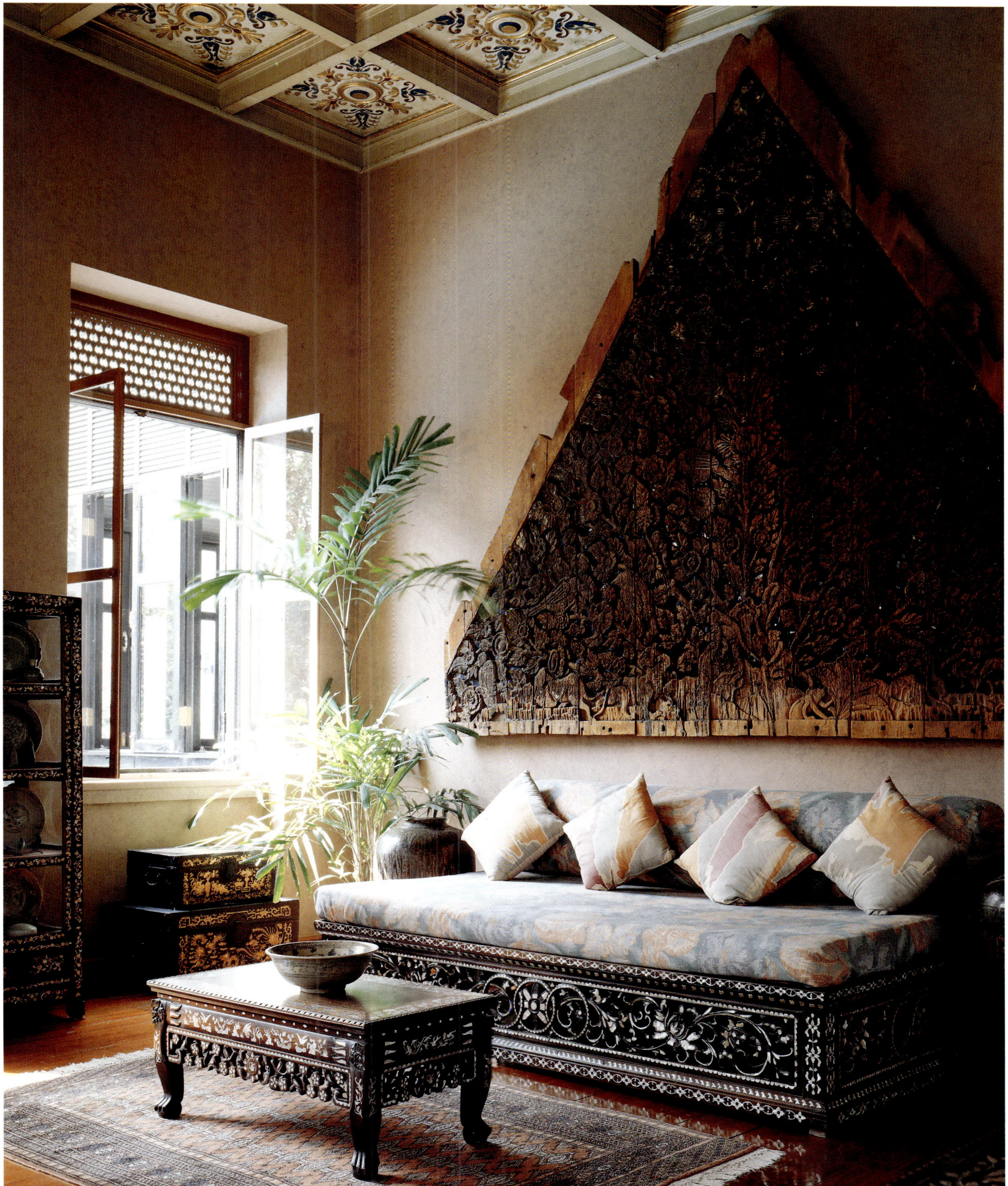

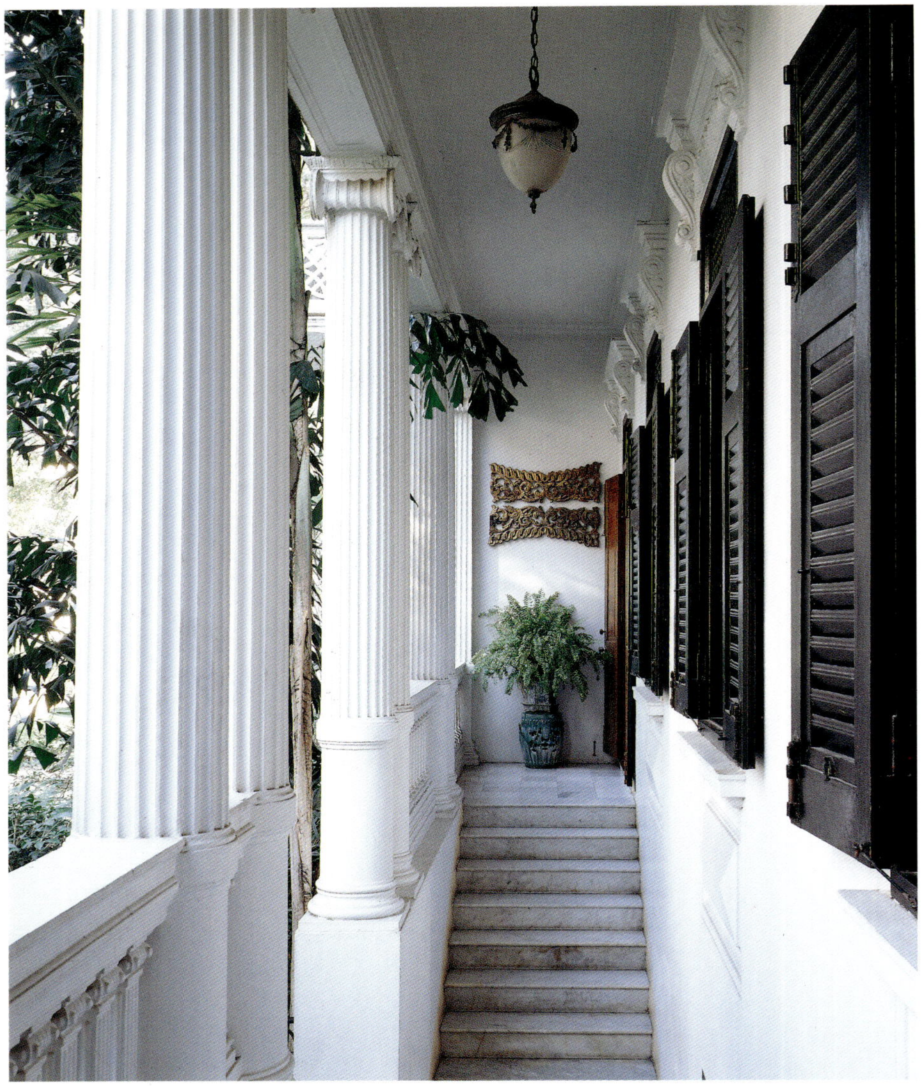

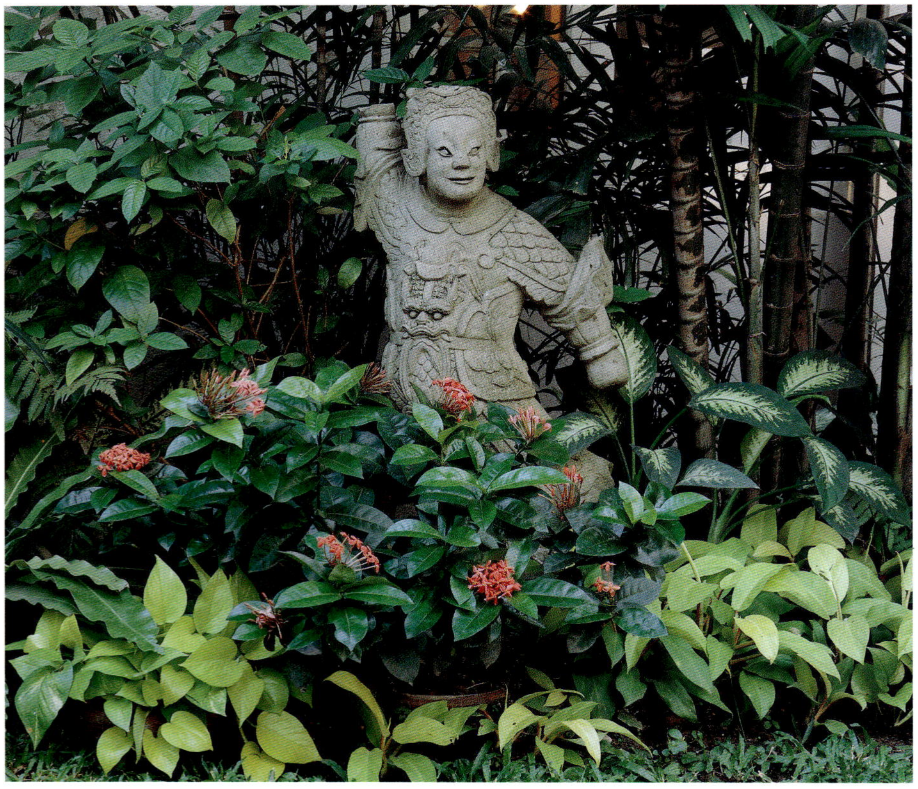

Right : *Front view of Devavesm Palace, built during the reign of King Rama VI for Prince Devawongse Varopakarn.*
Above left : *Entrance stair, with classical columns on the left; the palace was designed by an Italian engineer.*
Left : *Chinese guardian figure, used as a garden decoration; many such statues came to Thailand in the 19th century.*

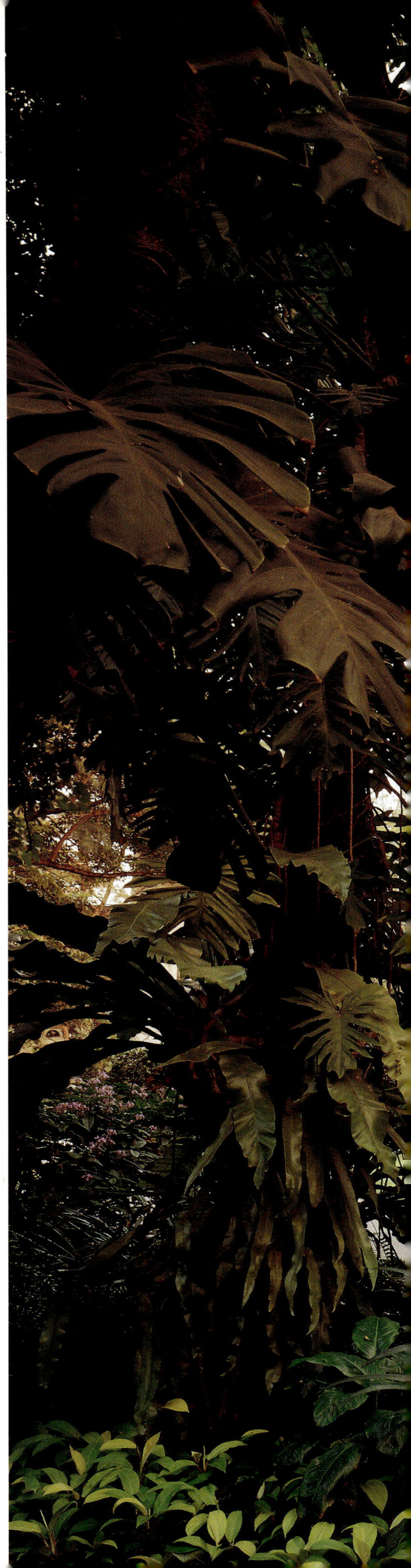

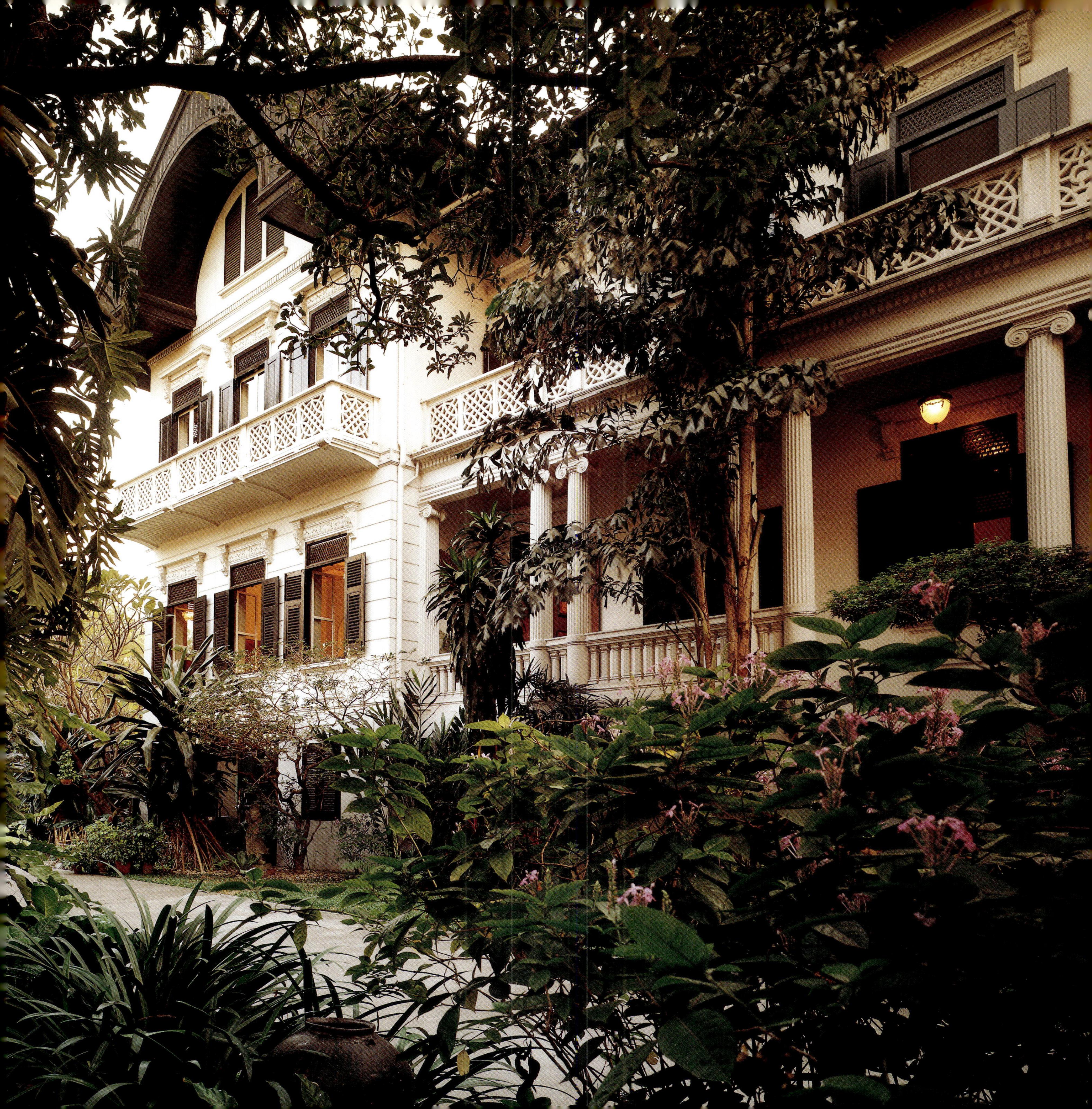

Abdulrahim House

Located on Rama IV Road across from Lumpini Park, in what is today one of Bangkok's busiest areas, the Abdulrahim House stands as a nostalgic reminder of an era long past but not yet entirely forgotten.

It was built by H. Abdulrahim, a Thai-born Indian merchant whose father's shop, founded in 1872, became so well-known for fine imported merchandise that it came under royal patronage in 1902; several decorative items from the shop, such as marble vases, were used in furnishing the Ananta Samakhom Throne Hall. The family lived at the time on the upper floor of the shop, on Fuang Nakhon Road opposite Wat Raj Bophit, and it was to escape the heat and congestion of the old city that H. Abdulrahim acquired ten rai of land in the Saladaeng area in the first decade of the present century. Though the Royal Bangkok Sports Club had recently opened not far away—by 1908, it had a race track and some 300 members—Saladaeng was then regarded as suburban; the property bought by H. Abdulrahim was being used as a Chinese vegetable garden, with Klong Hua Lamphong running along the front, Rama IV Road was a mere dirt track, and the future Lumpini Park consisted of rice fields.

A bungalow-style house was built on the land, with a lower level open to the garden and wooden stairs leading to a second floor entirely made of wood. The rooms were located in two wings on either side of a large, airy verandah, and the decorations included woodwork featuring Islamic patterns of a crescent moon and star and intricate fretwork on the gables and brackets in a style popular on such residences at the end of King Rama V's reign. Here the family retreated for holidays to relax and enjoy the fresh air, a long carriage ride away from the bustle of Fuang Nakhon Road.

Later the house was leased to a succession of Europeans working for the government, among them a Financial Advisor and the Manager of the Wat Lieb Electricity Office. Shortly after the death of H. Abdulrahim, in the early 1930s, the family moved in permanently and has remained there ever since. The present owner is Khun Prachoom Abdulrahim, who was born in 1907 and who has watched the many drastic changes that have gone on around her home. In the garden stands a white pillar with the name "H. Abdulrahim" inscribed on it. This was one of a pair that once stood on the bridge that led to the house across Klong Hua Lamphong; when Rama IV Road was widened in the 1960s, the bridge was destroyed but the pillar was rescued by Khun Prachoom's sister and survives, like the house itself.

Several years ago, now occupying only two rai of its former ten, the house underwent a major renovation, during which the lower level was re-paved and two small servants' rooms enlarged. No major structural changes were made, however, due to the owner's desire to preserve its original form. Indeed, such was her concern that she herself approached the Fine Arts Department and requested that the house be registered as a National Historic Building so that it cannot be torn down or inappropriately altered in the future.

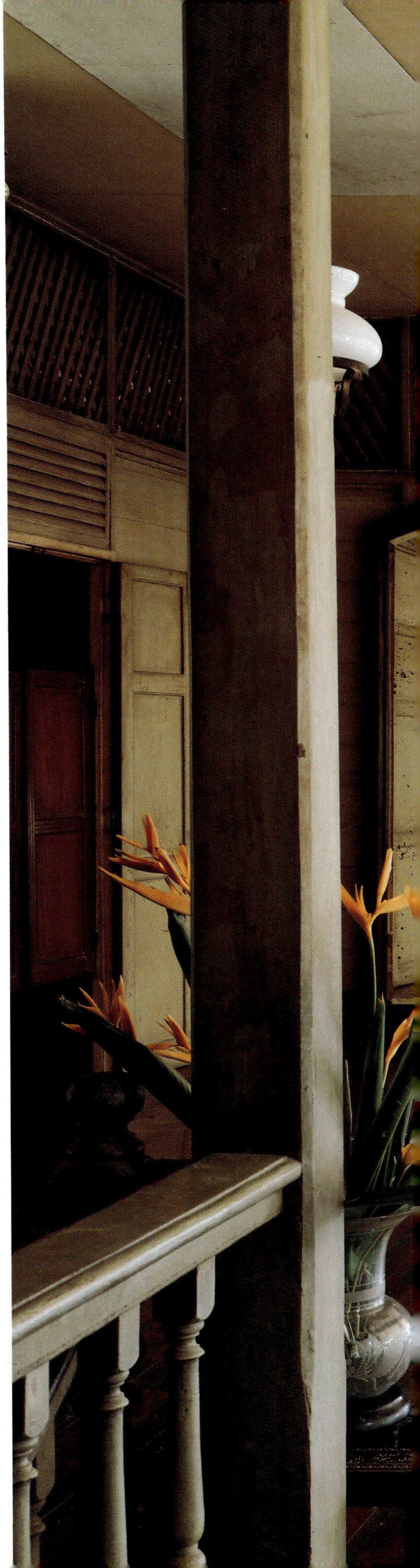

Right : *Open verandah in the center of the Abdulrahim House, flanked by two wings.*

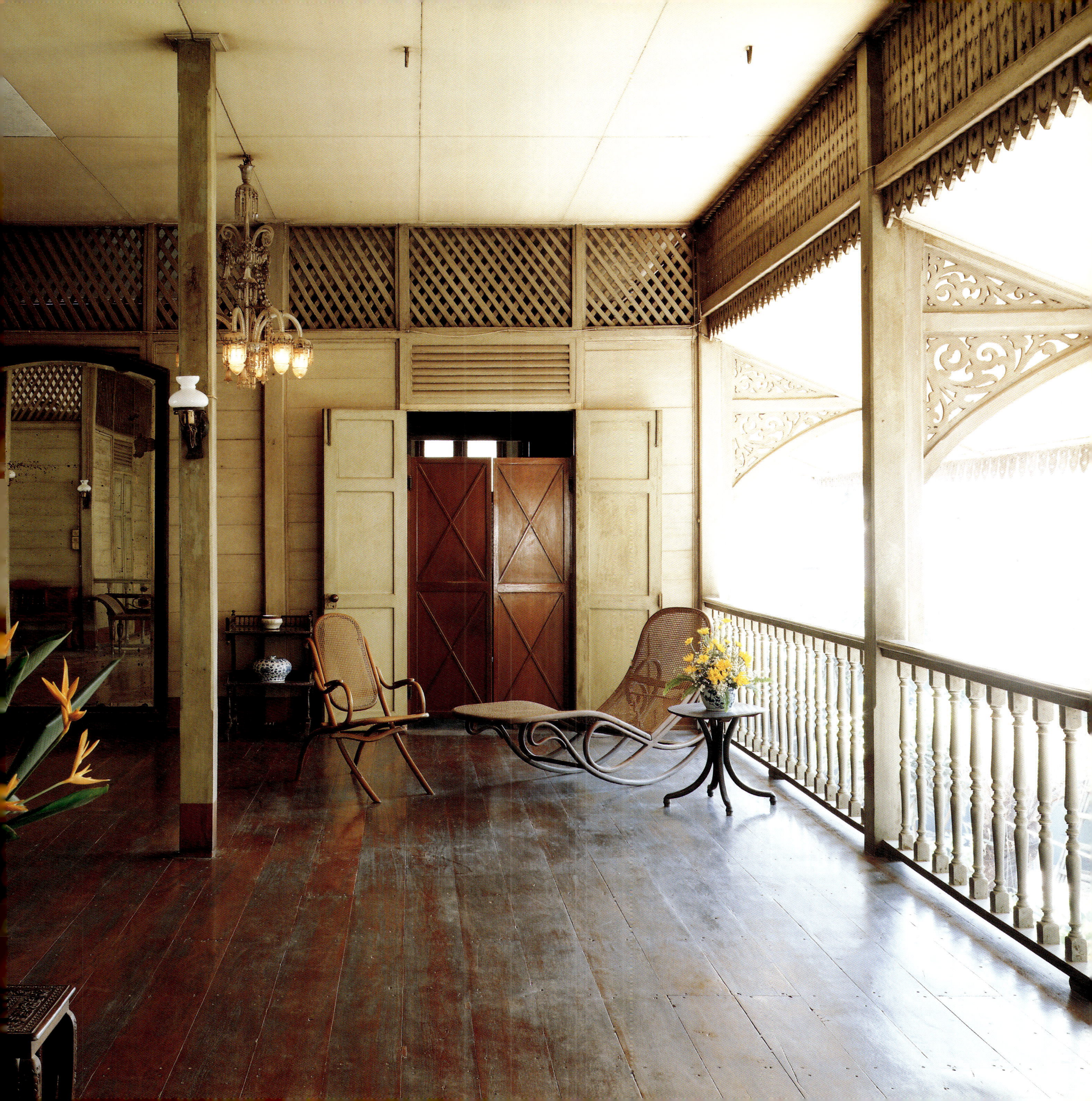

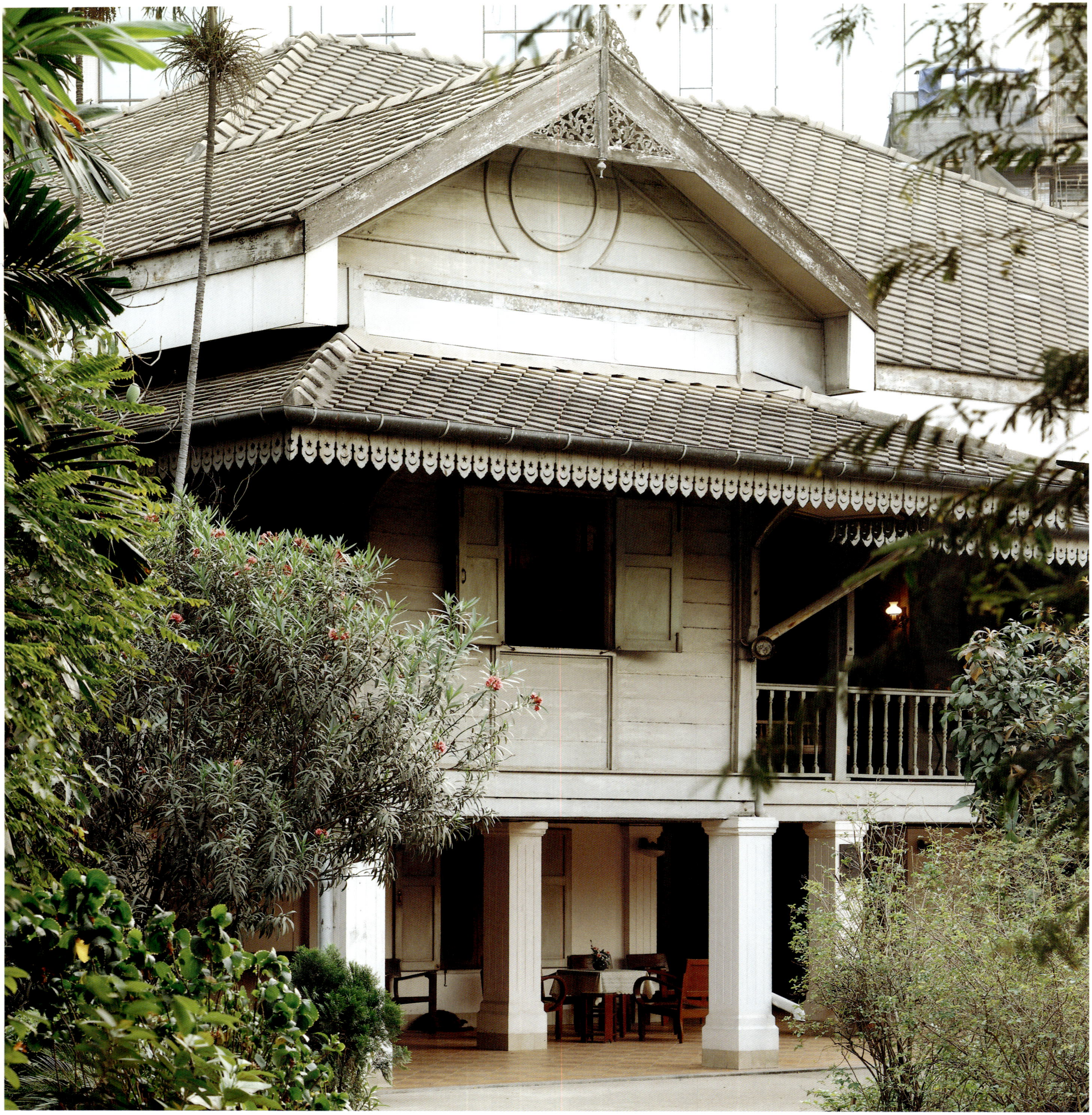

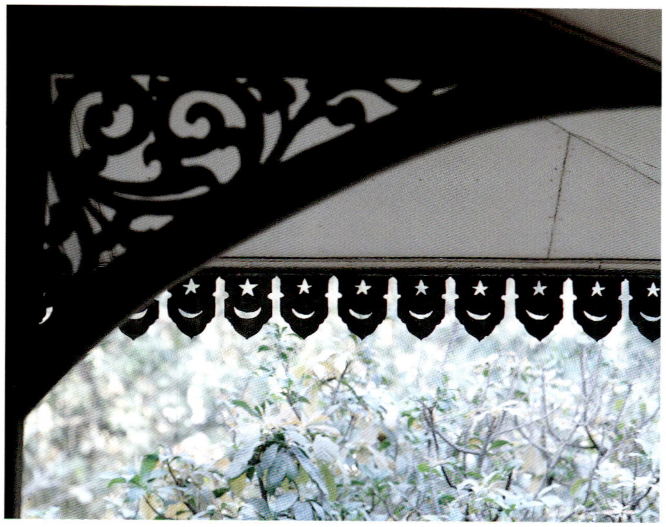

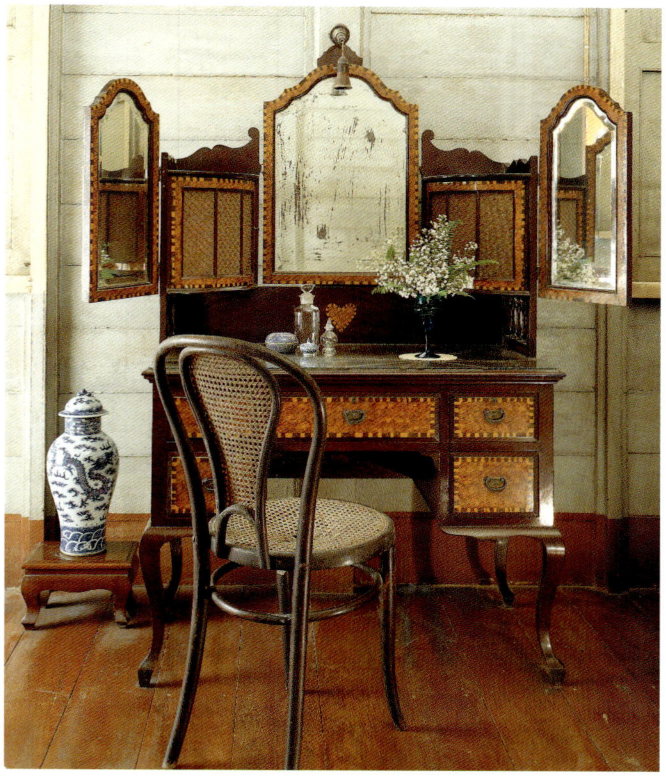

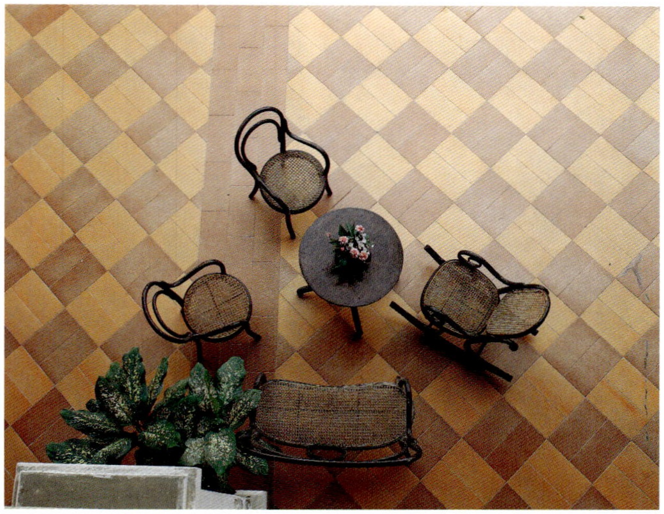

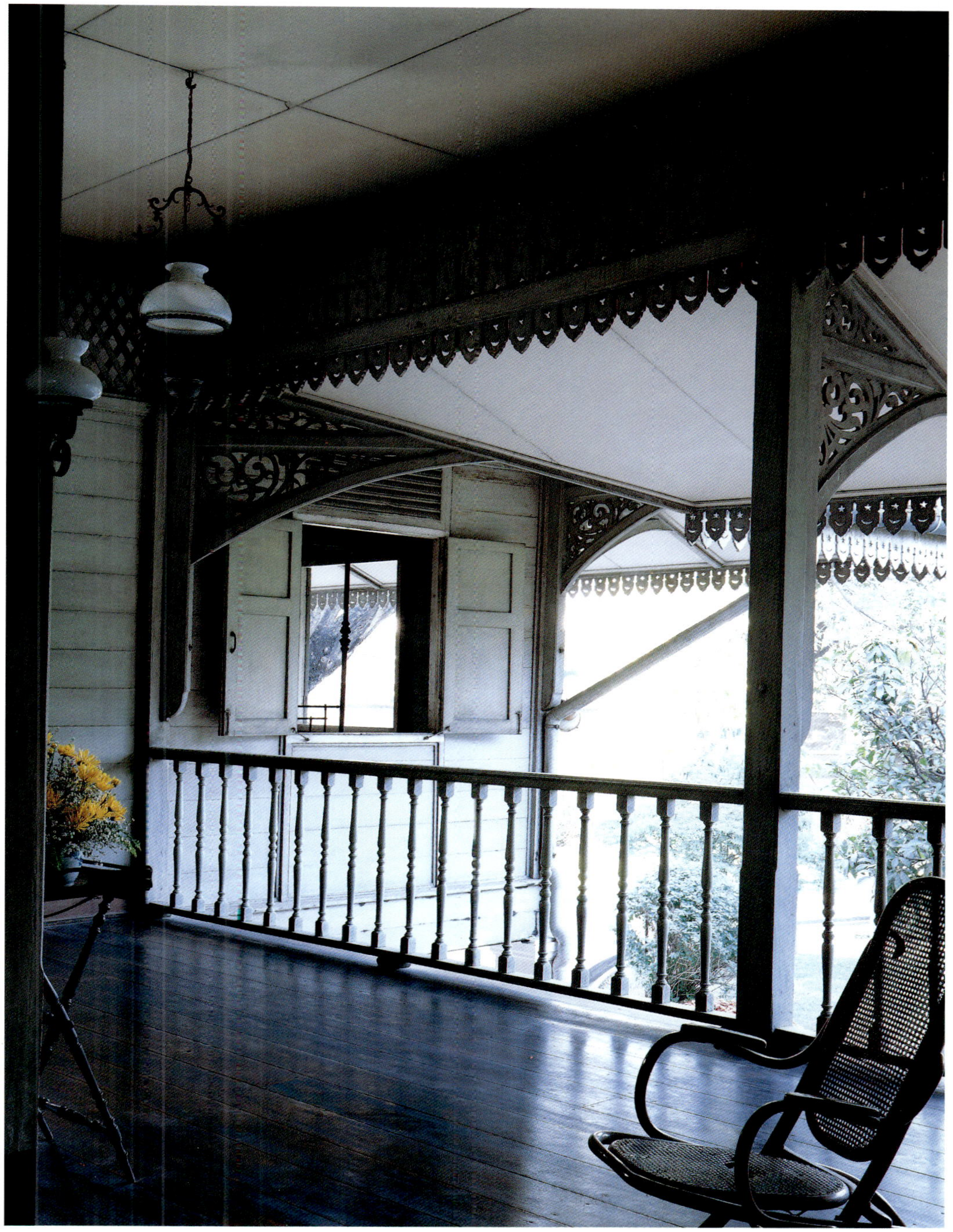

Opposite page : *Front of the Abdulrahim House facing Rama IV Road, built in the early years of the present century.*
Above : *Upstairs verandah, showing carved brackets and gingerbread decorations.*
Top left : *Ornamental woodwork featuring Islamic patterns of crescent moon and star.*
Middle left : *Antique dressing table in upstairs bedroom.*
Bottom left : *A tiled lower level with children's chairs once sold at the Abdulrahim store on Fuang Nakhon Road.*

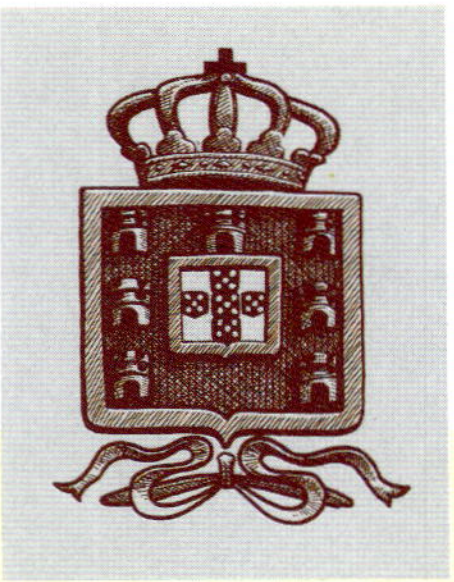

The Portuguese Embassy Residence

In the early 16th century, during the Ayutthaya period, the Portuguese were the first Europeans to open trade relations with Siam. They were also the first Westerners to be granted land for a "factory," or trading post, and subsequently a consulate on the east bank of the Chao Phraya River in Bangkok. The Letter of Concession is dated 1820, and shortly afterwards the first buildings were constructed on the site.

According to F.A. Neale, an Englishman who came to work with the Thai Navy in the early 19th century, the consul's early residence "was very indifferently constructed with bamboos, poles, lath, and plaster, but it was an extensive house, cleanly whitewashed, neatly furnished, and situated in one of the pleasantest positions in Siam. It was the original intention of the Portuguese Government to construct a splendid brick palace as a fit residence for their envoy at this illustrious court, and so far had they progressed towards the carrying out of their intention that a vessel laden with the finest bricks, and accompanied by Portuguese masons and artificers, actually sailed from Goa (the Portuguese island on the Malabar coast) bound for the city of Bangkok. But alas! she was tempest-tost in the China Seas, and finally stranded on some hidden shoal, from which the crew with difficulty emerged with their lives. The vessel went down, the bricks sunk with her, and so did the hopes of the poor Portuguese consul, for his Government could but ill afford to risk such another cargo, and so [the consul] hoisted his flag on a flagstaff more fitting for his intended consulate than it was for the very unpresuming house he occupied."

Dr. Dan Beach Bradley, who came in 1835, notes that "the Portuguese Consulate was at that time situated very nearly in the place it now occupies [i.e., the 1870s, just before Bradley's death], and its buildings were of the antique bungalow style." As this suggests, the present building dates from somewhat later and was probably constructed in several stages. It faces the river, with an open, tiled area below and, as was typical of the period, a large, airy verandah above flanked by wings containing the bedrooms. As in many old houses in Europe, the rooms lead to one another without the use of interior corridors.

Several recent ambassadors have renovated and restored the house, which is possibly the oldest Western-style residence in Bangkok and certainly one of the most impressive.

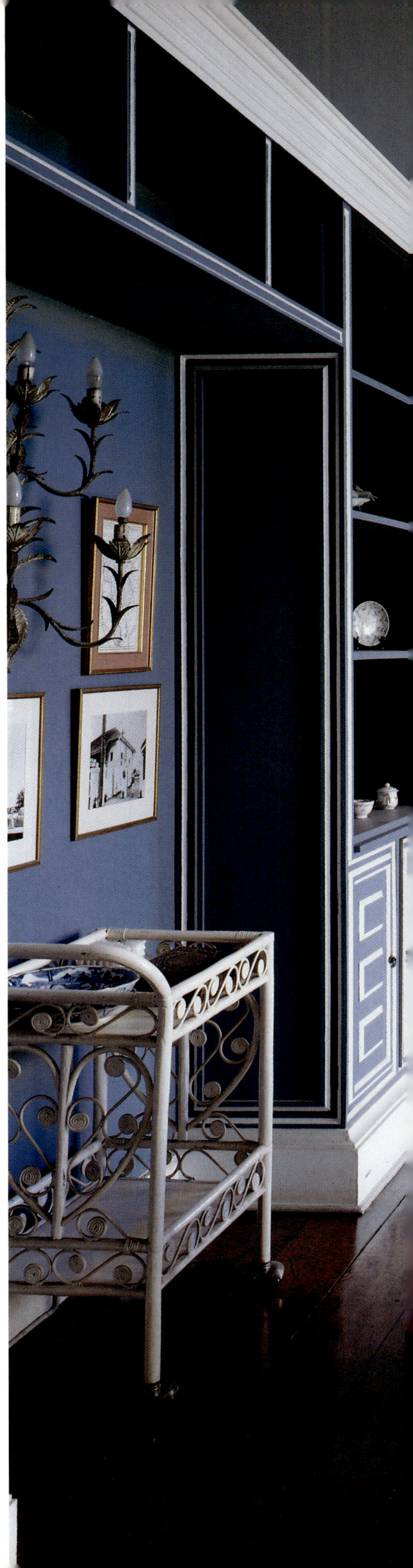

Right : *Upper floor of the Portuguese Embassy Residence, with arched windows, louvered shutters, and rattan furniture; dating from the early 19th century, this is the oldest embassy in Thailand.*

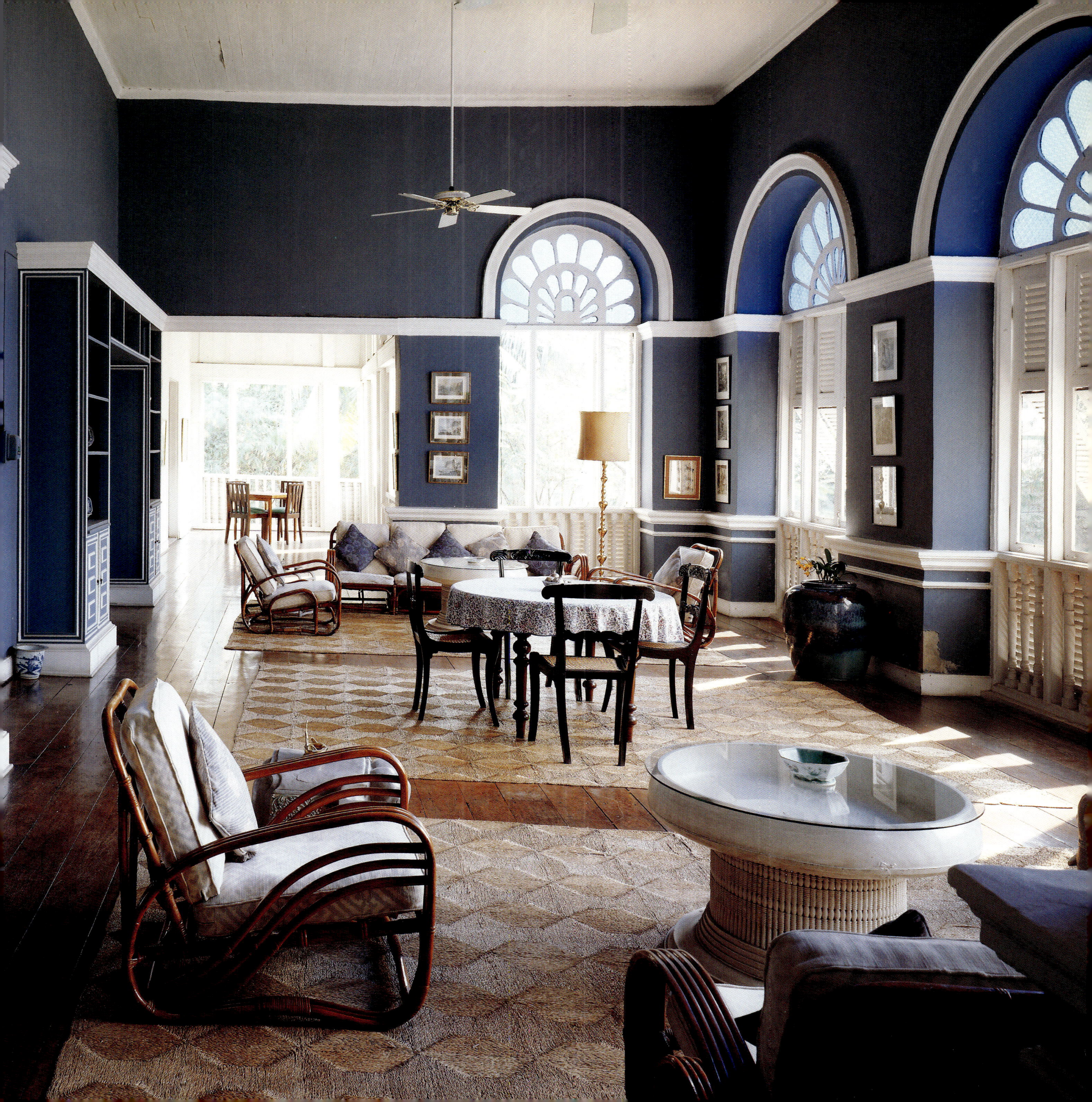

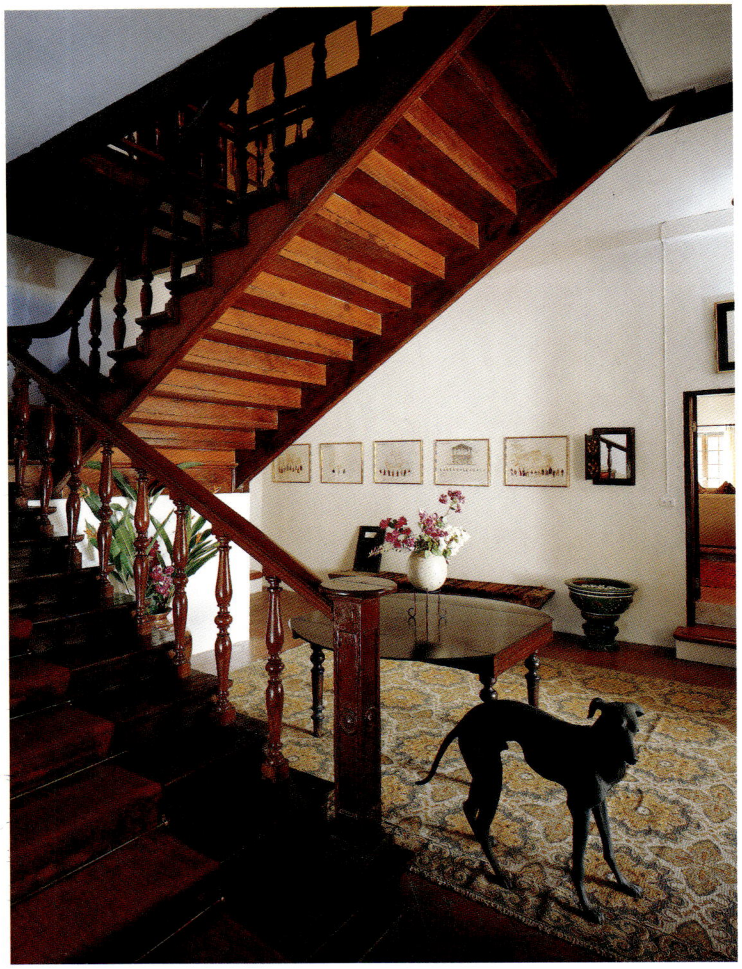

Right : *Facade of the Portuguese Embassy Residence, facing the Chao Phraya River.*
Left : *Teak staircase leading to the upper floor.*
Below : *Tiled terrace on the lower level of the Residence, facing the river.*
Bottom : *Lower living room with thick walls and teak roof beams, probably the oldest part of the building.*

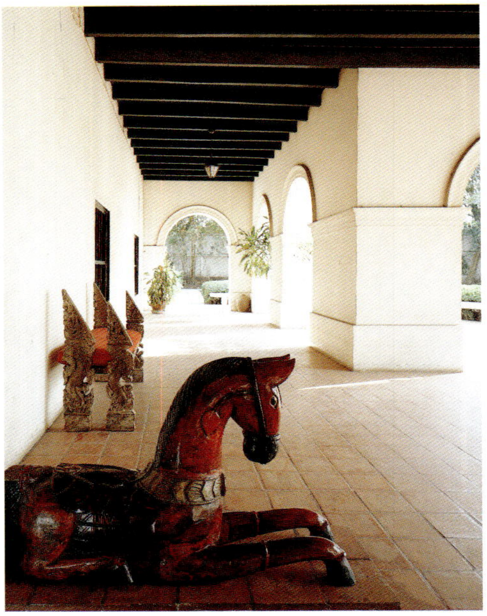

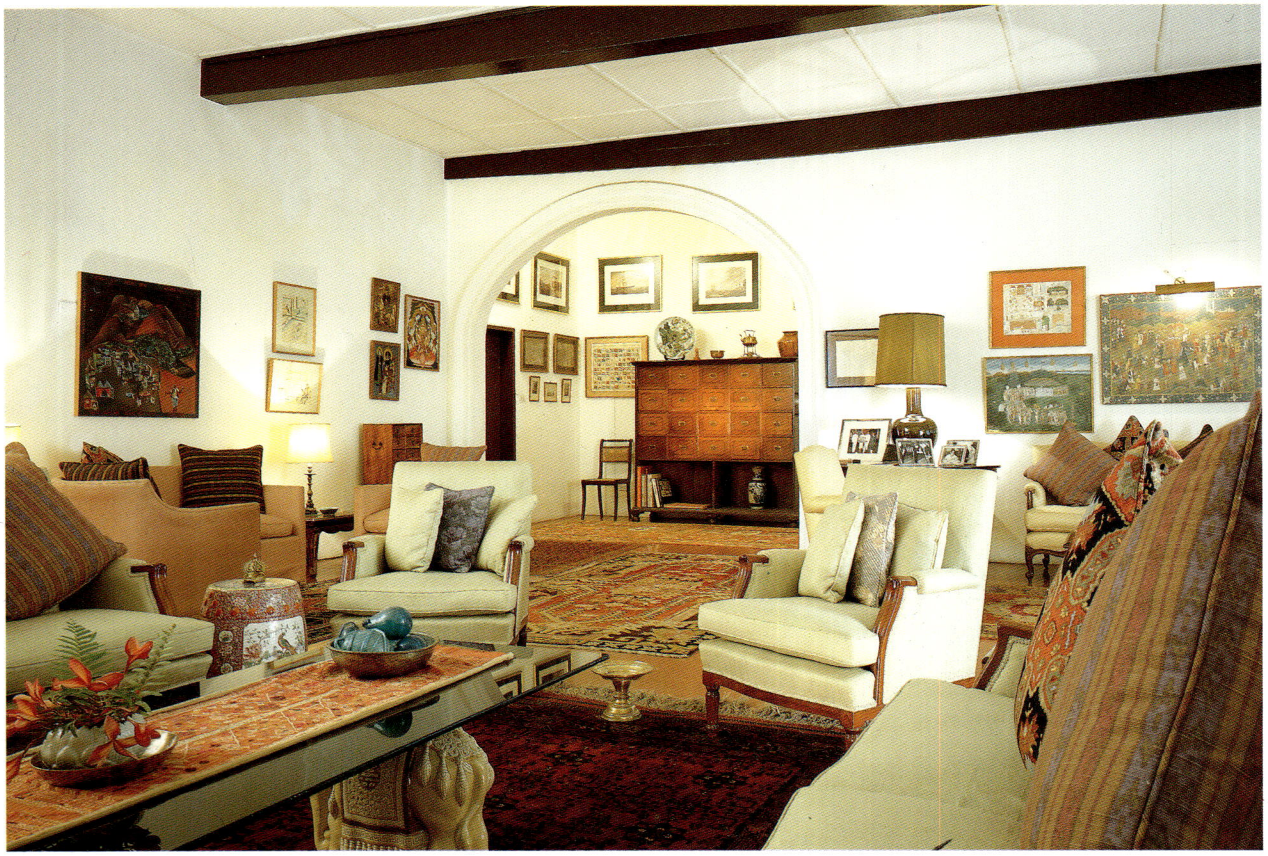

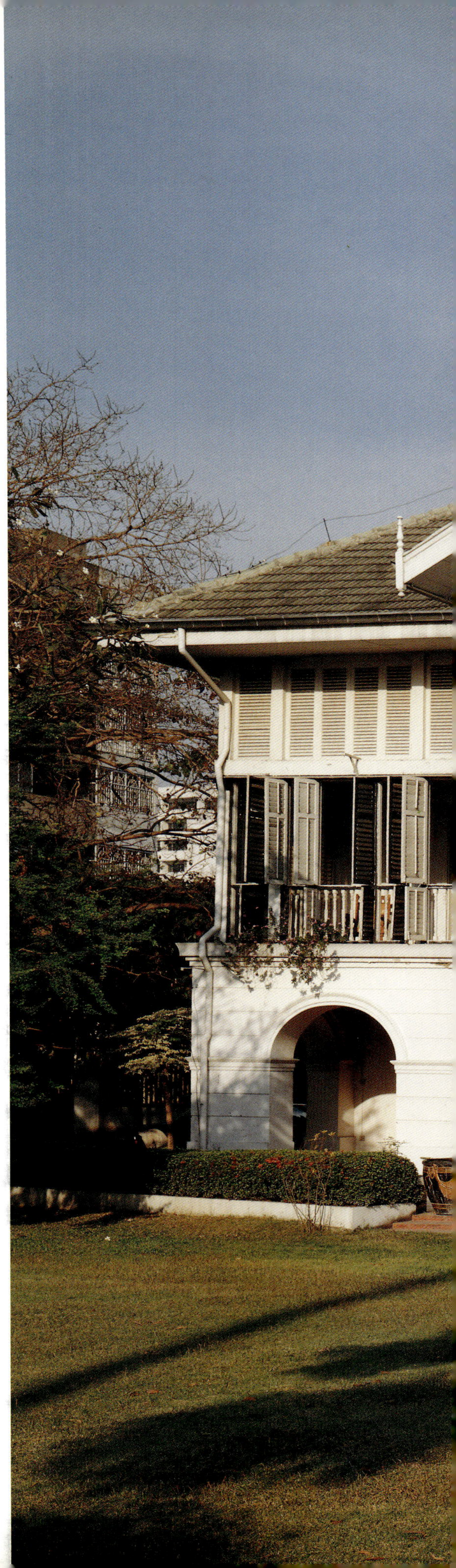

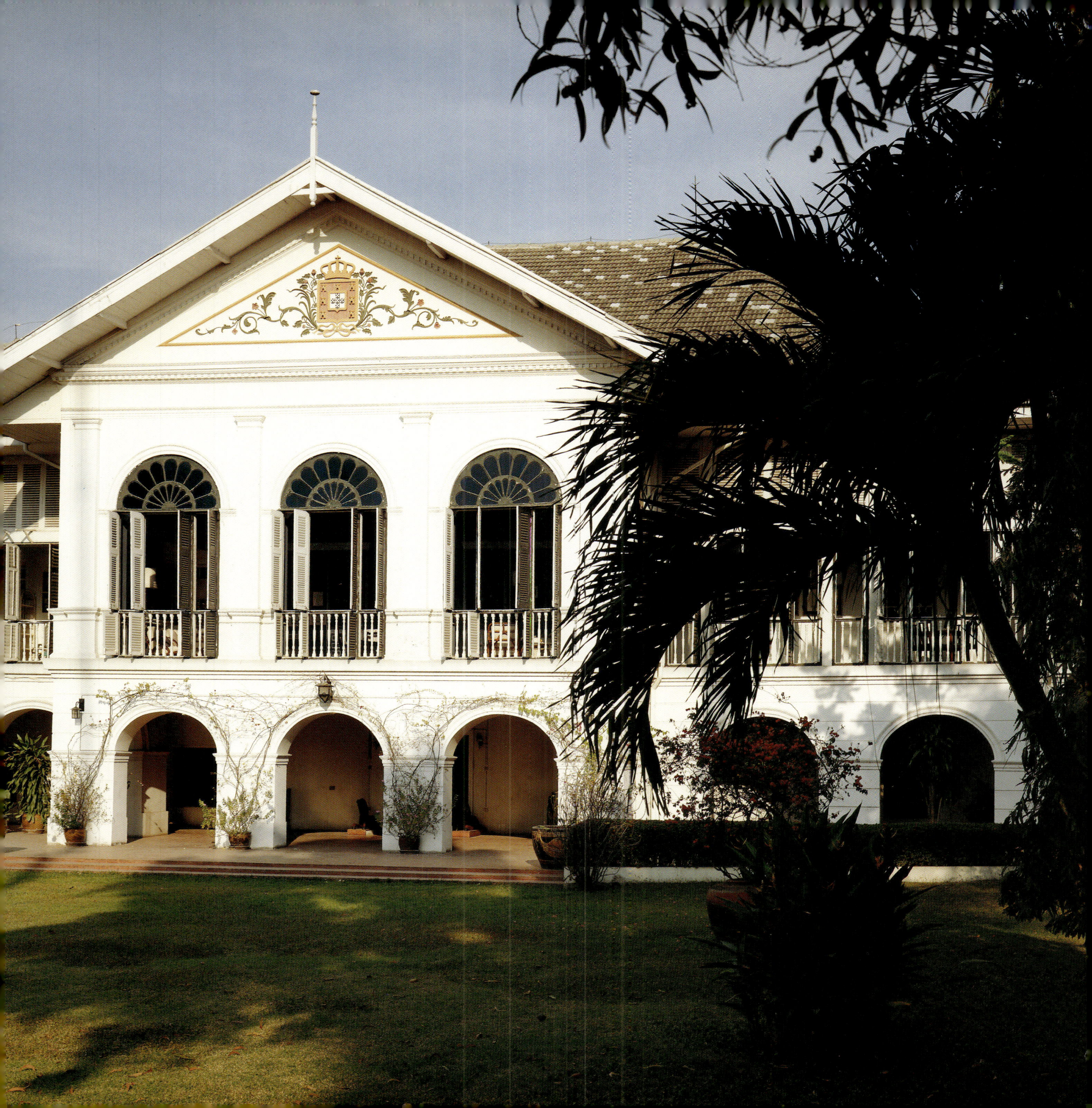

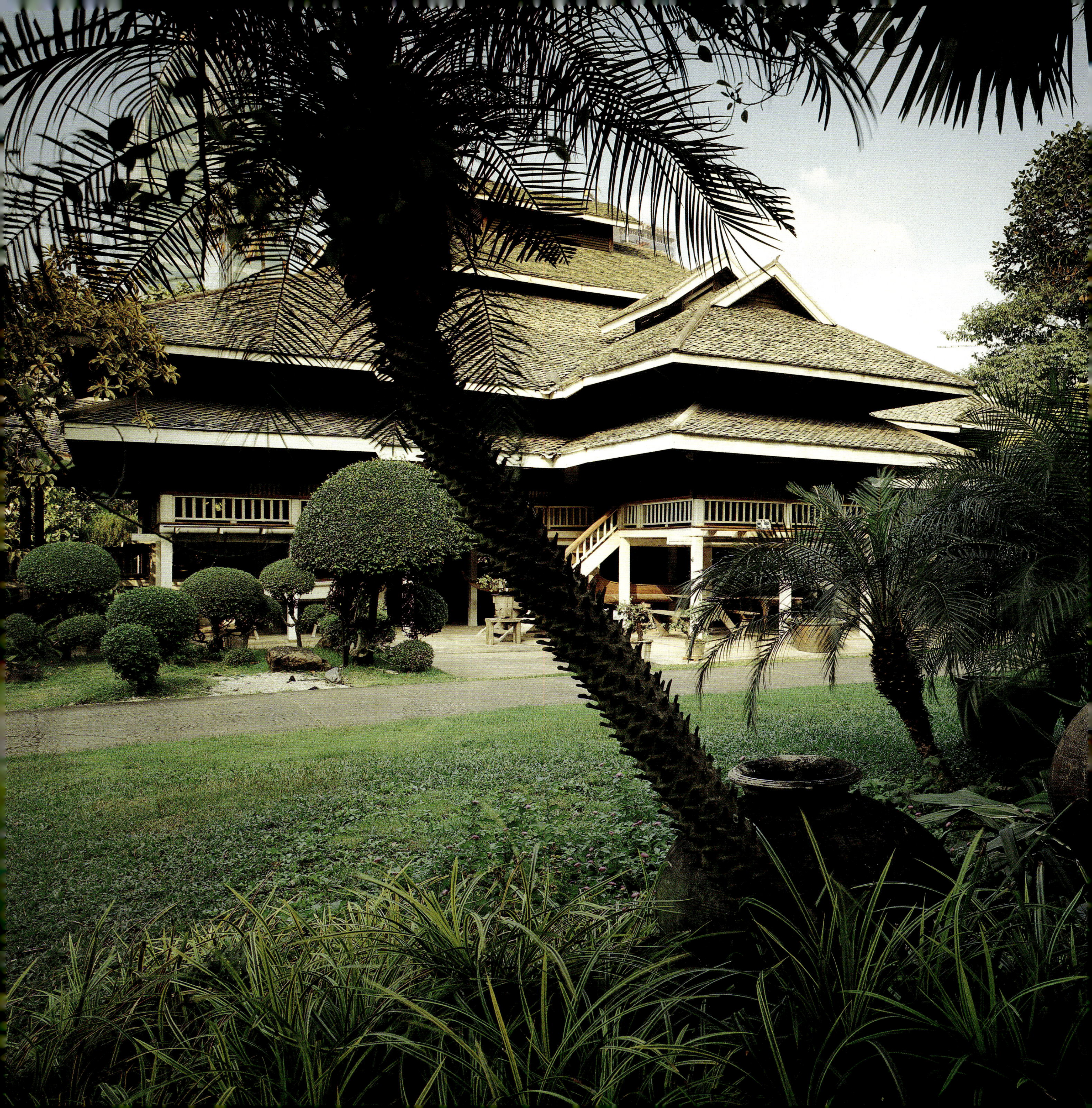

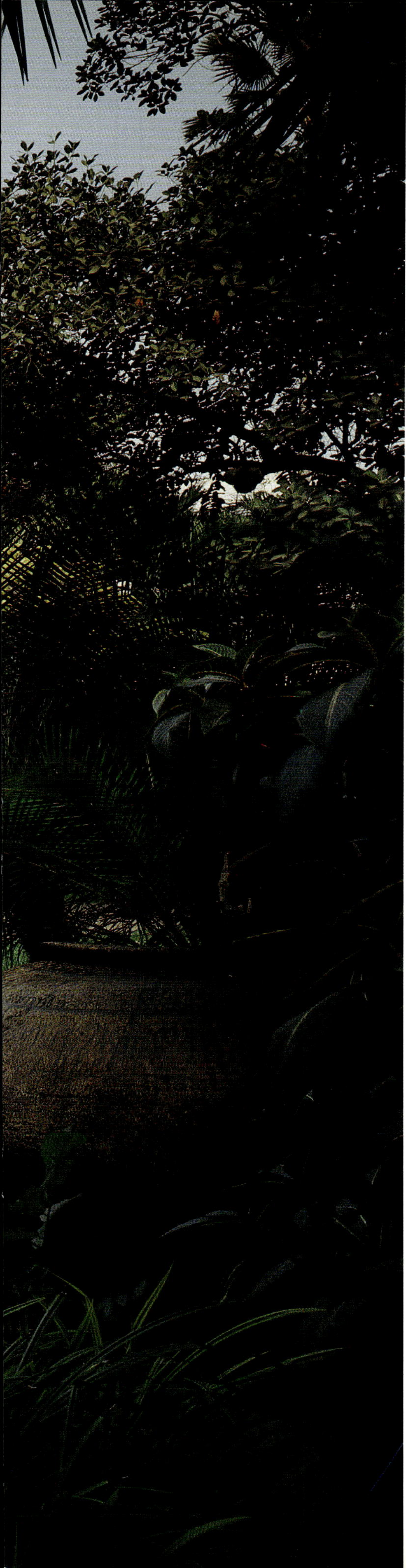

The Nai Lert House

Lert Sreshthaputra, better known as Nai Lert, was a successful businessman when, in 1915, he acquired 65 rai of land in the Ploenchit area of Bangkok from a member of the royal family. This was then regarded as a rather distant suburb, the principal means of access being by water along Klong Saen Saep, but Nai Lert had the prescience to see that Bangkok was expanding eastward and away from its traditional center along the Chao Phraya River. He laid out streets on the property, planted Rain Trees along them, and, in time, sold off most of the land; one large plot was acquired by the British Embassy when it decided to leave its original riverside site. Retaining another large piece for himself, he began construction of a house where he and his family and friends could relax and enjoy the fresh country air on weekends.

The house is often described as being in Burmese style, perhaps because of its layered roofs, but there is no evidence of any such intent in the family's recollections. Instead it seems to have been inspired by the spacious bungalows that were then common in Bangkok. Vents between each of the roof layers encouraged air circulation, which meant there was usually a breeze even on the hottest days, and the deep overhangs on all sides protected the interior from both sunlight and rains.

The house was constructed in two stages. The first, now the rear section, was essentially a large airy pavilion raised about eight feet off the ground on hand-hewn columns. In the 1920s, by which time the family was spending increasingly longer periods there, a second structure was added, almost identical in exterior appearance but with several enclosed bedrooms and bathing facilities. Nai Lert moved permanently to the house in 1927, several years after the British Embassy had gone up across a large pond on one side of the property.

Toward the end of the Second World War, the house was struck by a bomb intended for Japanese in the embassy compound. Despite considerable damage, no one was seriously injured and no fire resulted; the house was soon rebuilt and Nai Lert continued to live there until his death on December 15, 1945.

Today, surrounded by an extensive garden of tropical plants and some of the original Rain Trees planted by its founder, the Nai Lert House is being preserved by his daughter Thanpuying Lursakdi and her husband Khun Binich Sampatisiri. Inevitable changes have taken place due to contemporary city life; several of the interior areas, for example, have been glassed in to allow air-conditioning; but the house retains its open quality, with garden views from almost everywhere, and remains one of Bangkok's most distinctive private residences.

Left : *The older of the two linked pavilion-like units of the Nai Lert House; at left is a planting of trees clipped in the traditional Thai style.*

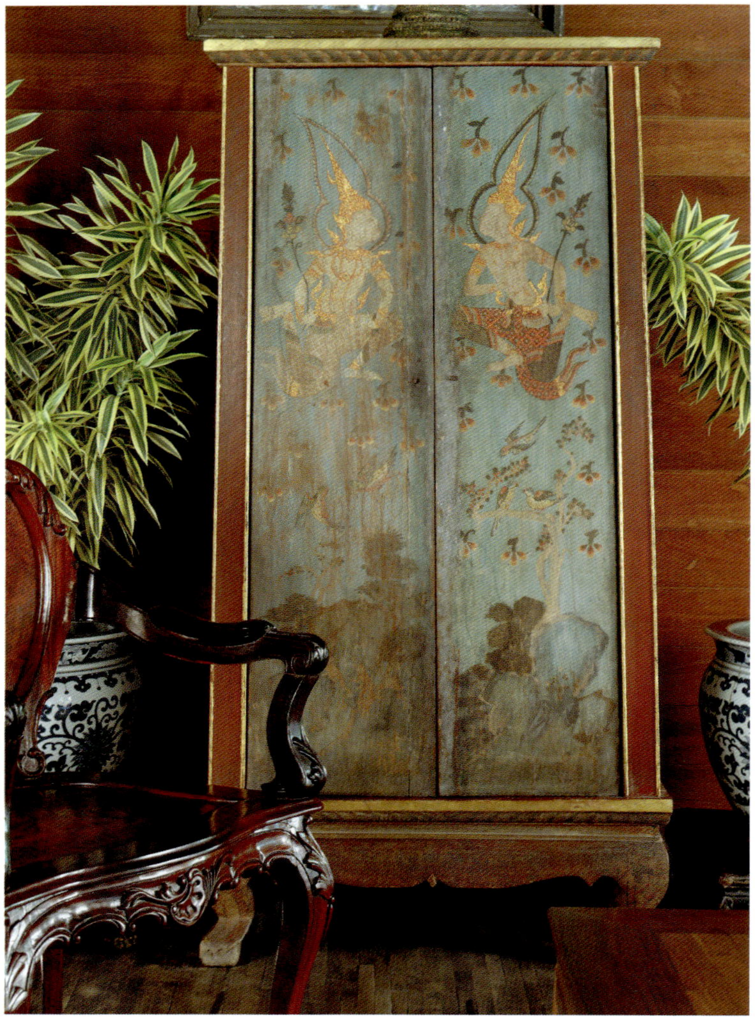

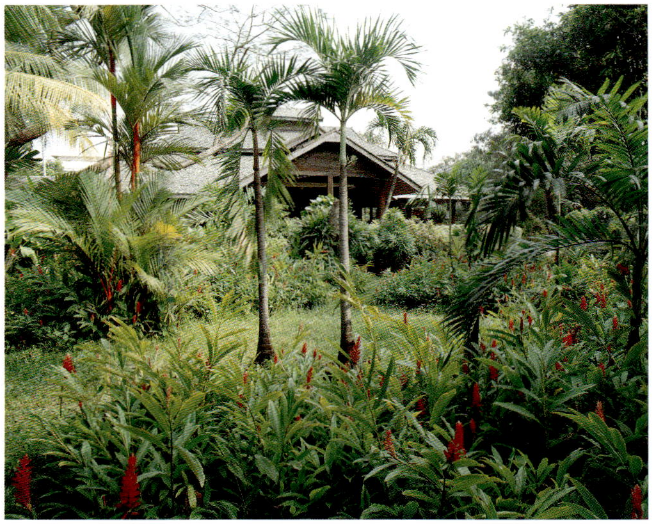

Right : *Verandah overlooking the garden; the deep roof over hangs provide protection from both sunlight and rain.*
Below : *Drawing room with a fine covered Bencharong jar.*
Left : *Antique cabinet, painted with celestial figures.*
Above : *Part of the extensive garden; Red Ginger* (Alpinia purpurata) *is seen in the foreground with various types of palms.*

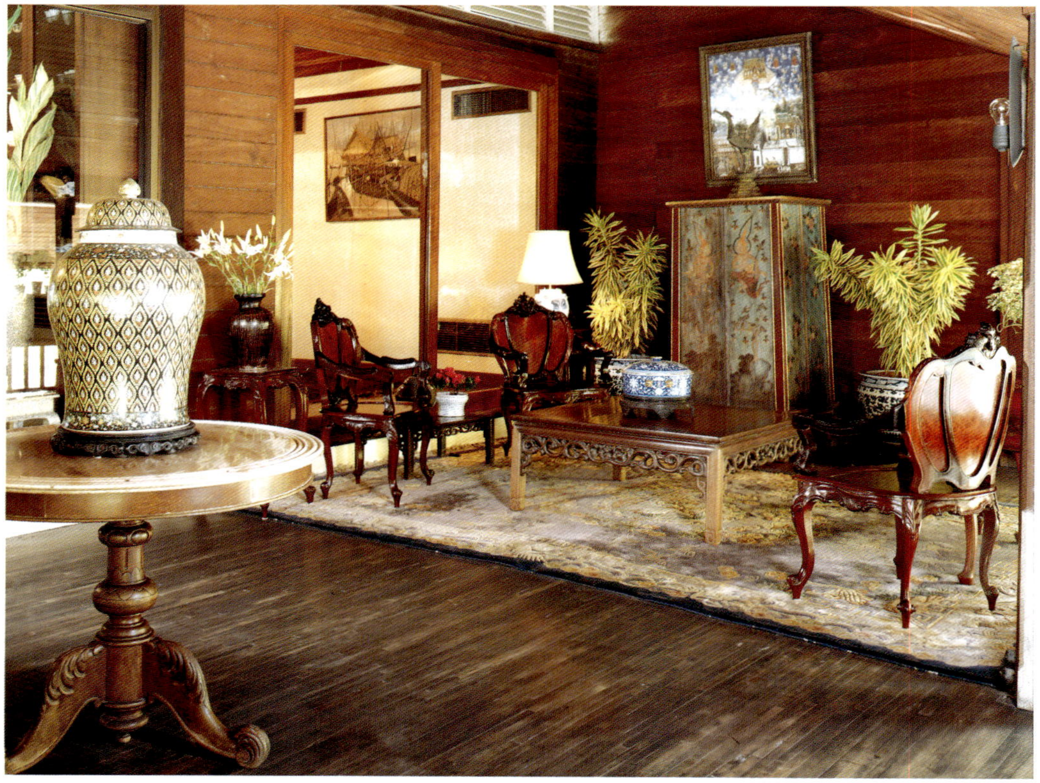

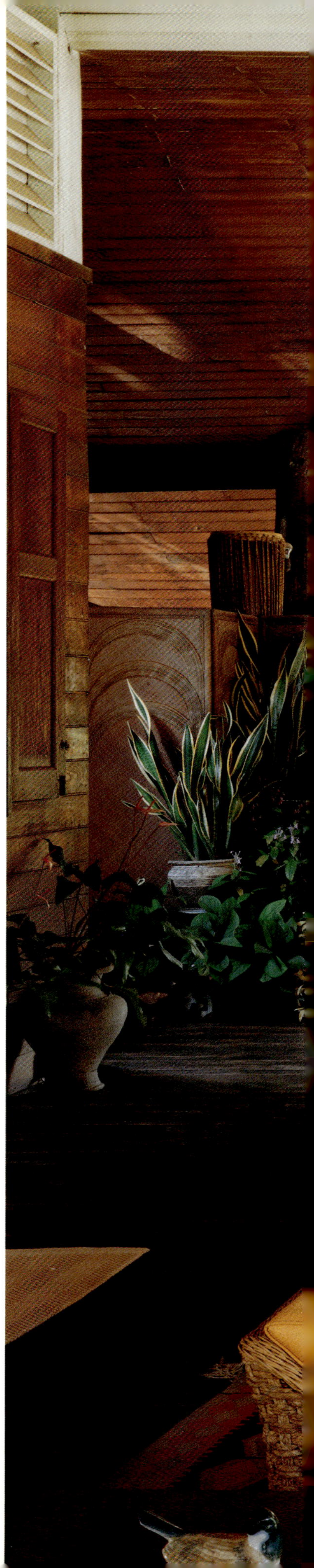

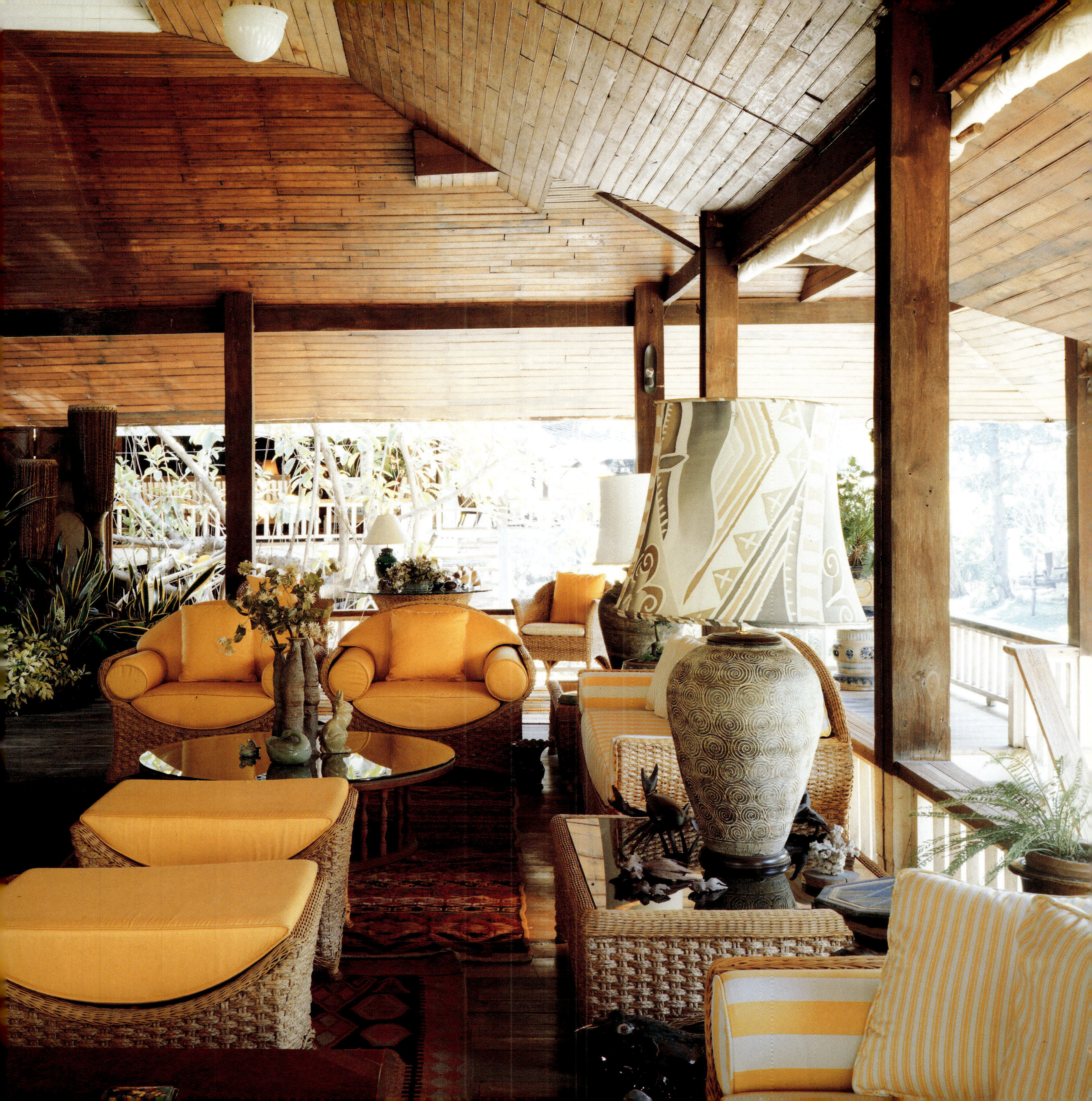

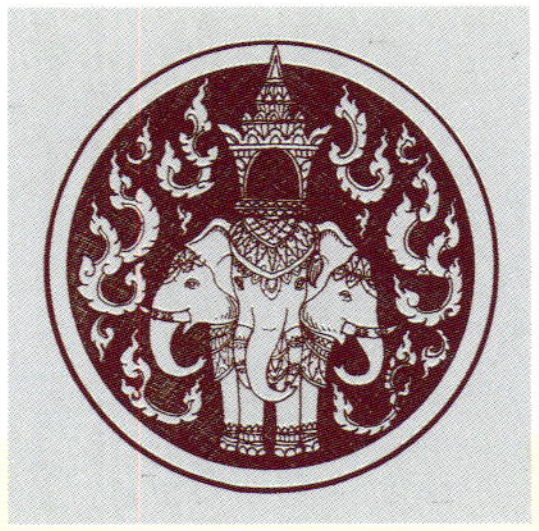

Chateau William

The name of this house might strike some as a trifle odd, but according to present tenant, Ms. Pia Pierre, it was in fact used during one period of the building's long history. Phya Vichitnavee, who lived in the house from 1867 to 1923, was originally named William Punyakalin and it was he, presumably, who so called his residence. He was associated with the Royal Thai Navy and perhaps got the idea while he was studying abroad.

Located in Thonburi on Klong Mon, convenient to the nearby naval headquarters, the Western-style house was constructed in three stages as the family expanded. The oldest part, now in the rear, dates from the end of the reign of King Rama IV, and additions were made in the reigns of King Rama V and King Rama VI. The original rooms are on a lower level than the later ones, suggesting that then, as now, the land along Klong Mon was subject to seasonal flooding. Colored tiles cover the ground floors in the older section, while Italian marble—which became popular toward the end of the fifth reign—are used in the other areas.

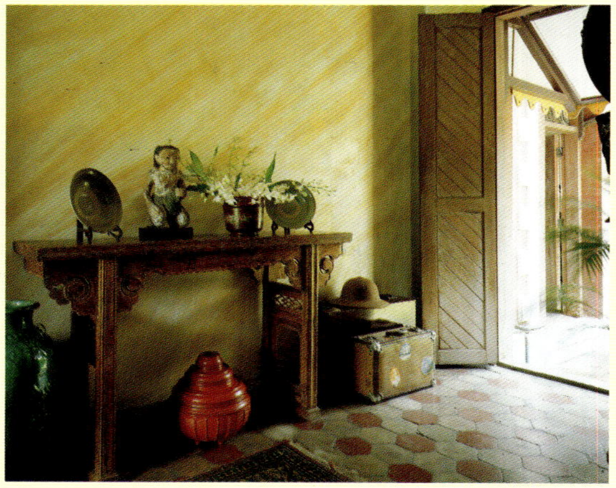

Decorative features include carved wooden valances over the windows, grillwork to increase air circulation, Victorian fretwork, and ornate iron balustrades on an upstairs verandah. A royally-bestowed insignia showing a three-headed elephant, a popular navy symbol, is displayed on the gables of the old section. The house is divided into a complex network of rooms large and small on two levels and also includes third-story rooms on either end of the front side facing the canal.

Phya Vichitnavee's descendants sold the residence about 35 years ago and, except for a few periods, it remained uninhabited for a long time. Ms. Pierre, who rents it from the current owner, has spent a considerable sum on restorations and where additions were unavoidable— modern bathrooms, for example, and air conditioning in several rooms—has taken pains to ensure that they harmonized with the spirit of the original structure.

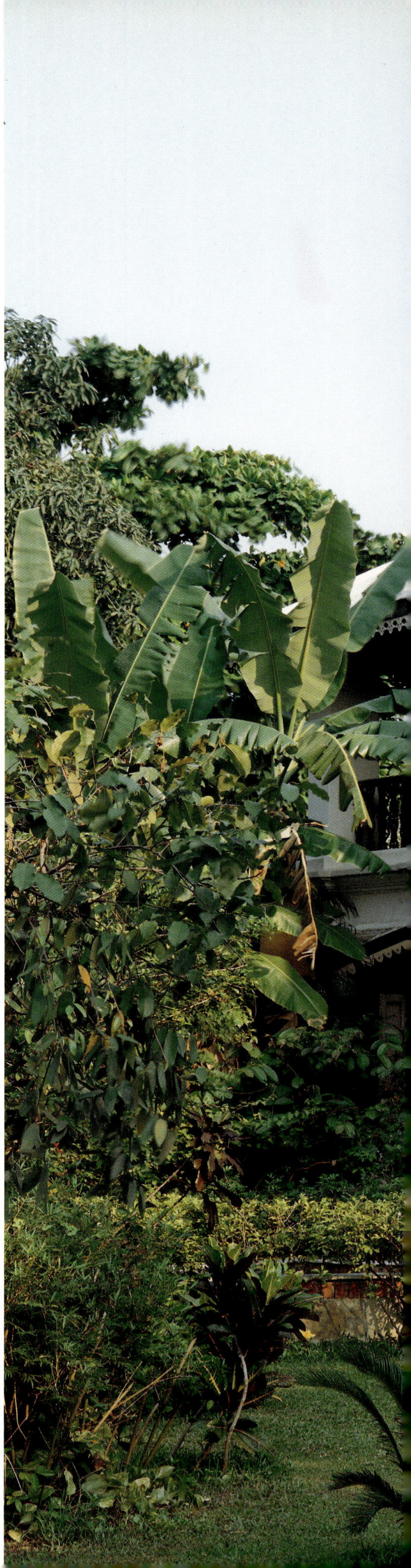

Right : *Front view of Chateau William, built in various stages and facing Klong Mon in Thonburi.*
Above : *Antique Chinese altar table; on the right is a set of old luggage and a vintage solar topee.*

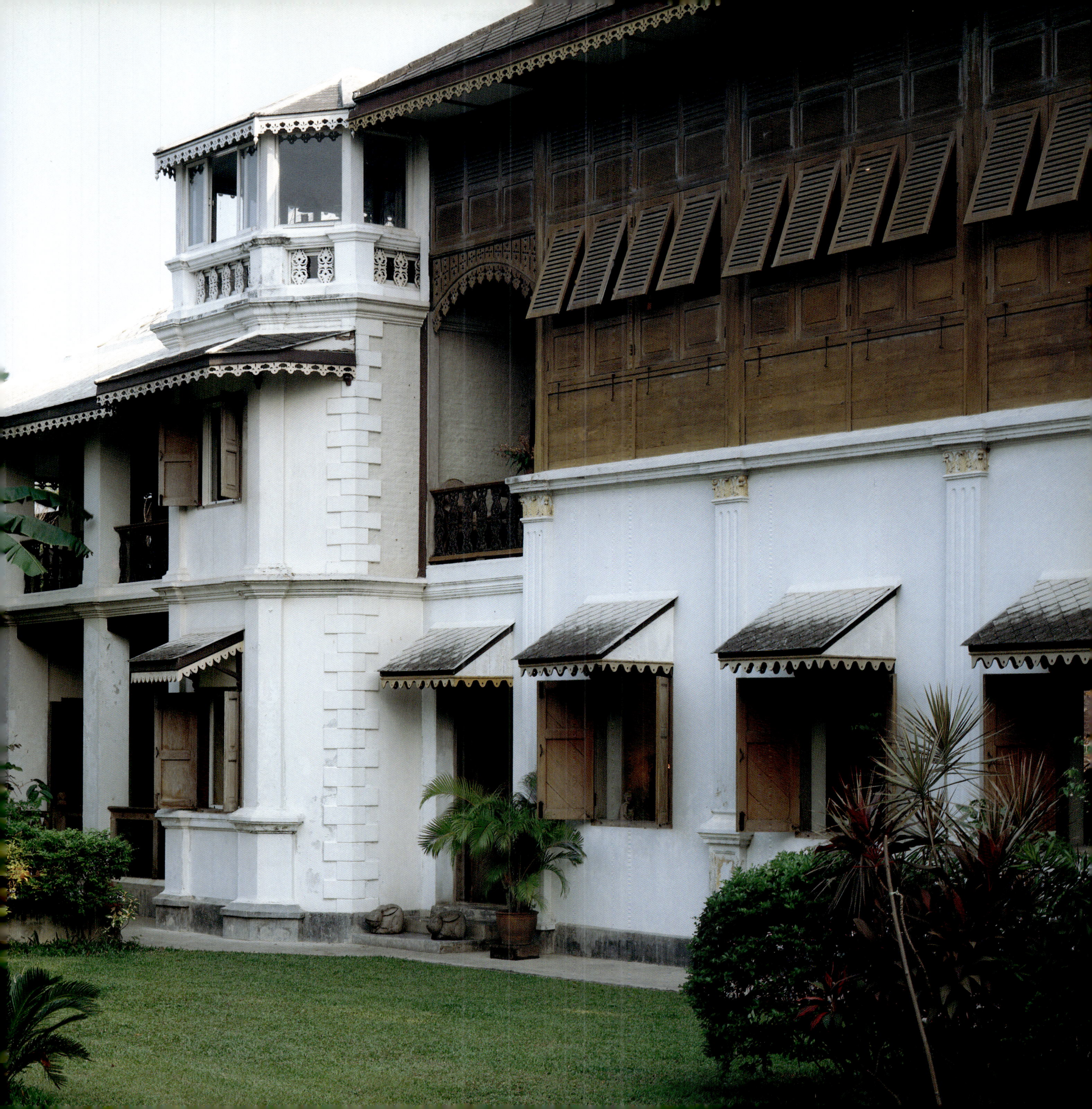

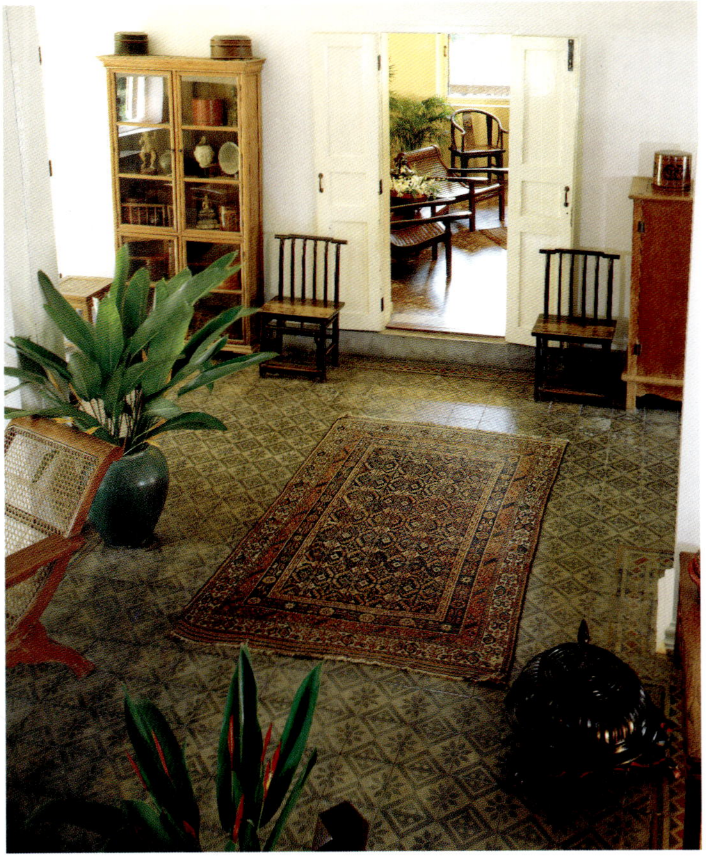

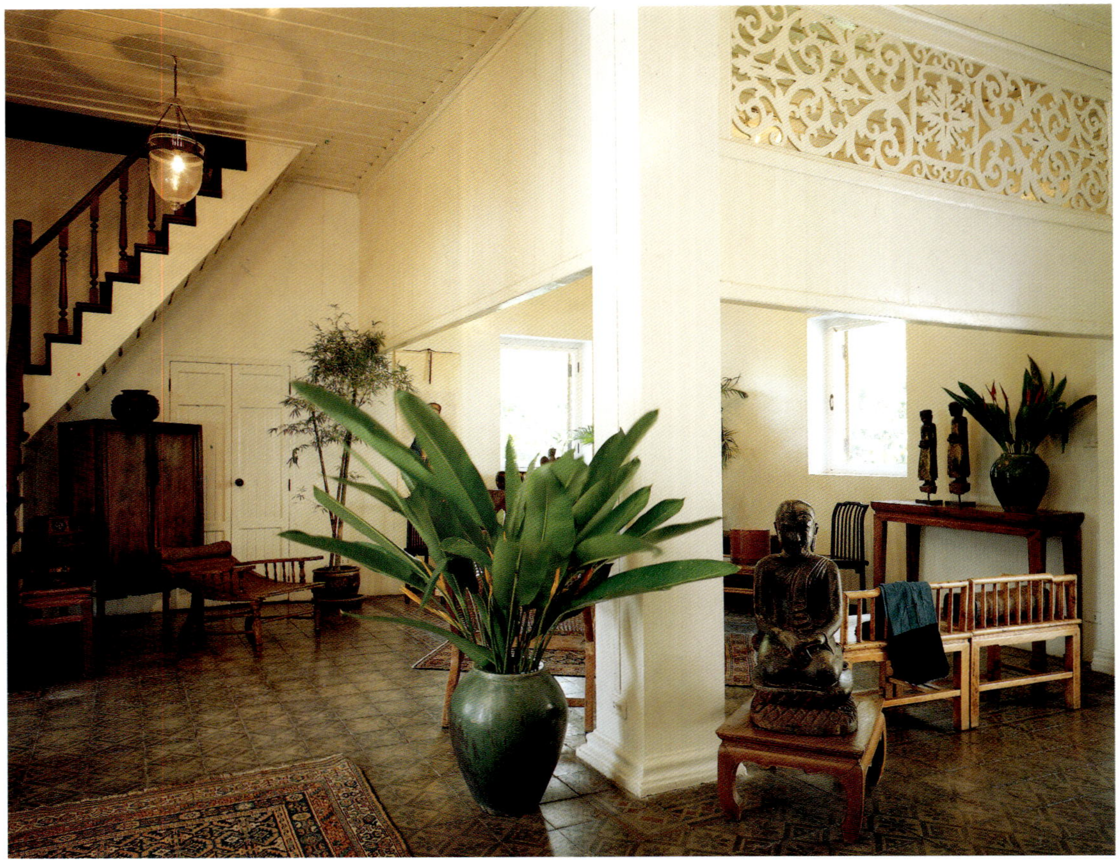

Above left : *Oldest room in the house, built toward the end of the reign of King Rama IV; the raised section in the rear dates from the following reign.*
Above right : *Another view of the oldest section, with decorative carvings with a floral design that served as air vents.*
Opposite page : *An antique chandelier, installed by Ms. Pia Pierre, matches the ambiance of the house.*
Right : *Display of silver betel nut boxes and an old wooden figure from Burma.*

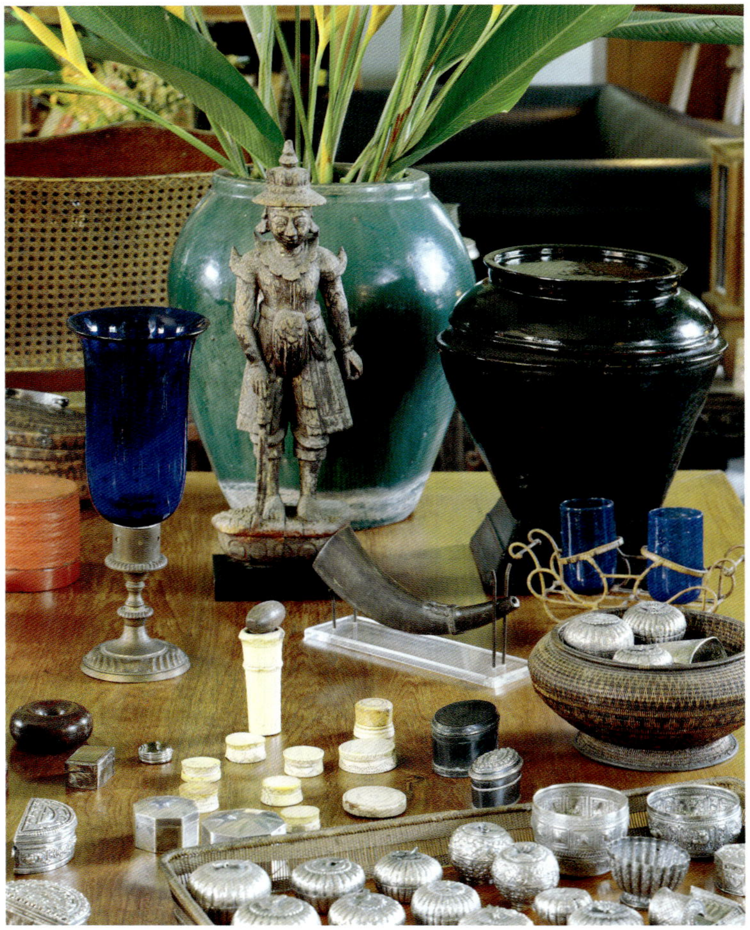

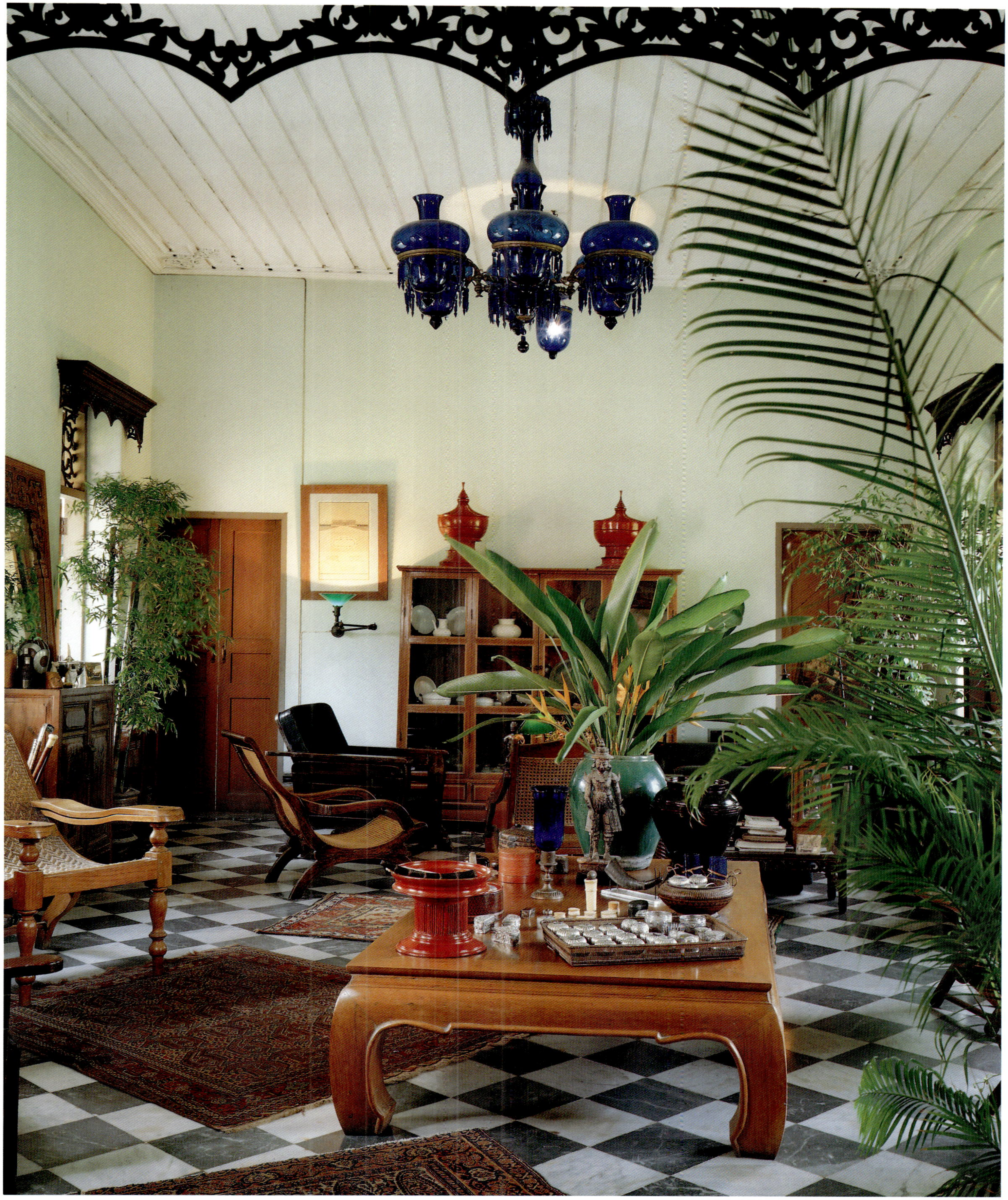

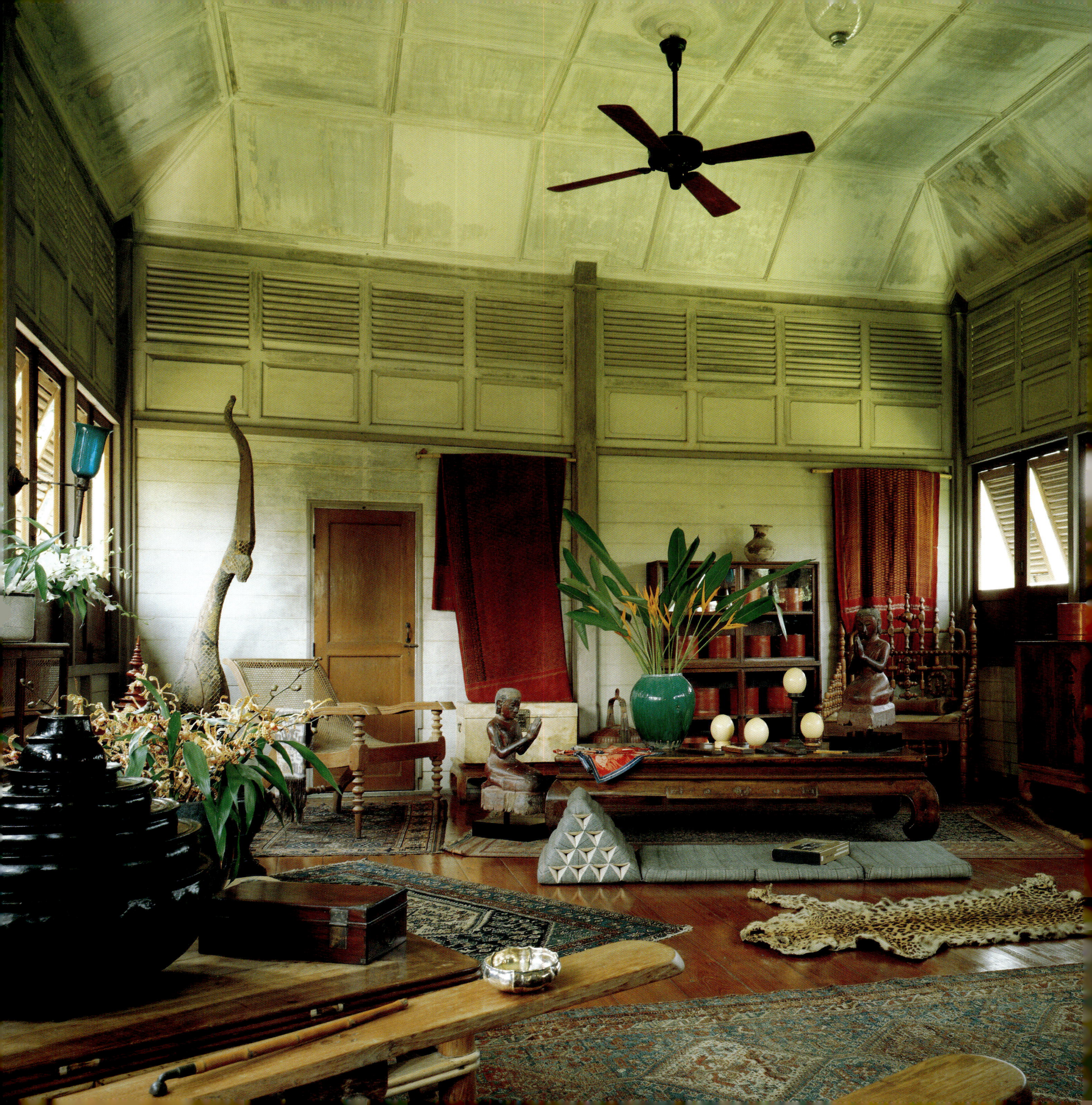

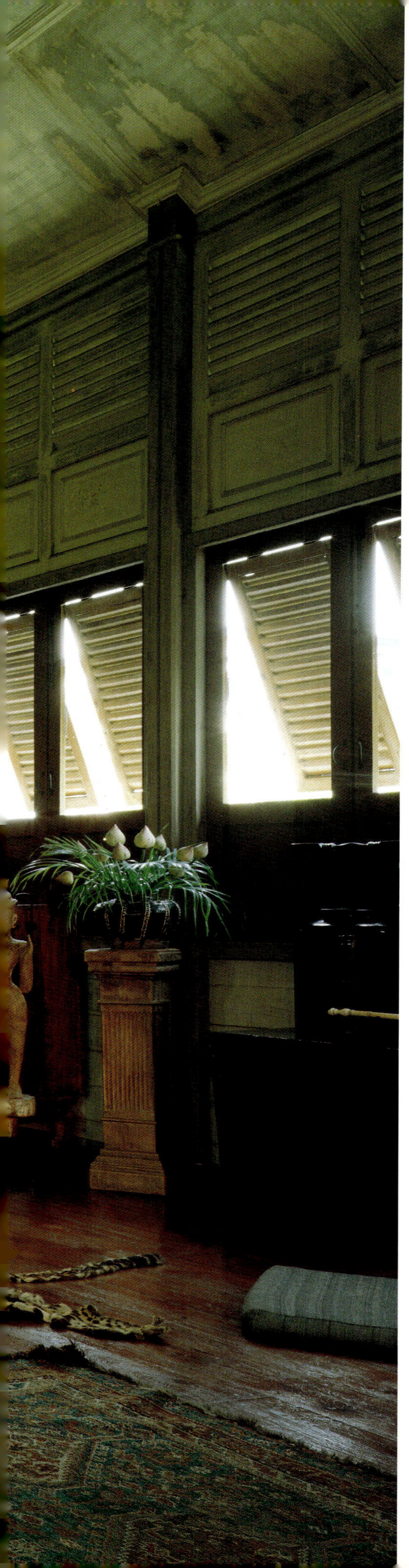

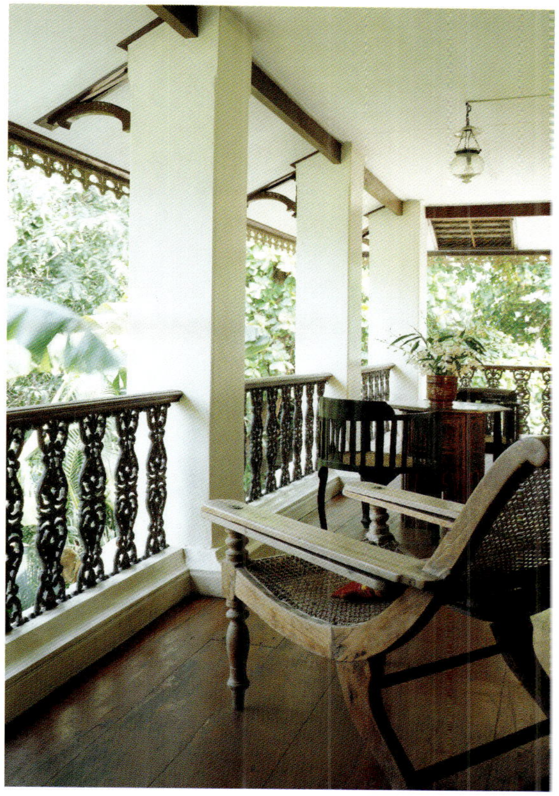

Opposite page : *Display of objects collected by the present tenant in the second floor sitting room.*
Left : *Verandah overlooking the garden, with decorative wrought-iron railings.*
Below : *Rear portion of house, constructed partly of wood and partly of brick and masonry.*

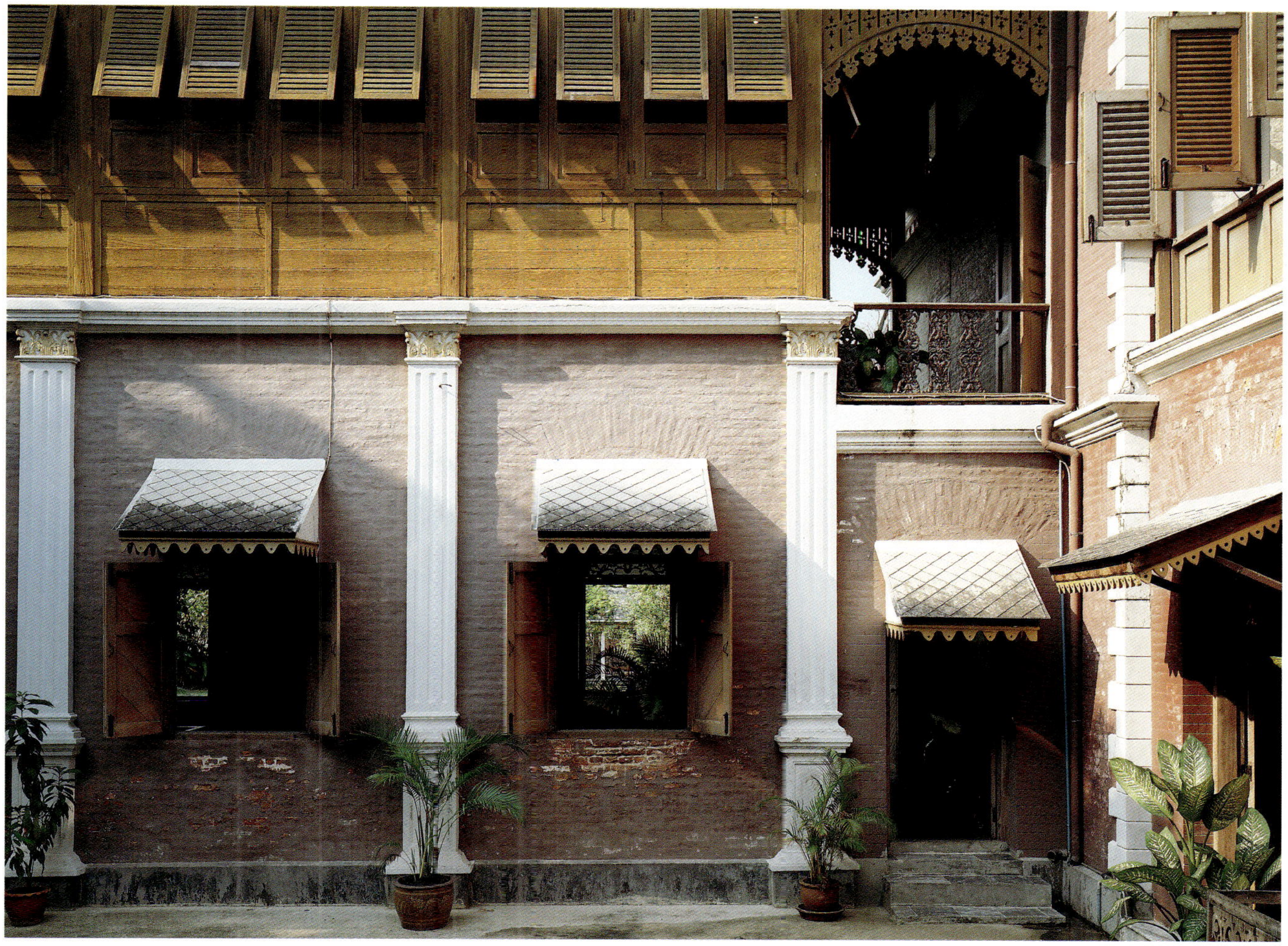

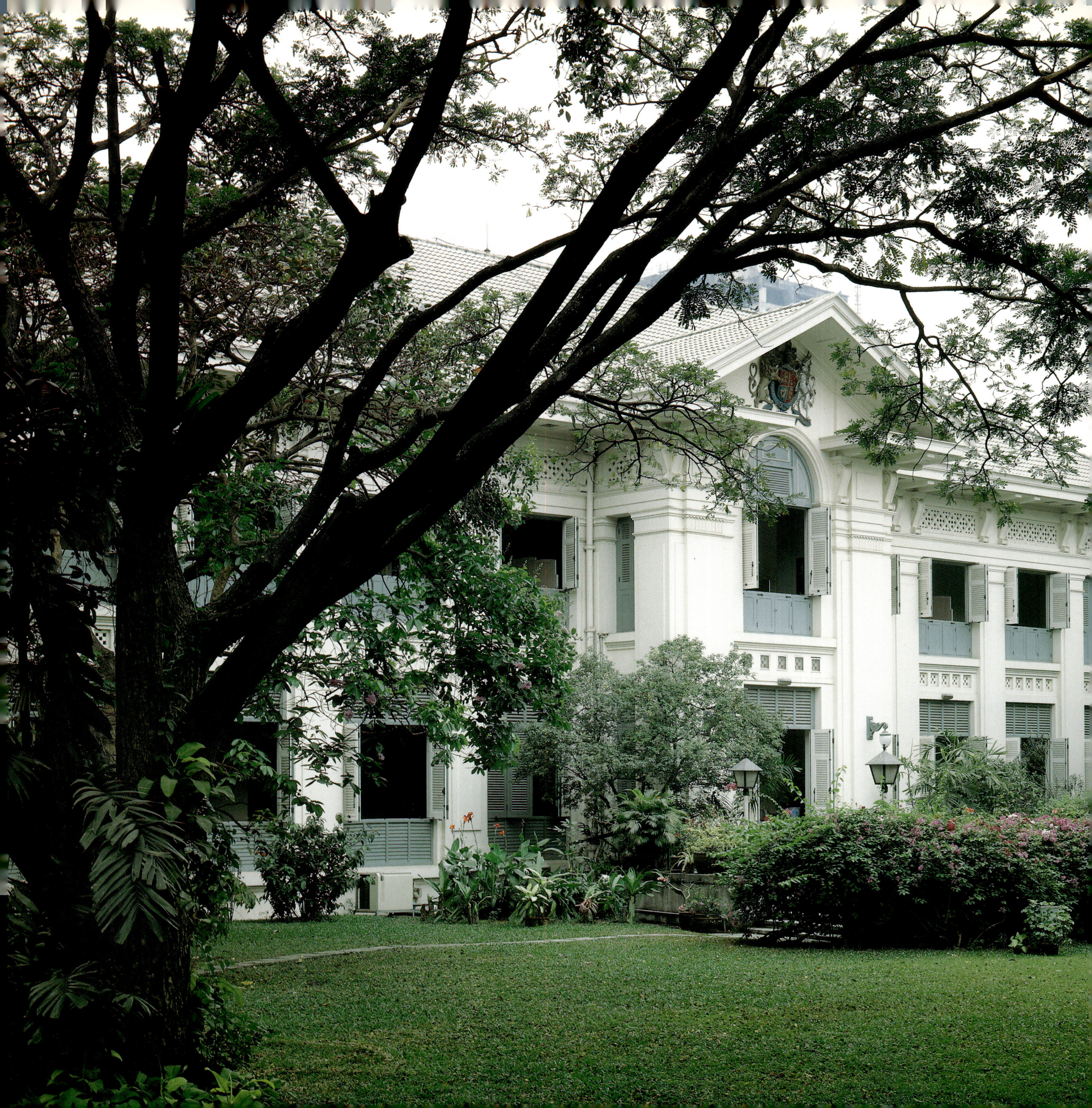

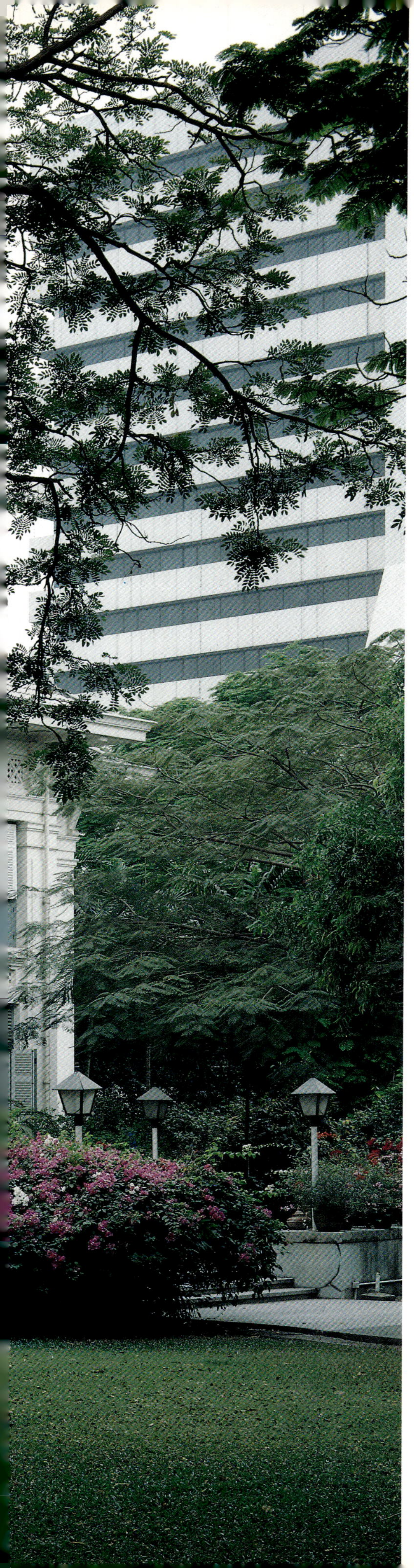

The British Embassy Residence

Like most other foreign legations, the first British Consulate was located on the bank of the Chao Phraya River, on the site presently occupied by the Post Office. As early as 1902 there was talk of a move, due to the noise from rice mills on the opposite bank of the river and the general congestion of the area, but for various reasons definite steps were not taken until 1922 when some 12 acres (28 rai) of land on Ploenchit Road was acquired from Nai Lert, who had begun developing the area. As this was then regarded as being on the outskirts of Bangkok, it was possible not only to buy the land but also pay for the cost of the new buildings out of the money paid for the old site.

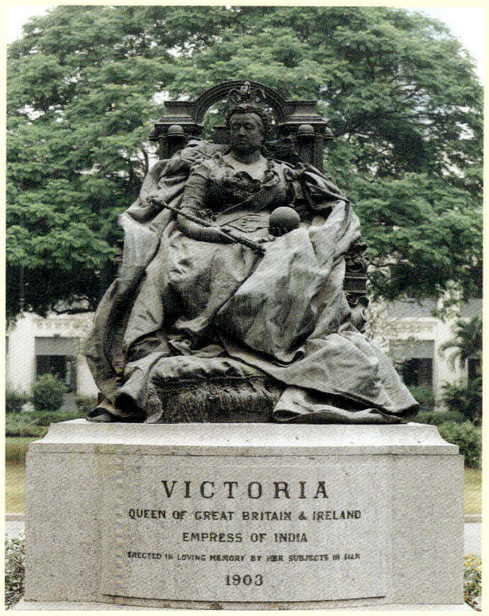

It is said that Sir Robert Greg, who arrived as Minister in 1921, was less than enthusiastic over the idea of the move. He and his wife liked the old riverside residence and were, moreover, "horrified at the thought of being obliged to live in a house designed by an architect from the Ministry of Works whose achievements elsewhere were widely regarded as architectural monstrosities."

Relief was fortunately at hand in the person of W.A.R. Wood, Vice-Consul at the time and later the author of several well-known books on Thailand. Wood, who had been responsible for the draft plans of new Consulates in Songkhla and Chiang Mai, visited England in 1922 and was able to apply his talents to the plans for the new main Residence, with results that finally overcame Sir Robert's objections.

A statue of Queen Victoria bearing the inscription "erected in loving memory by her subjects in Siam 1903" was moved to the new site, as was a steel flag staff reputed to be the tallest of its kind in Southeast Asia. In 1923, a War Memorial subscribed for by British residents was erected, and the new buildings were completed in the autumn of 1926. It was a little later than Sir Robert expected, but as he noted in a letter to the Foreign Office, "what is a few weeks' delay when you have built almost for eternity?"

Designed by both Thai and British architects, the Residence is in a style similar to others built by the British in tropical countries at the time, with huge, lofty rooms and deep verandahs. Air-conditioning has now been installed and the old ceiling fans removed—one punkah, however, was retained in the dining room—but the building has lost none of its stately charm and remains the grandest of all the foreign embassy residences in Bangkok.

Left : *The British Embassy Residence, completed in the autumn of 1926; inside the gable can be seen the Royal Insignia.*
Above : *Statue of Queen Victoria, moved from its old riverside site to the new compound several years before the buildings were completed in the mid-1920s.*

Right : *Sitting room; since the residence is now air-conditioned, the ceiling fans are rarely needed.*
Left : *Staircase; above the window can be seen some of the building's fine stucco decorations.*
Below : *The Visitor's Book, containing the names of many notable guests.*
Bottom : *Central hallway of the residence, showing double staircase leading to the living quarters on the second floor.*

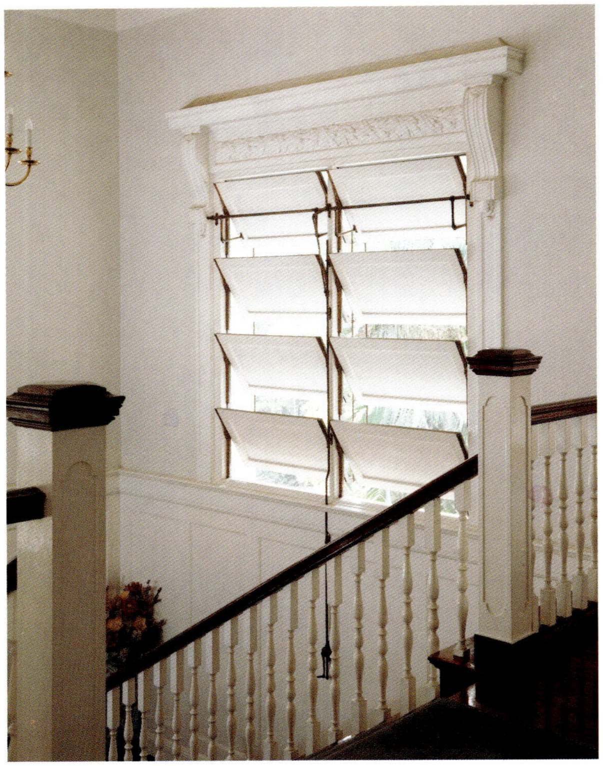

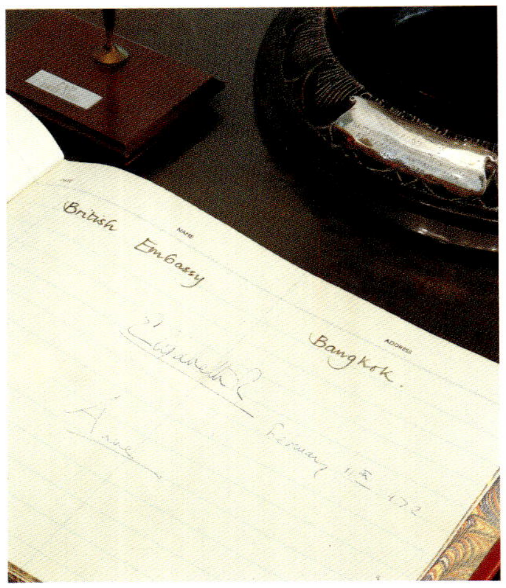

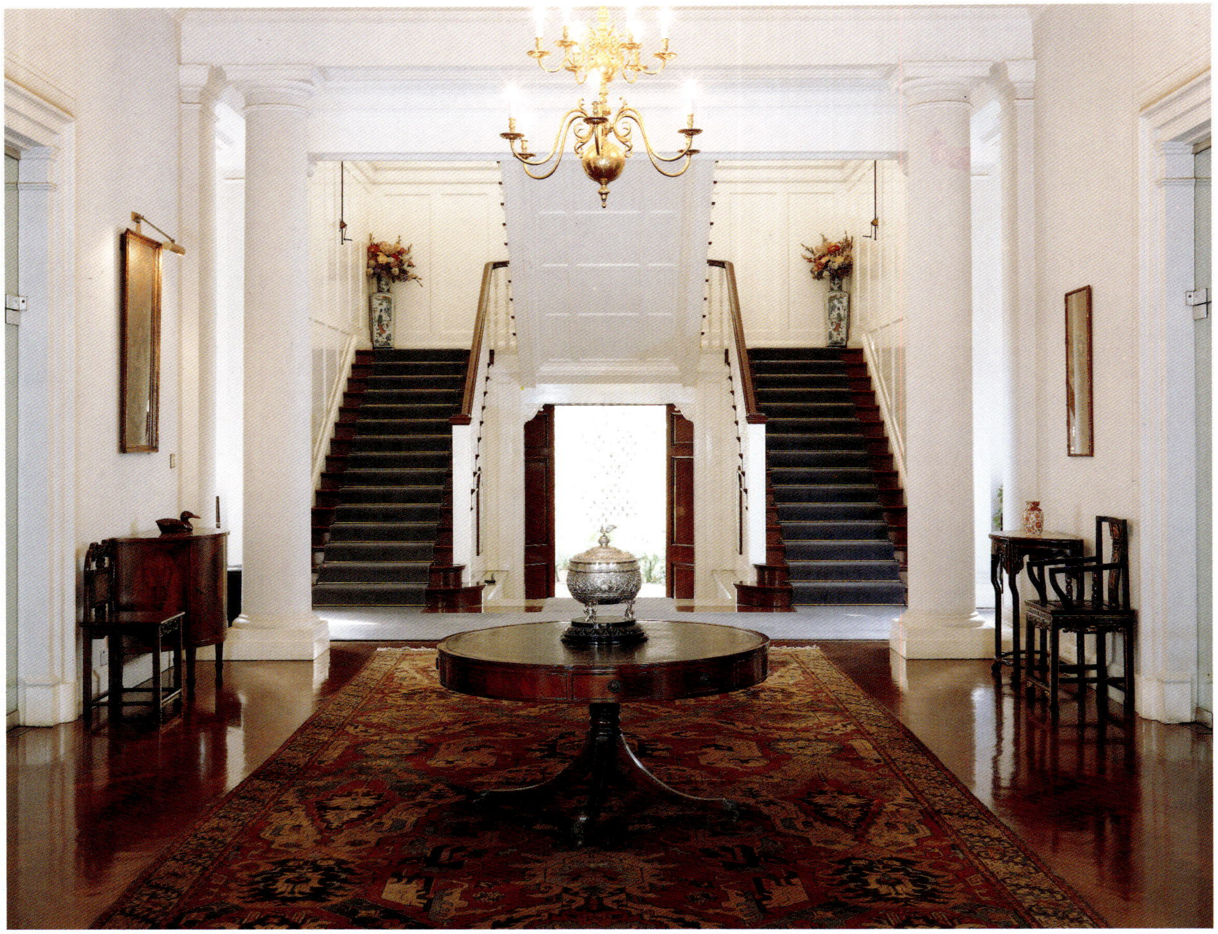

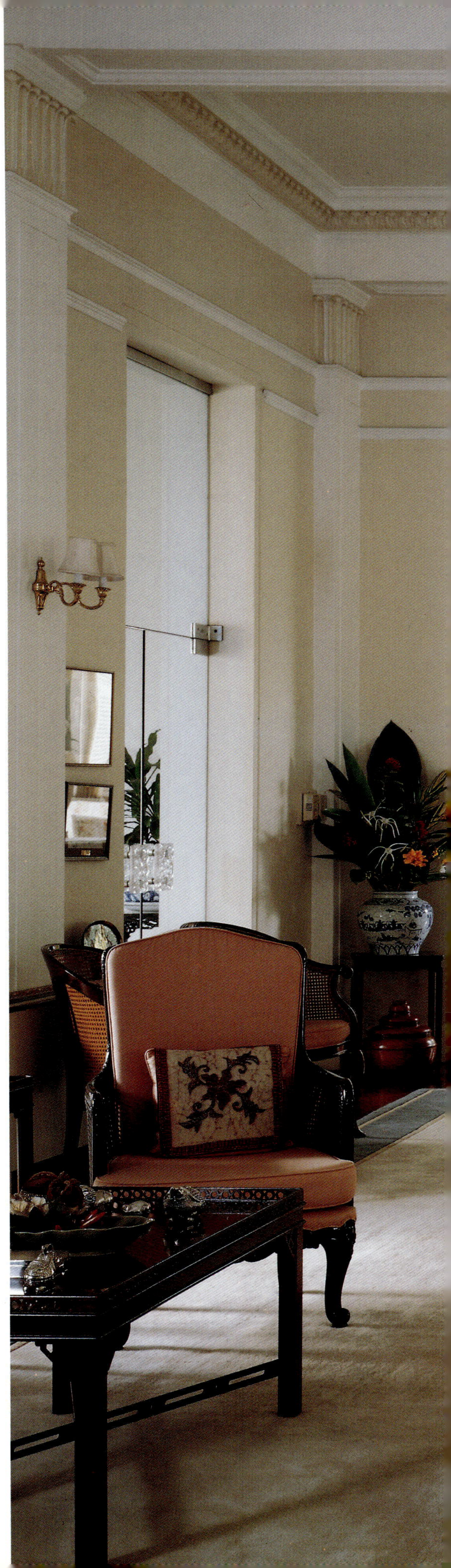

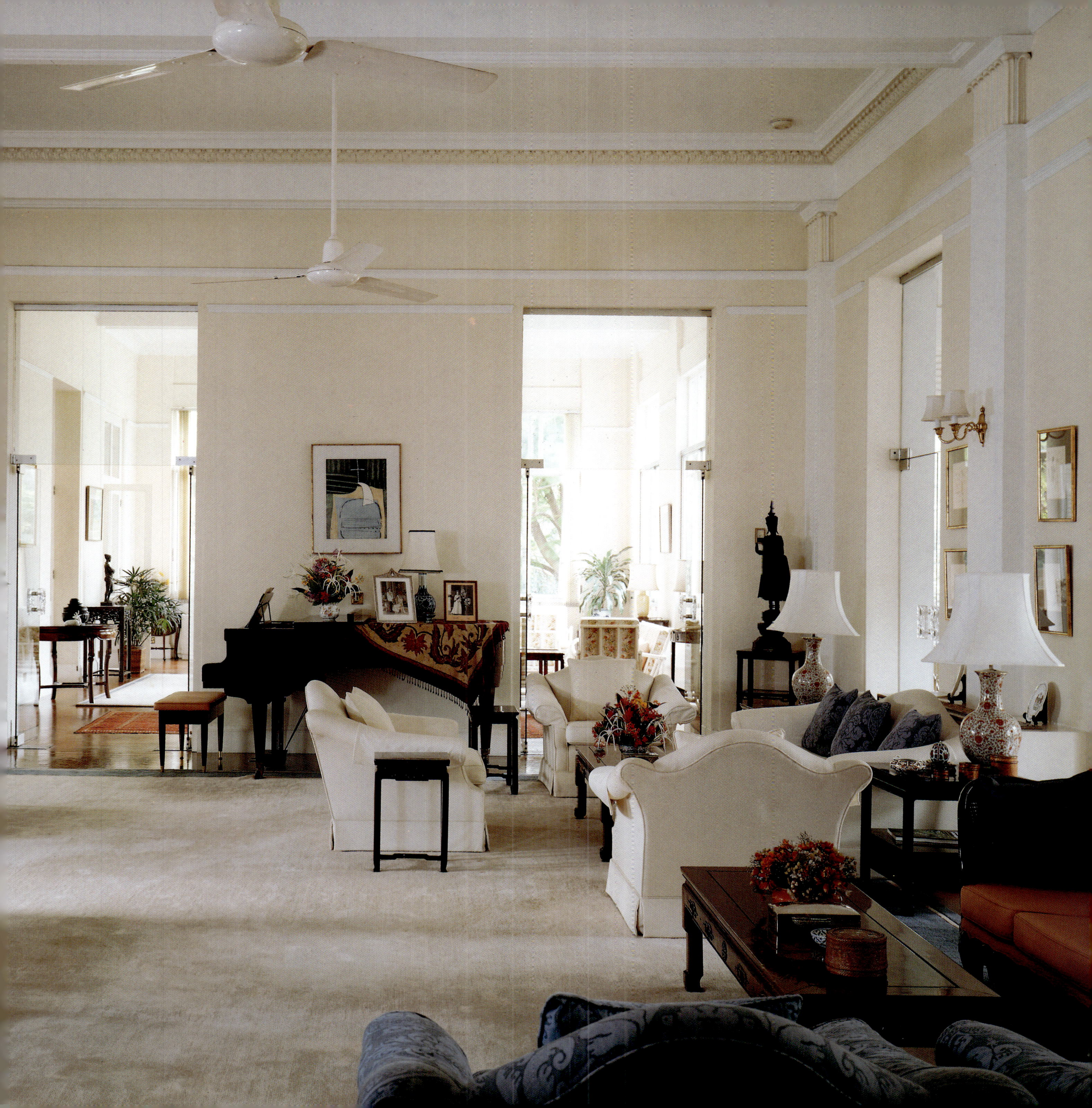

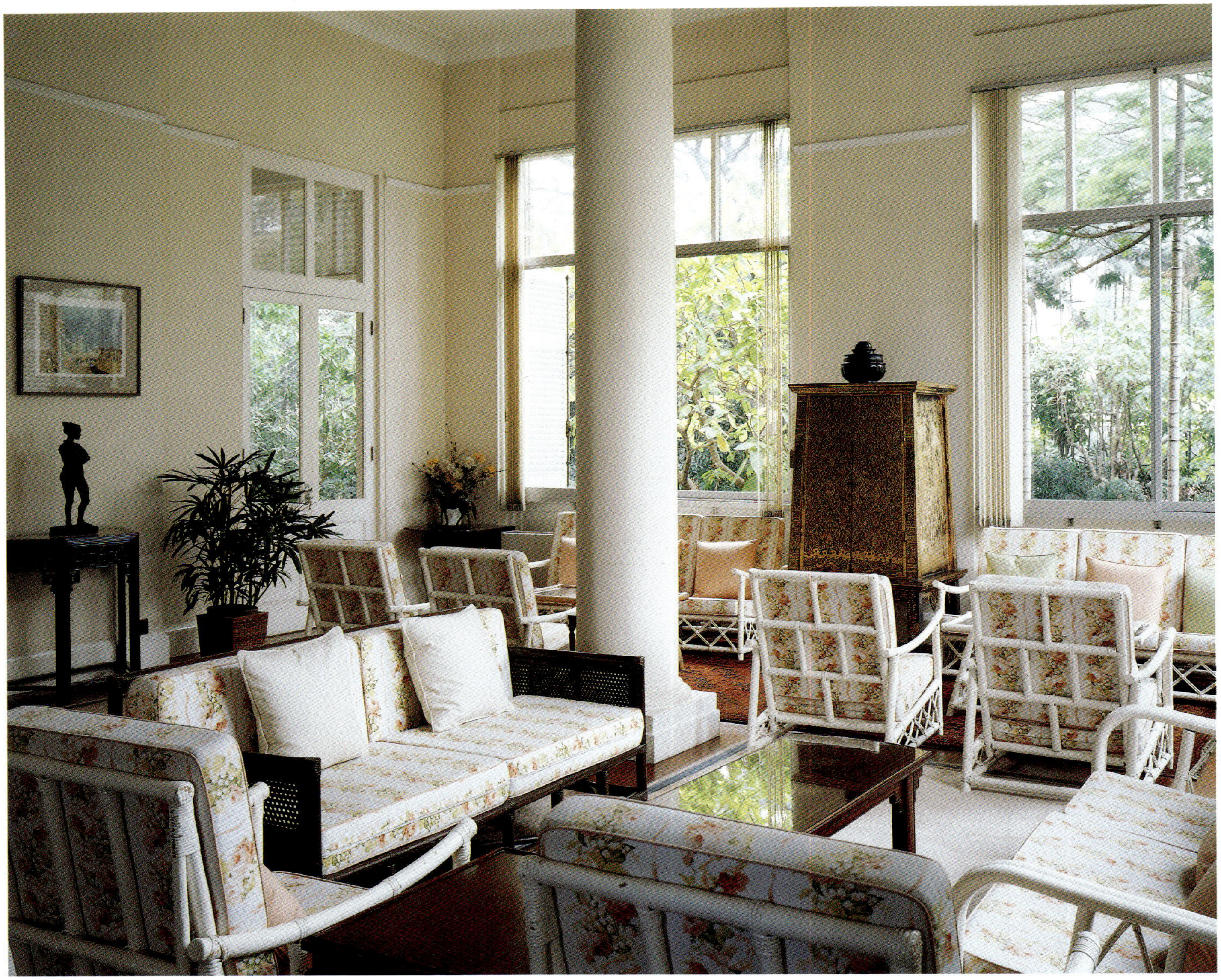

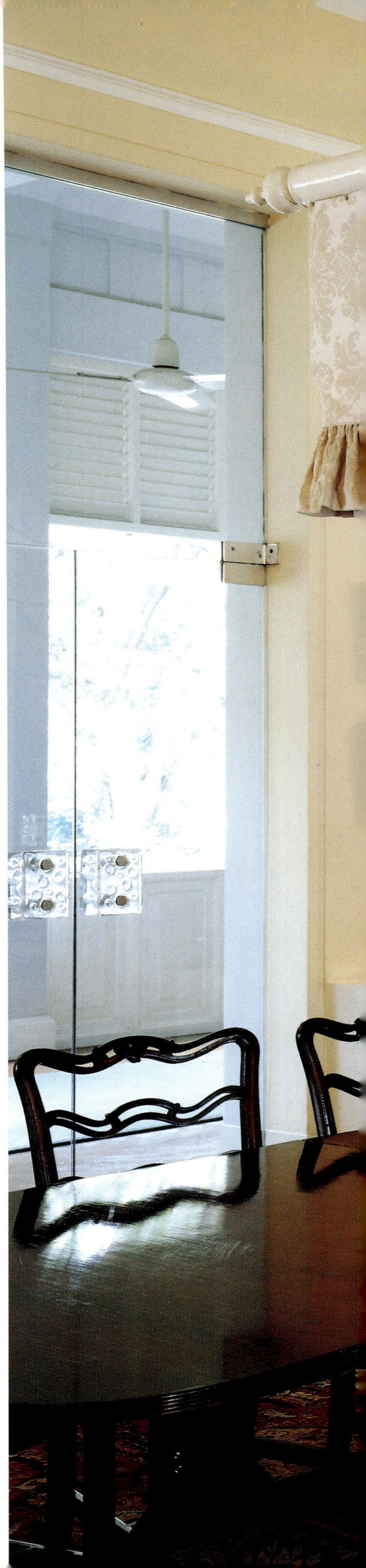

Right : *Dining room; suspended from the ceiling are two of the old punkahs used for cooling the room in the days before air-conditioning.*
Above : *Garden room, with light rattan furniture.*

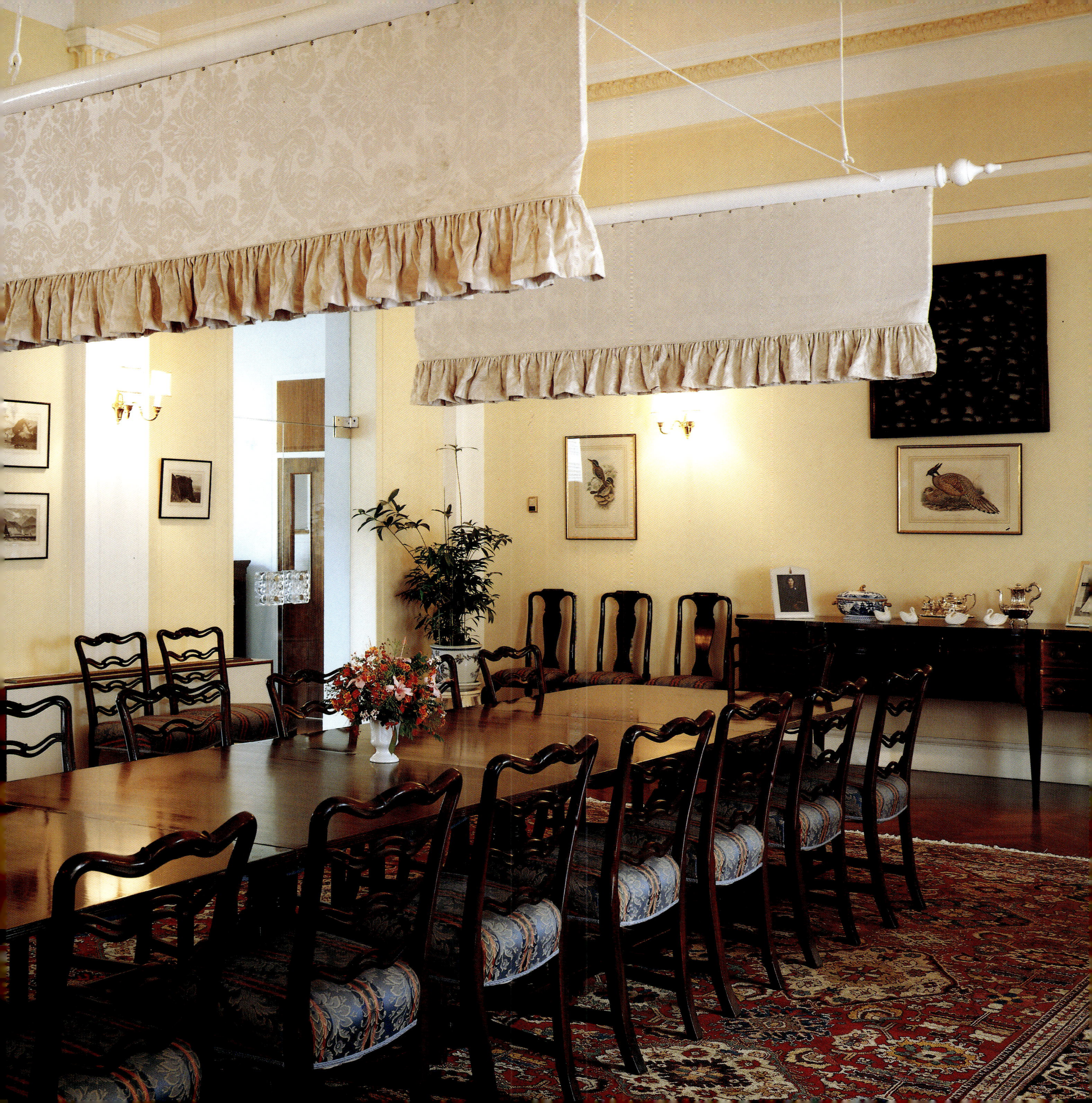

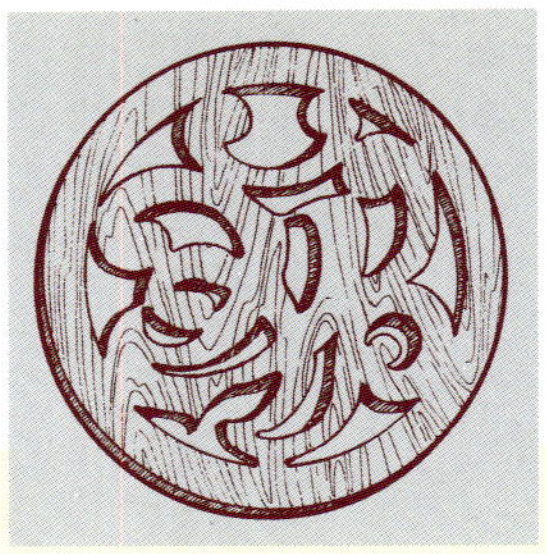

The Gingerbread House

This residence, so called because of the elaborate carved decorations which adorn it, stands on a small street near the Giant Swing and is currently owned by Thanpuying Petchara and Dr. Sidhi Techakampuch. The area was once noted as a center for Brahmins, who took part in many ceremonies, and there is still a Brahmin temple across from the house.

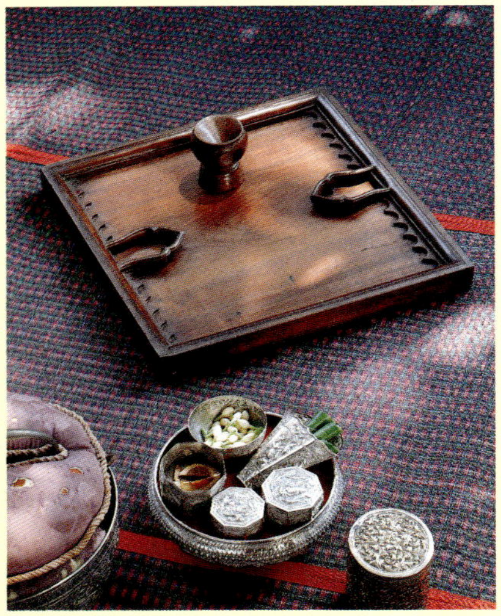

The structure was built about 83 years ago by Thanpuying Petchara's grandfather, Khan Yuwakanit, a nobleman whose official name and rank was Khun Prasertthabean and whose wife, Amdang Nai, owned the land. The name "Khan" appears repeatedly in a circular decorative motif throughout the house above all the doors and windows, as well as along the fence outside. The house consists of two stories and is basically rectangular, though with a hexagonal-shaped wing at one end which was used for bedrooms. The hip roof and extensive gingerbread decorations were popular features of houses built during the latter part of King Rama V's reign and also during that of King Rama VI.

Over the years, the building was altered in a number of ways. When she inherited it in 1990, Thanpuying Petchara decided to restore it as much as possible to its original form, a task that involved the collection of many old photographs as well as interviews with surviving relatives for any information they might provide. The restoration included raising the structure by 30 centimeters to correct leaning, replacing several old teak posts, reconstructing an outside staircase that had been torn down, and replacing the roof tiles with others of the same kind.

After the work was completed, the family decided to call it the Gingerbread House, which was appropriate in view of its decorations but which also led to many visitors asking whether the confection was in fact being sold there. It no longer serves as a residence but is used for various family ceremonies.

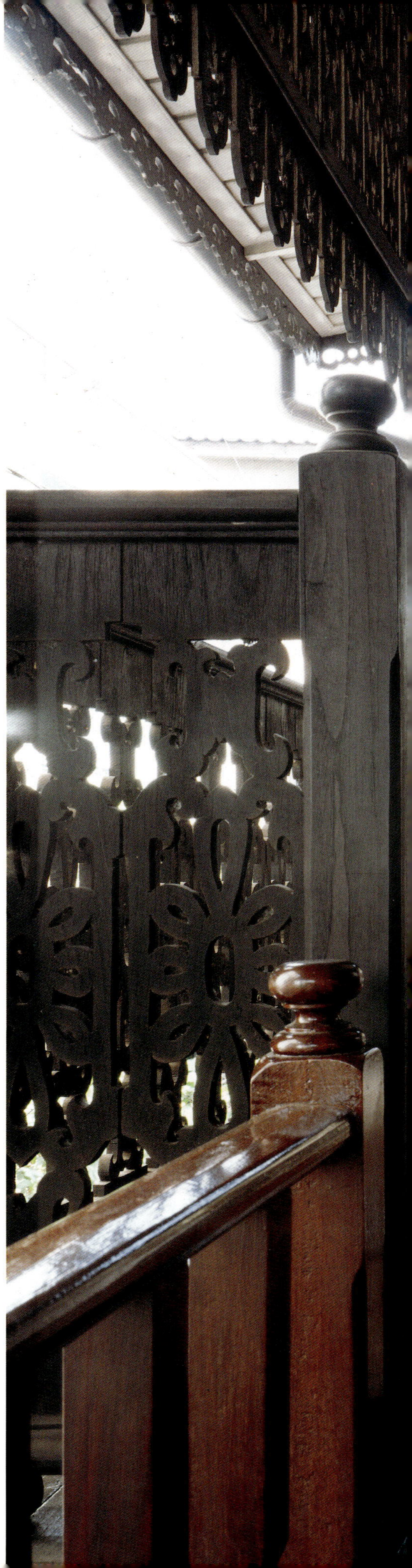

Right : *A verandah between the two stories of the Gingerbread House*
Above : *An old Siamese game board which belonged to the original owner of the house, while in the foreground is an elegant silver betel-nut set.*

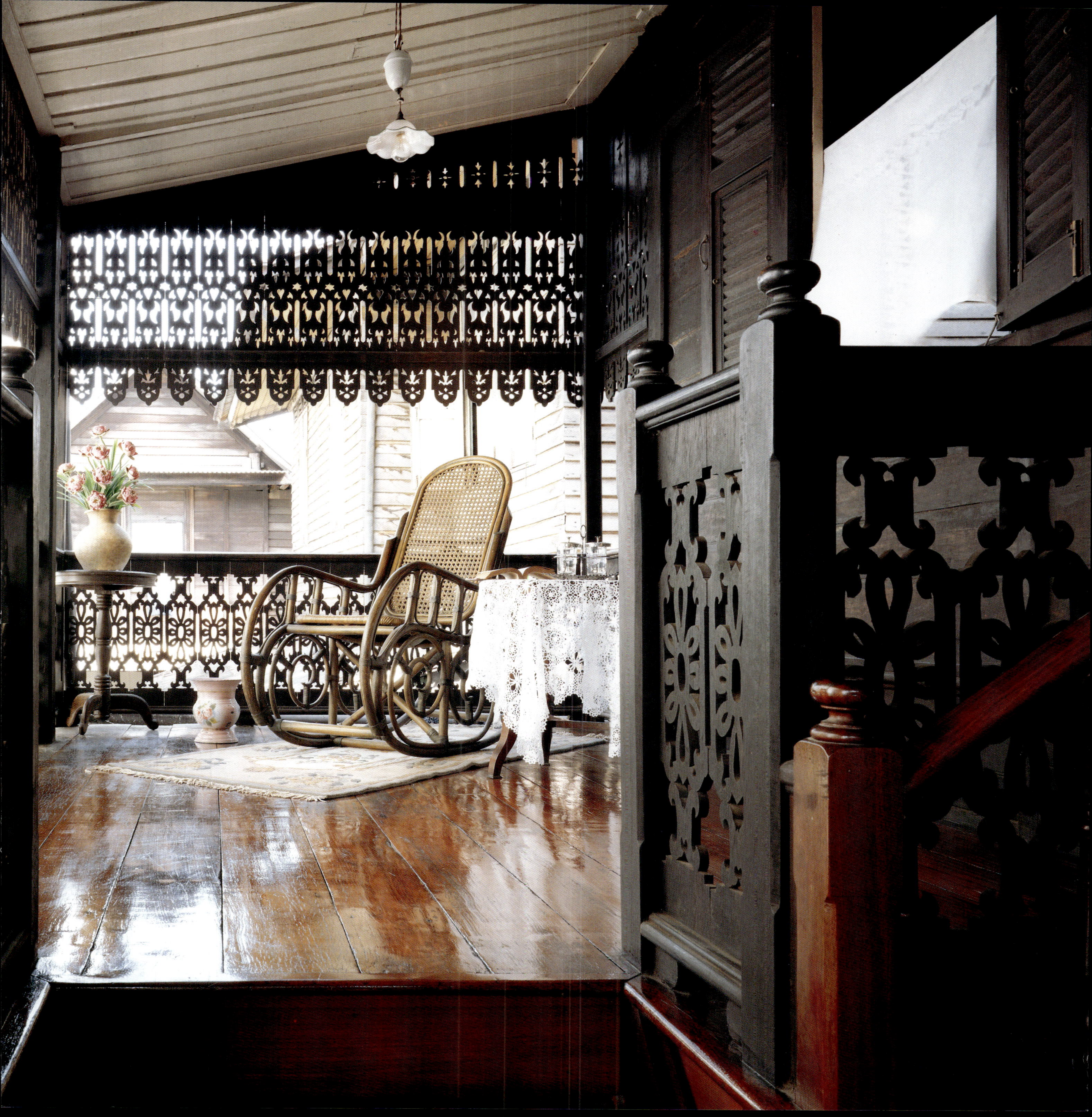

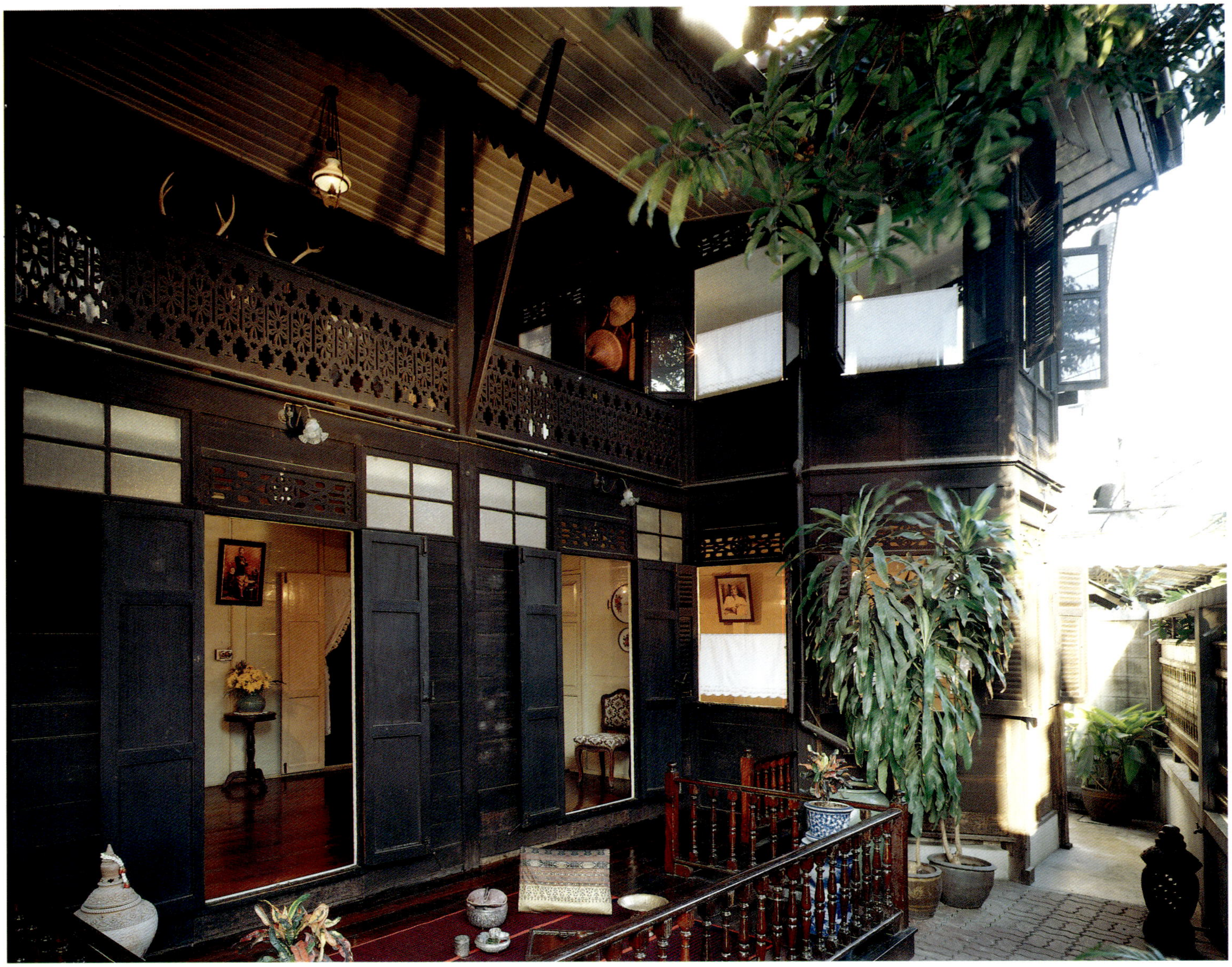

Left : *Exterior of the Gingerbread House; on the right is an hexagonal wing which contained bedrooms.*
Below left : *View of the downstairs terrace.*
Below right : *Bedroom in the hexagonal wing.*

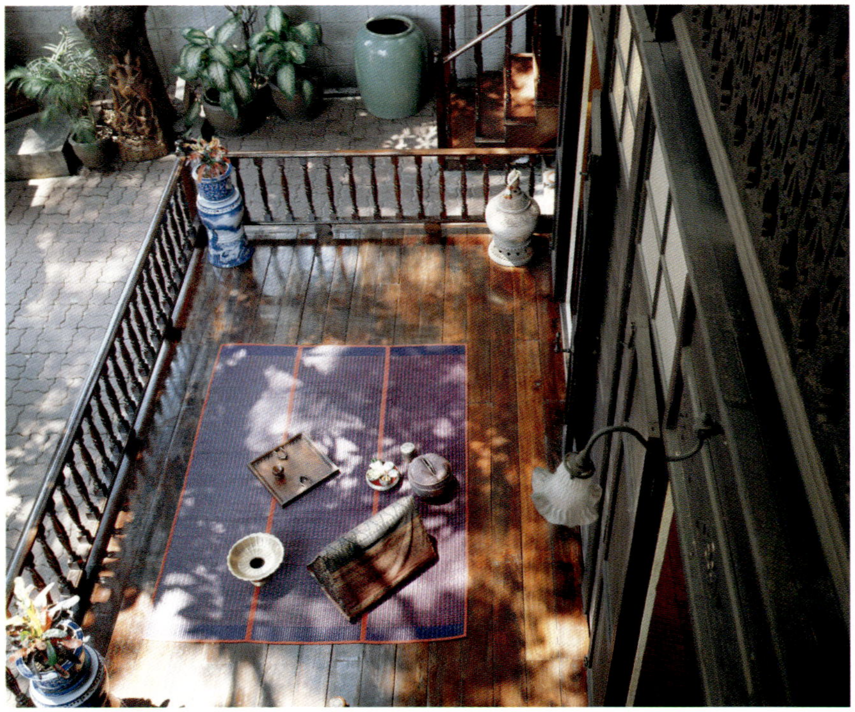

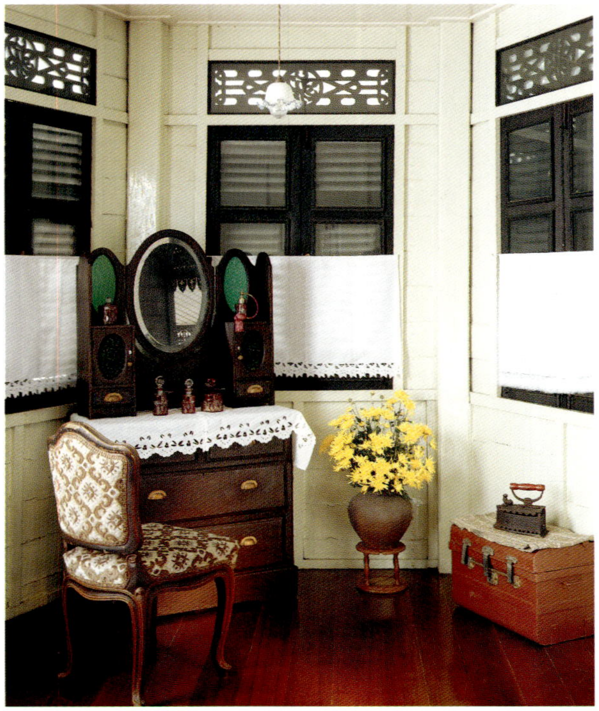

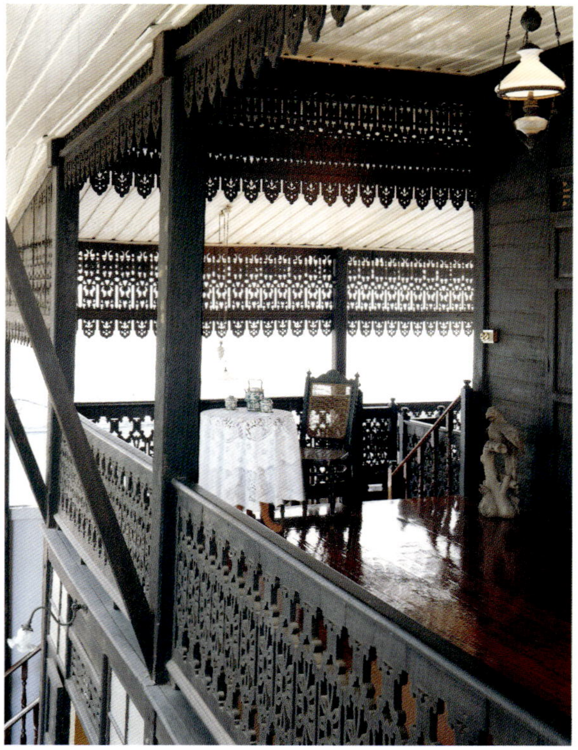

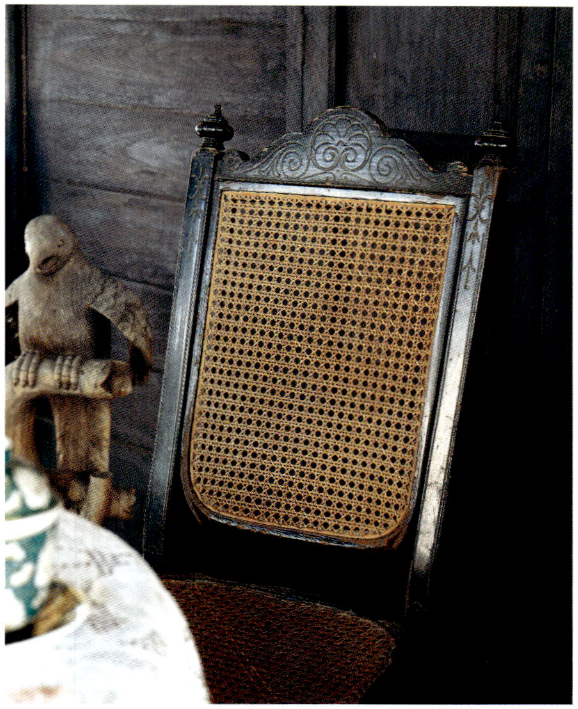

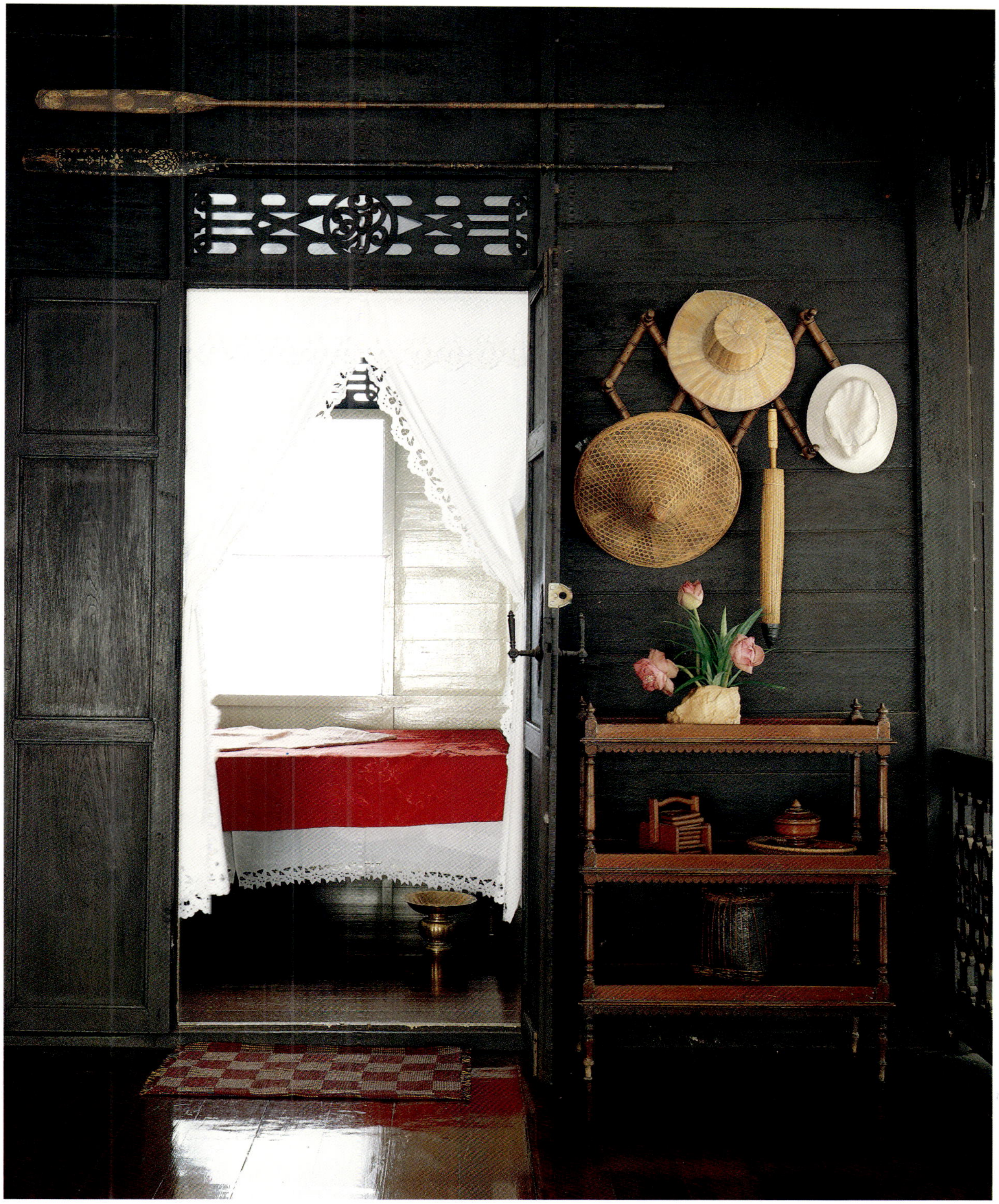

Above : *View into one of the bedrooms from the upstairs verandah.*
Top left : *Upstairs verandah, lavishly adorned with gingerbread carvings.*
Above left : *Detail on an antique chair.*

Suriyanuvat House

Suriyanuvat House, located near Klong Krung Kasem, was originally built for Phya Suriyanuvat (Kerd Bunnag), who is known as Thailand's first economist and who also had a distinguished career as an ambassador, a permanent secretary, a minister, and a privy councilor. The land was given by King Rama V in gratitude for Phya Suriyanuvat's help when the future King Rama VI became ill while studying abroad; the King also lent three elephants to help compact the earth on the site, as well as educational grants for Phya Suriyanuvat's children.

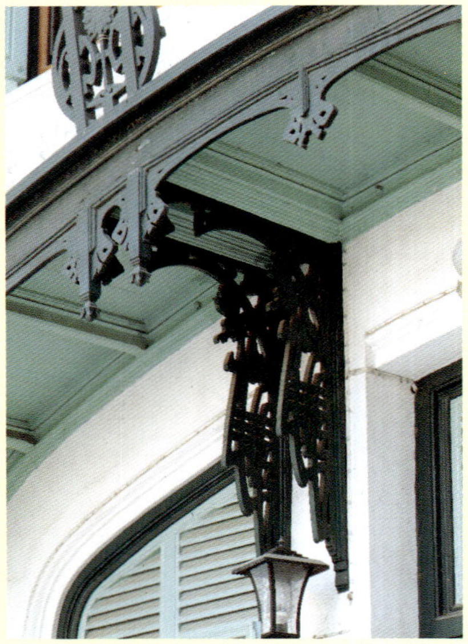

Designed by an Italian architect who worked on the Ananta Samakhom Throne Hall, the house was constructed between 1905 and 1909; after its completion, Phya Suriyanuvat lived there until his death in 1936, when the government acquired the building for official use. In 1950, it became the permanent office of what was then called the Economic Council (now the National Social and Economic Development Board). The structure was later declared a National Historic Building by the Fine Arts Department and underwent an extensive renovation costing some 12 million baht between 1990 and 1992; Khun Prachong Bunnag, the only surviving daughter-in-law of Phya Suriyanuvat, donated some of the funds for this effort, as well as antique silverware and other items belonging to the family now on display in the house.

The house is in European style, consisting of a central section flanked by two wings of different sizes. Besides many Art Nouveau decorative details characteristic of residences built at the time—particularly on stair railings, brackets, and doors—it also has the original parquet flooring designed by Phya Suriyanuvat. This was one of the numerous ideas he had acquired during his long service abroad; another was a dairy farm with 40-odd cows of an imported breed which he began on the grounds of his residence to provide fresh milk for his household and other members of the nobility.

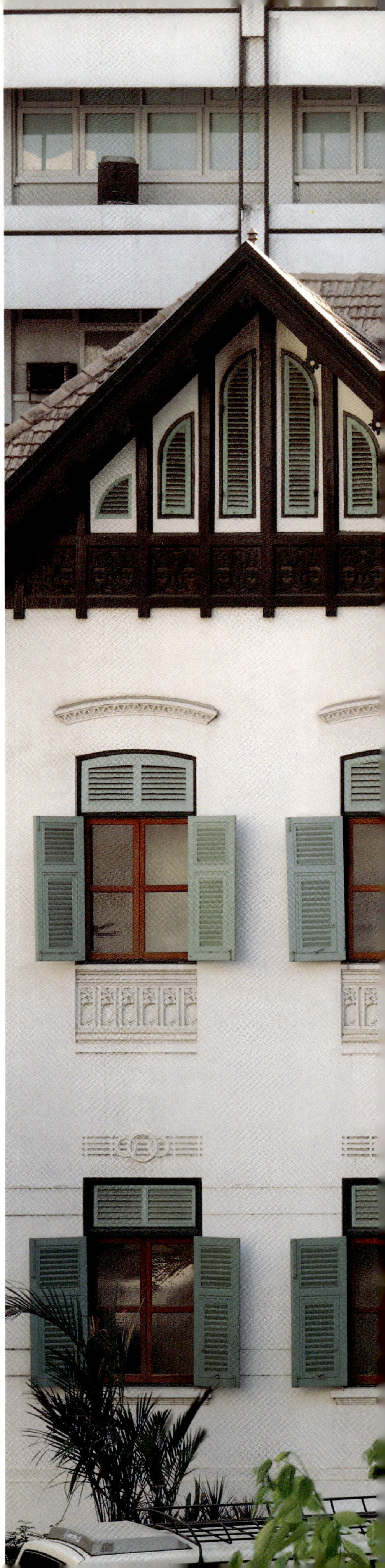

Right : *Front view of Suriyanuvat House, built between 1905 and 1909 on land given by King Rama V.*
Above : *Graceful bracket in Art Nouveau style at the entrance to the house.*

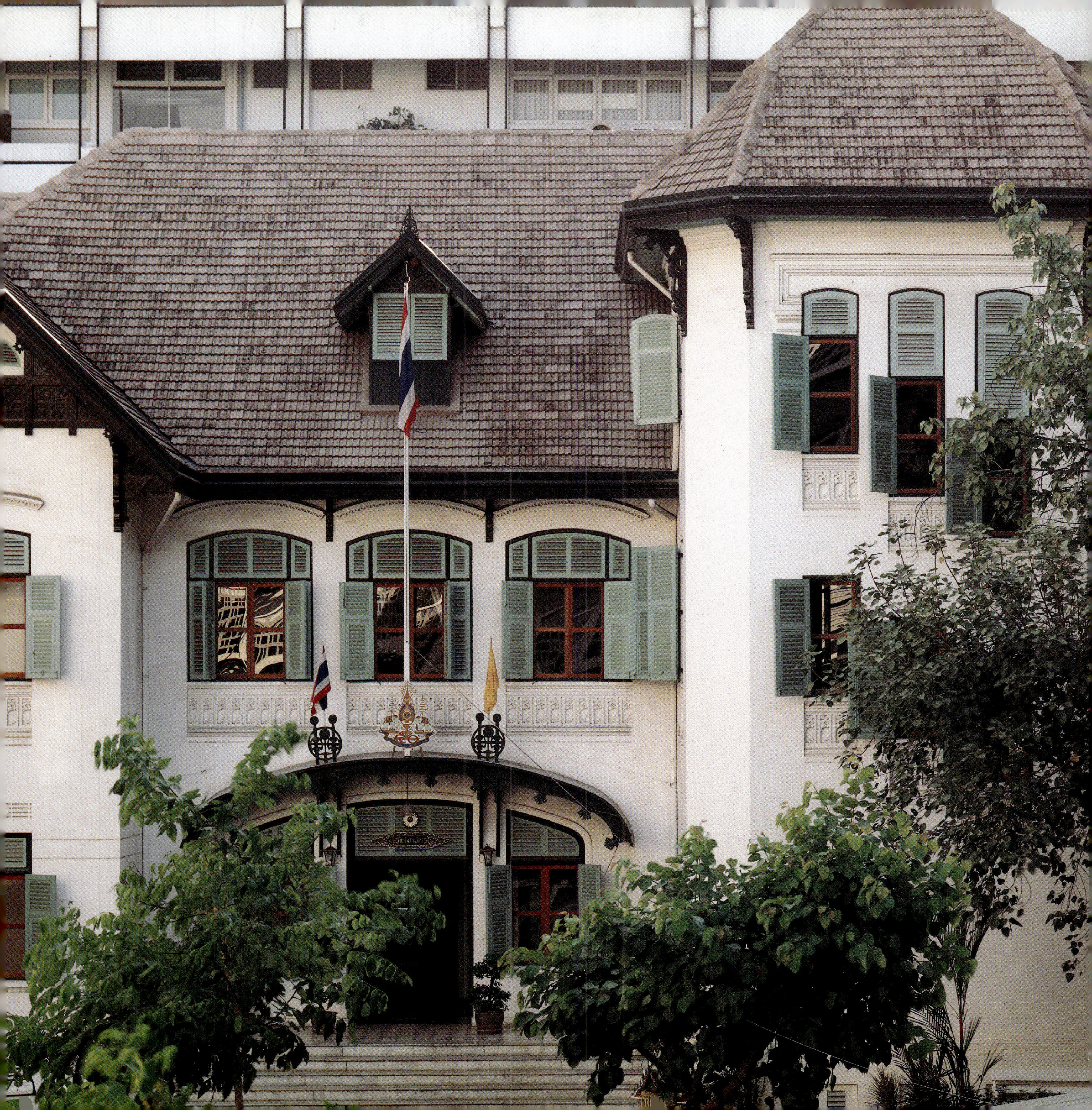

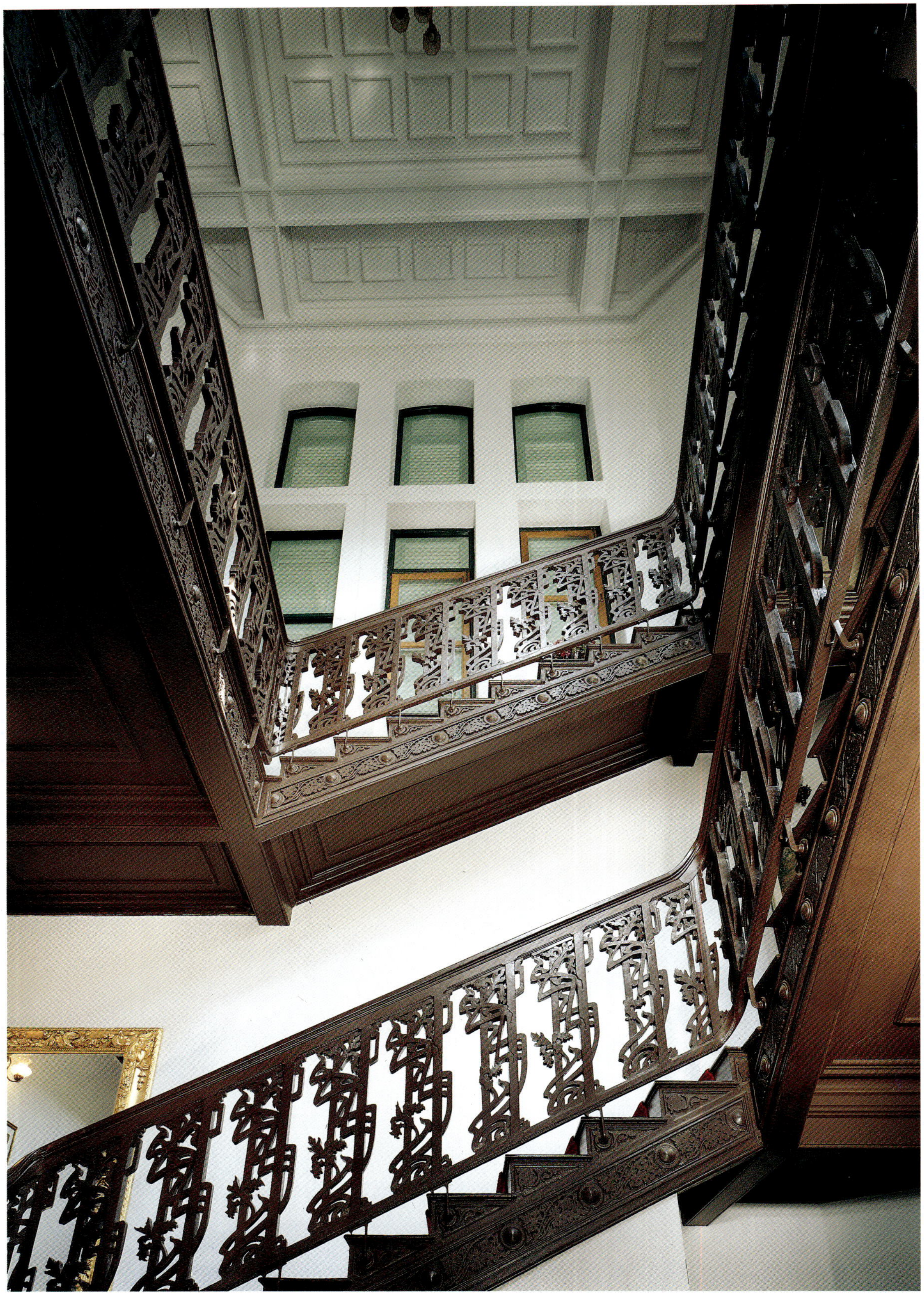

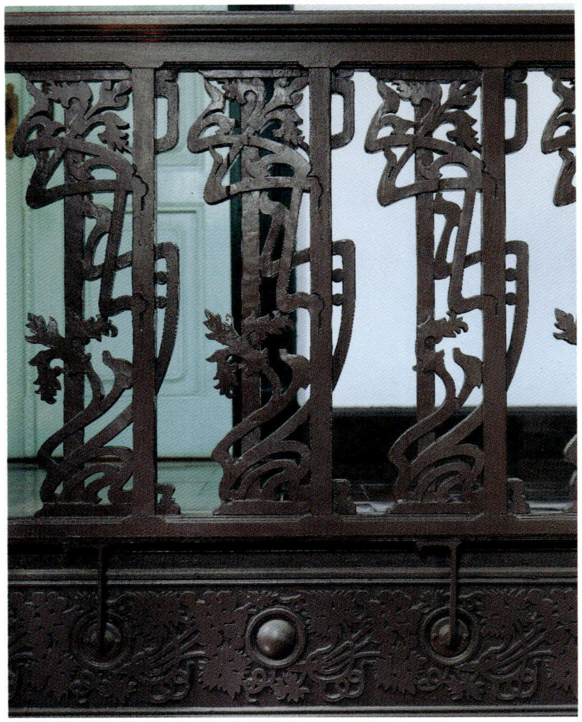

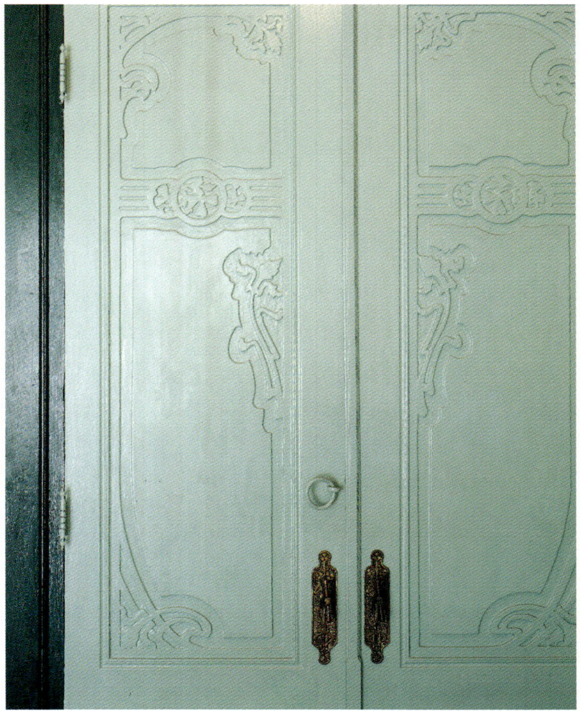

Right : *A sitting area, with pierced decorations above the entranceway.*
Left : *The staircase, with Art Nouveau railings.*
Above : *Detail of Art Nouveau decorations on stair railings and doors.*

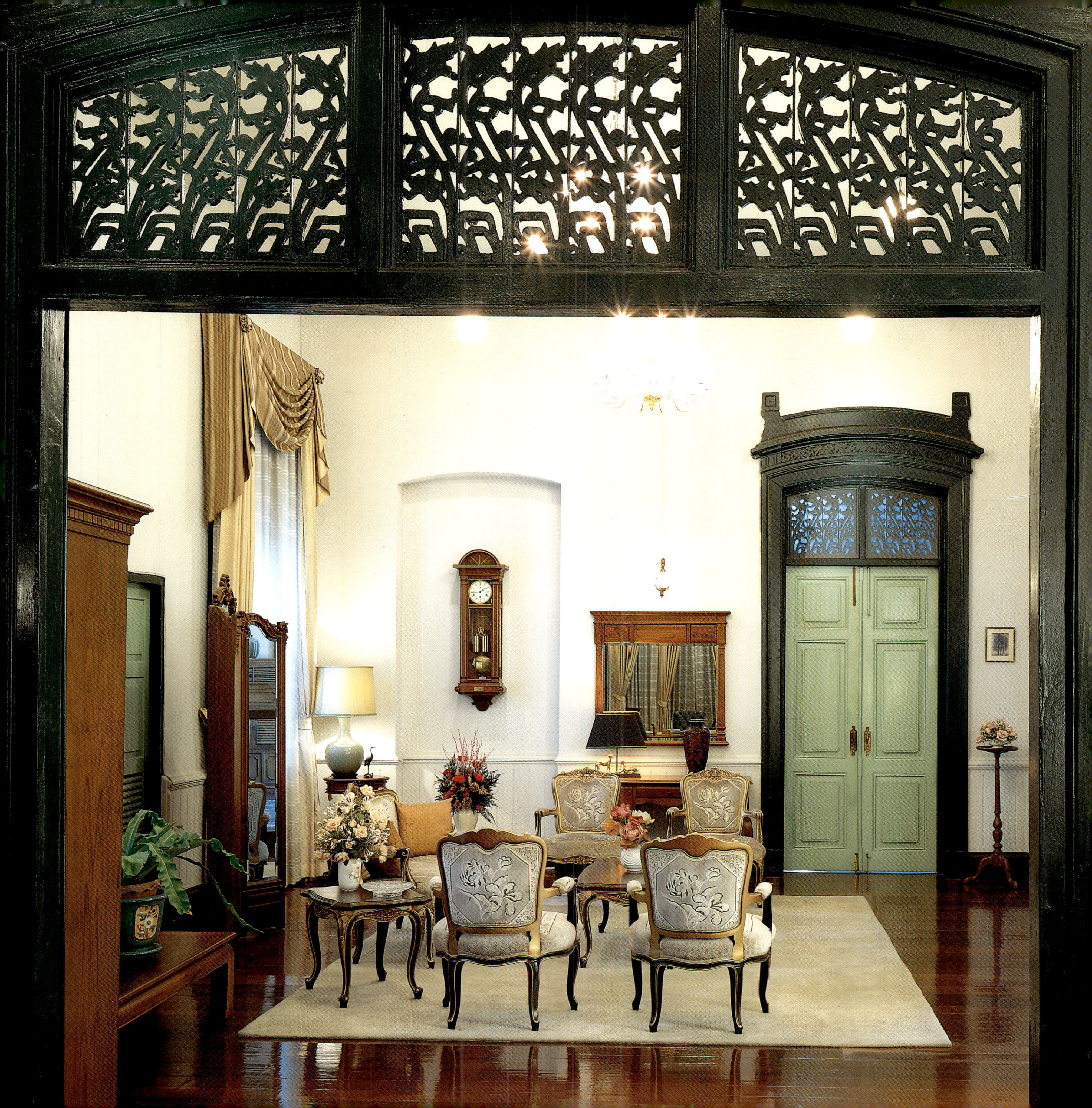

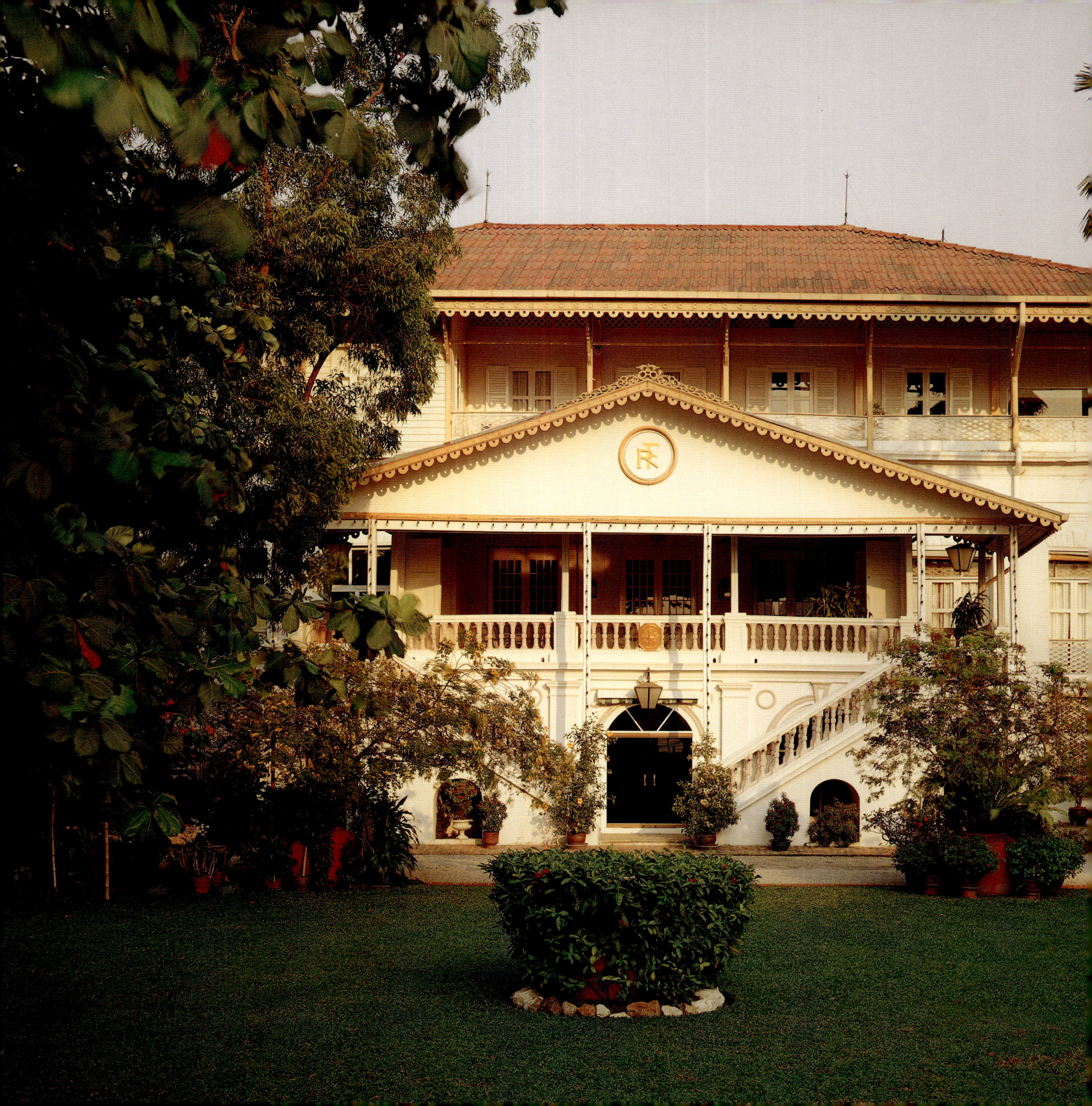

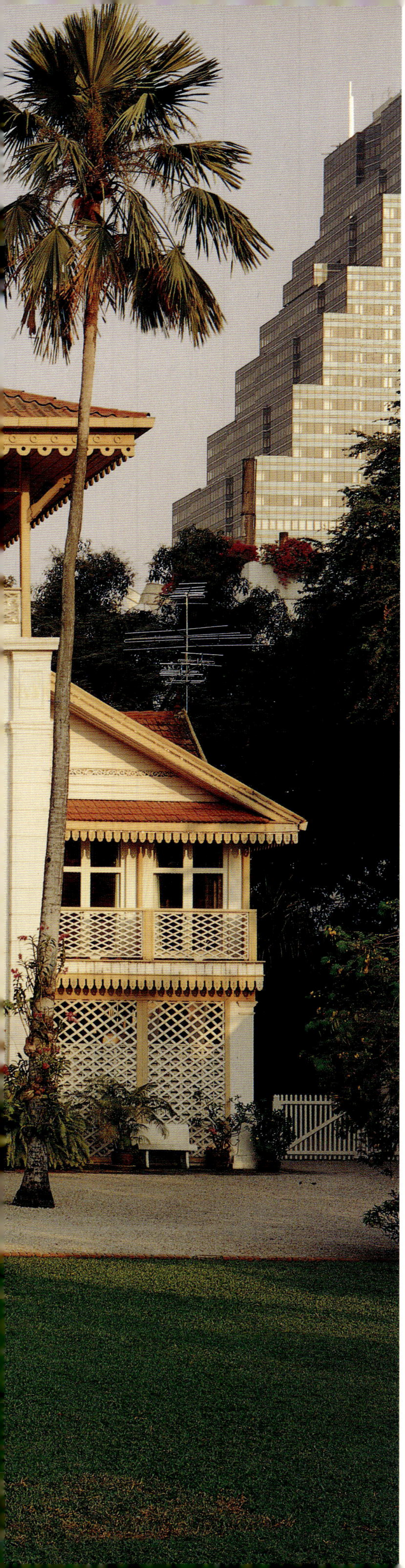

The French Embassy Residence

Little information appears to be available about precisely when or by whom the present French Embassy Residence was built. Records, however, show that the building originally belonged to the Crown and that the French Consul was living there as early as 1857. In 1875 the house and land was officially donated to the French Government by King Rama V.

The residence was the focus of considerable local attention in 1893, during a dispute between France and Thailand over territory in Indo-China, when a French warship breached the defenses at the mouth of the Chao Phraya River and anchored just outside the embassy in a show of force. "Every evening," Phya Anuman Rajdhon wrote in his memoirs, "crowds flocked to see that battleship in front of the Department of Customs (then situated next to the French Legation on the north) while the crew were taking their bath in the river, naked since they did not know how to use the loincloth. The spectators, when seeing the French soldiers shamelessly exhibiting their nude bodies outdoors, could not withstand their disgust at such a sight and reacted angrily...Eventually the authorities had to calm them down for fear that they would lead to uncontrollable consequences."

For almost a century, the building was used as both the Ambassador's residence and also for embassy offices; since the construction of a new office building, it has served only as the residence. By 1959, the structure was in a poor condition, prompting extensive restorations over the next decade. It is now listed as a National Historic Building.

Architecturally, it is similar to a number of residences built by or for Westerners in the mid-19th century, elevated off the ground on pillars and with verandahs, louvered shutters, and gingerbread decorations. The only access in the early days was by river, though later a road led down to it from New Road.

Left : *Front of the French Embassy Residence, facing the Chao Phraya River*

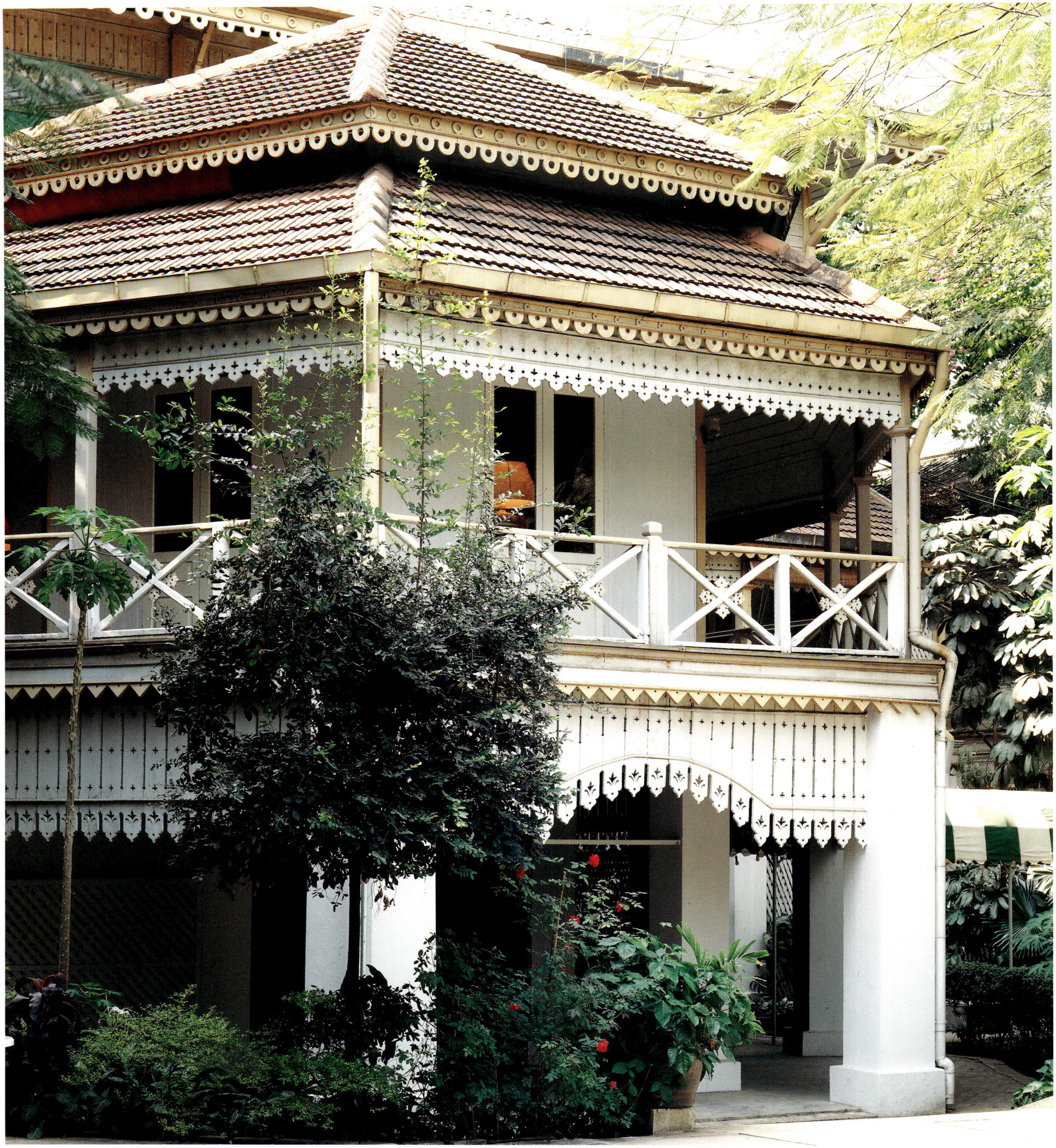

Left : *Side entrance; the gingerbread decorations and surrounding verandah were typical of Western-style house built in Bangkok in the second half of the 19th century.*
Above right : *Detail of the upstairs verandah and decorative fretwork.*
Above far right : *Part of the verandah that runs around the upper floor.*
Right : *Sitting area on the upper verandah of the residence.*

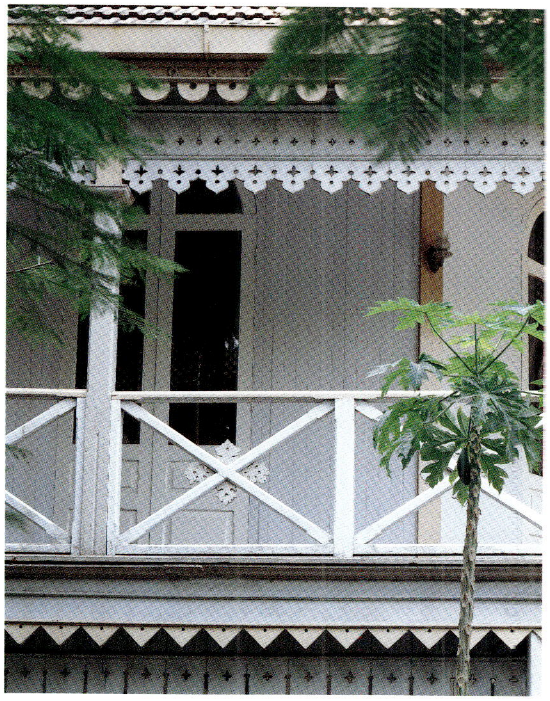

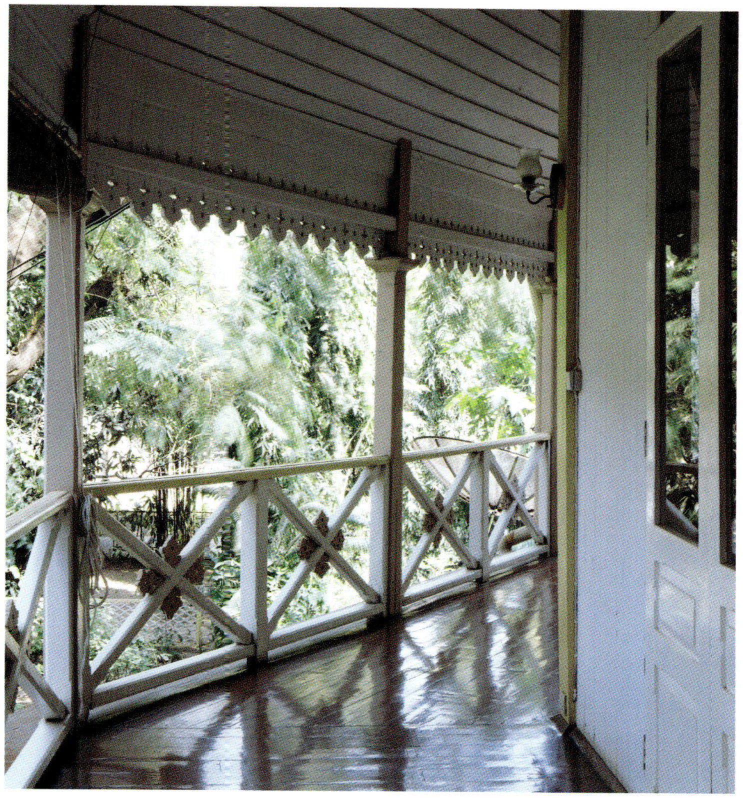

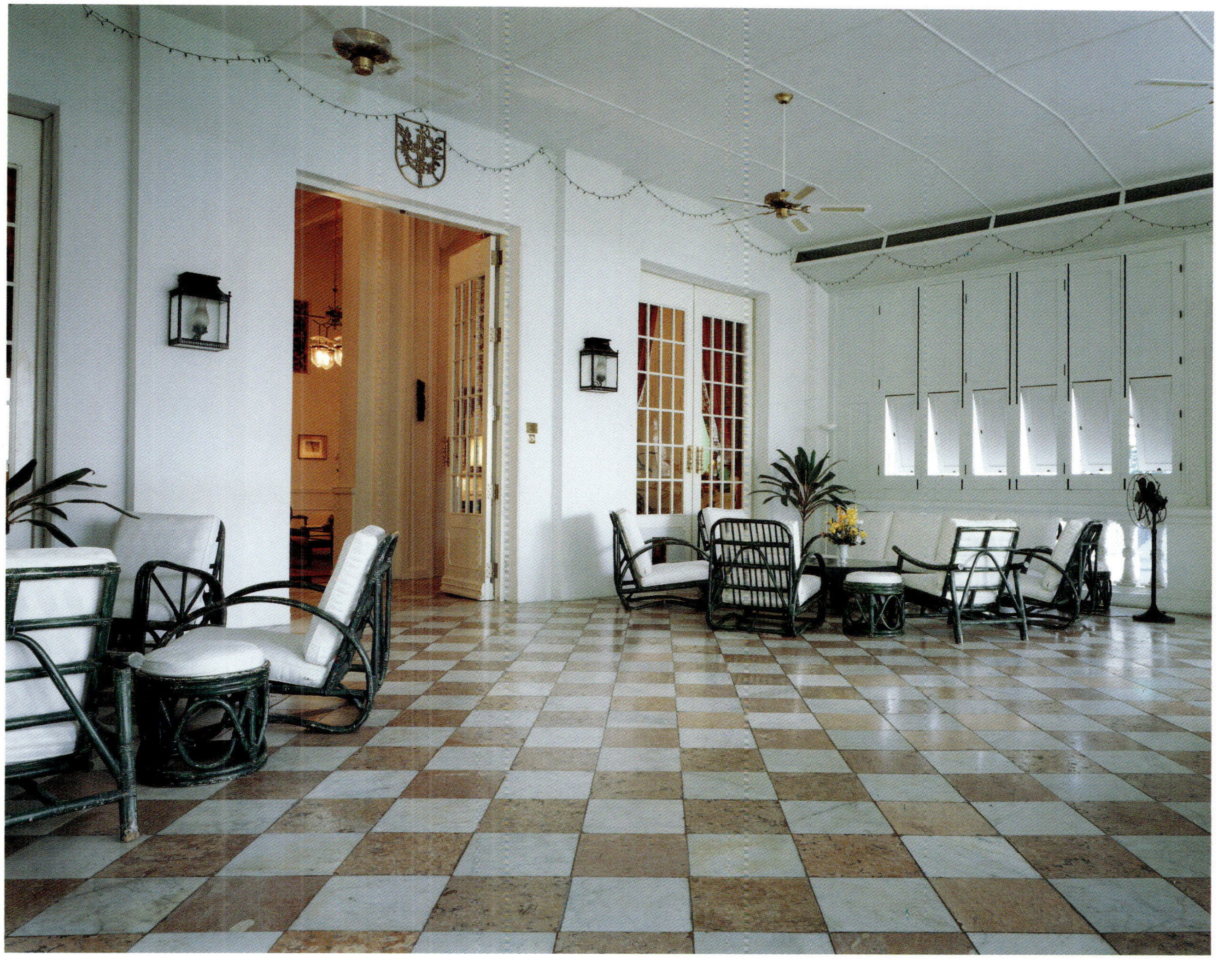

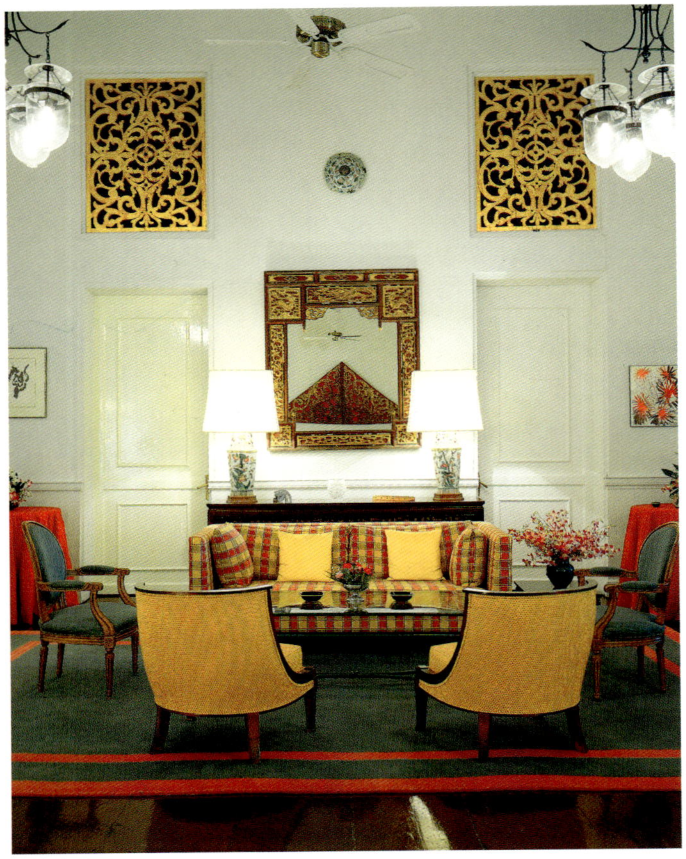

Right : *The dining room, overlooking the garden and river.*
Below : *Sitting room of the residence; the carving on the wall is northern Thai.*
Left : *The sitting room, showing decorative vents above the doors.*

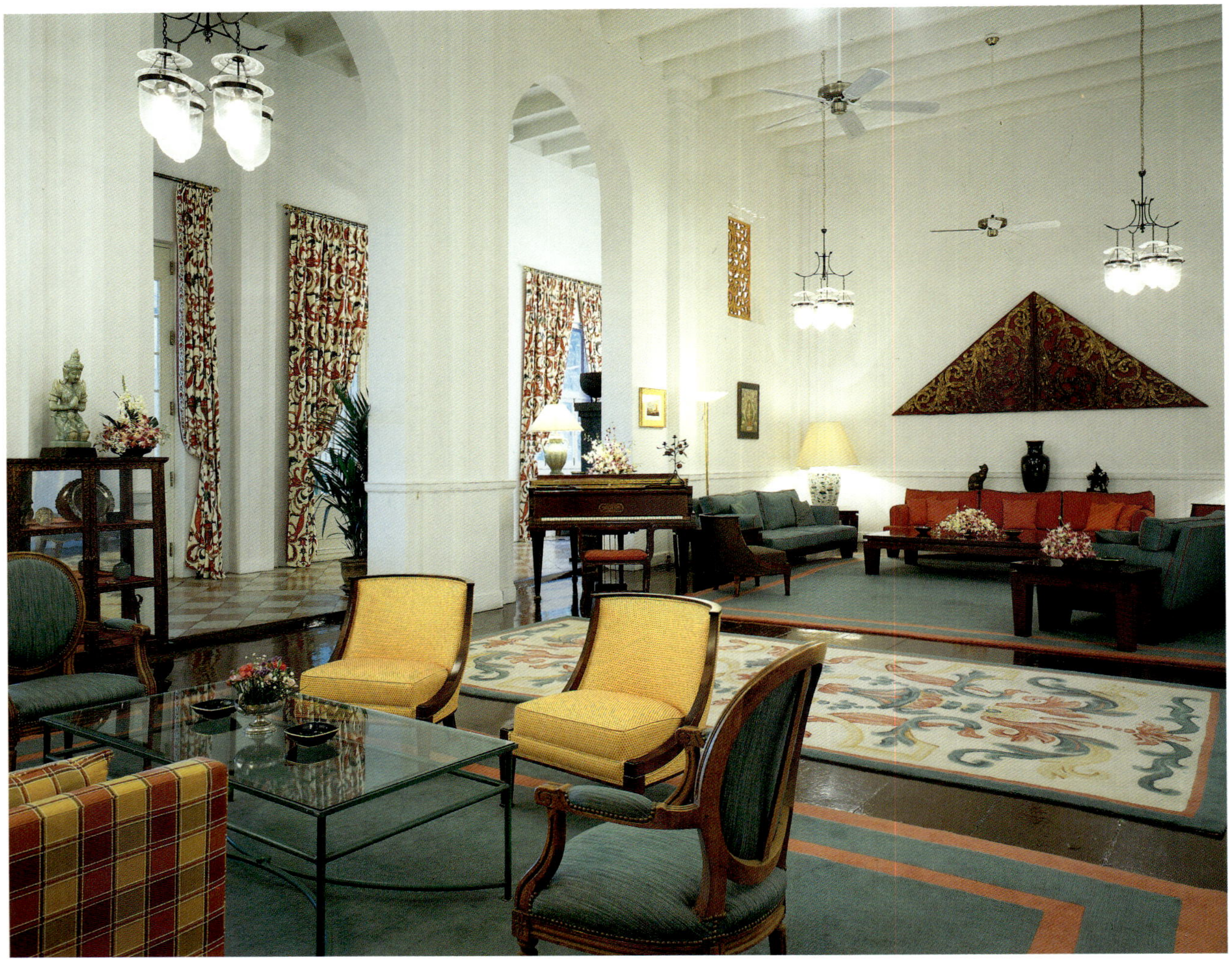

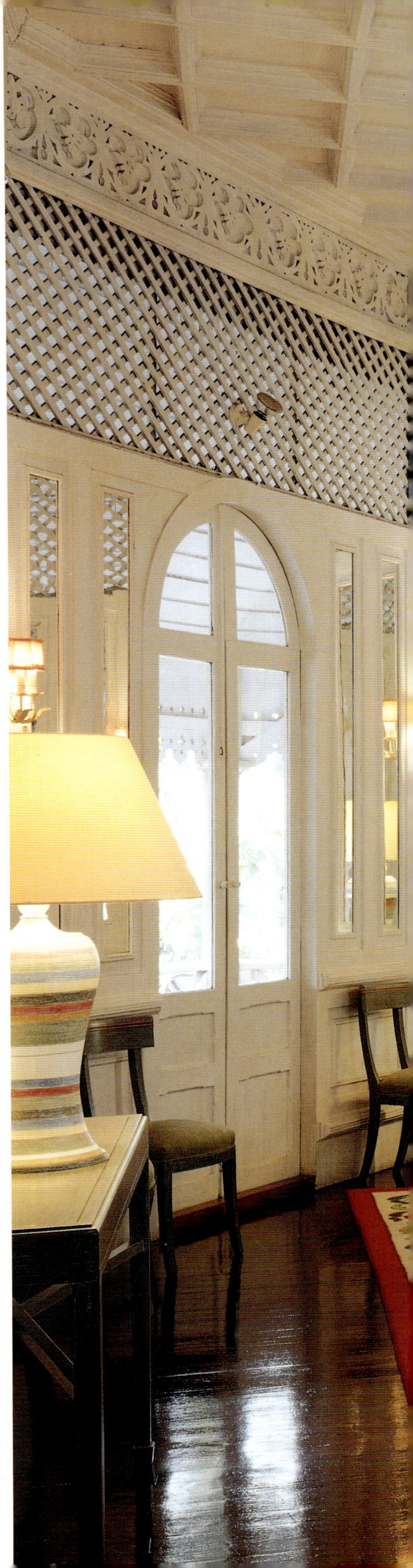

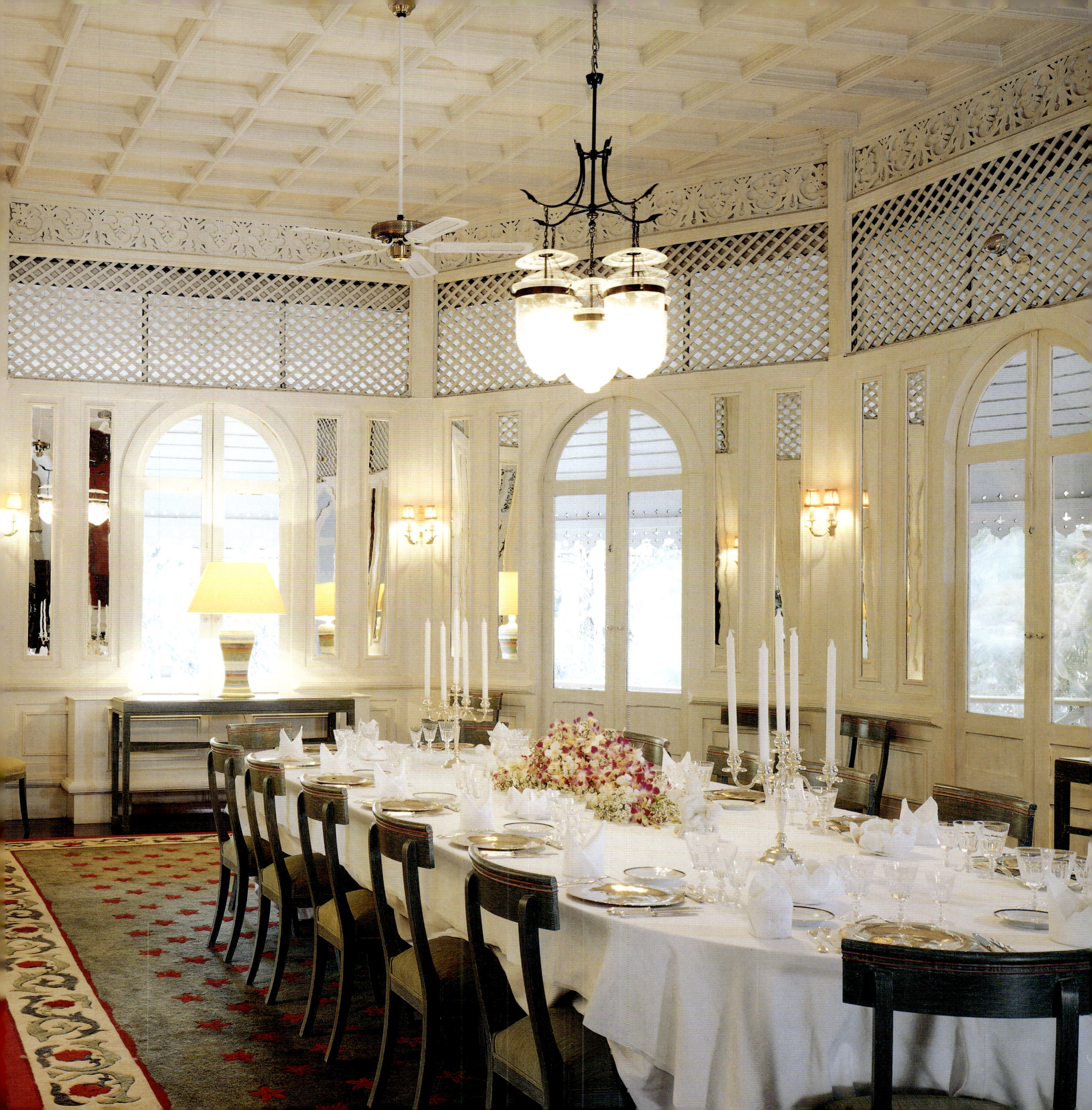

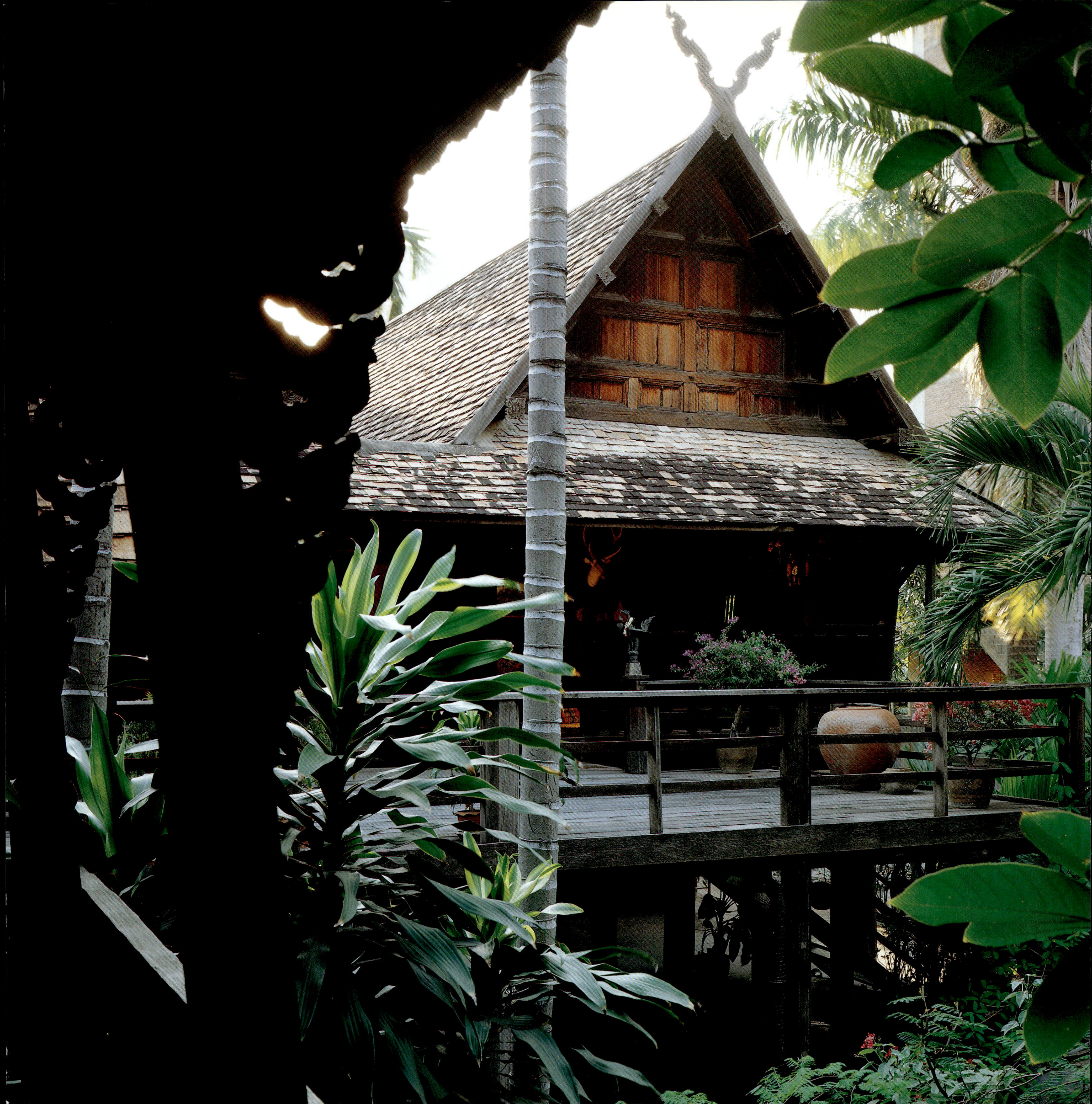

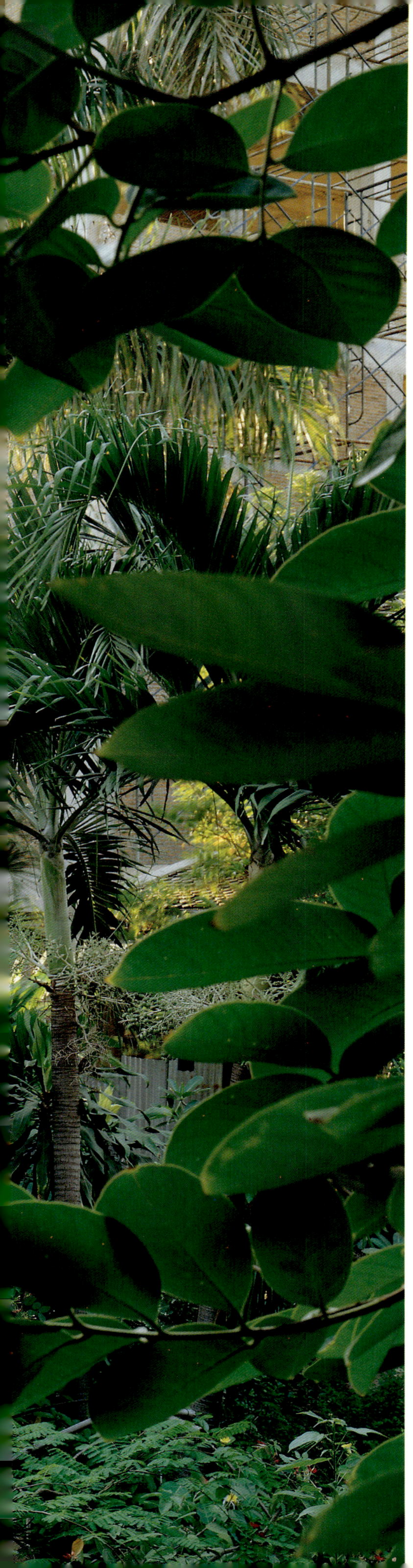

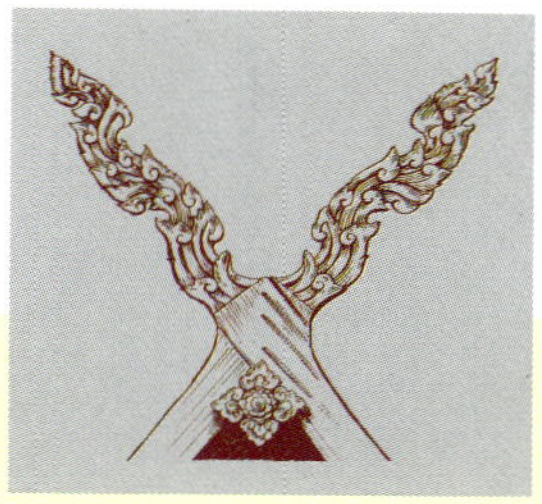

The Kamthieng House

When the Siam Society was founded, in 1904, one of its original goals was the establishment of an ethnological museum. Not until 1963, however, did plans actually materialize when Nang Kimhaw Nimmanahaeminda of Chiang Mai offered her ancestral teak house to the Society to serve as such a museum.

Built in the mid-19th century on the east bank of the Ping River, the house is a fine example of the traditional northern-style *ruen luang*, or "large house". It consists of two rectangular units with a common floor, as well as a covered verandah and walkway leading to the kitchen and a working balcony, the entire structure elevated on 36 octagonal teak pillars. The walls slant outward from the floor to the lower edge of the peaked roof, the ends of which are adorned by V-shaped designs called *galae*. The outward shape has been compared to a buffalo, with the pillars serving as legs; houses of similar design are found in a number Asian countries, among them Northwest India, Laos, and Burma. Walls, gables, doors, and windows are prefabricated and attached with wooden joints, meaning that the structure can be dismantled and moved to a new location with relative ease.

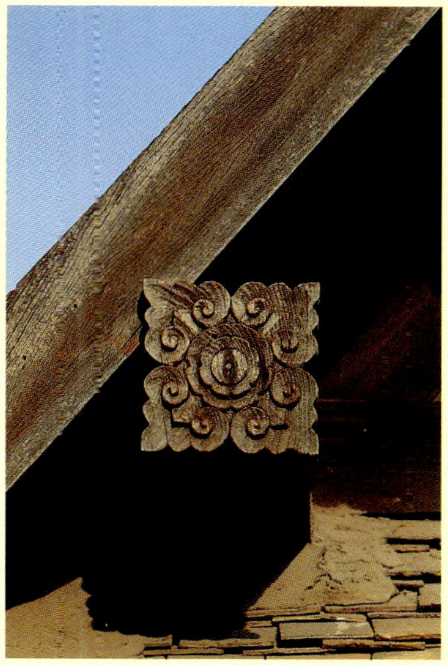

Also characteristic of northern domestic architecture are the carved lintels, or *ham yon*, above doorways leading to the inner room. *Ham*, in the old Lanna Thai language, means "testicles," and *yon* is derived from the Sanskrit yantra, or magic formula for warding off evil spirits; Khun Kraisri Nimmanahaeminda, Nang Kimhaw's son, has written that the lintels protected the hidden strength of the owners and became more powerful as the house aged.

Funds for moving the house to the Society's grounds in Bangkok were provided partly by the Asia Foundation of San Francisco and partly by private donations. The outer verandah, or *toen*, was added to the structure, while two northern rice granaries were also acquired from Chiang Mai. The entire process took two years, and the Kamthieng House, displaying a collection that ranged from textiles and lacquer ware to woodcarvings and cooking utensils, was officially opened by His Majesty King Bhumibol Adulyadej on November 21, 1966.

Left : *View of the Kamthieng House from the rice granary, showing the distinctive northern roof decorations called* galae.
Above : *Decorative carving on the bargeboard or* pan-lom.

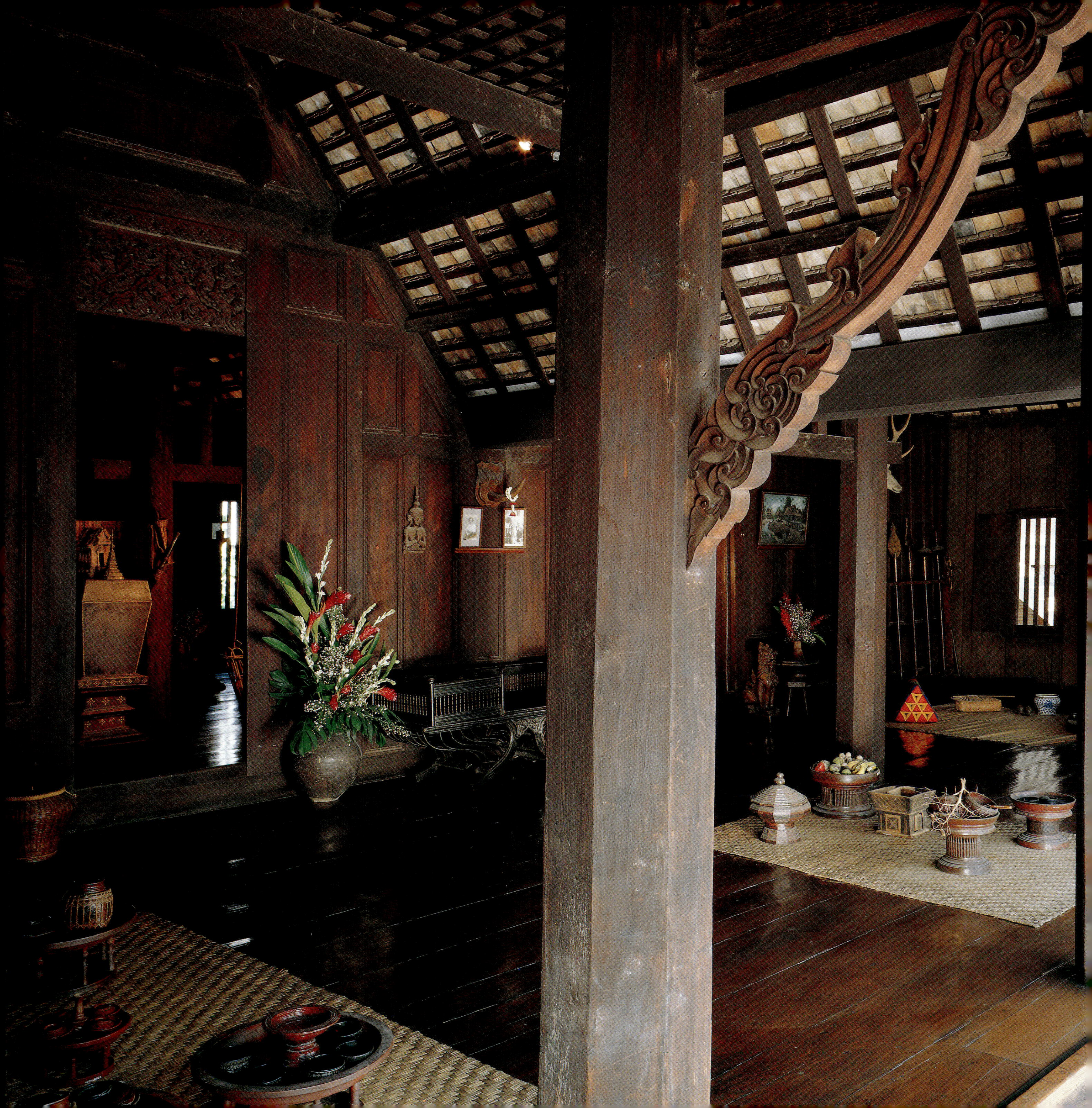

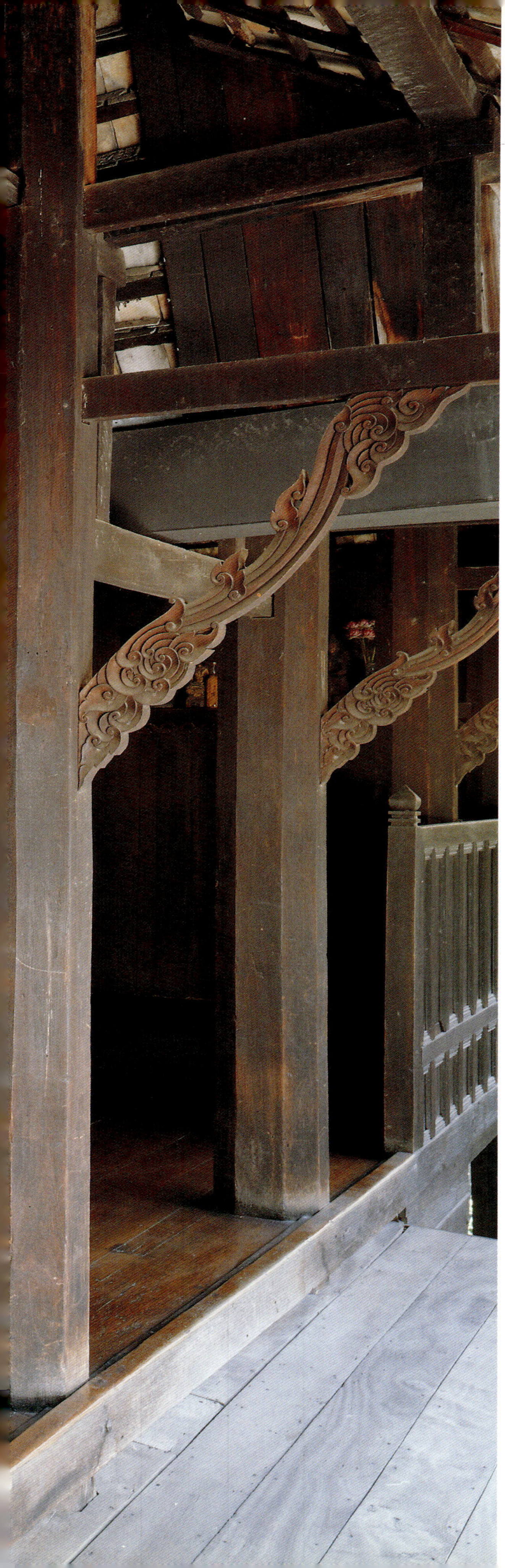

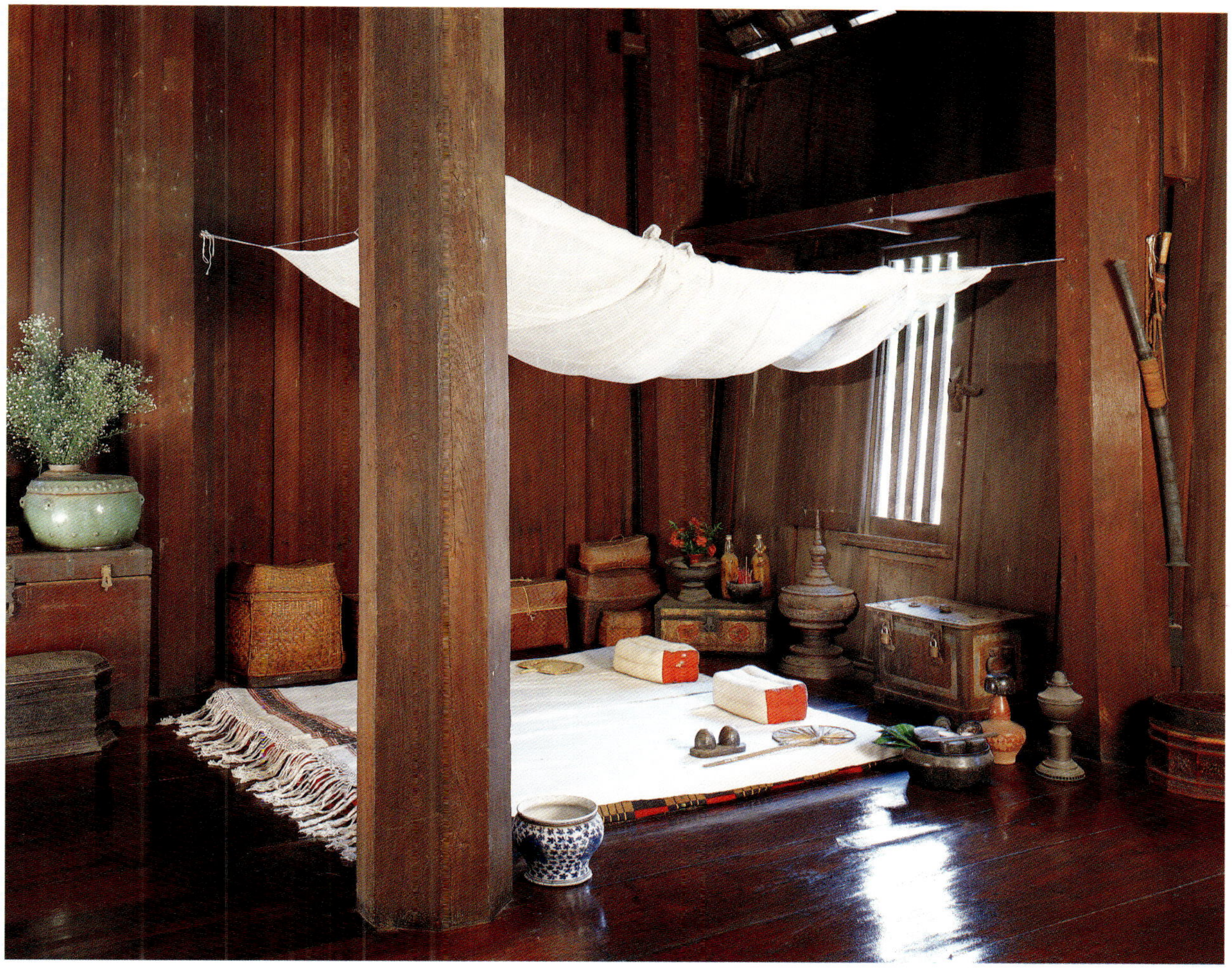

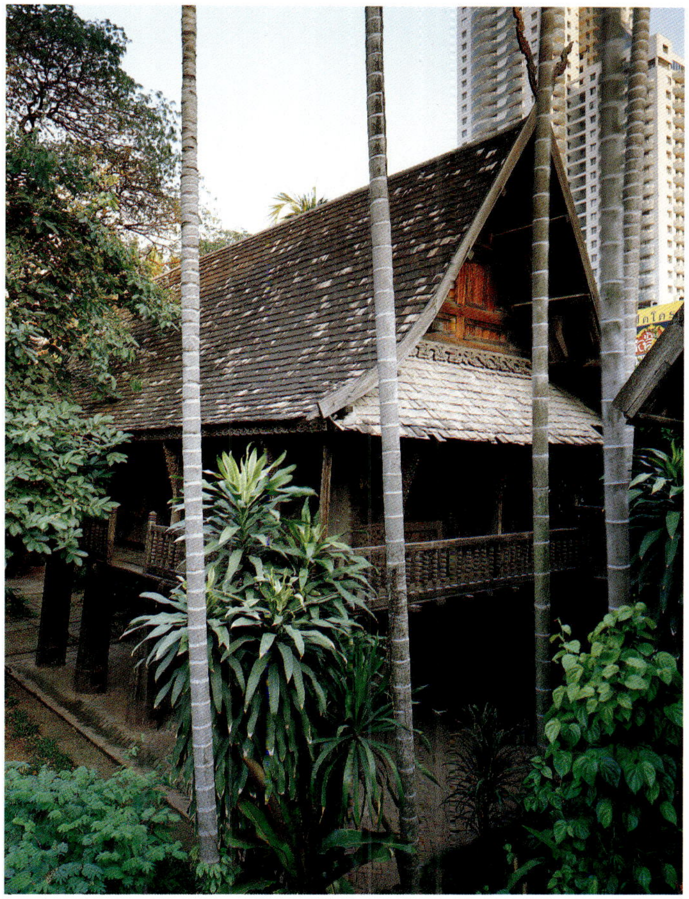

Opposite page : *Living area off the verandah, where northern furniture and other items are displayed.*
Above : *Sleeping area for owners of the house; according to northern tradition, this is located in the northeastern corner of the main room.*
Left : *The rice granary, acquired from Chiang Mai and dating from around the same period as the house.*

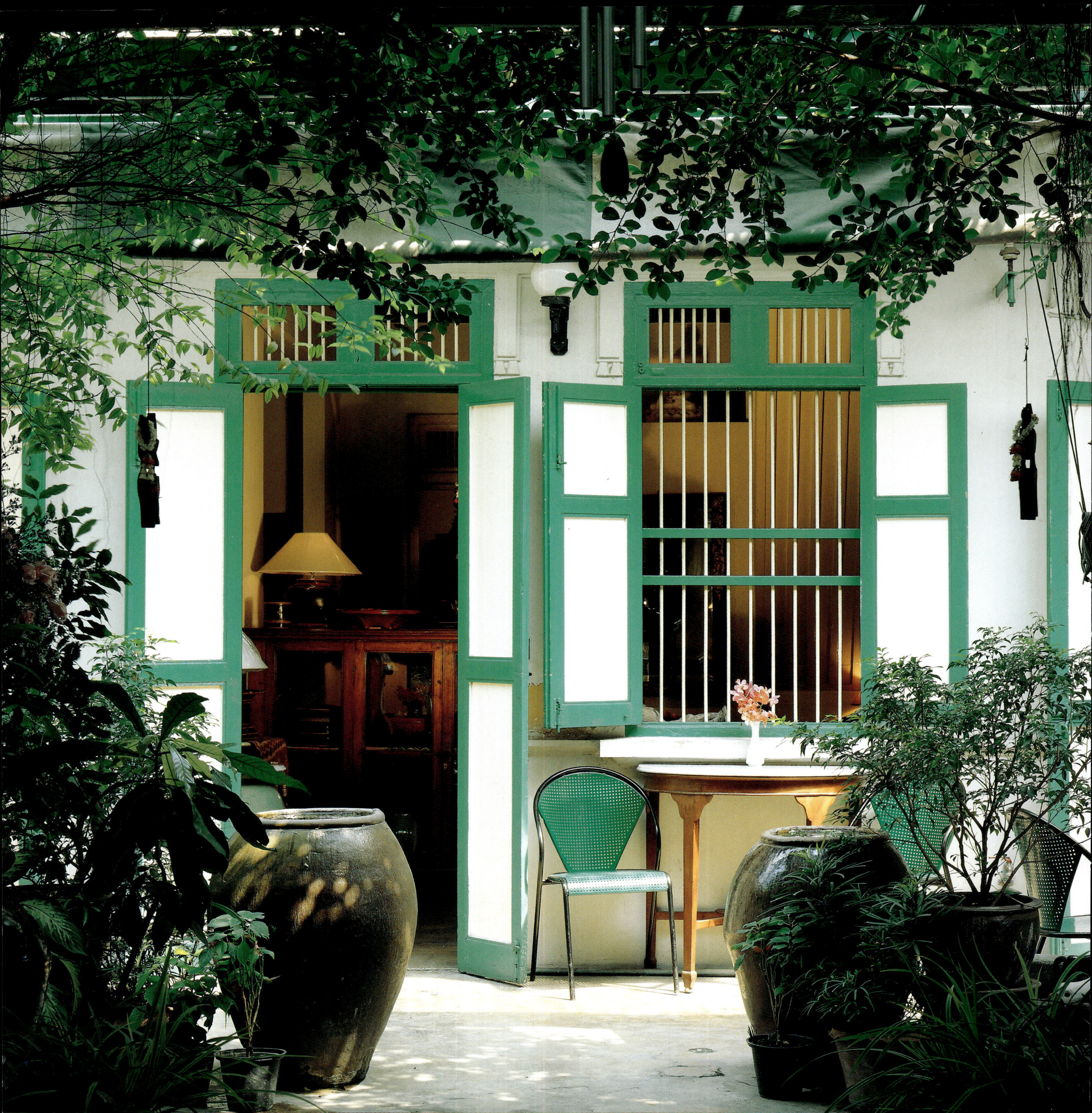

Bangkok Shophouses

Charoen Krung, popularly known as New Road, is generally described as Bangkok's first proper street, though in fact Rama IV Road preceded it by several years, having been built on earth removed when Klong Hua Lamphong was dug. In any event, both appeared during the reign of King Rama IV and, even before being paved, were soon lined with shophouses owned mostly by Chinese. At first these were simple, two-story affairs with the shop below and living quarters upstairs, largely devoid of any decorative features. Later, during the next reign, they became larger and more elaborate, sometimes in the Sino-Portuguese style of Malacca and Penang.

Phya Anuman Rajdhon, in his memoir "Looking Back," recalled that in the early years of the present century the New Road shophouses on either side of an entrance to Assumption College could be divided into two styles. "North of the entrance," he wrote, "were contemporary two-story shophouses. South of the entrance were Chinese-style two-story shophouses, called Chup-poey Kuey, which means 18-room building. This was because the shophouses had 18 units. The name was also used to refer to the district in those days."

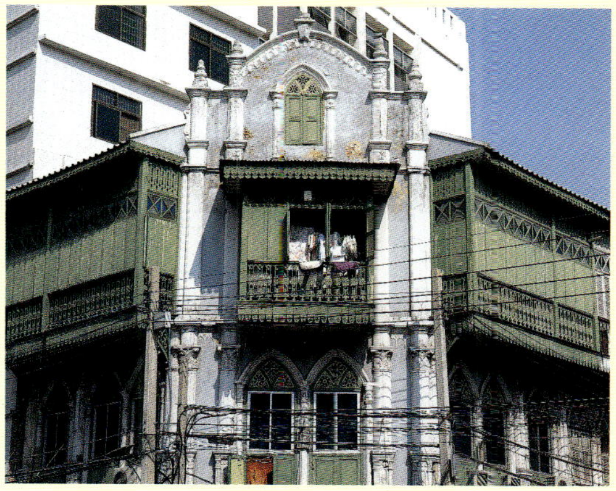

Bangkok's old shophouses have managed to survive more successfully than many of its grander residences, usually because they are located in areas less tempting to developers but also, occasionally, because they have been actively preserved by their present owners or tenants.

One, which now houses the Harmonique Restaurant on Soi Wat Muang Kae off New Road, is located near the Chao Phraya River and is built in European style. As the importance of the river declined with the expansion of Bangkok, it and others in the area were left to deteriorate or used for storage. Around 1988, the current owners, Khun Boonma Phanvivattana and Jacques Deen, converted the front section for use as a restaurant; this proved so successful that in 1992 they expanded into the back area, also embarking on an effort to restore the building to its original condition.

Some walls were so damaged they had to be removed, but the original floor and parts built of teak were in good condition. In general, the owners say, it would have been easier and less expensive to put up an entirely new building; once the restoration was complete, however, it became a source of pride to them as well as an object of admiration to their customers.

Another well-preserved shophouse is "123 Baan Dee" on Fuang Nakhon Road, connecting Ta Now and Baan Mor Roads, in an area where some of the earliest structures date from the early 1860s. The building was rented out for a considerable period, but when the lease expired about five years ago two descendants of the original owner, Khun Suwanee Jenpanichkarn and her niece Khun Pongkwan Sukwattana, decided to restore it. As architects, they were well-suited to the job and now operate an antique and gift shop on the premises.

Several elements, among them a teak balcony and the ceiling, were in good condition and only needed slight repairs. The floor had to be redone, though with old patterned tiles similar to the original ones. Markings indicated that arches above the windows had been removed; these were restored, using the same elegant design found on neighboring shophouses. A rear courtyard open to the sky at the top was part of the original design. The house was recently cited by the Association of Siamese Architects as an outstanding example of cultural preservation.

Other shophouses of architectural merit and historic value can be seen along Na Phra Larn, Maharaj, Phraeng Nara, Phraeng Phuthorn, Adsadarng, Ta Now, Bumrung Muang, and Baan Mor Roads.

Left : *Harmonique Restaurant, occupying a restored shophouse just off New Road.*
Above : *Gothic-style shophouse on Songwad Road, dating from the reign of King Rama VI.*

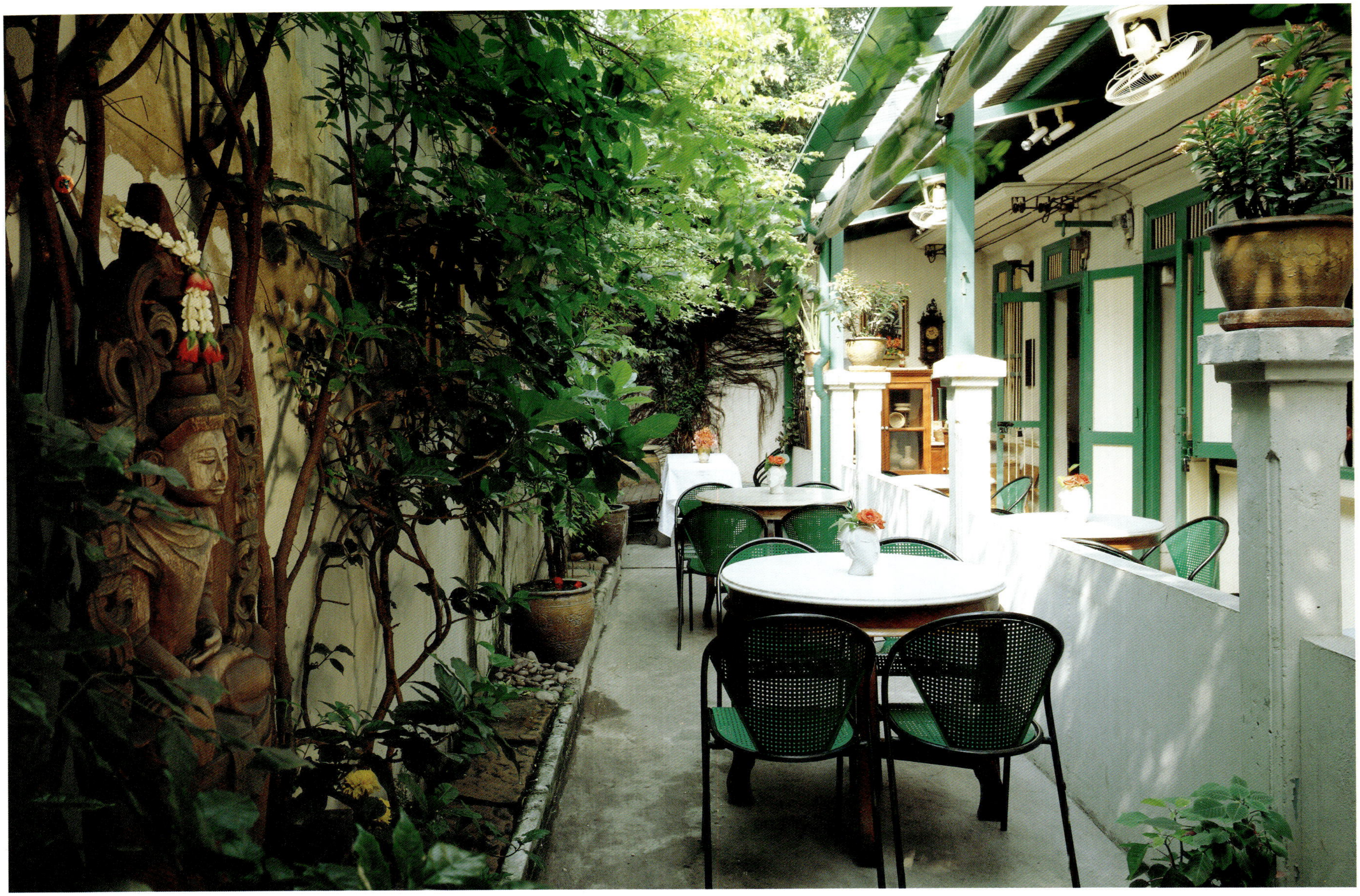

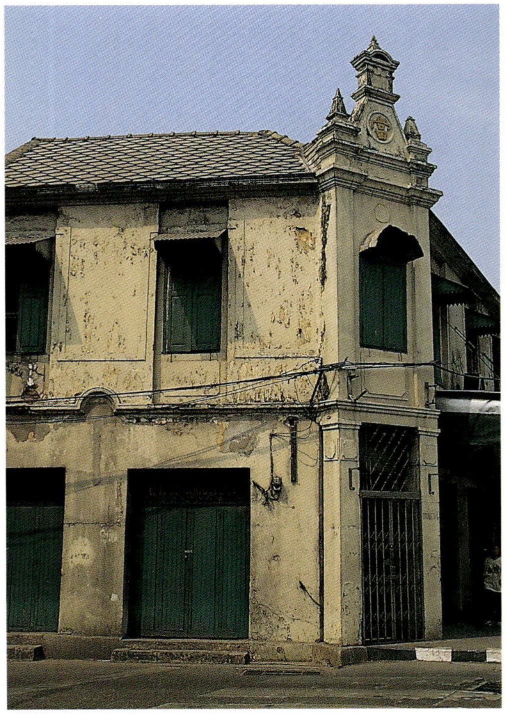

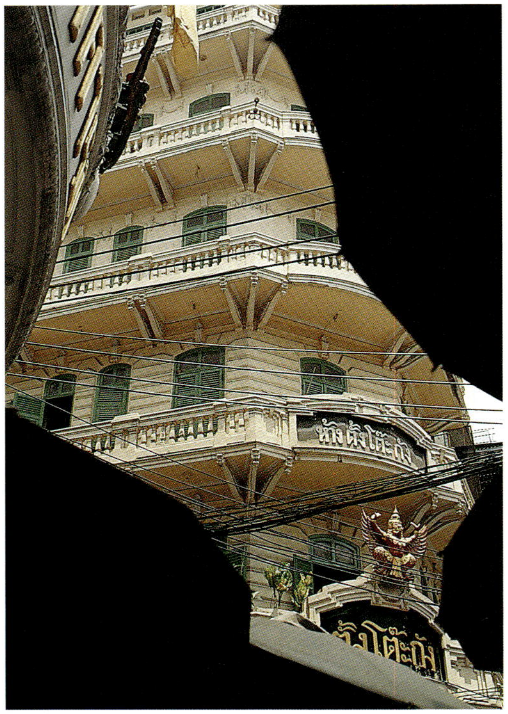

Above : *Courtyard of Harmonique Restaurant.*
Far left : *Oldest style of two-story shophouse on Bamrung Muang Road.*
Near left : *Shophouse dating from around 70 years ago in the Sampeng area of Chinatown.*
Opposite page : *Above is a detail of stucco work on a Songwad Road shophouse, showing Thai fruits and vegetables above windows, while below left is a shophouse along Klong Lawd on Adsadarng Road dating from the reign of King Rama V, and below right an old Chinese pawn shop on Baan Mor Road.*

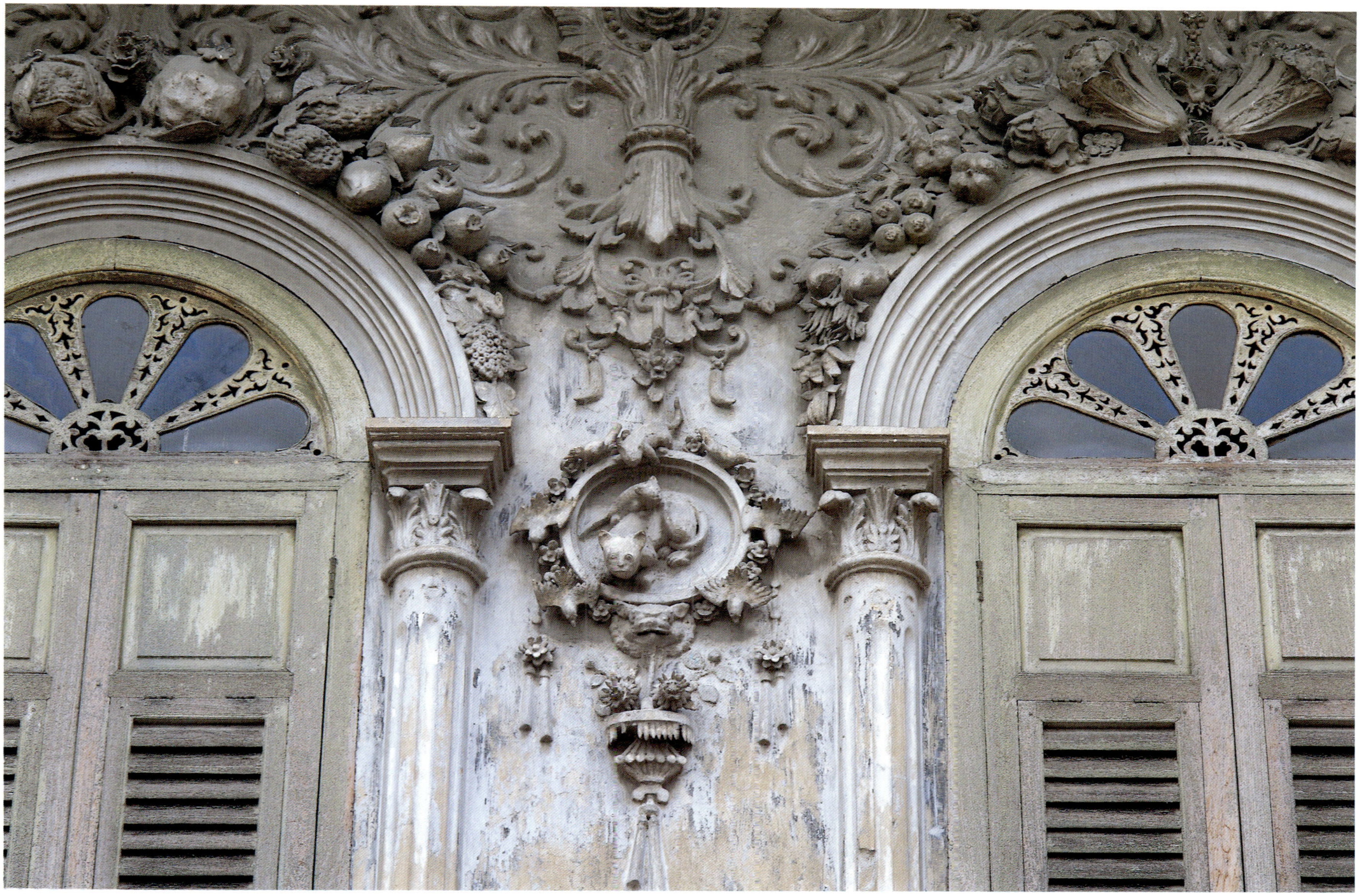

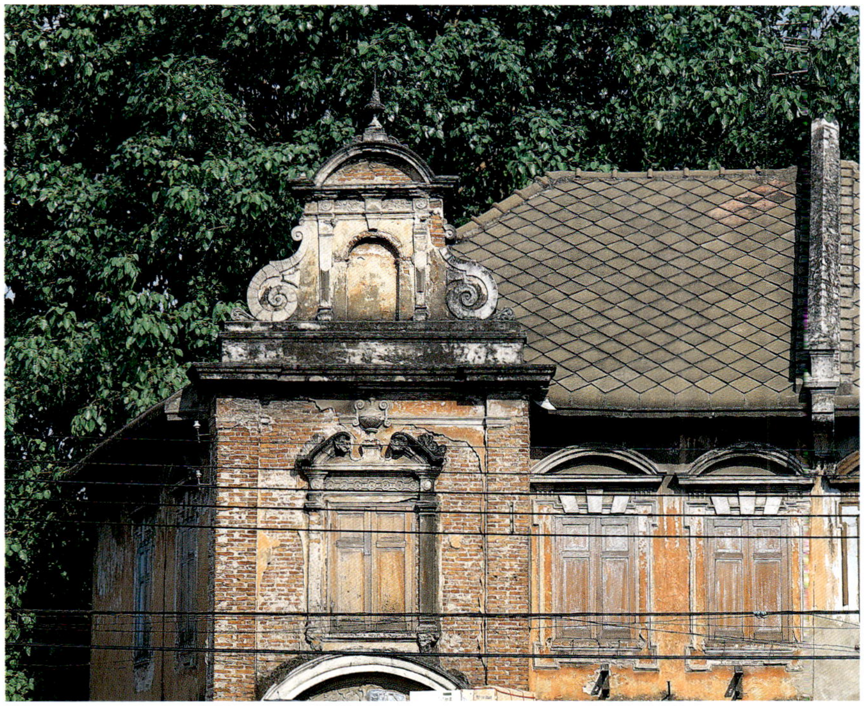

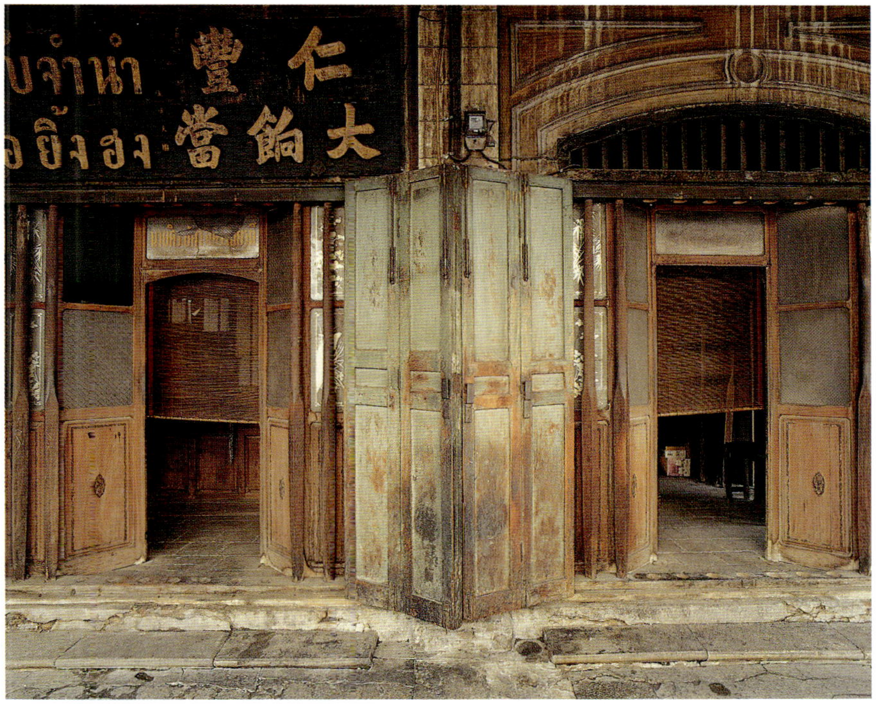
仁豐
大餉當

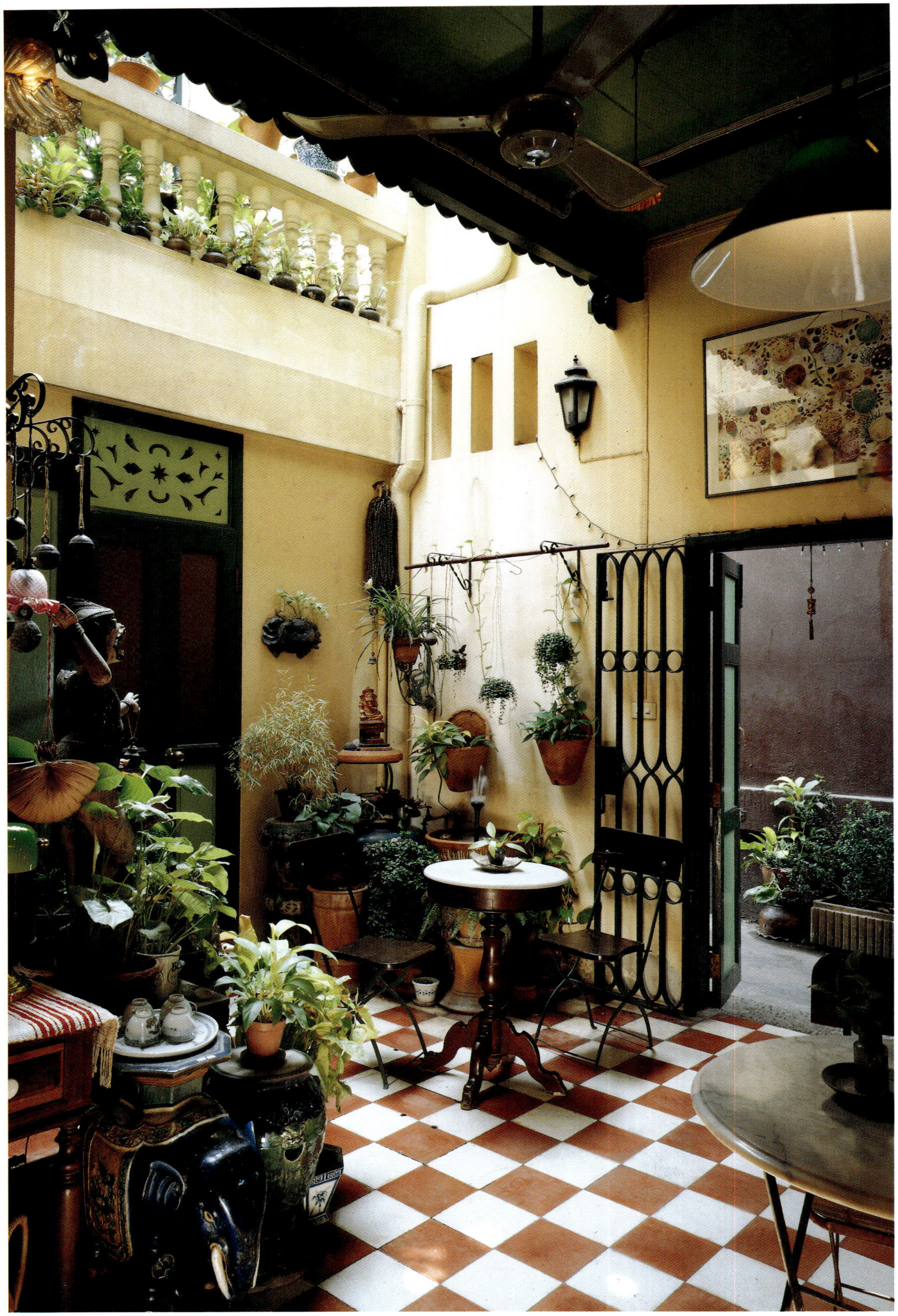

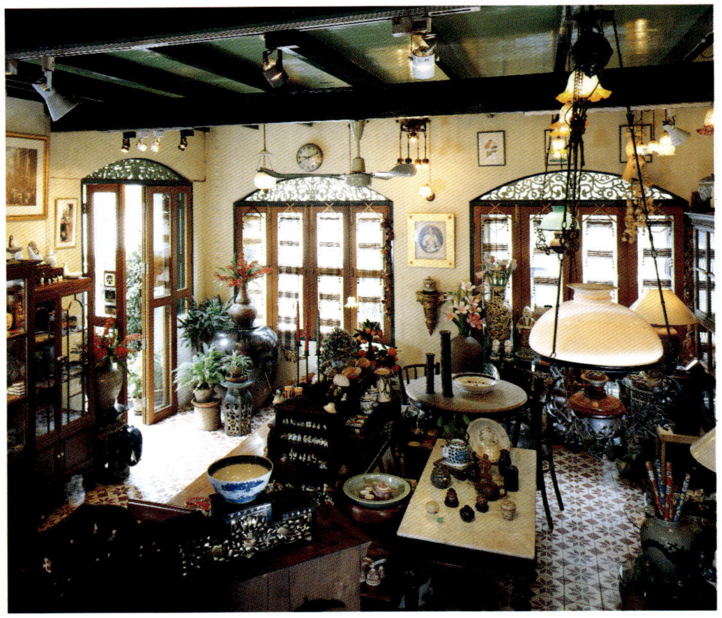

Above : *Interior of "123 Baan Dee", an antique and gift shop.*
Left : *Rear of the shop which is open to the sky.*
Right : *Exterior of "123 Baan Dee", an early-style shophouse facing Fuang Naknon Road.*

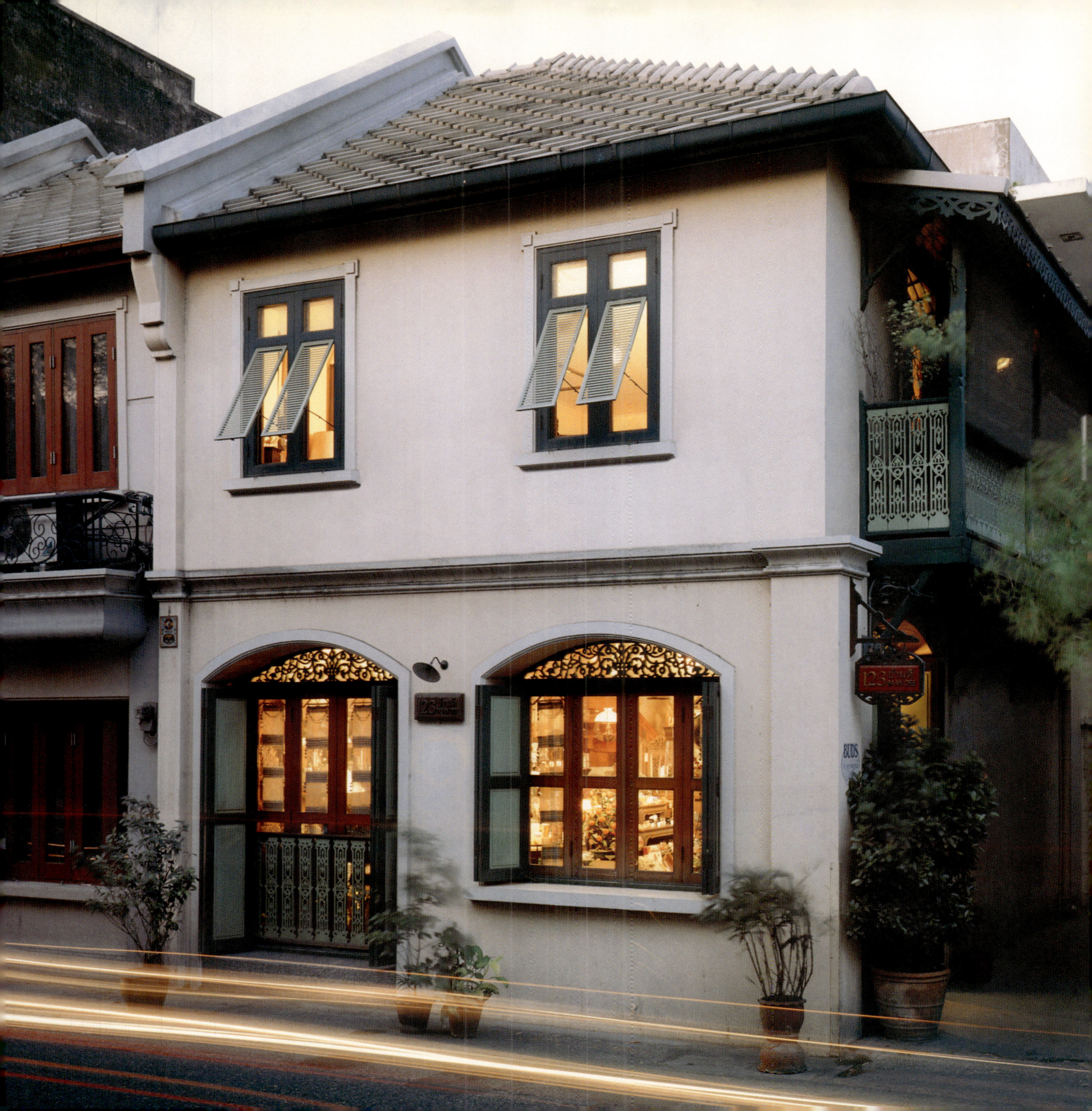
123
BUDS

Houses Along The Chao Phraya River

For close to a century after Bangkok was established as the capital, the Chao Phraya River remained not only its principal means of communication with the outside world but also the focal point of its daily life. Most buildings, residential as well as commercial, were located on or within a short distance of the river, steadily increasing in number as the city's population grew.

"A great proportion of the houses float on large rafters," wrote Sir John Bowring, who came in 1855, "and are sometimes seen moving up and down the river, conveying all the belongings of a family to some newly-selected locality...There are a few houses in Bangkok built of stone and brick; but those of the middle classes are of wood, while the habitations of the poor are constructed of light bamboos, and roofed with leaves of the attap palms. Fires are frequent; and, from the combustible character of the erections, hundreds of habitations are often destroyed."

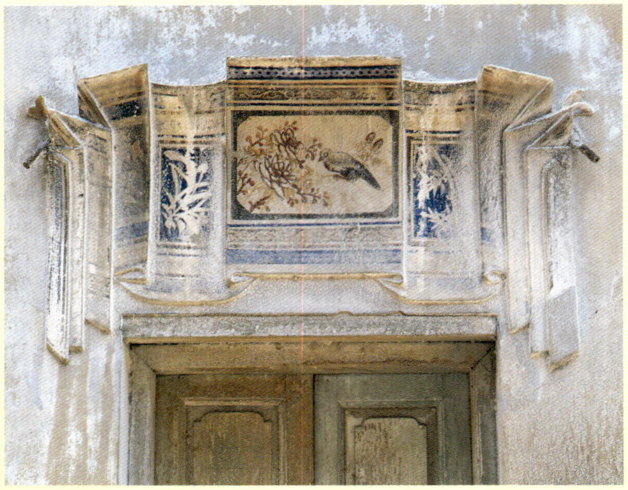

Bowring was staying in one of the few brick houses, a structure on the west bank near the present Memorial Bridge which he calls "the English Factory." It had been built by an adventurous Scot named Robert Hunter some 30-odd years before—"the first of European design to be built in the city," according to Dr. Dan Beach Bradley, a frequent guest—and was known to Thais as Hang Huntra. After Hunter was expelled in 1844 following a dispute with the government, his wife and son lived in the house for a time before it was taken over as an official guest house for distinguished visitors like Bowring. "I occupy two apartments above," he noted in his journal, "a sitting room, large and airy, and a bedroom, which has been newly papered, in which I sleep in a bed which is ornamented with drapery cloth of scarlet and gold, and from which garlands of flowers are suspended."

Hang Huntra vanished long before the end of the 19th century, but by that time other fine houses had appeared along the Chao Phraya, many of them built by Chinese immigrants who had prospered in trade. Due to congestion on the east bank, together with the fact that much of the land there was owned by the crown, most of these rose on the west, or Thonburi, side of the river, where property was less expensive and more readily available. Such residences, blending European and Chinese architectural styles, were often adjacent to the owners' sawmills, rice silos, and gowdowns, the visible sources of their wealth, which could still be seen in large numbers as late as the 1950s.

Today, thanks to increasing development on the Thonburi bank, nearly all the mills and silos have gone and only a handful of the old houses survive. A few, like the famous Wanglee House, have been restored and are still used for family gatherings; others, however, subject to floods and neglect, are sinking into semi-ruin and may well be remembered only through photographs by the end of the present century.

Right : *The Tamnak Nam at Chandhaburi Palace in the Deves district, originally a library and built over the water.*
Above : *Detail above the door of a Chinese house on the Thonburi side of the river near the Krung Thep Bridge.*

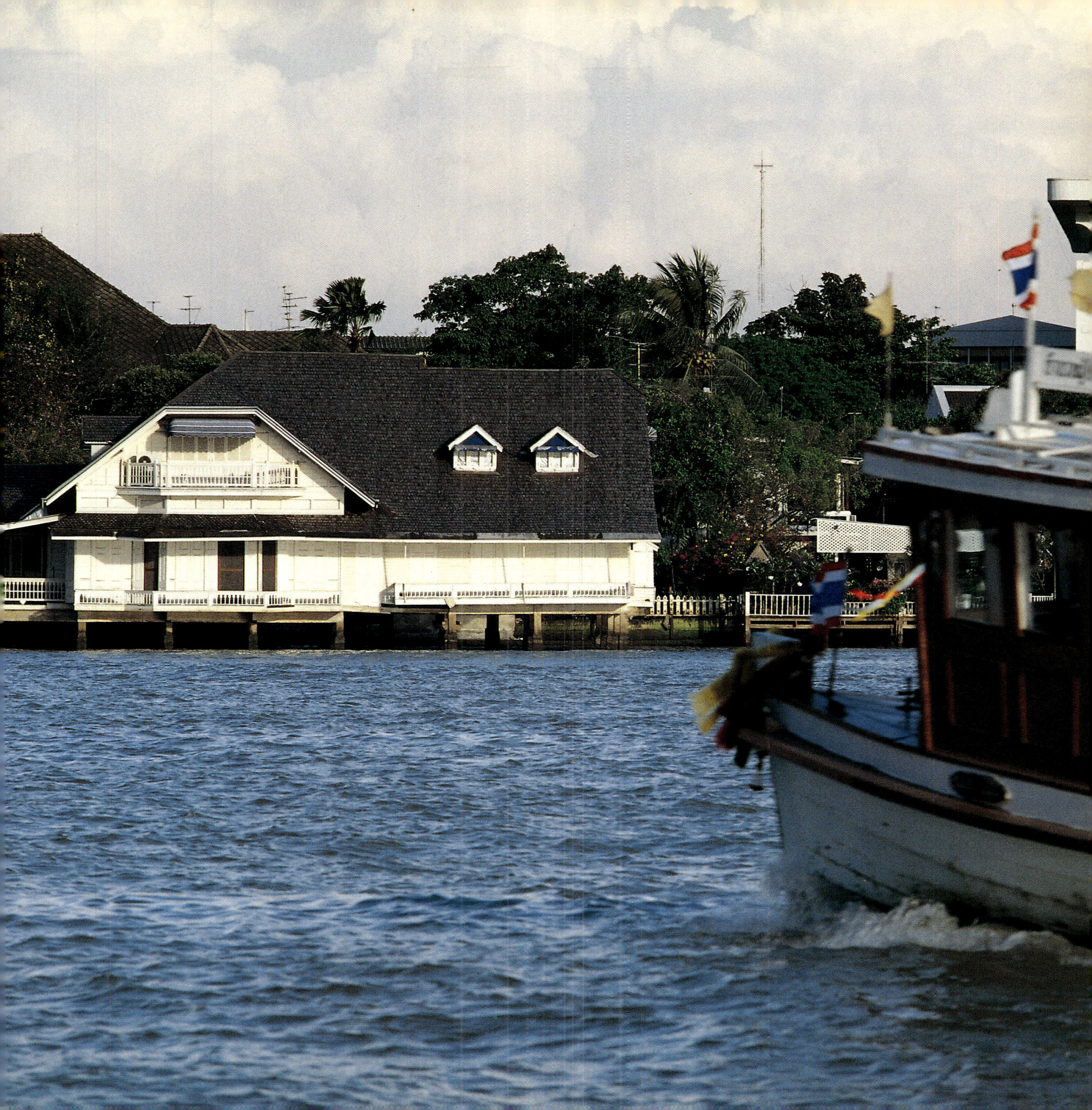

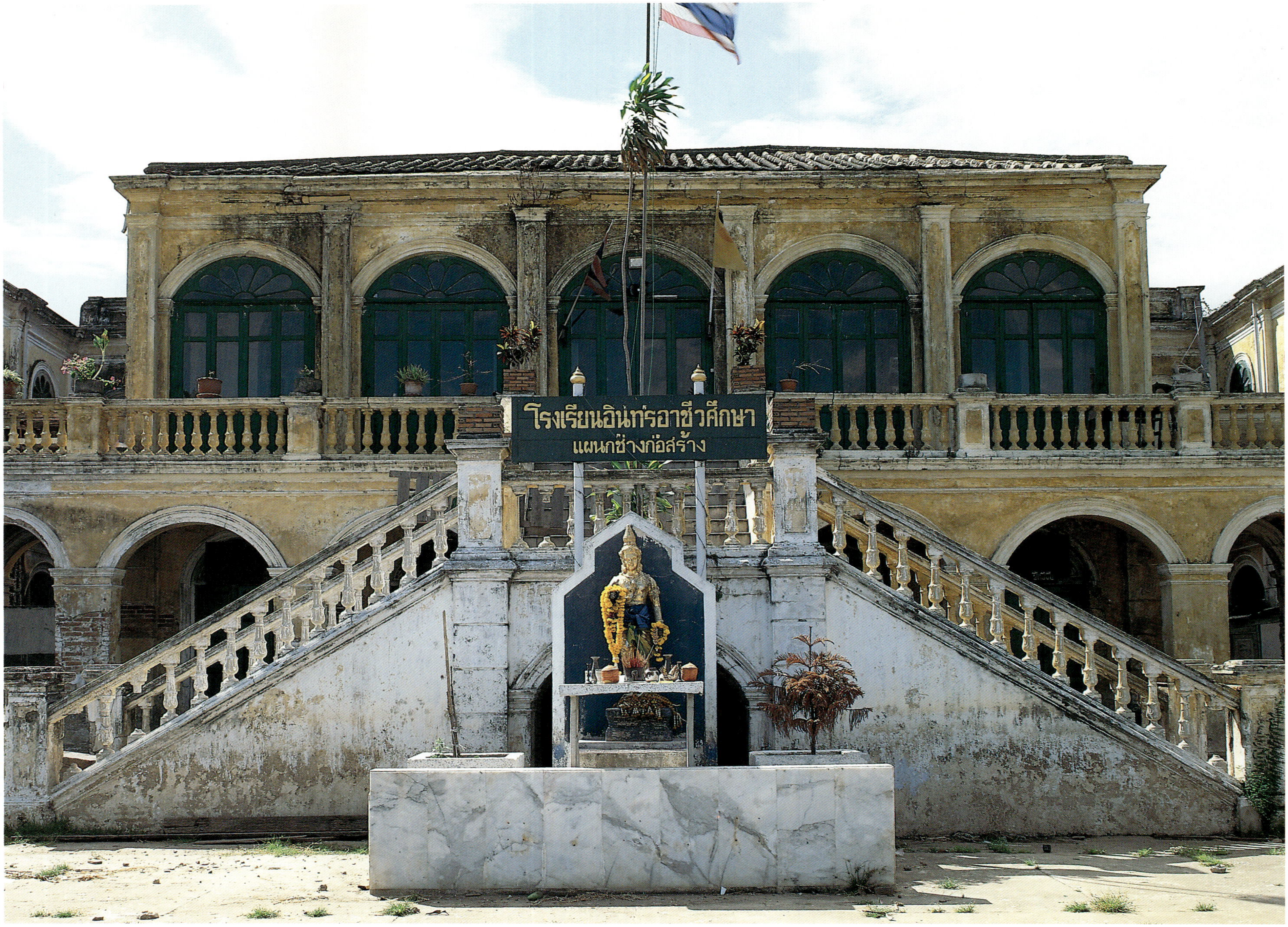

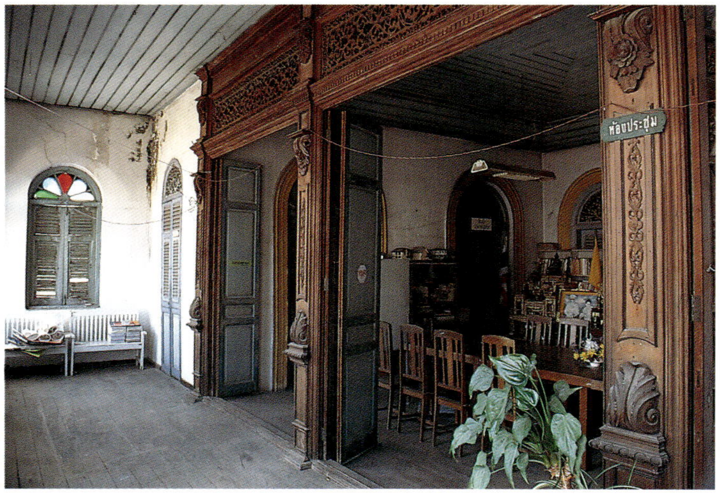

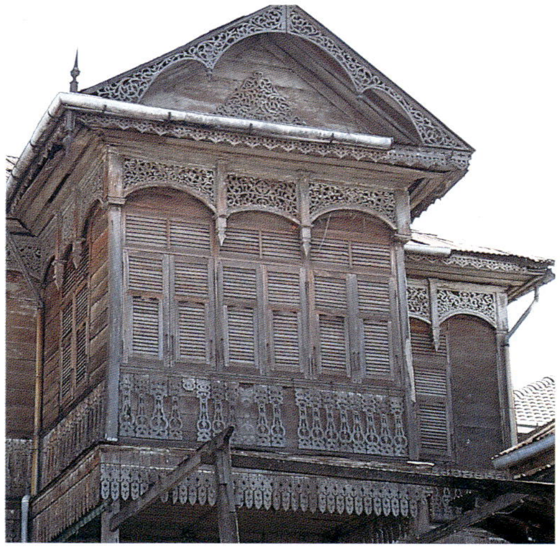

Above and far left : *Palladian-style villa built by Phya Chalabhumpanich toward the end of King Rama V's reign. It later became the property of the Anekavanija family until 1946 when it was sold and became a school.*
Near left and right : *Unidentified houses in a state of disrepair on the west bank of the Chao Phraya.*

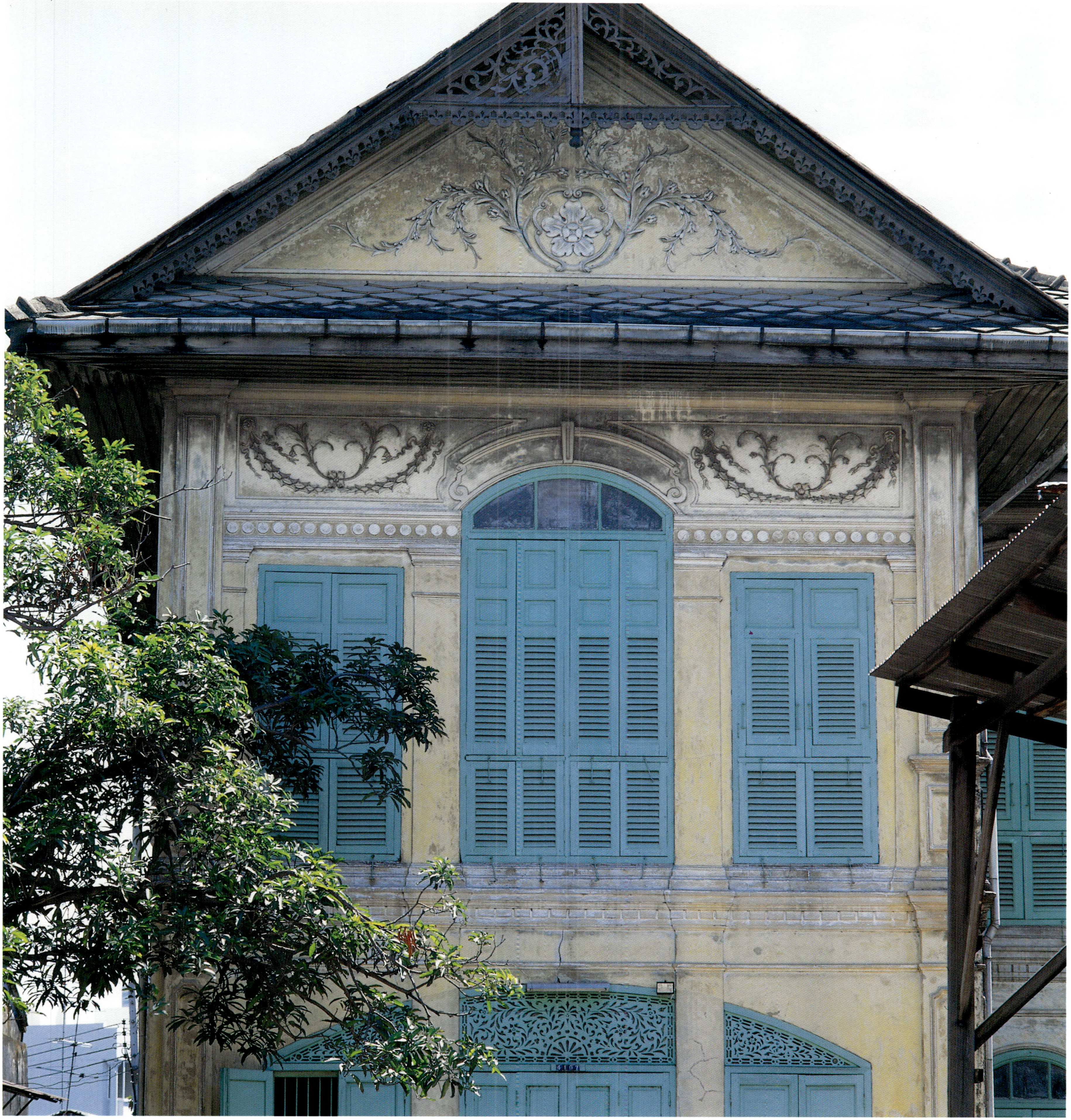

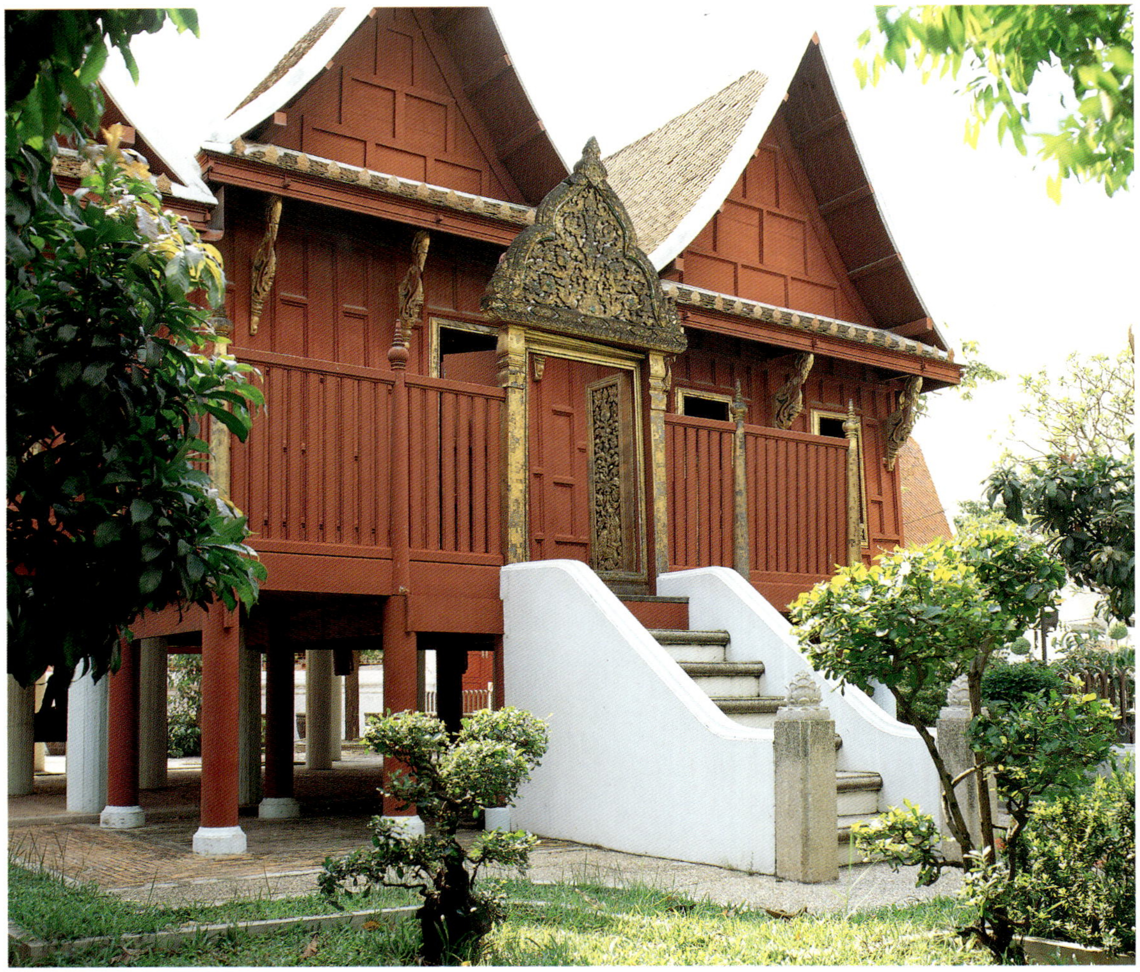

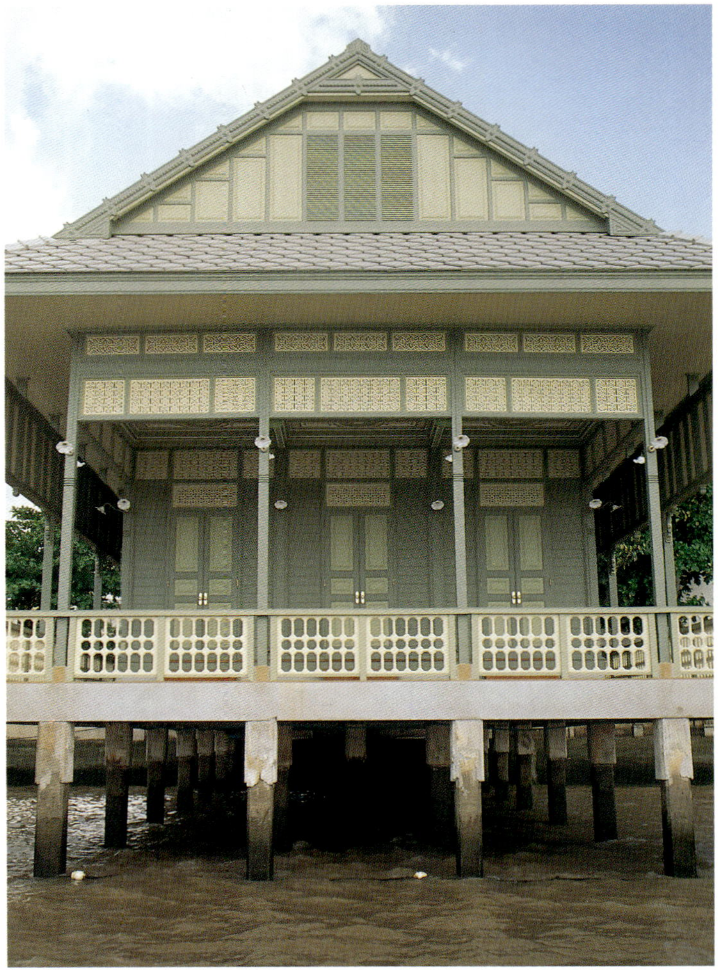

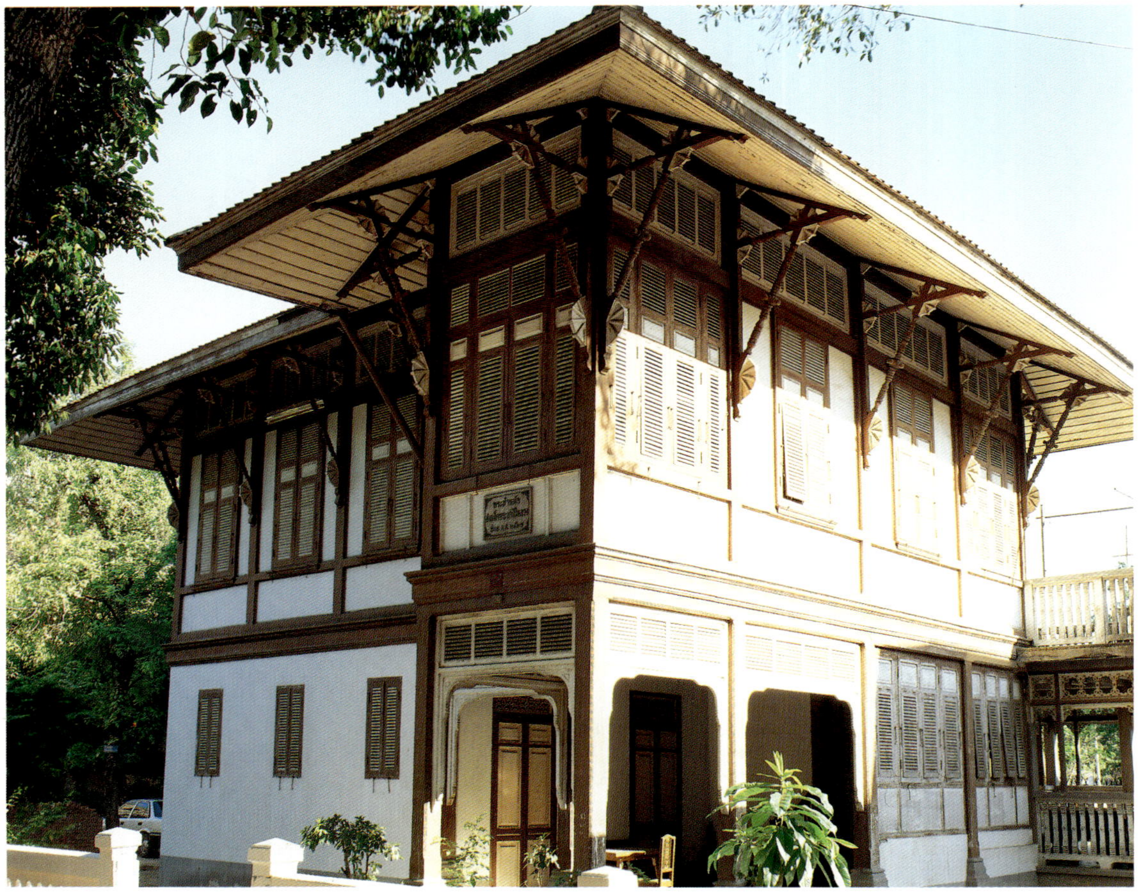

Right : *The old residence that now houses the Oriental Hotel Cooking School, formerly the home of Phya Mahaisawan who was the governor of Thonburi.*
Above left : *The wooden library at Wat Rakhang Kositharam, dating from the late 18th century, was the home of King Rama I before he became king.*
Above : *The river pavilion at Devavesm Palace, recently restored by the Bank of Thailand.*
Left : *Tamnak Phra Phanpeeluang in the compound of Wat Rachathiwas; built in English Tudor style, it formerly belonged to Queen Saowabha Phongsri and was moved to the site from Phyathai Palace.*

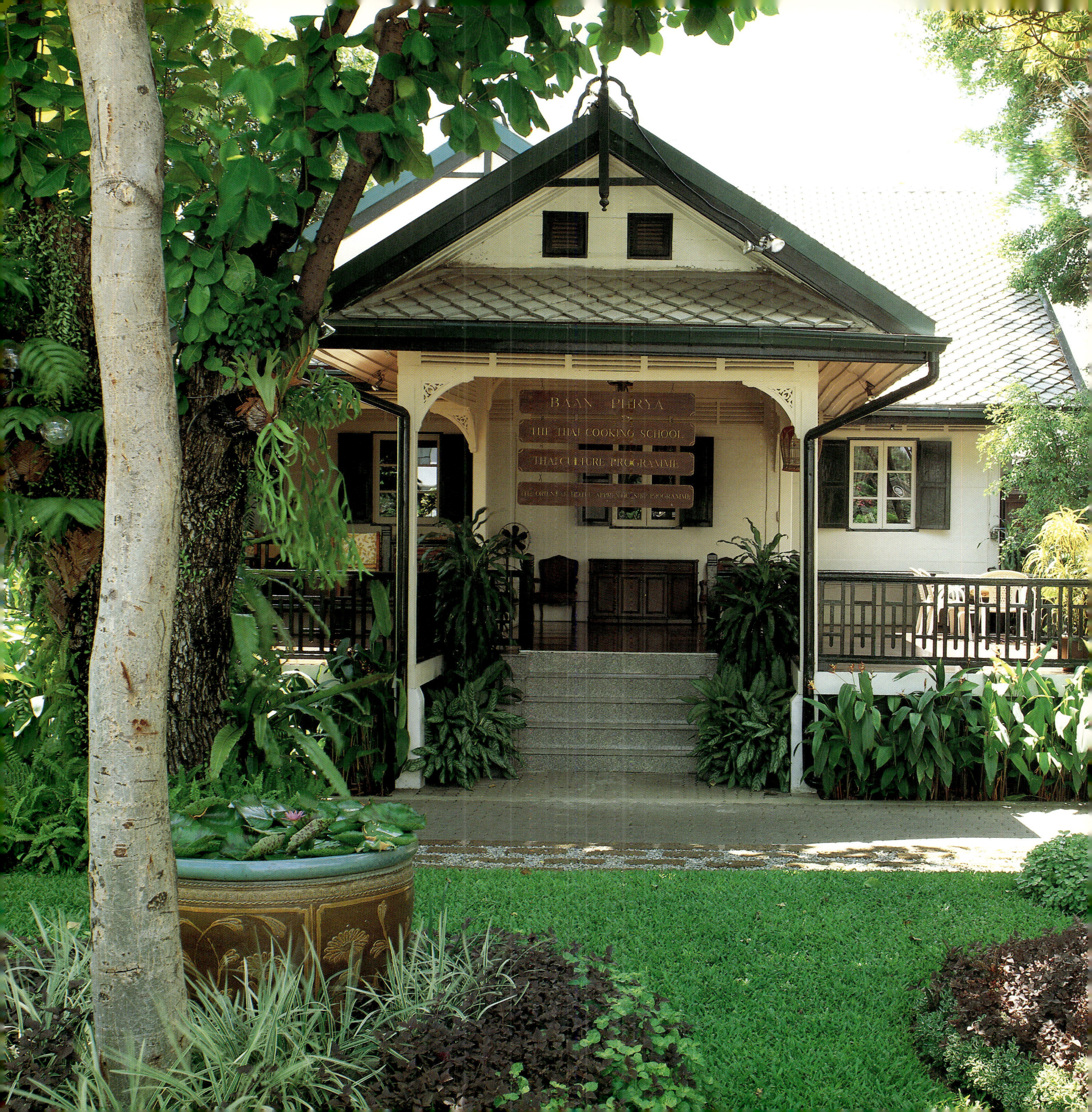
BAAN PHRYA
THE THAI COOKING SCHOOL
THAI CULTURE PROGRAMME

Baan Tha Sao
Ratchaburi

The original owner of Baan Tha Sao, a classic structure in the central Thai style, was Kim Hongthong ("Phuyai Kim"), headman of the village of Baan Tambon Tha Sao in Muang District, Ratchaburi Province. The village is located on the Mae Klong River, and Phuyai Kim was a prosperous merchant who dealt in timber, rice, and sappanwood.

Some 70 years ago, Phuyai Kim and his family lived in an older house. This was pulled down and donated to a temple, after which Baan Tha Sao was built; Phuyai Kim himself supervised the construction by local workers, one of whom, named Chang Imm, was noted for his carpentry skills. The wood used was of top quality, each of the long boards a single piece, and the house was built by the traditional tongue-and-groove method, the process taking about 10 months to complete. The roof was originally thatched, but as this had to be changed from time to time and thatch became harder to find, tiles were used instead.

Phuyai Kim's daughter, Khun Rabieb, recalls going into the forest with officials to select trees and how the wood was brought to the house on carts numbering as many as a hundred at a time. The family also opened a shop in Bangkok called Sathaporn Panich, near the Phan Fah Bridge, which sold wood transported by boat from Ratchaburi and which prospered until it was bombed during the Second World War.

After Phuyai Kim's death, most of the younger generation moved to Bangkok and the house began to deteriorate. It was subsequently sold to to the present owners, Khun Chanchai and Orawan Supanichvoraparch, who have a famous kiln producing ceramics in Ratchaburi. They in turn completely renovated the structure, replacing the wooden floorboards on the verandah with tiles but retaining the original wall panels as well as the classic Thai beauty of the house.

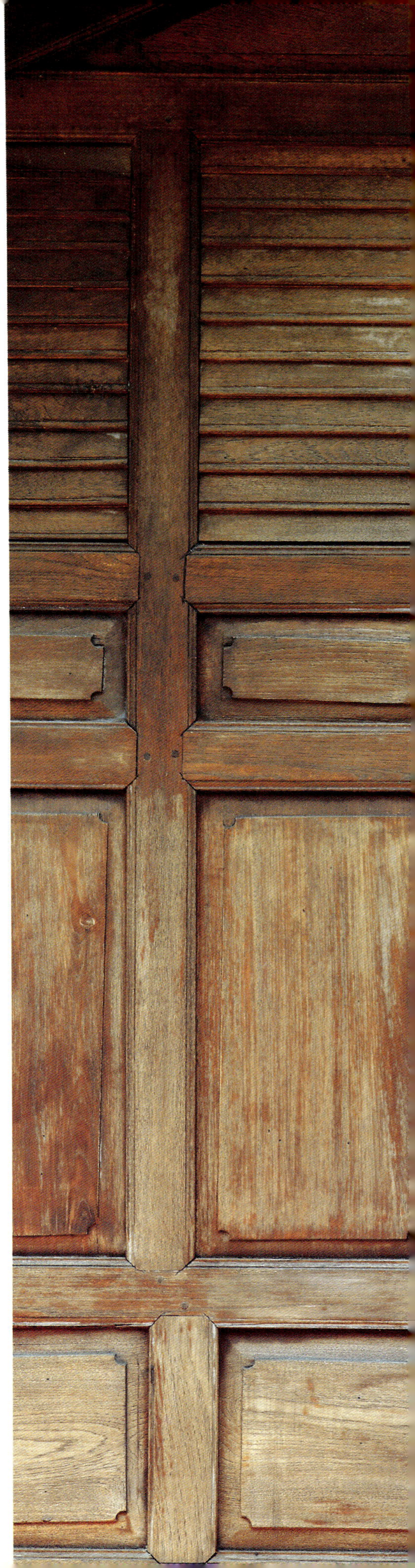

Right : *One of the original walls of Baan Tha Sao which was retained when the house was restored.*

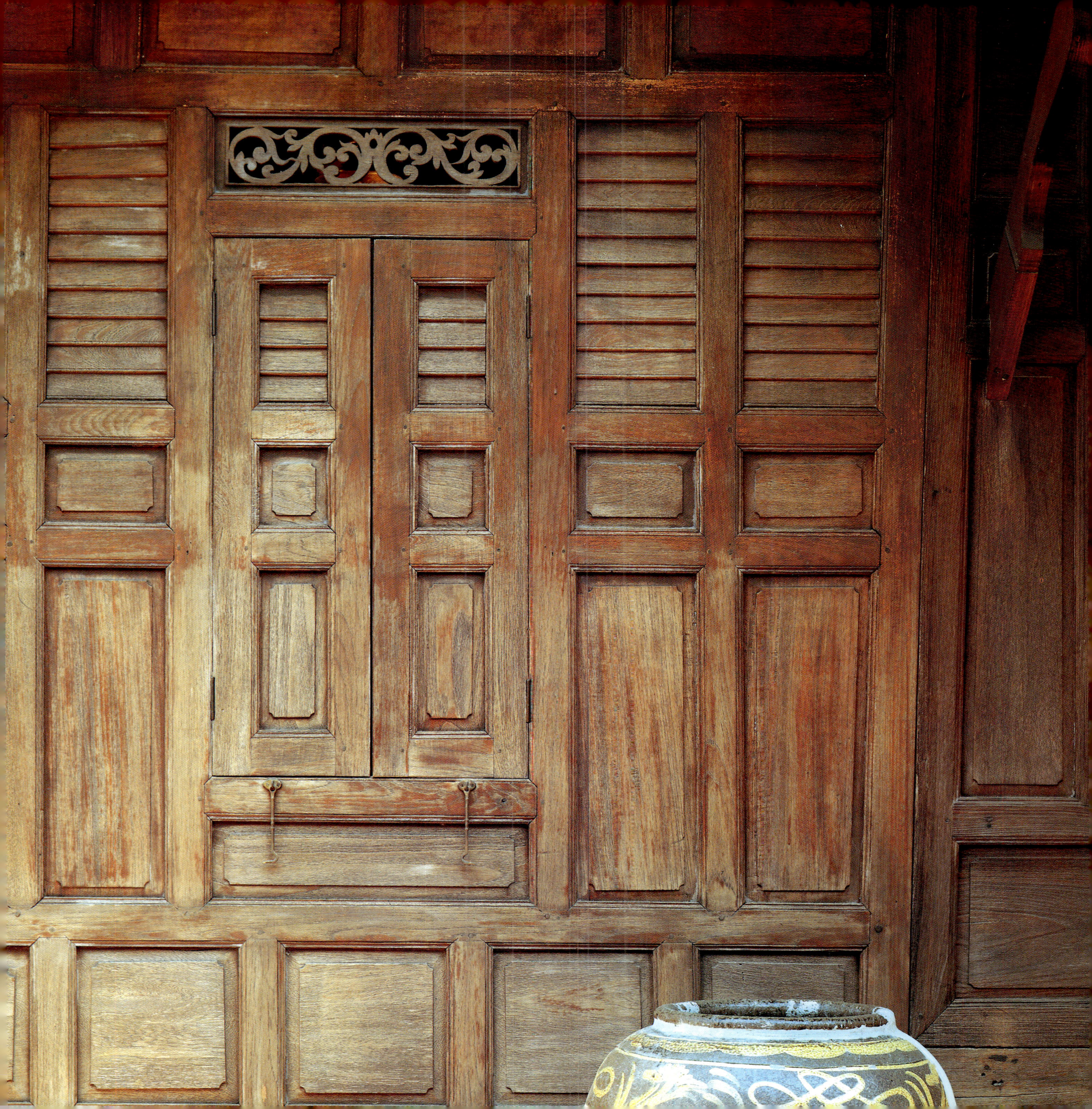

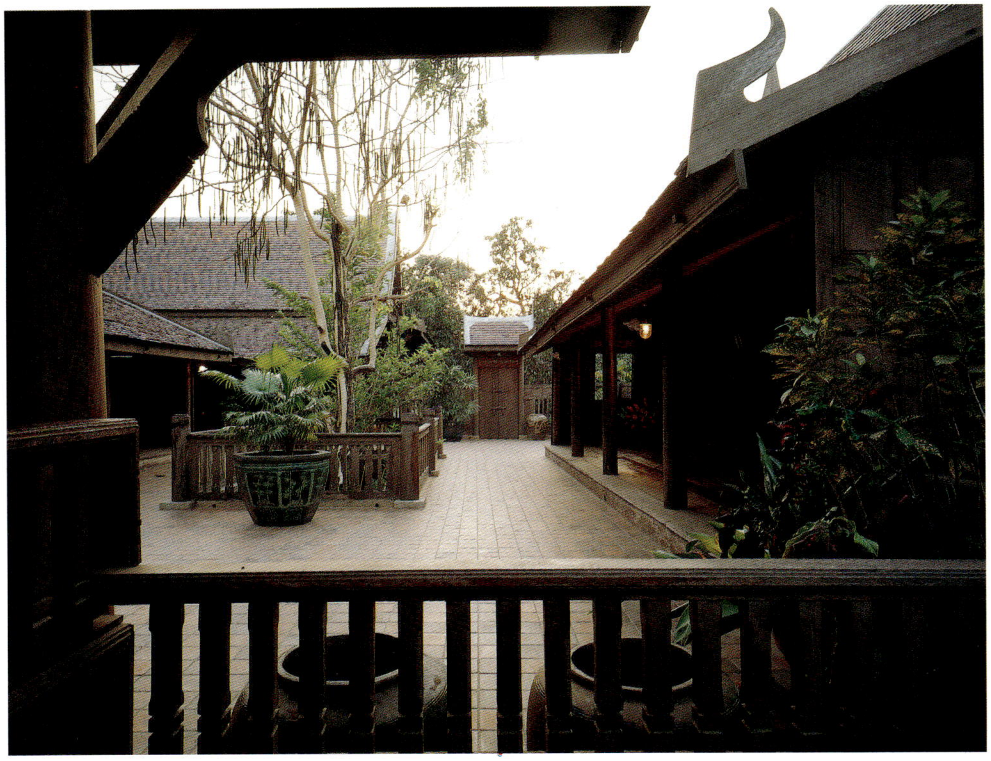

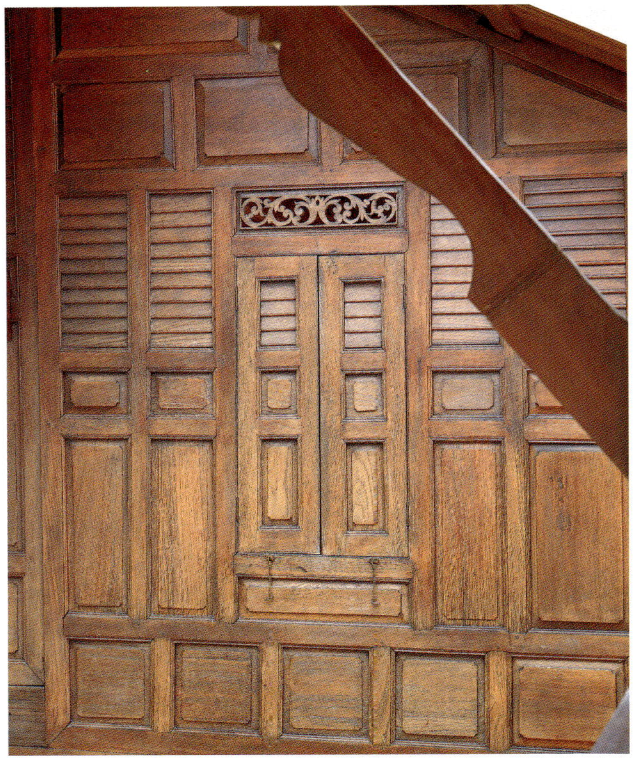

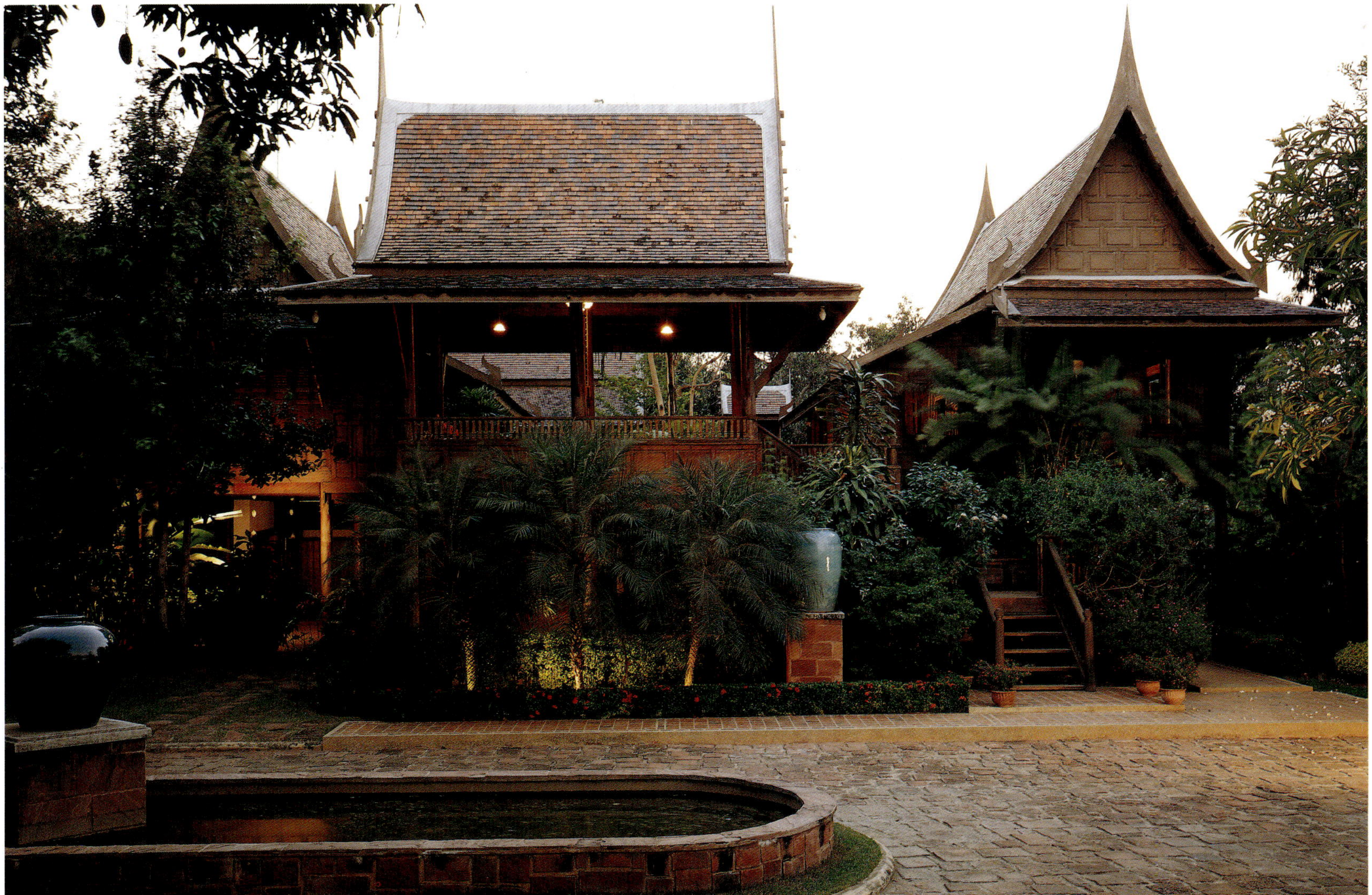

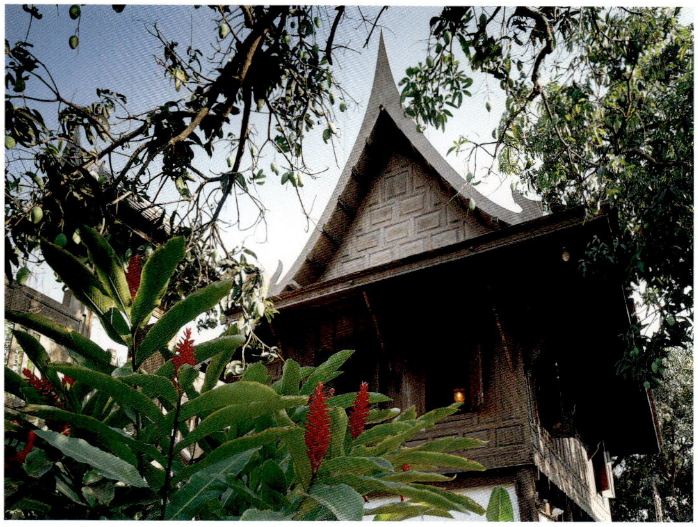

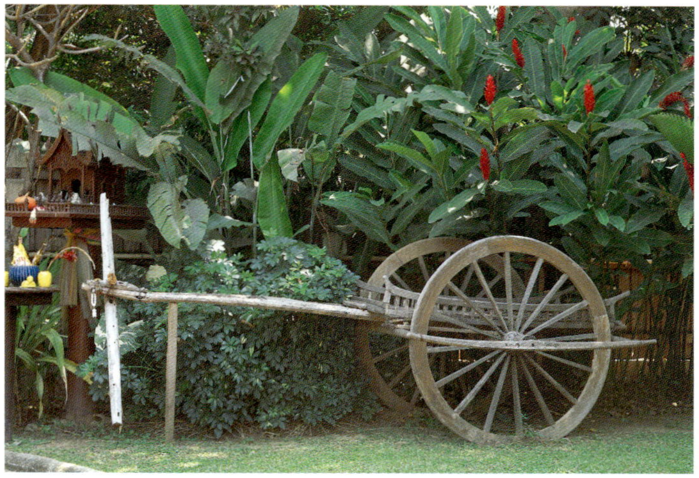

This page:
Top : *One of the units that comprise the house.*
Above : *Old ox cart used as a garden decoration; to the left is the spirit house of the compound.*
Right : *View from one of the rooms to the verandah; a carved air vent is above the door.*

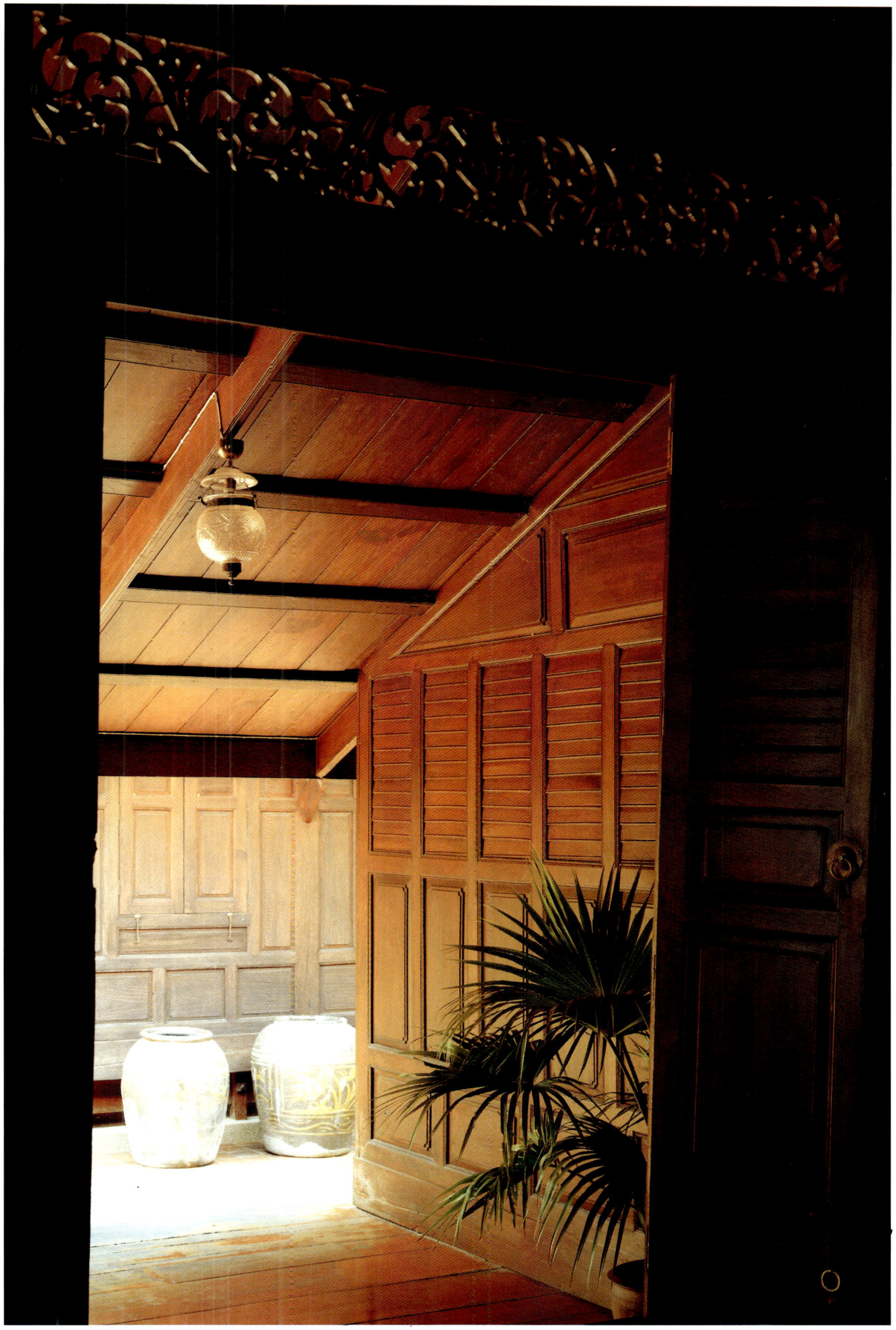

Opposite page :
Top left : *Open verandah now covered with tiles.*
Top right : *Wall showing carving above window.*
Below : *Front view of the house showing characteristic central Thai-style roof.*

Thap Charoen Villa
Nakhon Pathom

King Rama IV became the first Thai ruler to build a residence southwest of Bangkok, atop a hill in Petchburi Province. As better roads and, still later, a railway made the region increasingly accessible to the capital, more royal buildings appeared, among them Thap Charoen Villa, which was built to house members of King Rama VI's entourage in 1911.

The building was constructed in the same year as Sanam Chand Palace, south of the great *chedi* at Nakhon Pathom, where King Rama VI and members of his court frequently went for recreation. Around 10 other wooden structures were also built at this time as accommodations for the King's officials and courtiers, among them one that now serves as the Deputy Governor's Residence; only three of these were given the prefix "thap" instead of "ruen" (house), the other two being Thap Kwan and Thap Keow.

Thap Charoen originally served as a residence for Chao Phya Ramrakop, one of the King's attendants. During the reign of King Rama VII, it became the provincial Governor's residence and later was converted for use as the public health provincial office for Nakhon Pathom. In 1986, it was given by the city to Silpakorn University, which has recently established a new campus in the province.

Largely Western in appearance, a style which had become popular during the reign of King Rama V, the one-story wooden building is raised off the ground on high columns. The main structure and roof supports are made of teak, while the pillars are brick covered with plaster; the roof is in a 'hip' style, the lines meeting in a pyramidal fashion without a gable. The large structure faces east, is 28.5 meters long and 19 meters wide, covering about 425 square meters in all, and consists of 10 rooms with a spacious sitting room in the middle. All the rooms are connected by airy verandahs, the front one of which is bay-shaped and accessible by a staircase.

When Silpakorn University was given responsibility for Thap Charoen, it was in a considerable state of disrepair. One of the principal problems was roof leakage, which had led to wood rot and also ravage by termites, even on the strong teak; moreover, damp seeping up from the ground had damaged the plaster on the supporting pillars. The structure was carefully restored over several years and, on completion, became the Institute of Western Thai Culture.

Visitors today can see exhibits reflecting the culture of western Thailand, including work by Petchburi artists, puppets from Samut Songkram, basketry by the Thai Song tribe, and musical instruments. They also have a rare opportunity to enjoy the beauty of a well-preserved residence from the early years of the present century.

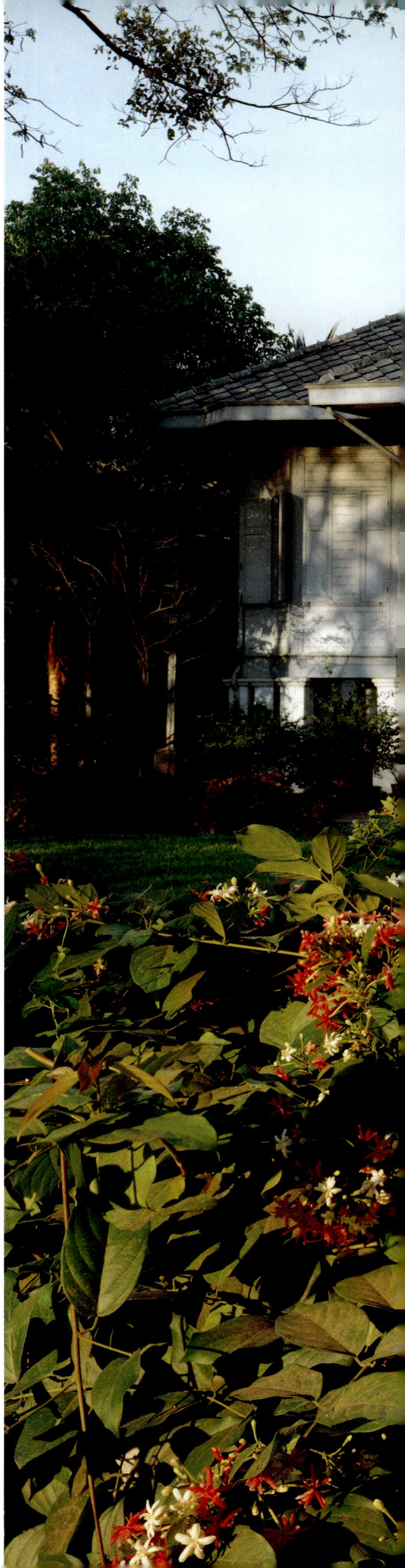

Right : *Front view of Thap Charoen Villa in Nakhon Pathom, built in 1911, which now serves as Silpakorn University's Institute of Western Thai Culture.*

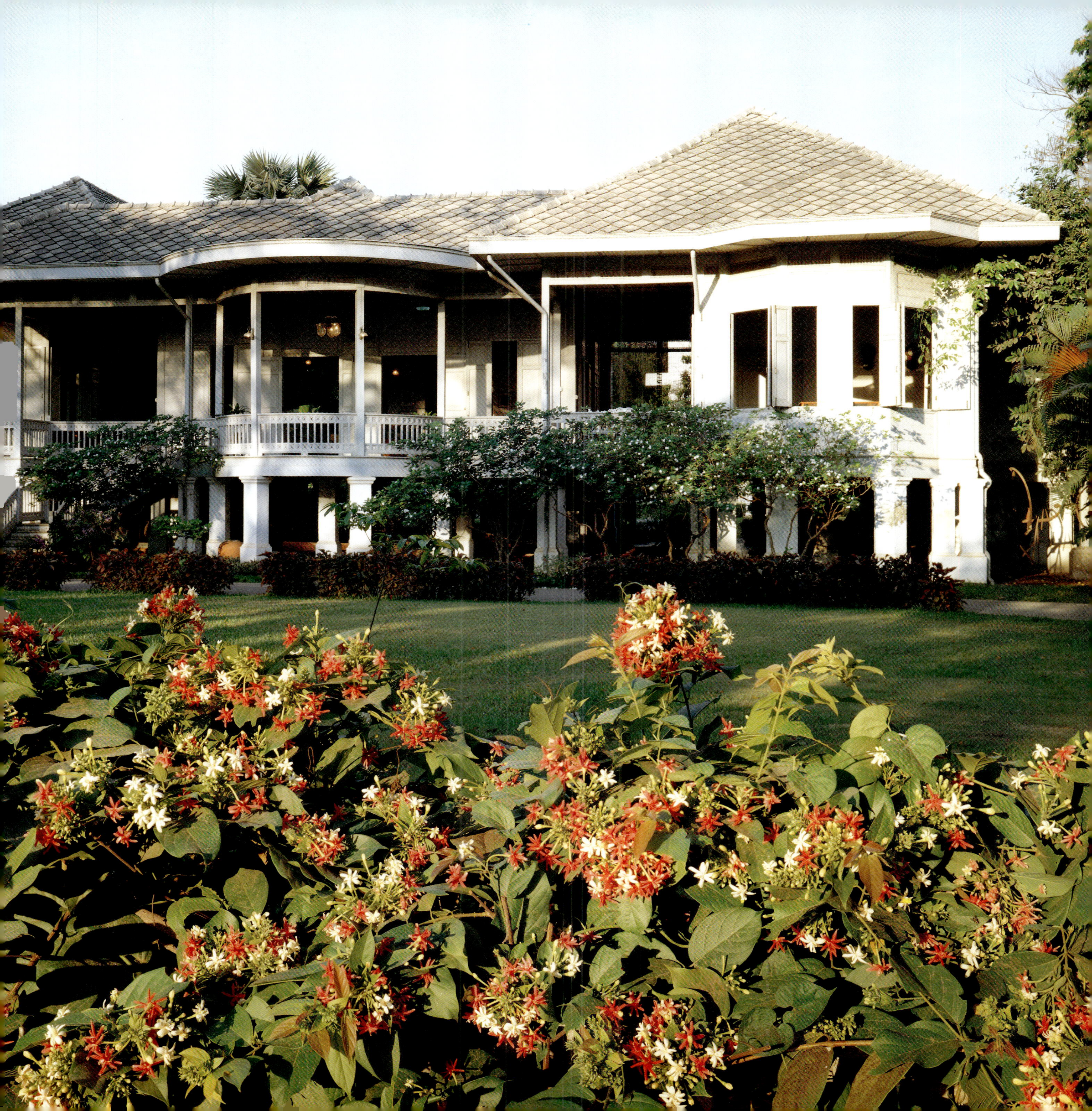

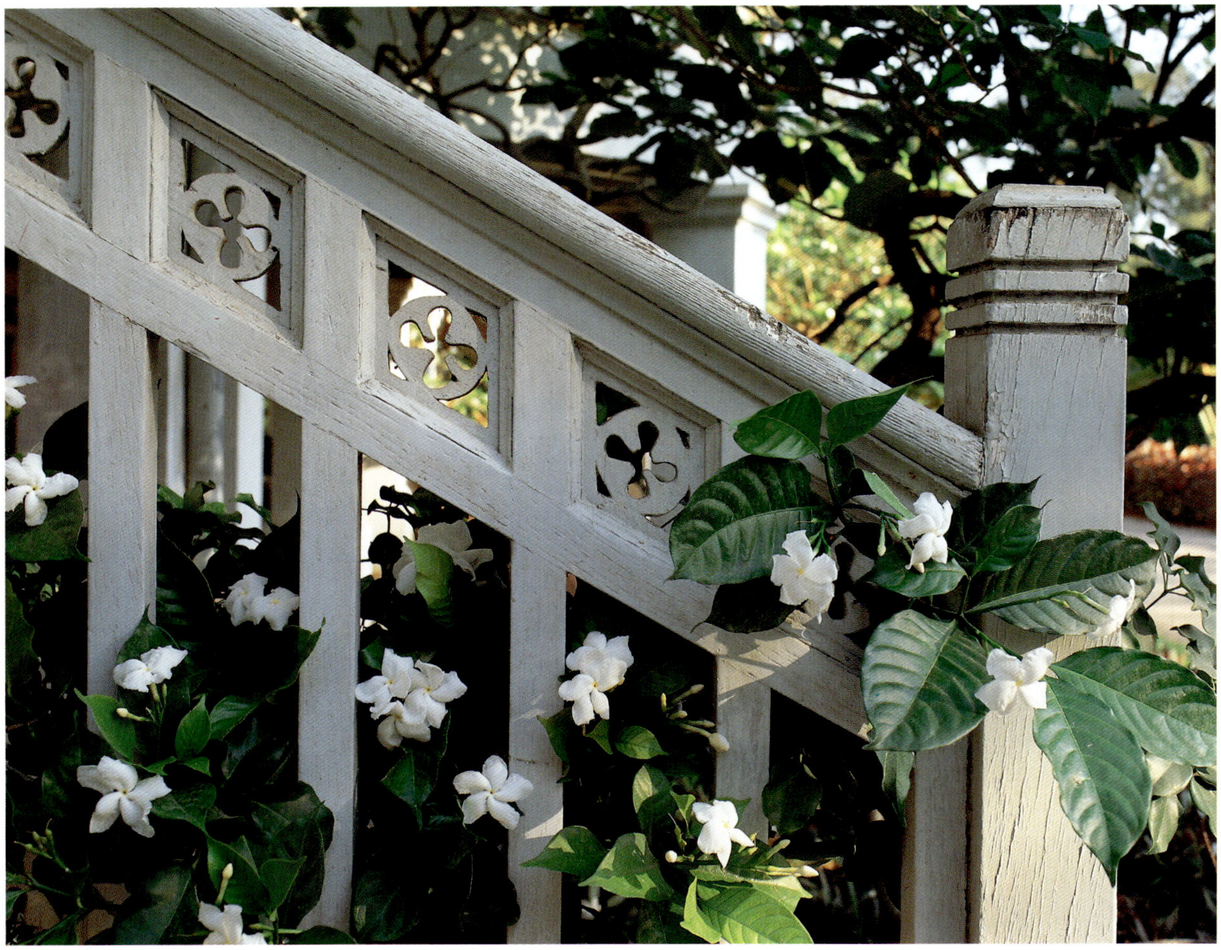

Left : *Detail of decorations on entrance staircase.*
Below left : *One of the three staircases at the rear of the residence.*
Below right : *Rear verandah overlooking the garden.*

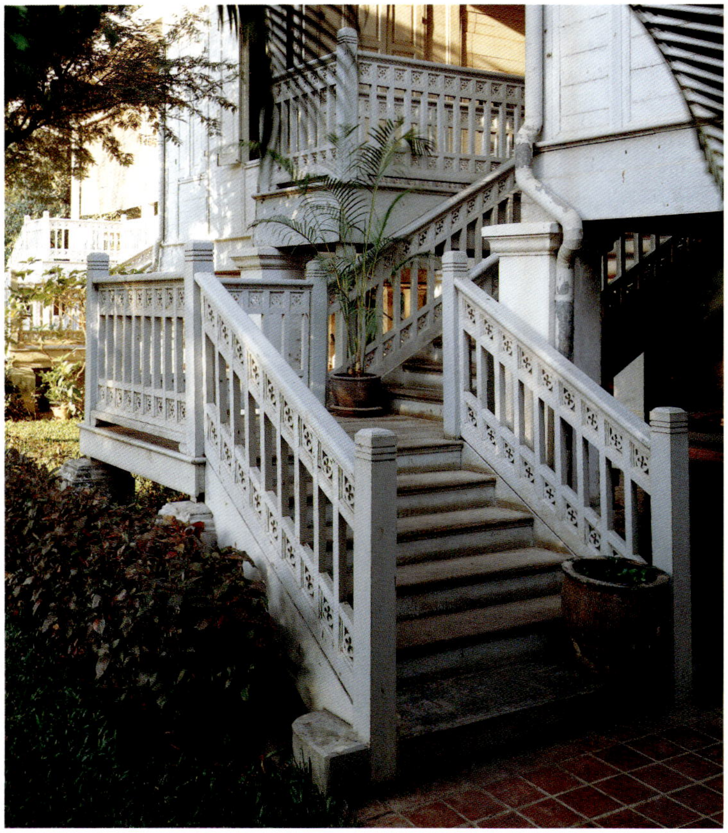

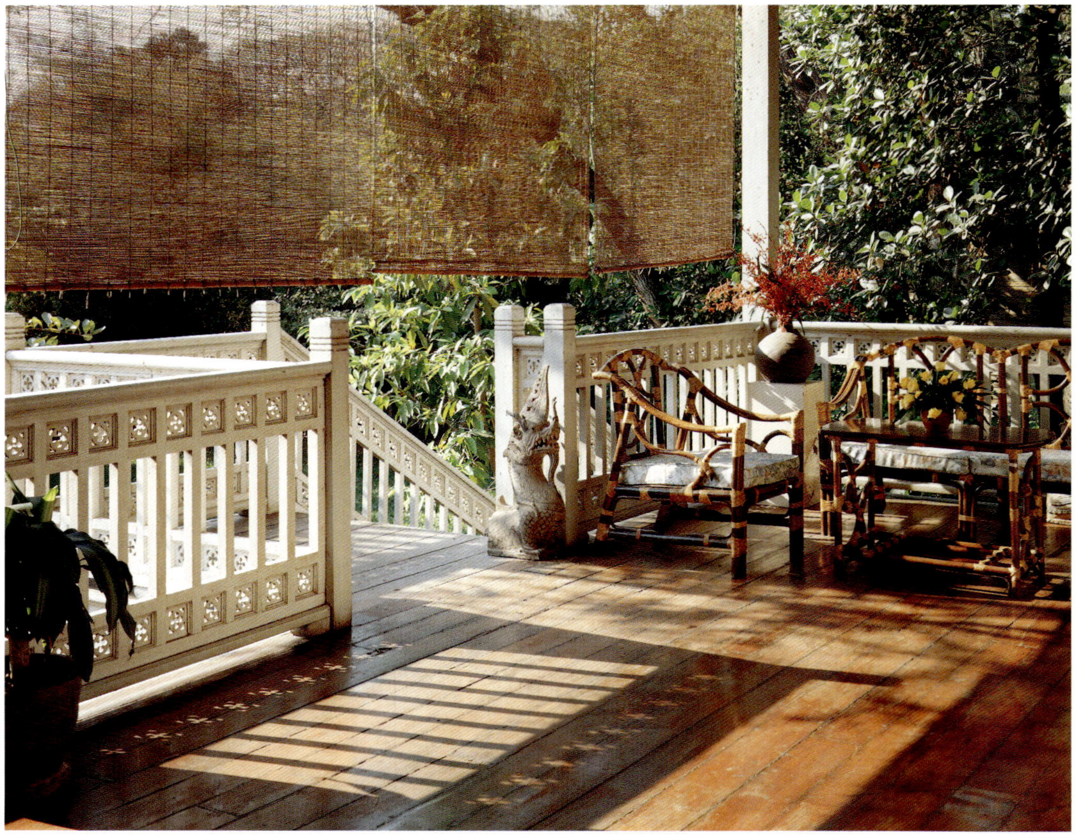

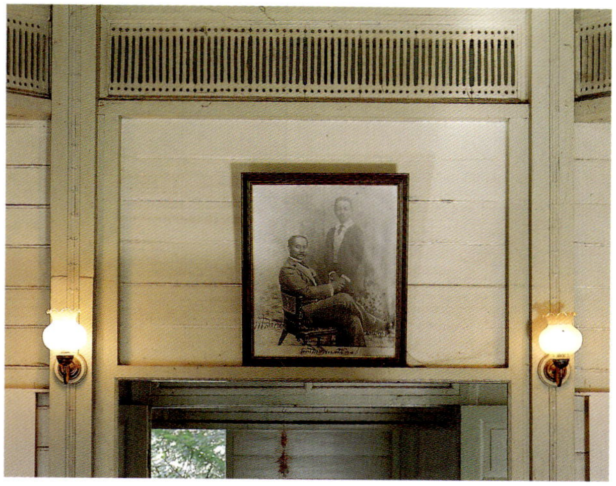

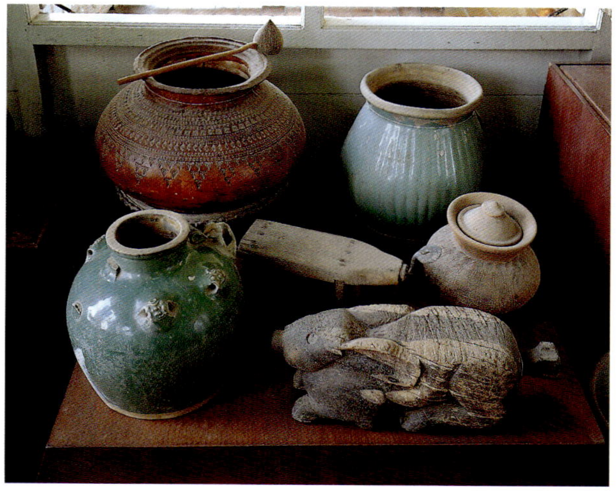

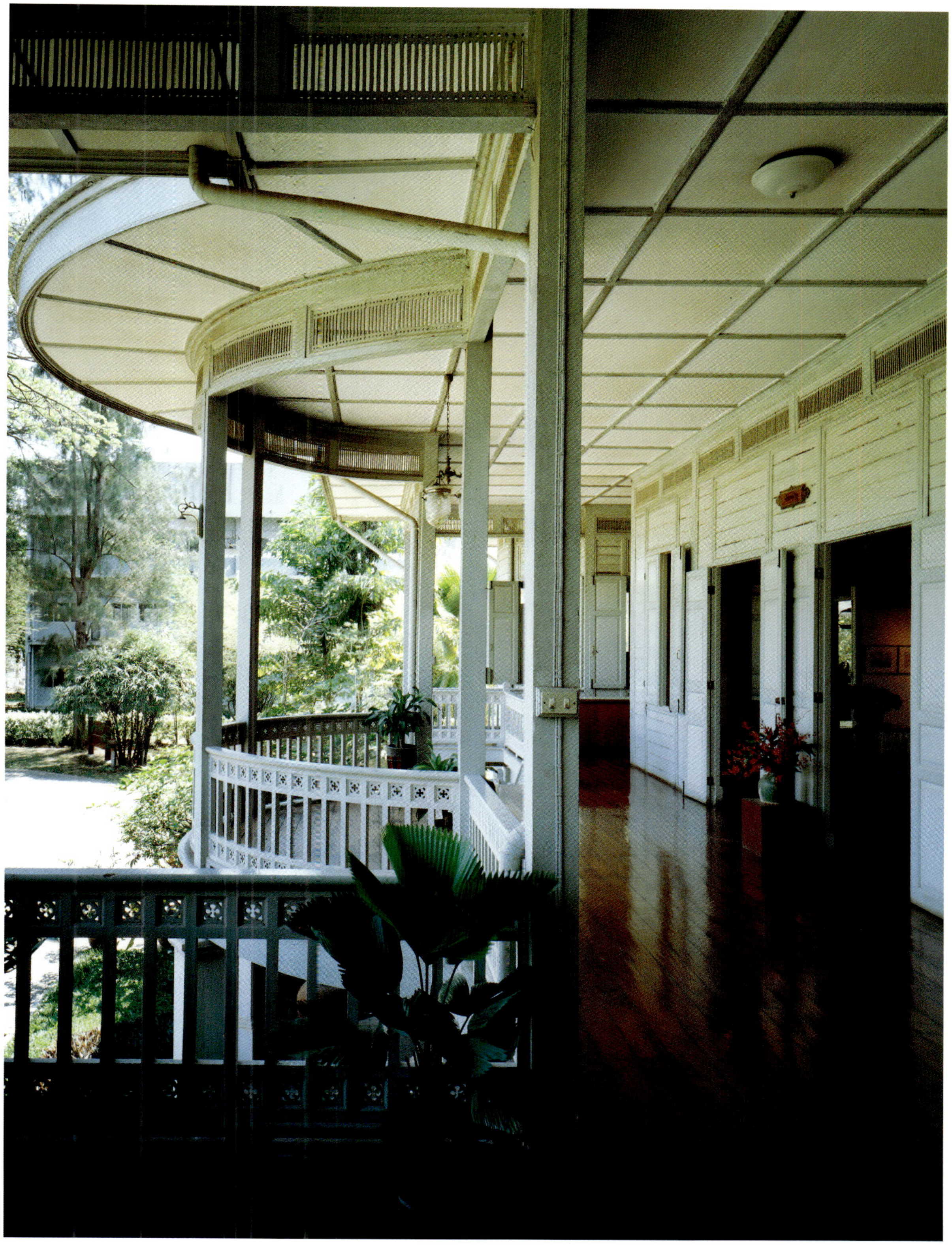

Right : *Airy verandahs connect all the rooms of the wooden building, which is raised from the ground on brick columns.*
Top : *Photograph of King Chulalongkorn and Crown Prince Vajiravudh.*
Above : *Artifacts from western Thailand in the Institute's extensive collection.*

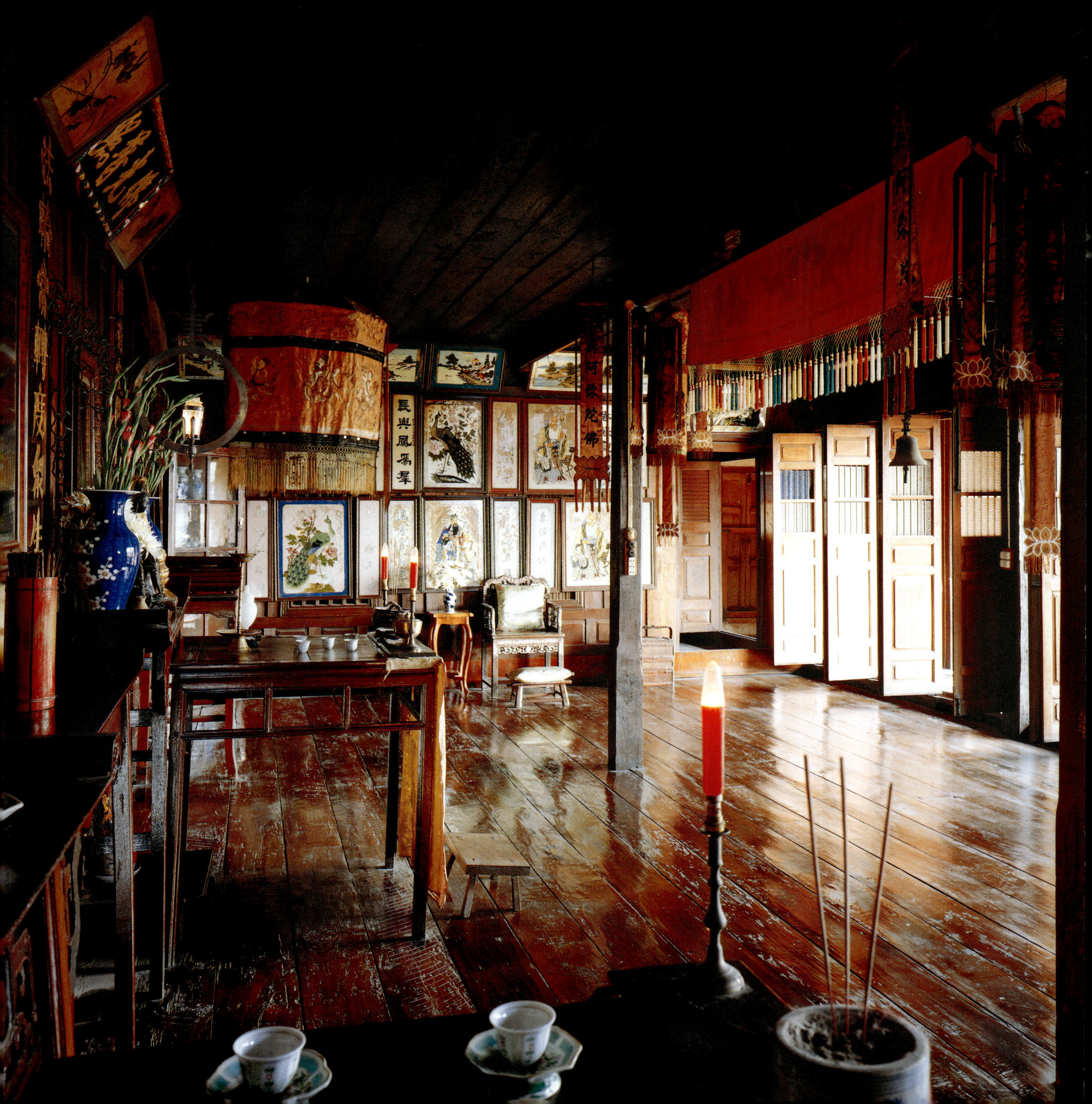

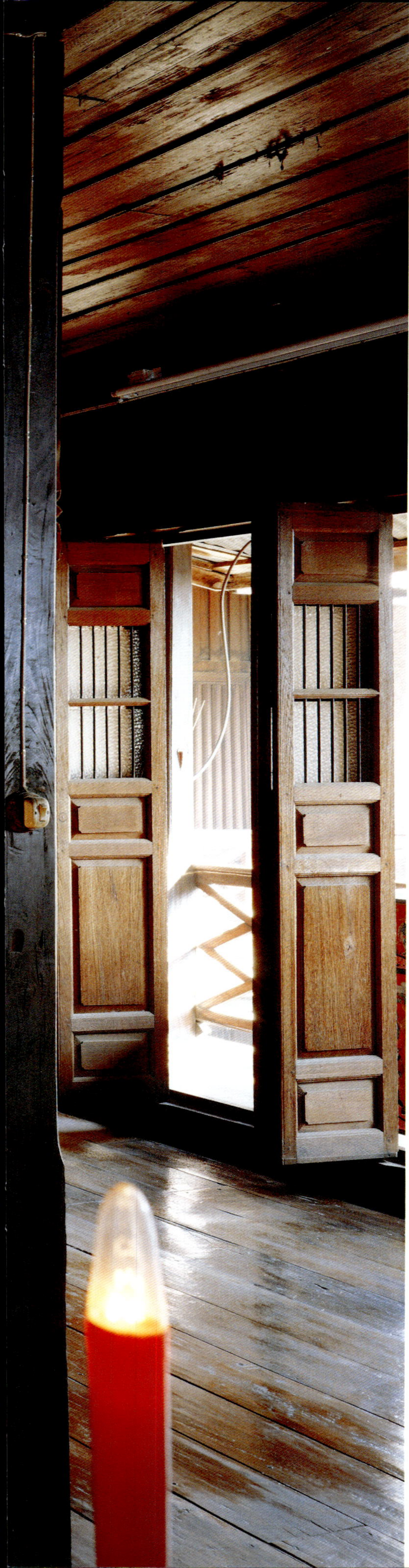

Hok Sha Tung House
Uthai Thani

Located in the town of Uthai Thani in the Central Plains, the Hok Sha Tung House is a wooden house that embodies an interesting aspect of Chinese culture. The precise age of the structure is uncertain, though it is believed to be at least a century old.

The first Chinese immigrants who established themselves here - in what was then the village of Sa Kae Krung - toward the end of the Ayutthaya Period, were mostly merchants who arrived on the cargo ships that called at various ports. The village was a prosperous market place, particularly for farmers of the area, who brought their rice in by ox cart, and the Chinese who became involved in trading and milling of the grain. As in most other parts of the country at the time, the Chinese formed a closed society with their own educational system and their own carefully preserved customs.

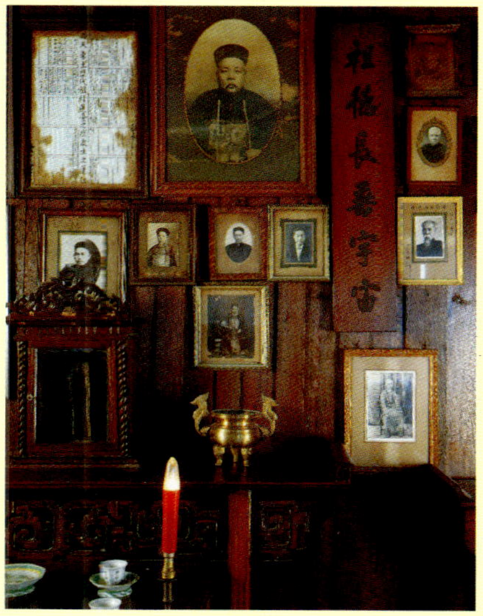

The Hok Sha Tung House was originally built as a meeting place for this community and also served as a center for various rituals associated with an annual week-long vegetarian festival. It was also used at one time as a Chinese medicine store which sold herbal remedies and trained traditional pharmacists. The building did not belong to any particular family, according to its present owner, Khun Sa-ngiem Palawatvichai, but was looked after by various ones in the past.

Constructed of teakwood in Chinese style, the house consists of two floors, with the shrine room on the upper floor. Other rooms on this level were used for storing musical instruments and ritualistic items used in the vegetarian festival. The lower level was used as a medicine shop, as well for the living quarters; a separate women's quarter was located in the rear part of the property. Local Chinese artisans are believed to have executed the fine, three-dimensional stucco work that adorns areas above the doors and windows of the house.

Left : *Shrine room on the upper floor of the Hok Sha Tung House; the central altar displays an image of the goddess Kuan Yin, a deity associated with the cult of vegetarianism.*
Above : *Altar displaying ancestral portraits.*

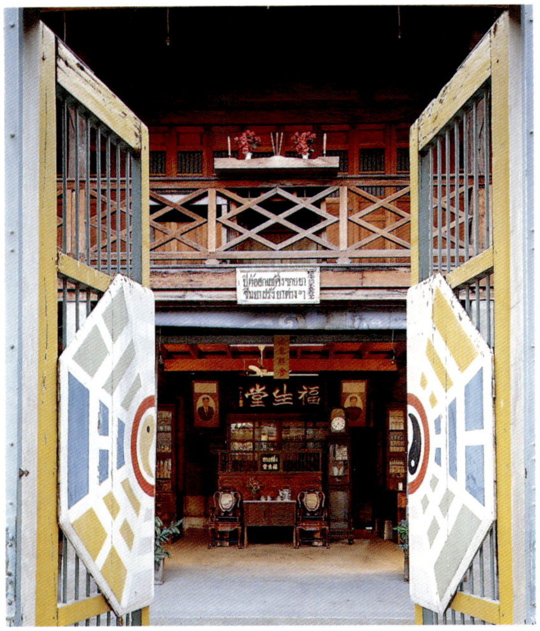

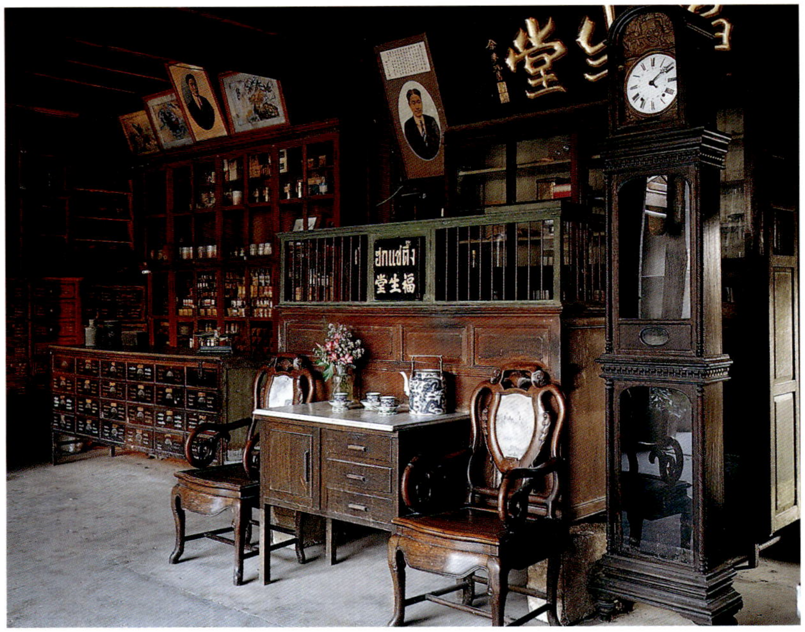

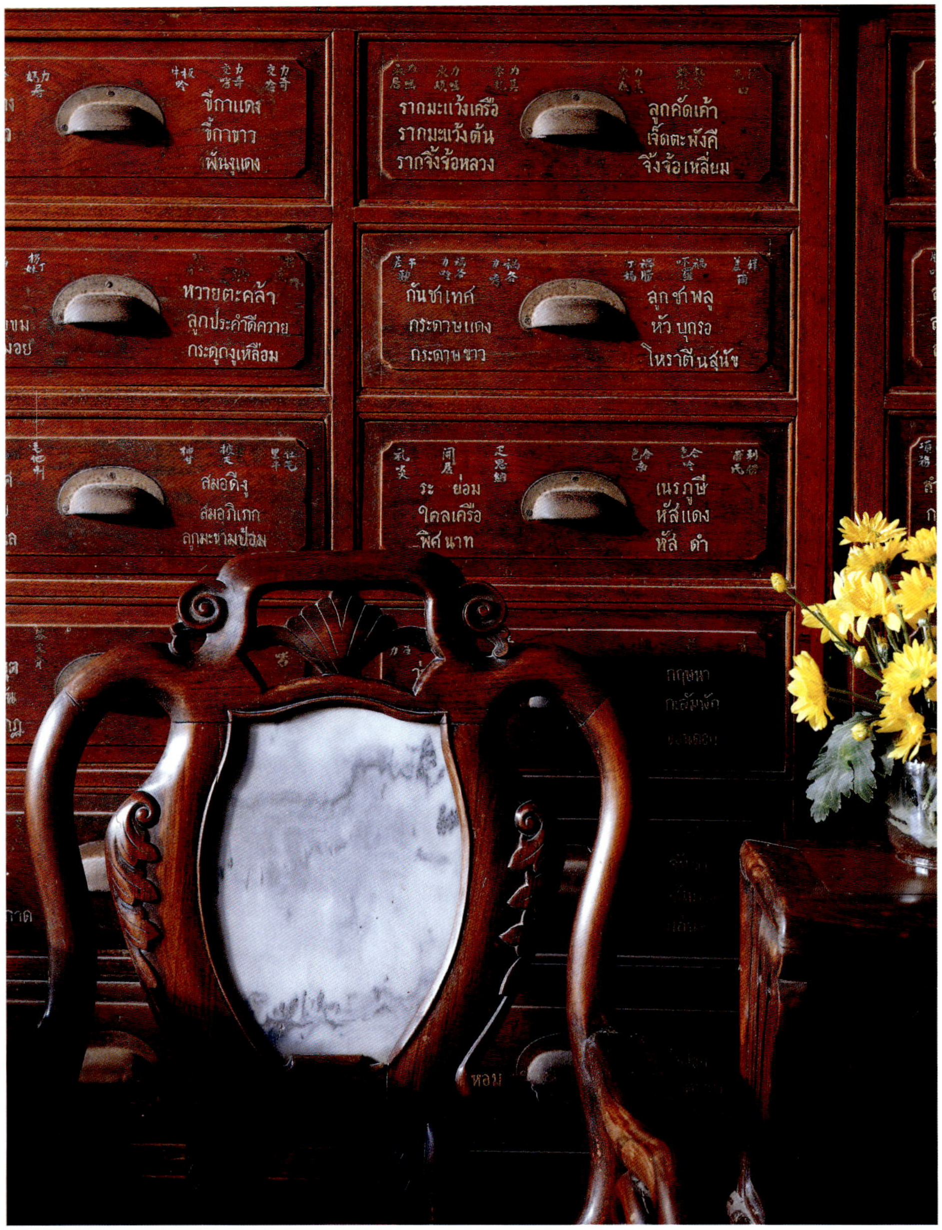

Right : *Lower floor of the building, showing an old cabinet used for storing herbal medicines.*
Above left : *Entrance gate to the house; downstairs is a herbal medicine store, while upstairs is a shrine room.*
Above : *Sales counter in the medicine shop.*
Left : *The drawers of the traditional medicine cabinet, labeled with such contents as "Bones of Python," "Foreign Cannabis," and "Indian Gooseberry."*

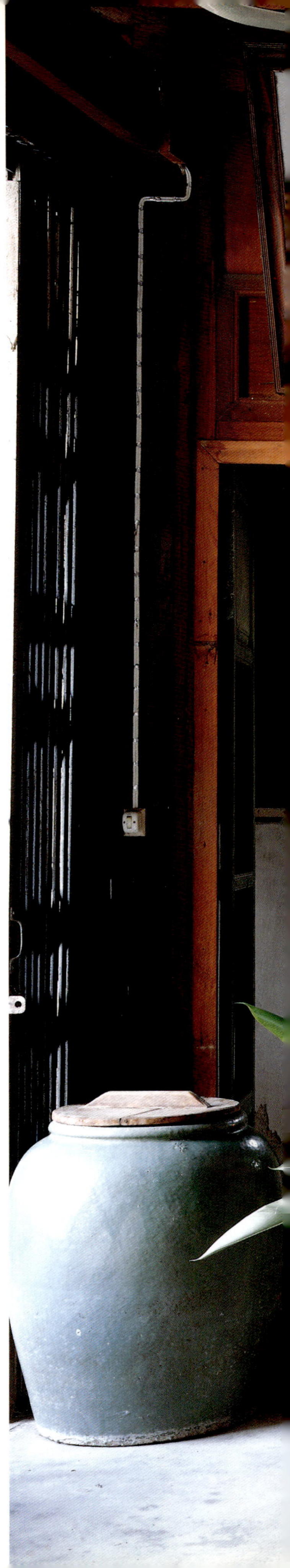

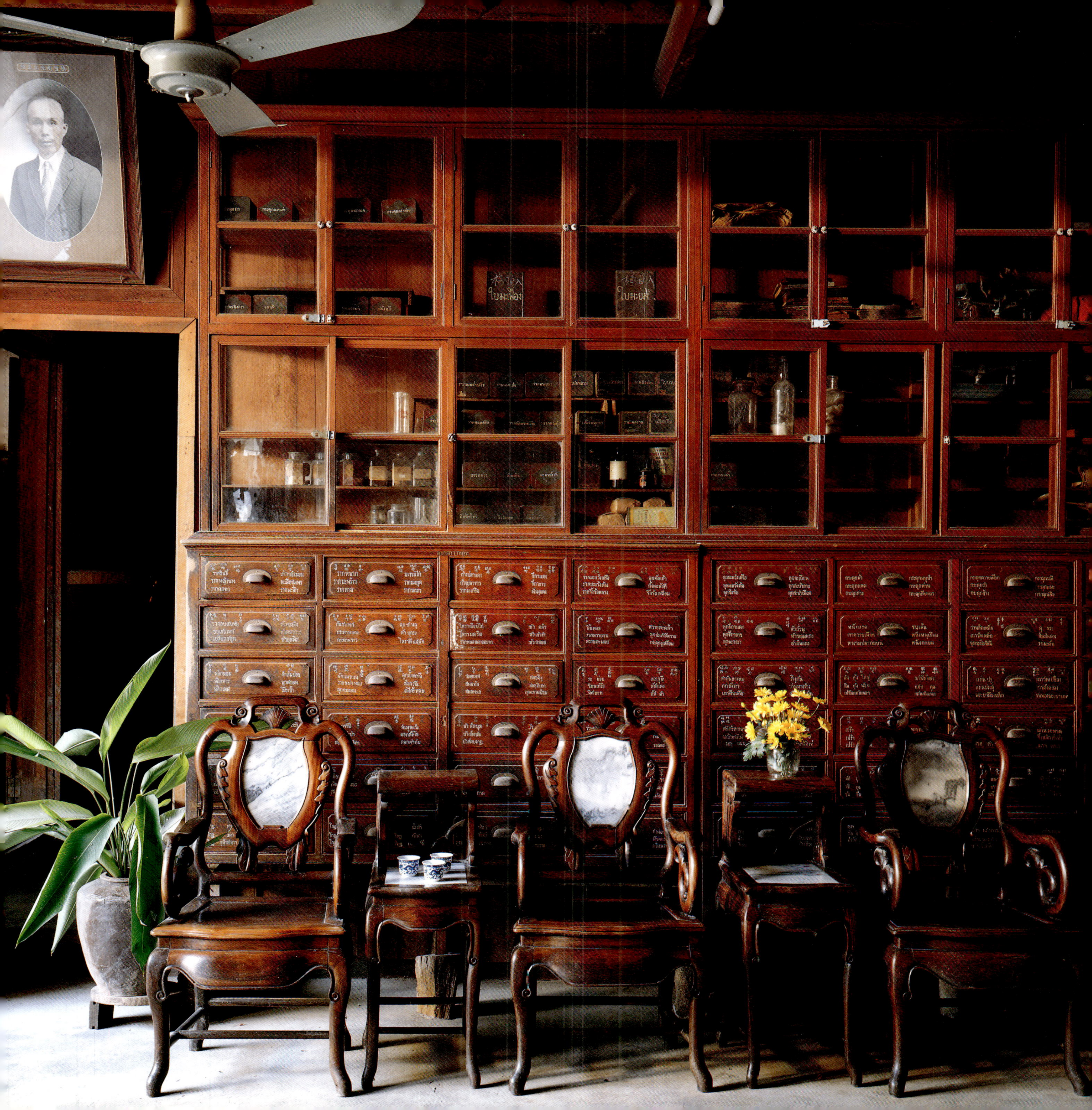
ใบมะเฟือง
ใบมะยม

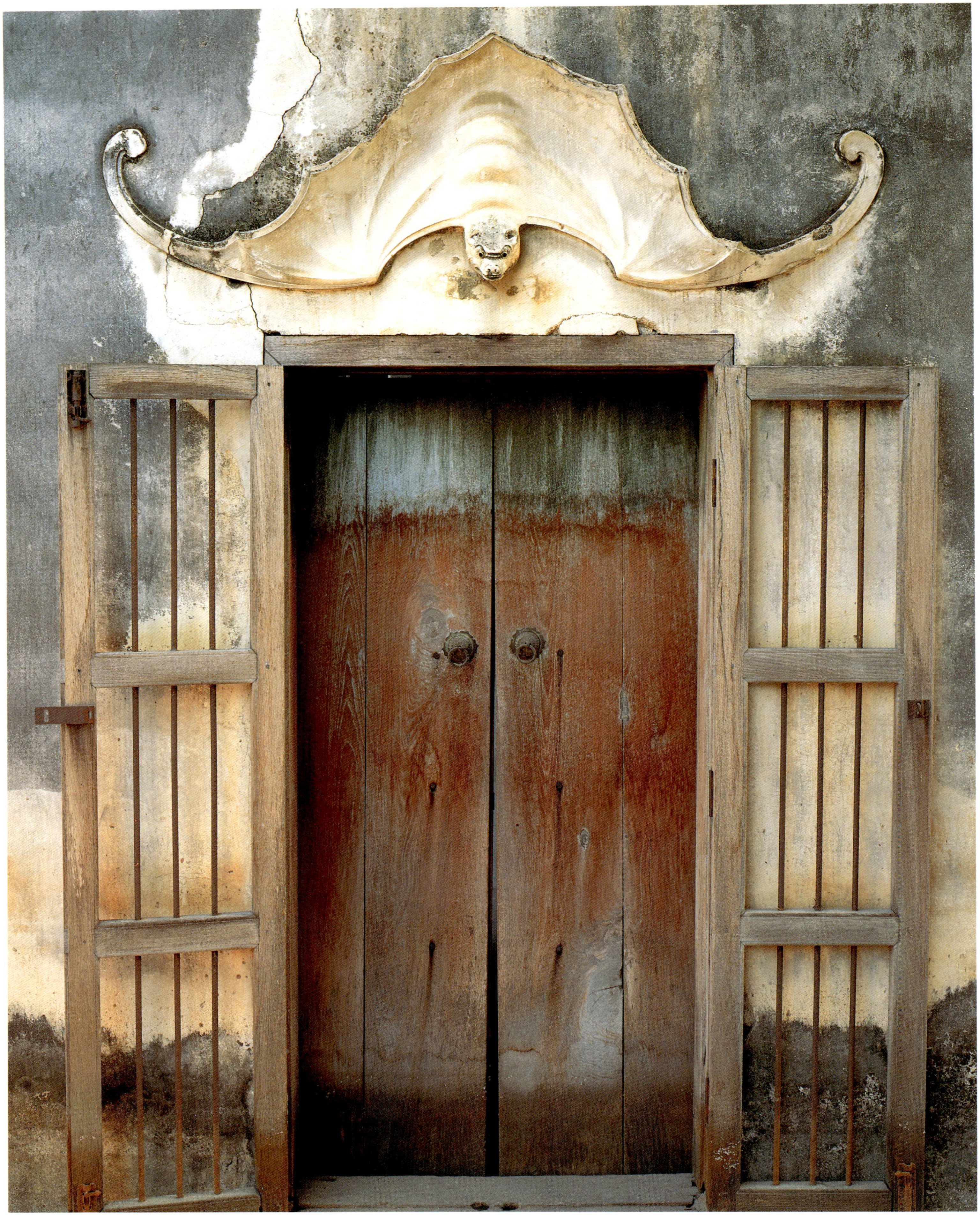

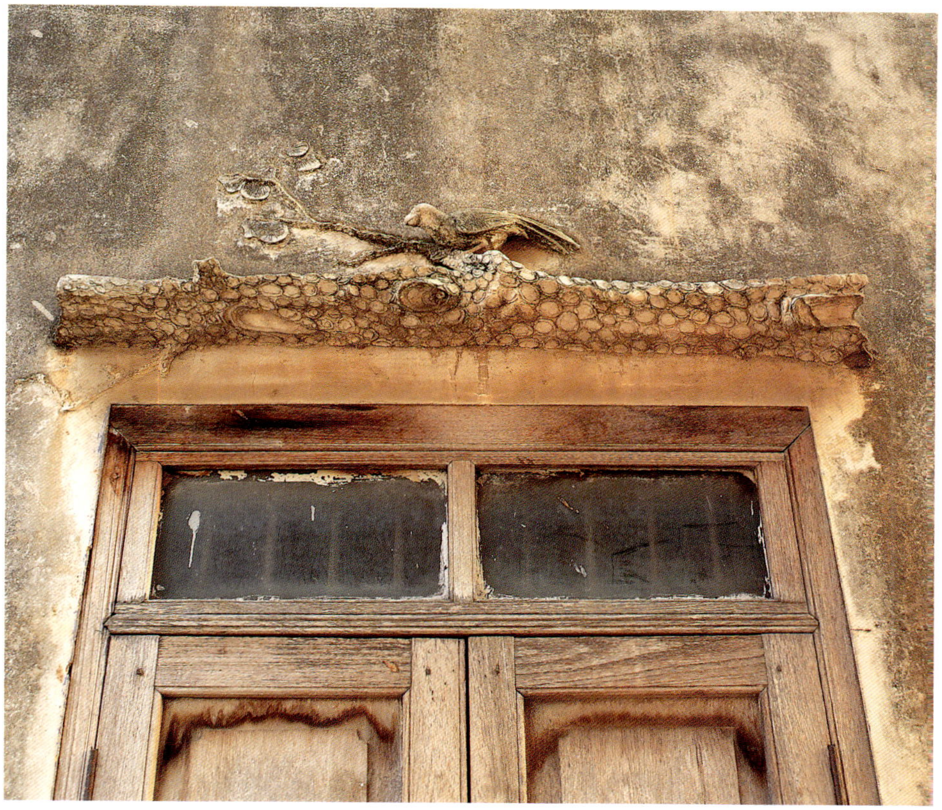

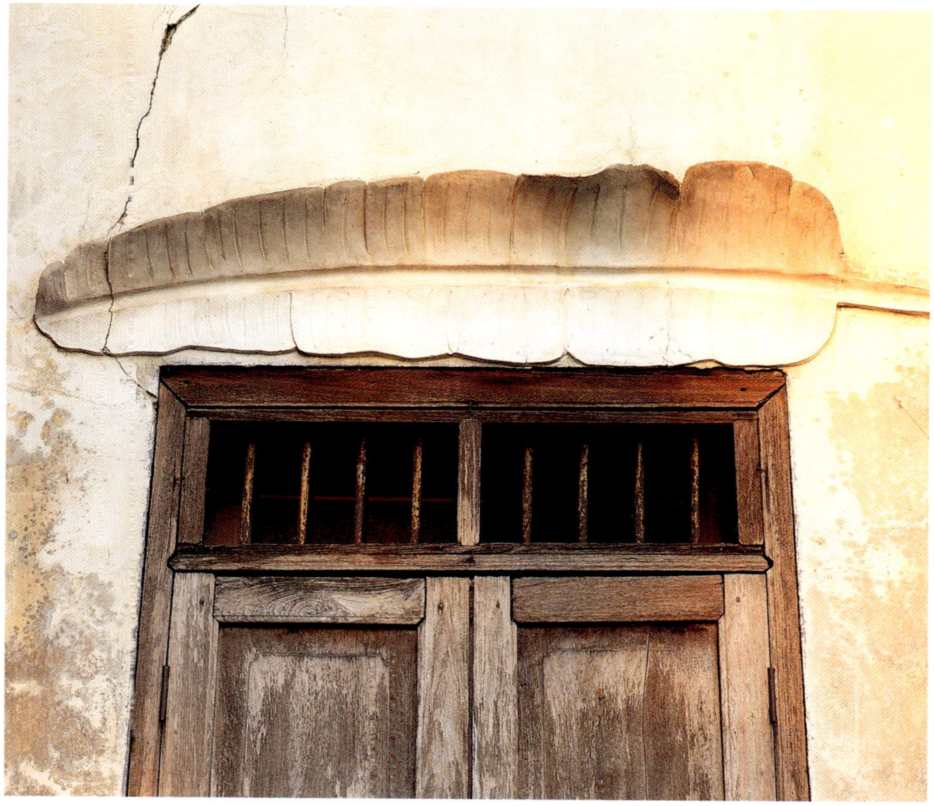

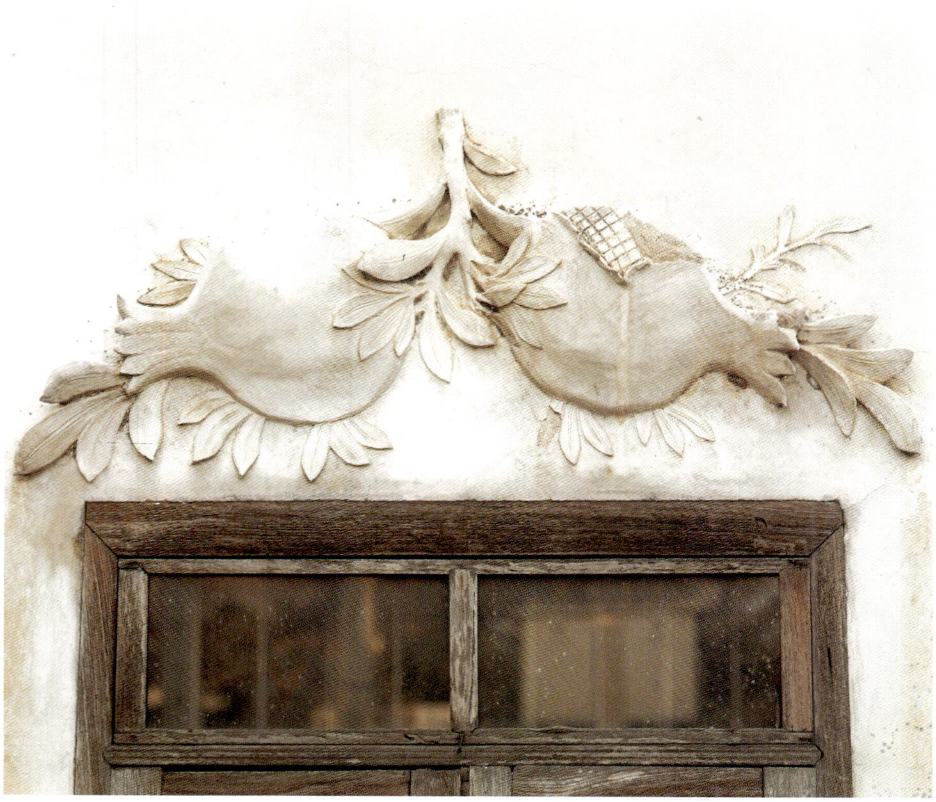

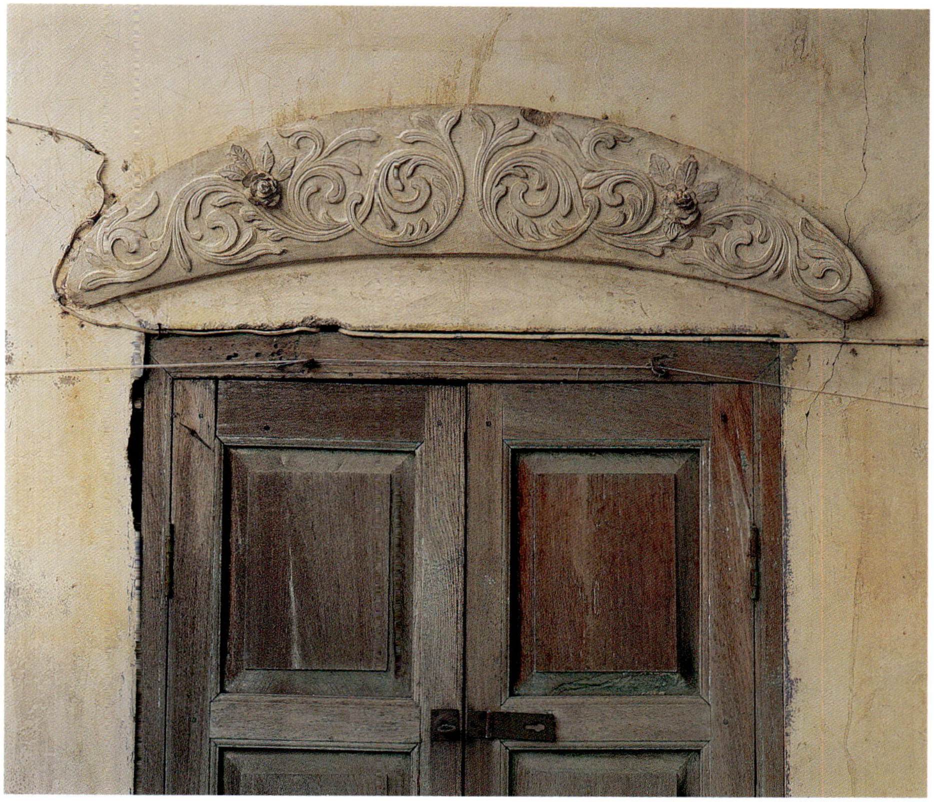

This and opposite pages : *Some of the fine stucco work with Chinese motifs that adorn windows and doorways; the bat, for instance, symbolizes happiness, while the banana-leaf represents self-taught knowledge (after a legend about a wise man who in his search for knowledge used banana leaves for writing paper) and the pomegranate symbolizes productivity (i.e., having many children).*

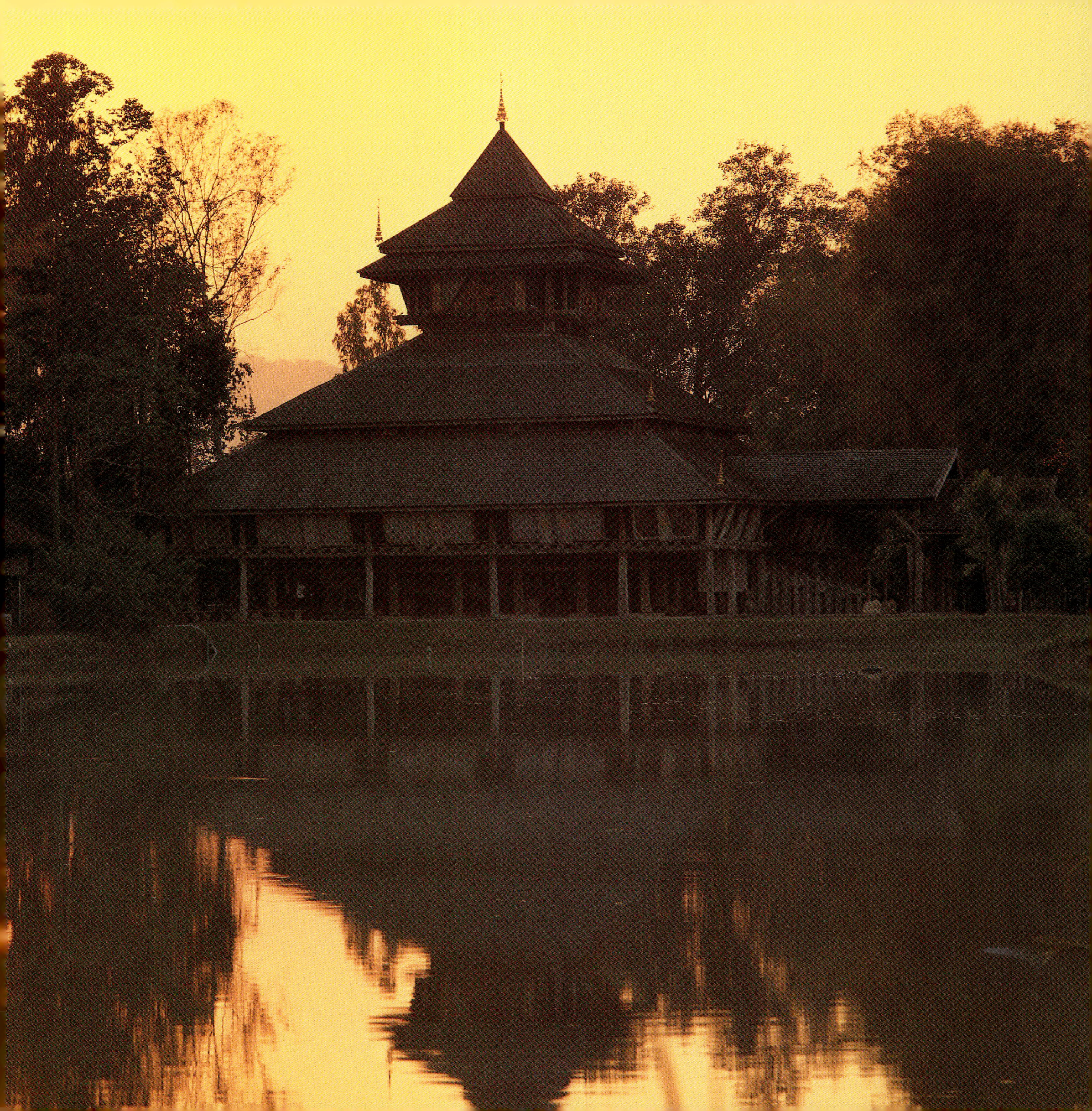

The North

Guarded by a high range of rugged mountains, the northern part of Thailand long remained remote from such centers of power as Ayutthaya and Bangkok in the Central Plains region. Some of the earliest Thai city states were established there, eventually forming a federation known as Lanna Thai centered around the city of Chiang Mai, and a distinctive form of Lanna architecture developed, both religious and domestic. For nearly two centuries, starting in 1556, Lanna Thai was a vassal state of Burma, and Burmese cultural influences became strong, with results that can still be seen today in the form of crafts and temple decorations.

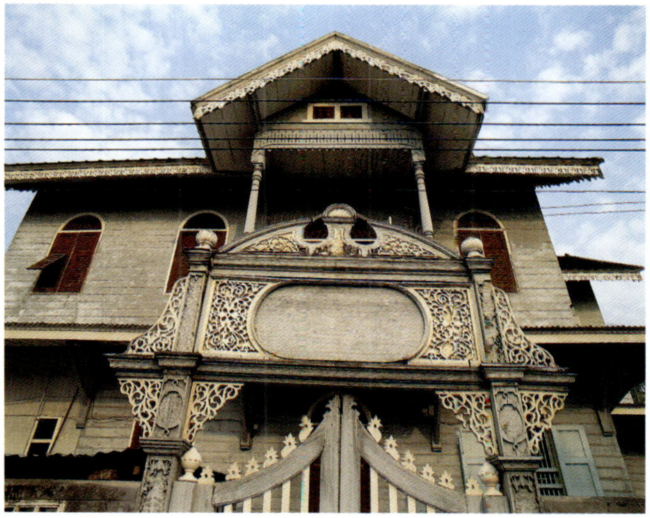

At the end of the 19th century and in the early years of the present one, when most of the houses shown in this book were built, prosperity returned to the north with the timber industry. Westerners and high-ranking Thais who were given concessions in the surrounding teak forests settled in cities like Lampang, Chiang Mai, Tak, and Phrae, along with numerous Chinese and Burmese, some of whom came as traders and others as builders. Dragged by work elephants to such nearby rivers as the Ping, Wang, and Yom, the logs were formed into huge rafts and floated down to sawmills in distant Bangkok for local use or export.

Not until the northern railway line reached Chiang Mai in 1921 did the region become easily accessible to central Thais; before that, a journey from Bangkok by river, bullock-cart, and elephant-back could take a month or longer during the rainy season. Outside architectural influences arrived much earlier, however, especially in the homes built by teak merchants and other affluent residents and also in those of Protestant missionaries, who came to the area in the 1880s. Using the readily available teak, these were often large bungalows of the type then common in Bangkok, elevated on brick or wooden pillars and surrounded by airy verandahs. Others were made of brick and masonry, nearly always lavishly adorned with the decorative woodwork that was a specialty of local carvers. In both cases, the original inspiration was probably the residences of colonial Malaya and Singapore, except that like the temples of the north, some showed pronounced Burmese influence due to the fact that either the builders or the owners came from that country.

In general, these houses survived longer than their counterparts in Bangkok. As recently as twenty years ago, numerous examples could be seen along the older streets of Chiang Mai, as well as near the Wang River in Lampang. The advent of tourism and uncontrolled development, especially in Chiang Mai, has resulted in the loss of nearly all, making the preservation of those that remain even more urgent. A similar fate has befallen residences in pure Lanna style, though a number of these have been moved from their original locations and reassembled so that they at least continue to exist in some form.

Left : *Inspired by northern Thai and Shan architecture, the Hor Kham at Mae Fah Luang Foundation in Chiang Rai was constructed from wood taken from 32 old houses in the locale; it serves as a museum displaying northern Thai artifacts.*
Above : *Built during the reign of King Rama VI, this house in Tak originally belonged to Luang Borirak Prachakorn, a teak merchant.*

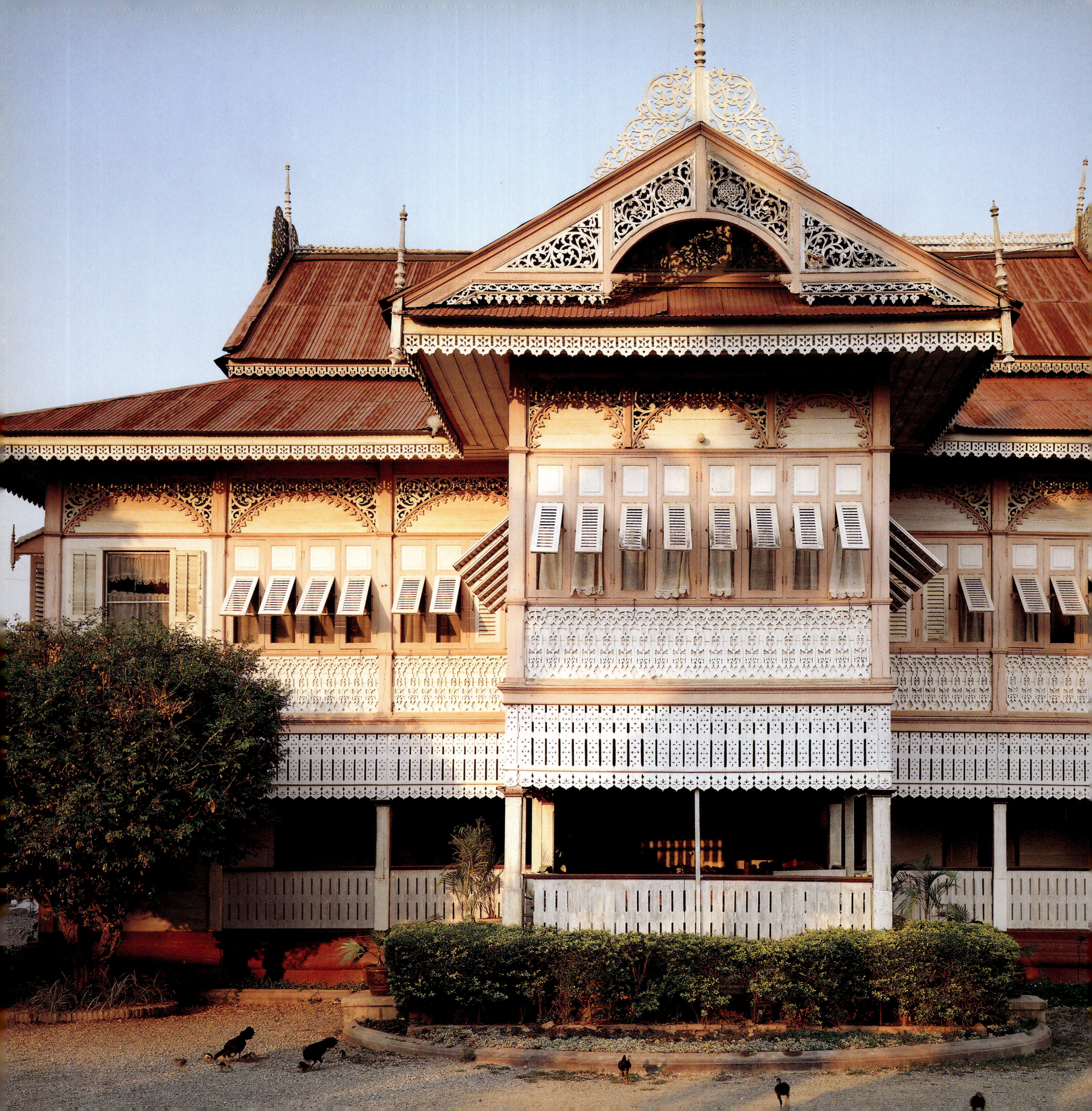

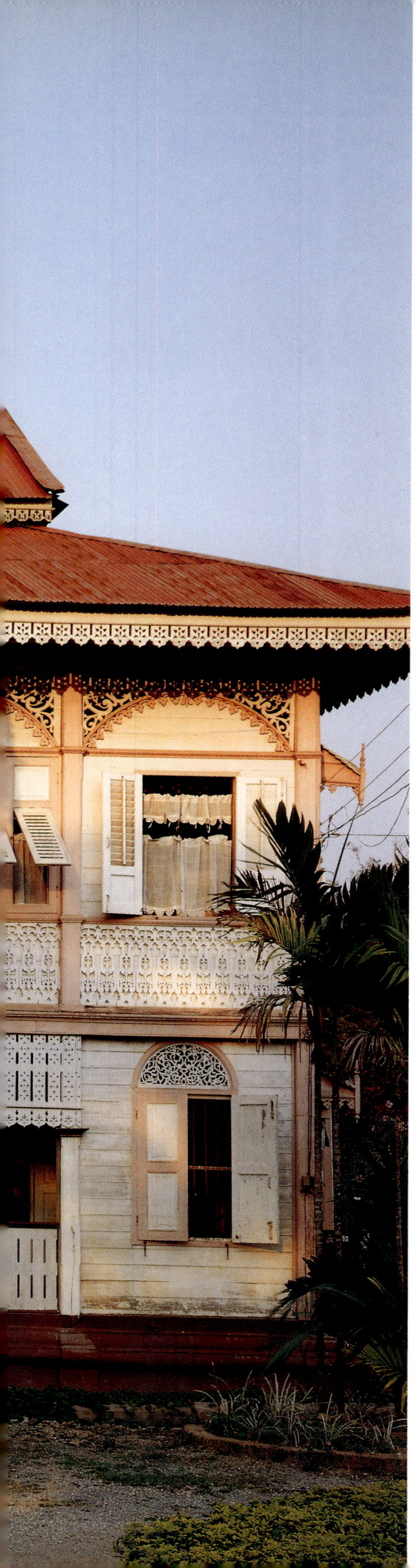

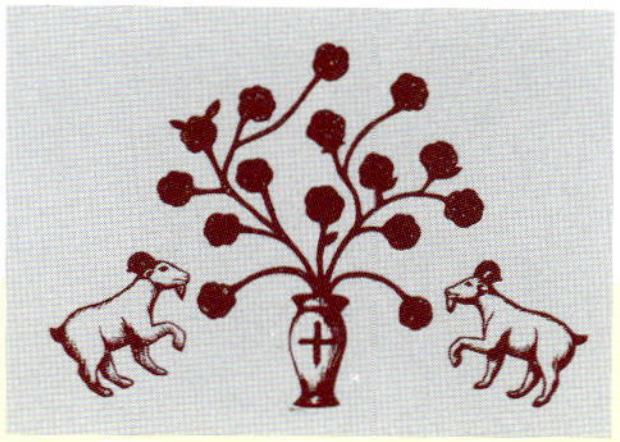

Vongburi House
Phrae

Phrae, located on the Yom River, is an ancient settlement, going back to 828 A.D. according to historical records. It served as a Burmese outpost during the Burmese occupation of northern Thailand, and, still later, attracted large numbers of Burmese and Laotian loggers who became involved in the teak trade toward the end of the 19th century.

Vongburi House was built in 1907 by Luang Phongphibul and his wife Mae Chao Sunantha, who held a teak concession in the city. The builder was a Chinese from Canton, using local carpenters for the job. The house has remained in family hands ever since, the current owners being Dr. Khanchai Vongburi, a researcher with the Department of Agriculture, and his wife Khun Watcharaporn.

A two-story teak structure, the house rests on a foundation of brick and mortar that elevates it approximately one meter above the ground. A double-tiered roof has a ventilation passage between the two levels to increase air circulation; since the house faces southwest, it is also subject to breezes during the hot season. There are 23 rooms, with high ceilings, covering 1,300 square meters of floor space. An originally open verandah on the front was later enclosed to create an additional room.

The outstanding feature of Vongburi House is its elaborate woodcarvings, which can be found on all its gables, eaves, balconies, and above doors and windows. Except for a few repairs and repainting them their original pink color, all the exterior carvings are original. The original roof of teak tiles, however, had to be removed in 1975 because of age; since the cost of replacing them would have been too high and since ceramic tiles would have been too heavy, corrugated iron was used.

On the front gate there is a stucco molding of two goats, commemorating the year in which both Luang Phongphibul and Mae Chao Sunantha, builders of the historic residence, were born.

Left : *Vongburi House in Phrae, built by a teak merchant in 1907.*

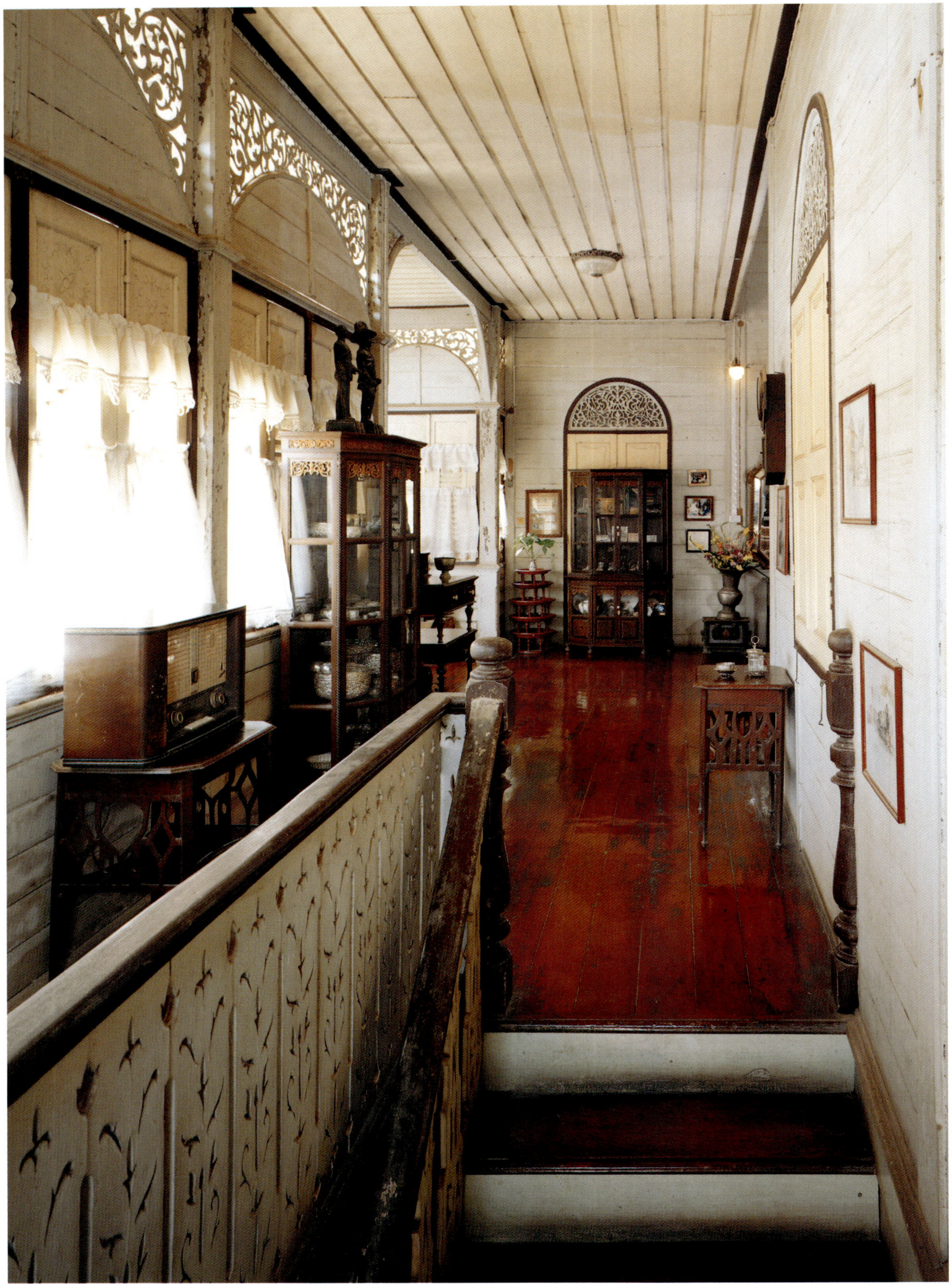

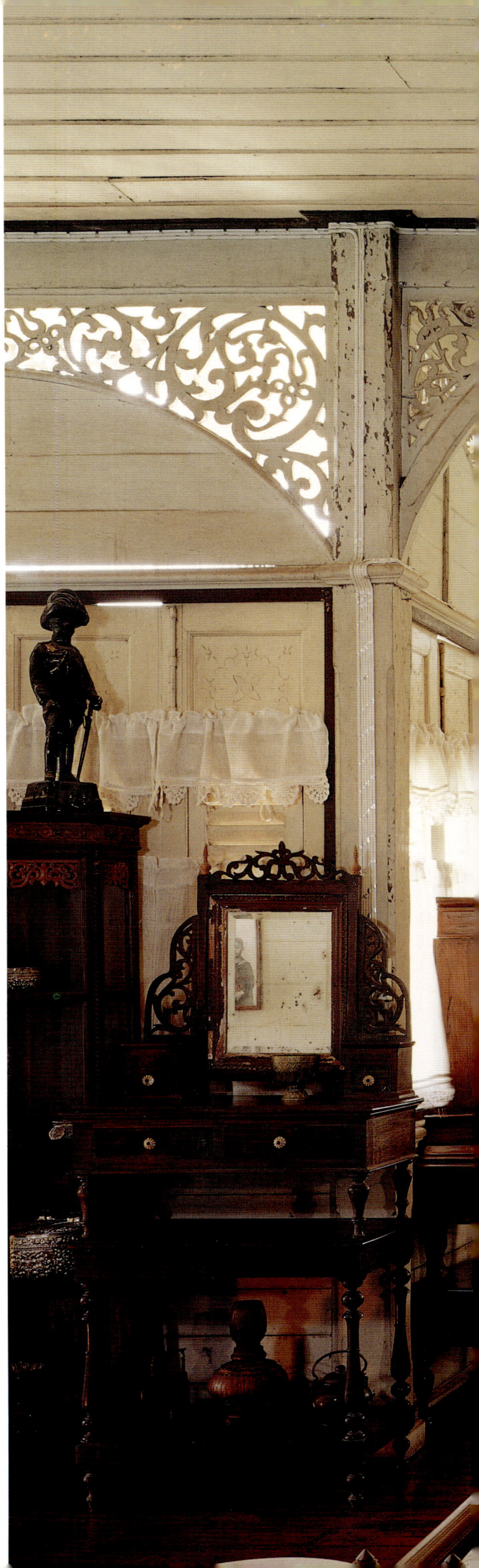

Above : *Former verandah at the top of the staircase; when the house was originally built the wall on the right faced the outside and the verandah was open.*
Right : *Enclosed verandah, now the living room; an antique elephant howdah stands below the windows.*

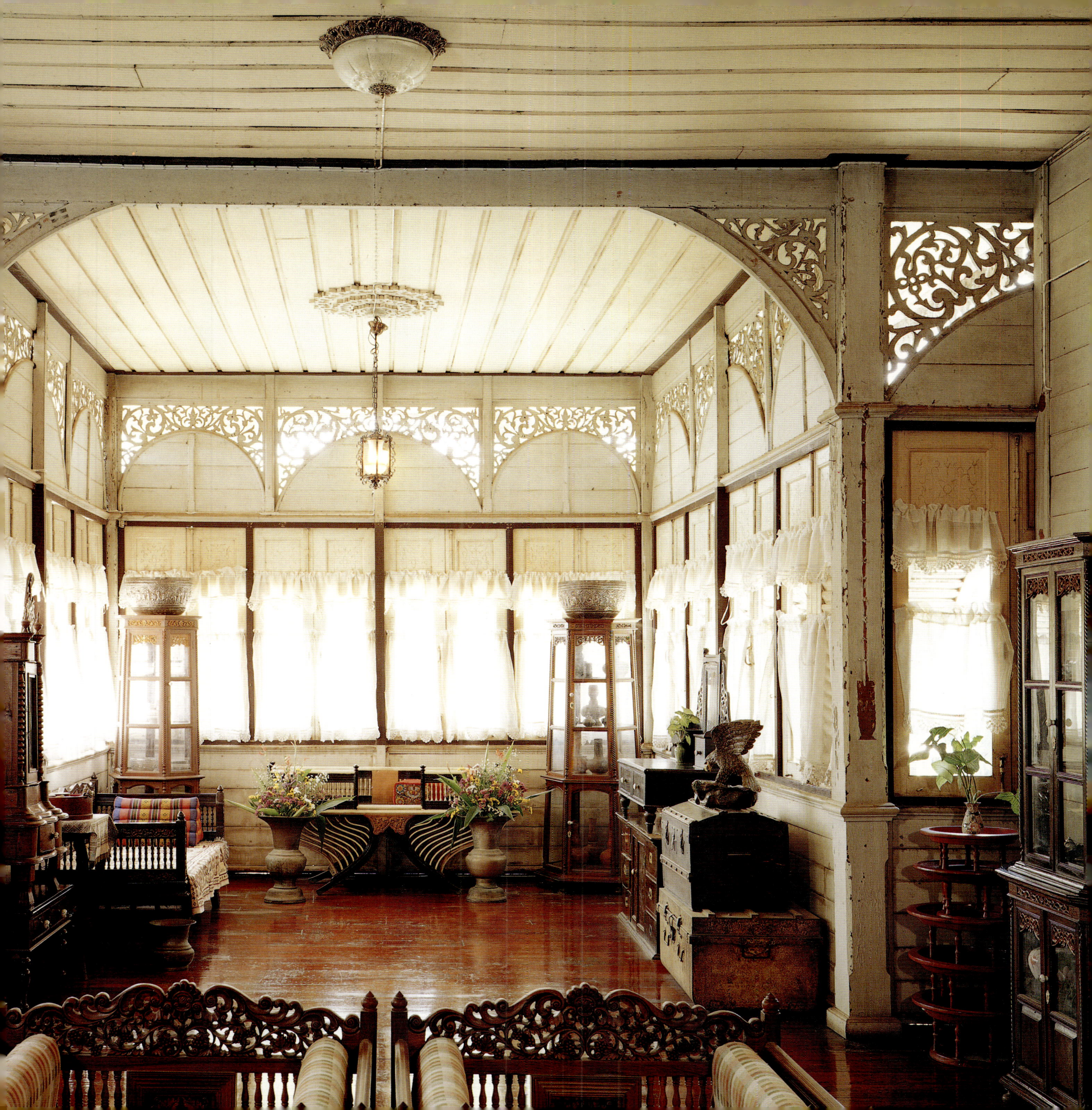

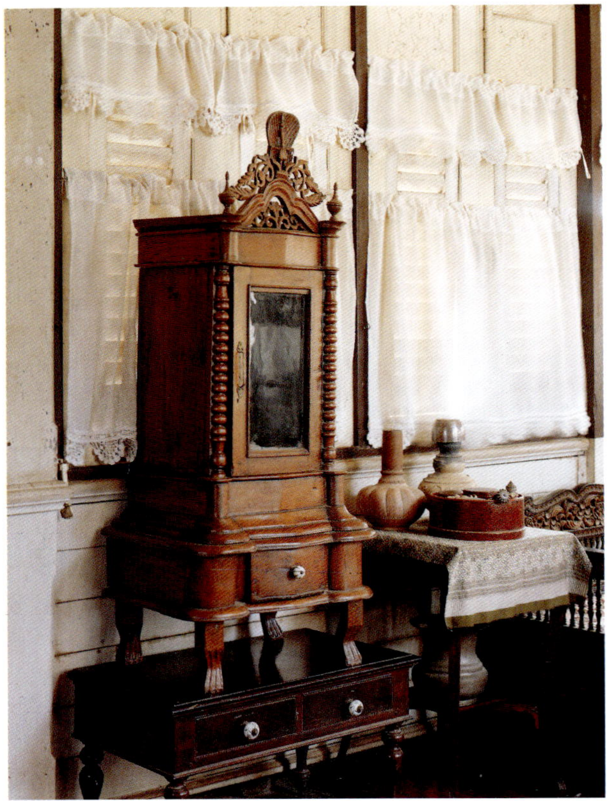

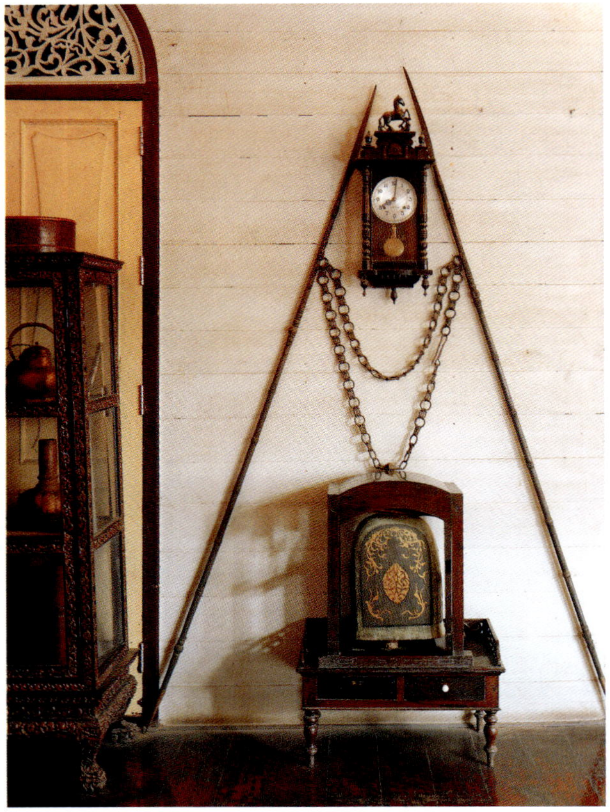

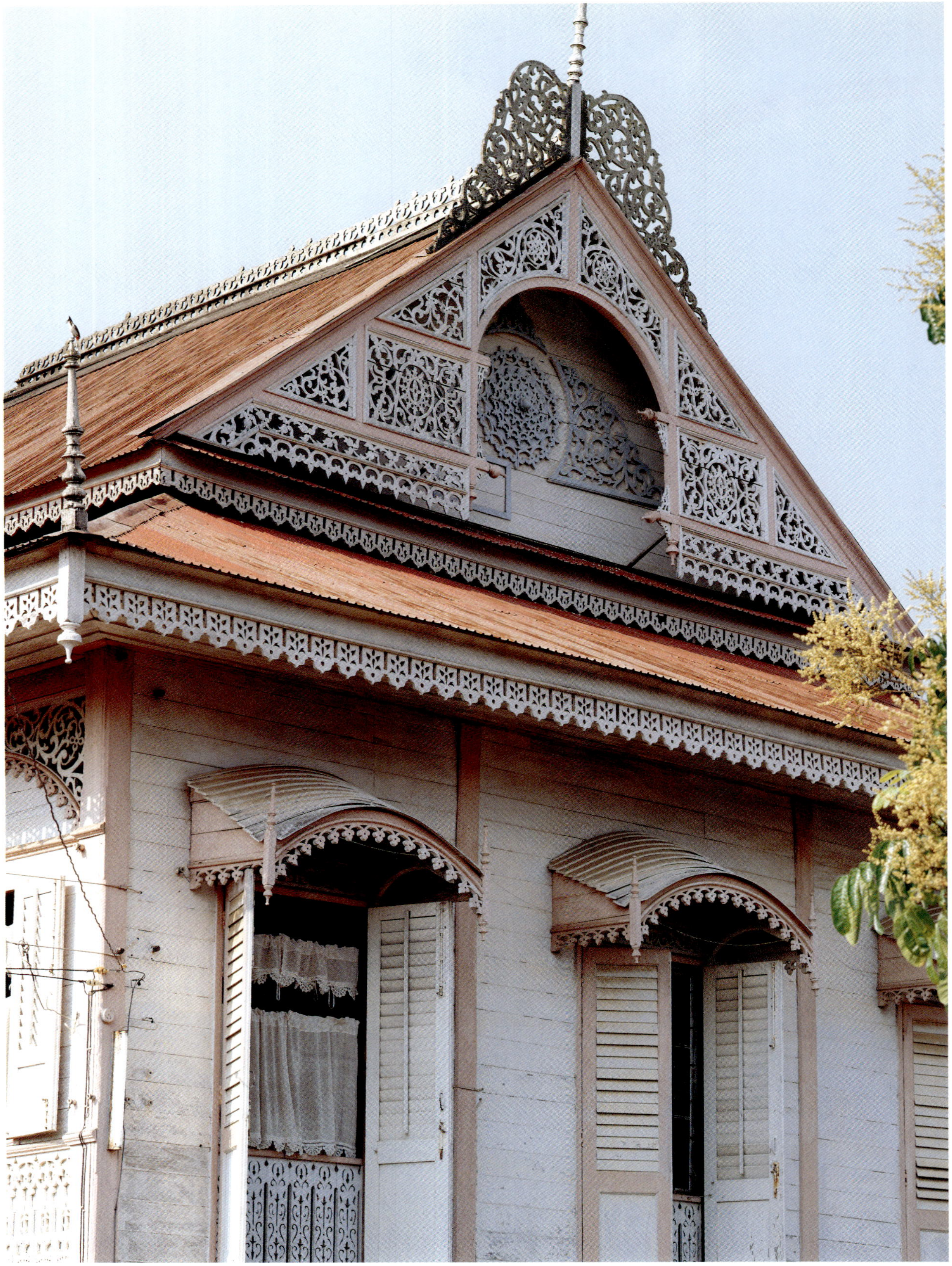

Right and above : *Detail showing the elaborate carvings that decorate the gables, eaves, and windows.*
Top left : *Antique Burmese manuscript cabinet in one of the houses' 23 rooms.*
Bottom left : *An old elephant bell and chain, together with spears used by soldiers who went to war on elephant-back.*

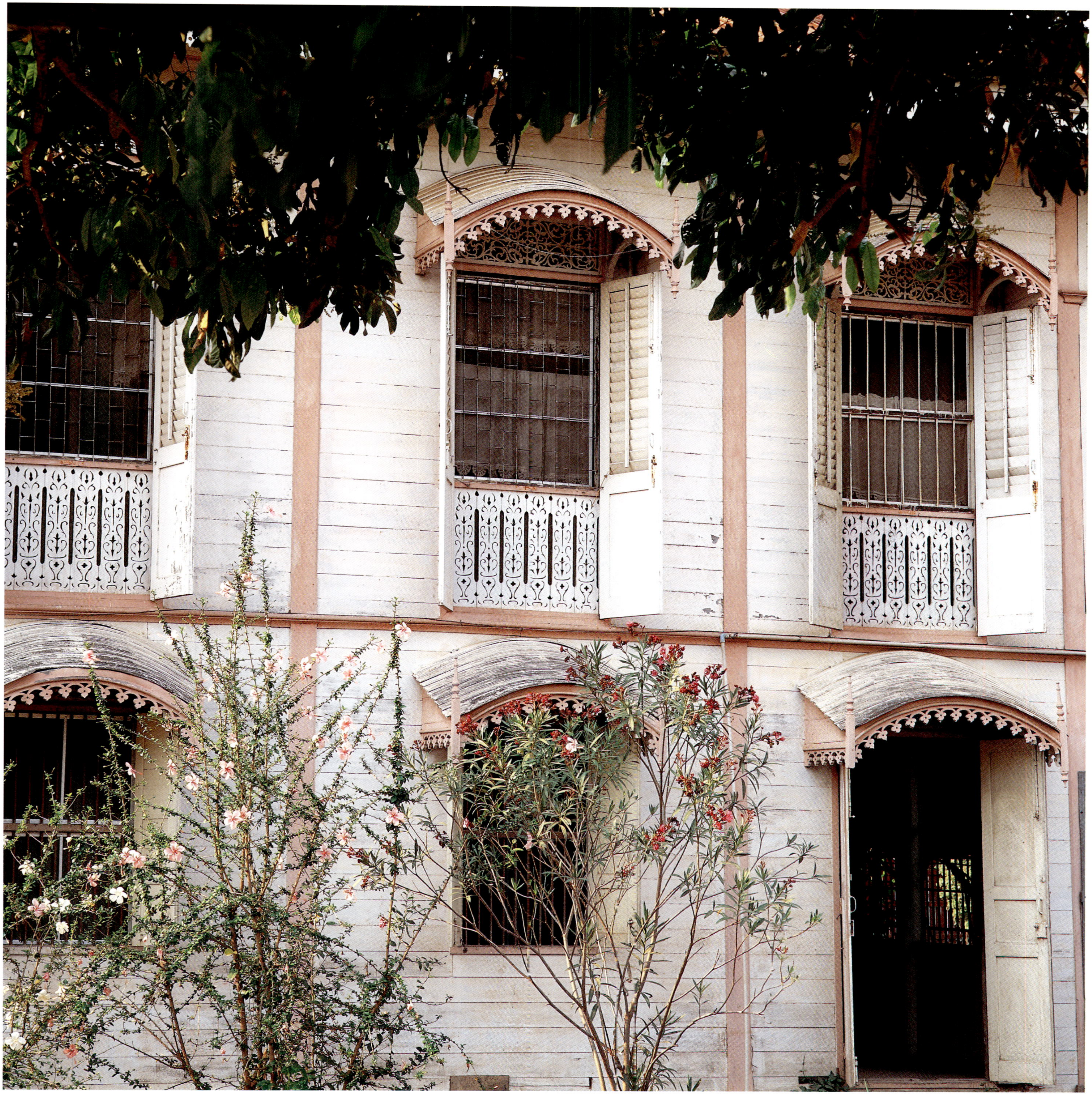

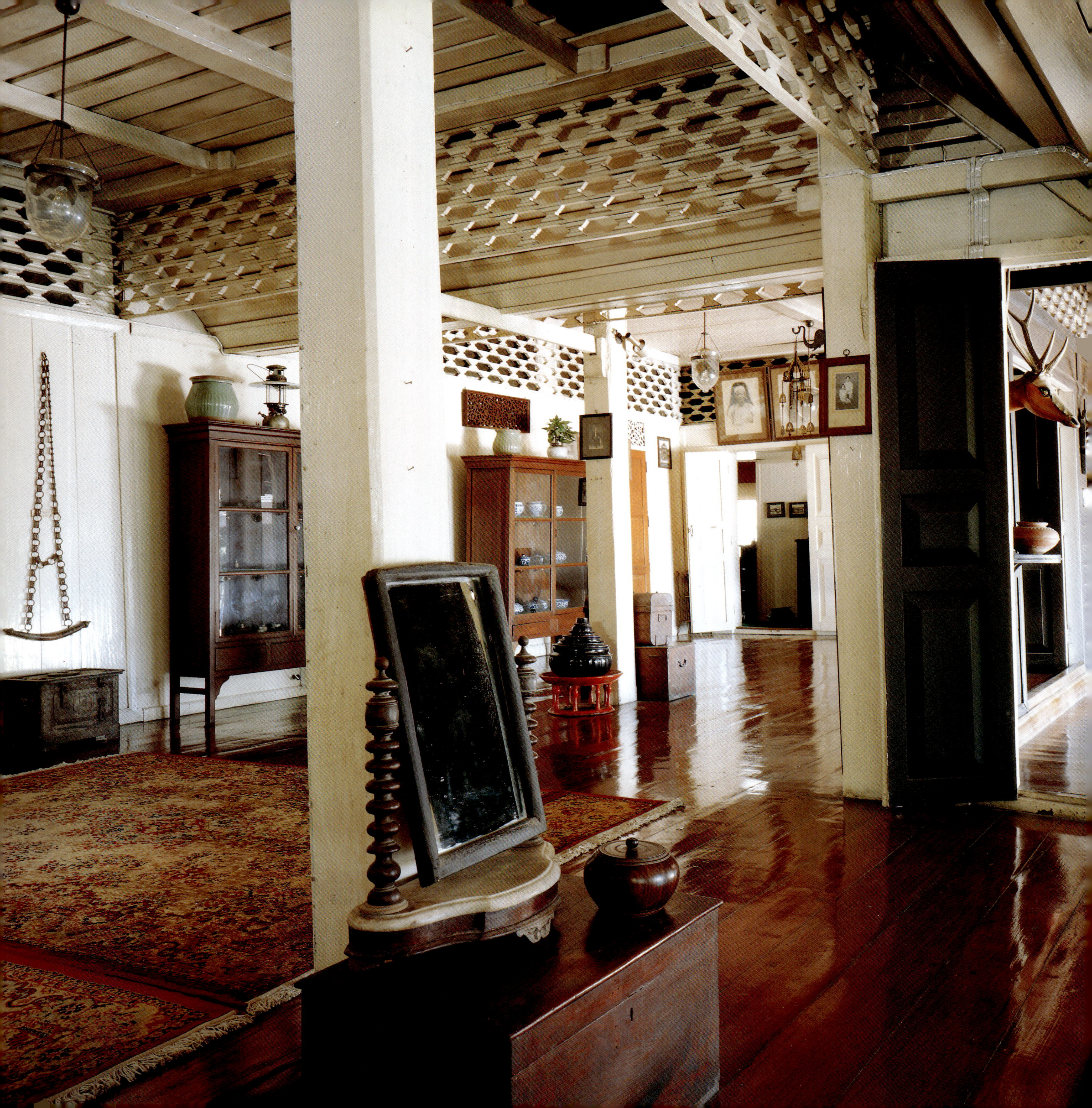

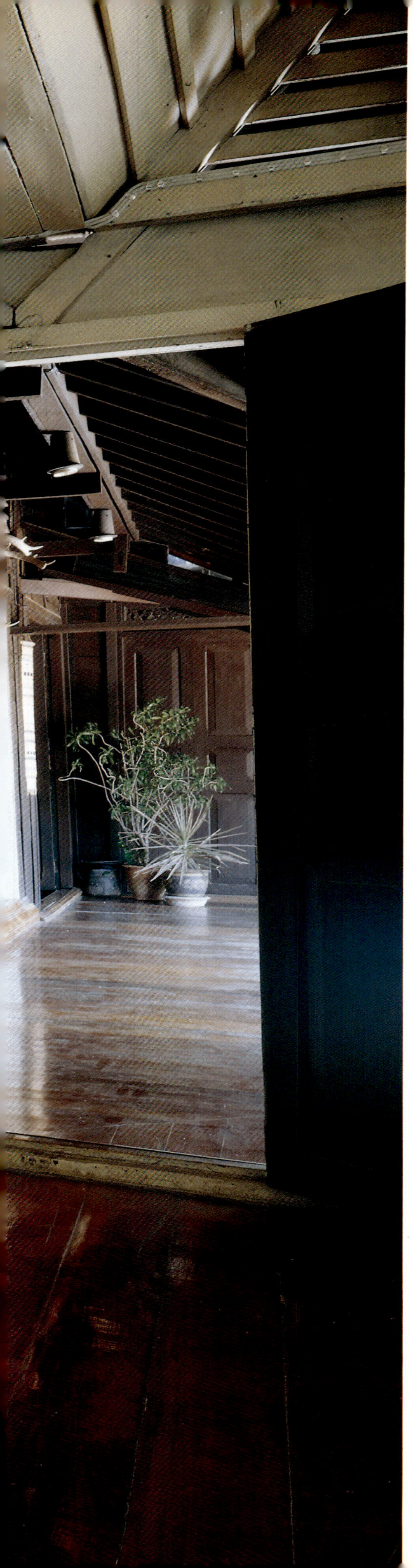

Baan Sao Nak

Lampang

Baan Sao Nak, literally "the house of many pillars," is one of the most famous structures in the northern city of Lampang. It was built in 1885 by Mong Chan Ong Chandraviroj, a Burmese who settled in Lampang during the period when it was a leading center of the teak industry, and displays both Burmese and northern Thai architectural styles. The verandah, for example, shows distinctly Burmese influence, while the roofs and general structure are typically Lanna Thai.

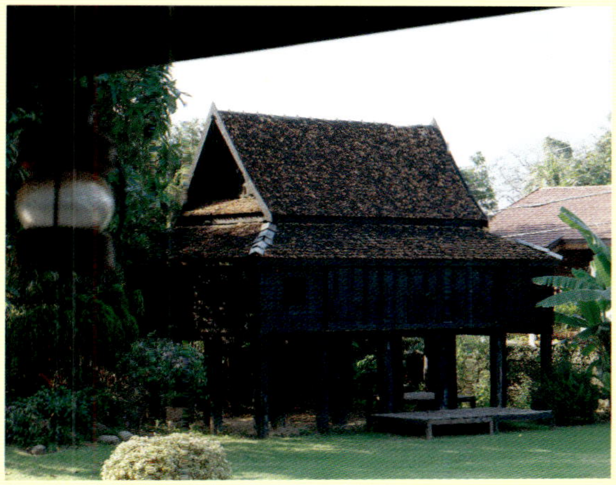

Two sleeping areas with connecting roofs and living quarters span the entire front part of the residence. The popular name, bestowed by the well-known radio and television personality M.R. Thanadsri Svasti, derives from the fact that it is raised from the ground on 116 stout teak pillars, an unusual number even for such a sizable structure.

By 1964, when the house was owned by Khunying Valai Leelanuj, a granddaughter of the builder, its age and weight were beginning to affect the structure. Extensive restoration was therefore carried out in consultation with Khunying Valai's younger brother, Khun Taweesak Chandraviroj, a well-known architect. The work, which took ten years, involved providing concrete plinths for the 116 pillars to prevent further subsidence, replacing the wooden floorboards of the verandah with tiles, and covering a teak gutter with galvanized iron.

In 1987, Khunying Valai decided to replace an old rice granary in the compound with another, dating from the same period and supported by 24 pillars. Completion of the barn was celebrated with a traditional Hong Khwan Ku Khao ceremony to encourage the return of any spirits who may have become lost during the building's relocation.

Since Khunying Valai's death a few years ago, the house and the large collection of northern handicrafts displayed in it have continued to be a popular Lampang tourist attraction.

Left : *Interior of Baan Sao Nak, now used as a museum to display northern handicrafts.*
Above : *Rice granary in the compound supported by 24 pillars.*

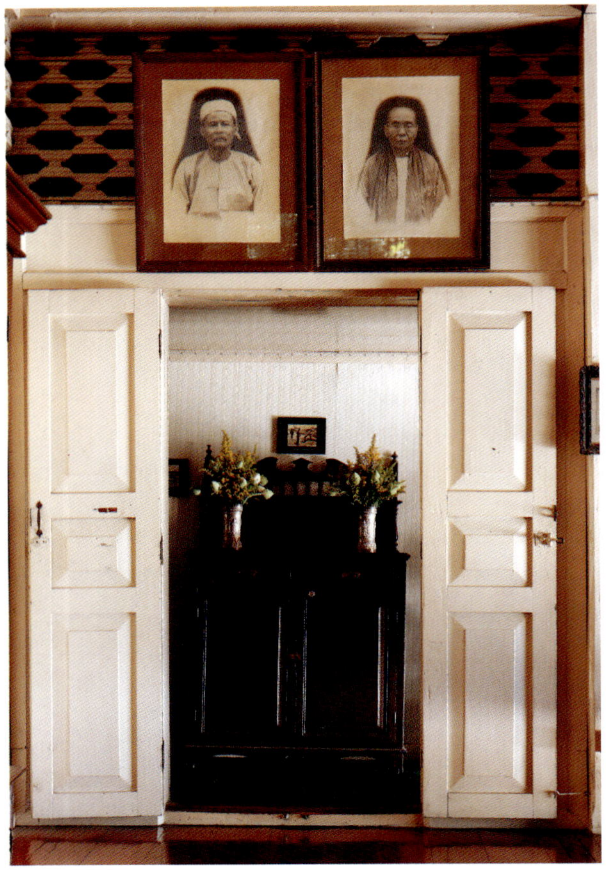

Right : *A photograph of Khun Mae Noi, great grandmother of the present owner and a lady of fashion in her day.*
Left : *Photographs of Mong Chan Ong Chandraviroj, who built the house, and his wife, hang in a place of honor.*
Below : *The tree in the front of the house is a 131-year-old Sarapee* (Ochocarpus siamensis) *and mats have been spread below to catch the flowers, used in making pot pourri and traditional medicine.*

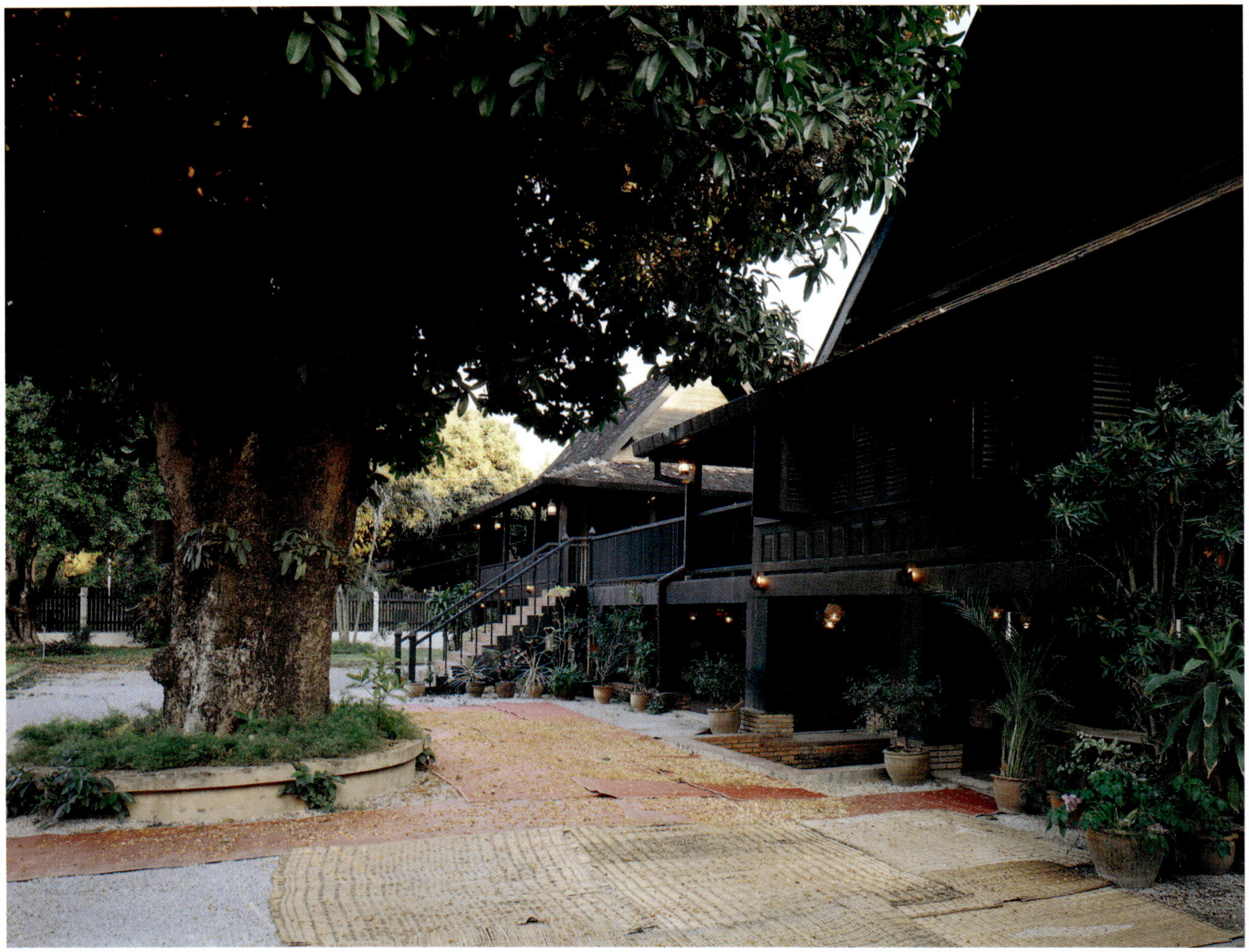

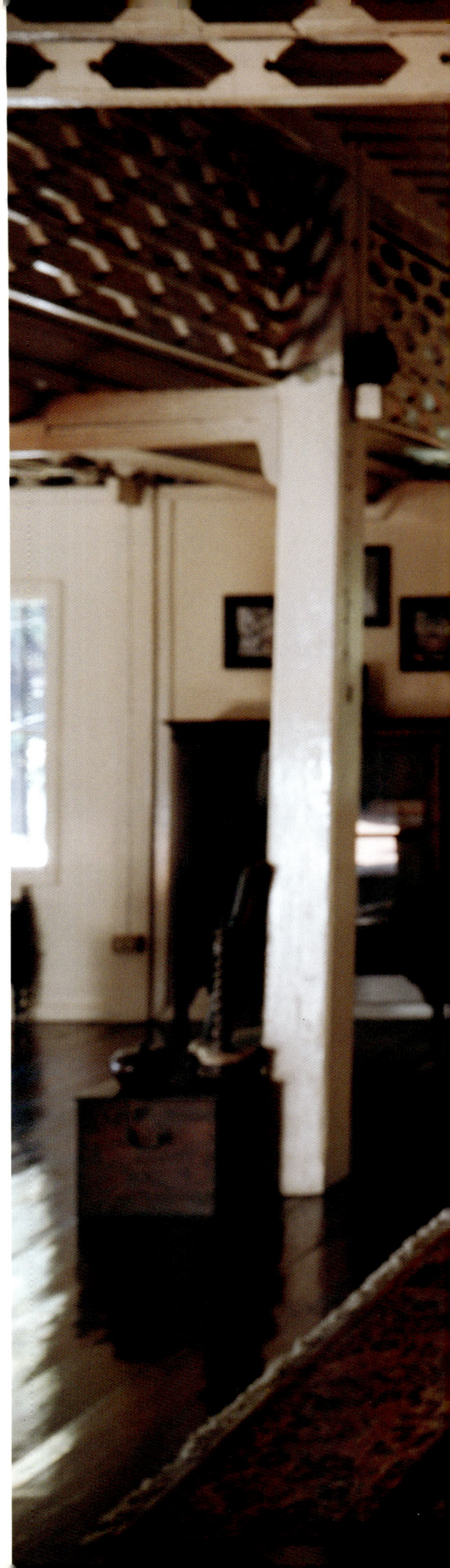

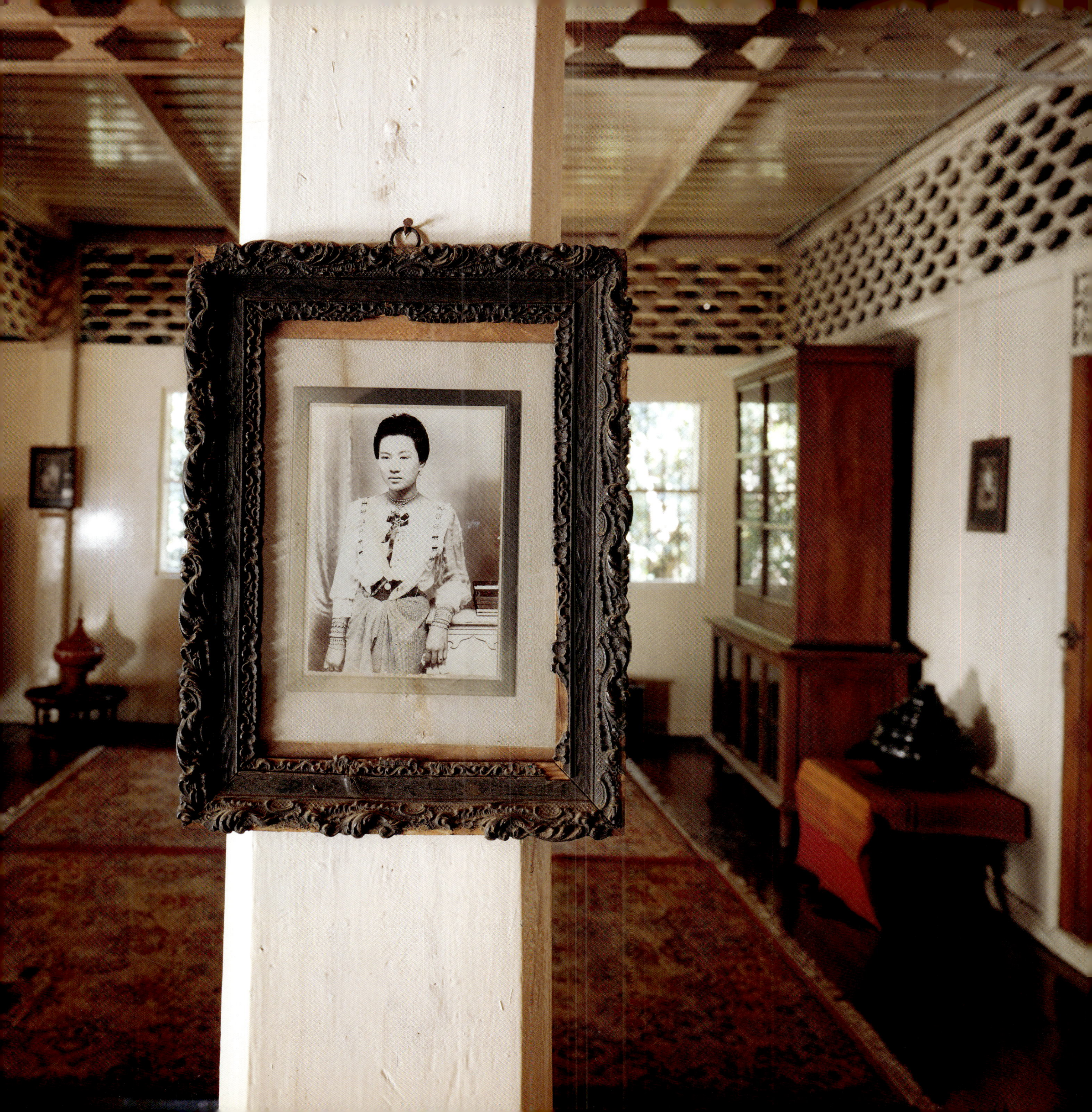

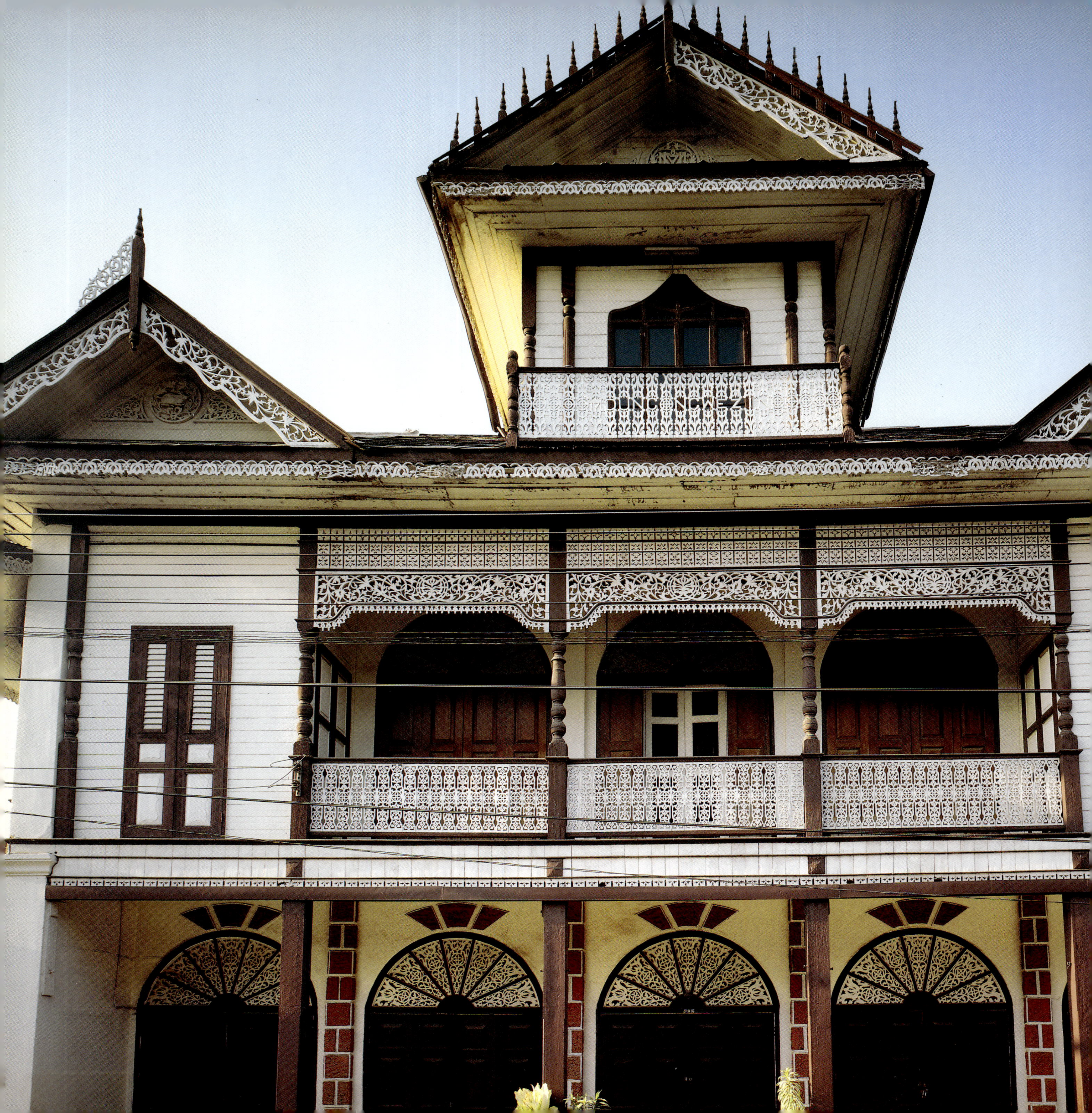
DUNC NCWE ZI

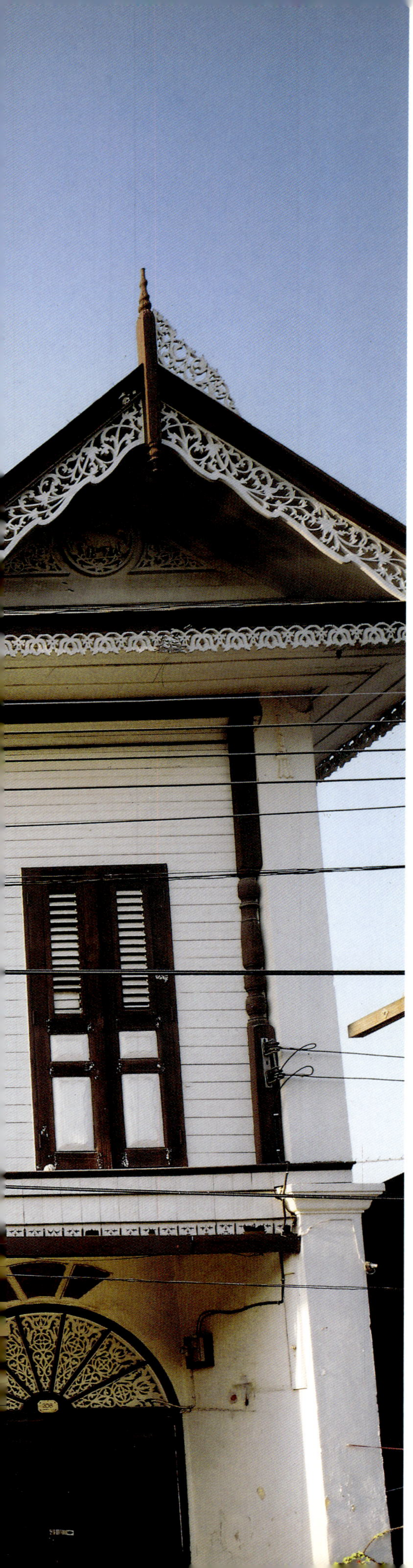

Lampang Houses

Lampang, currently northern Thailand's second largest city, is situated in the fertile valley of the Wang River, a tributary of the Ping. The traditional Lampang house design was different from that of the Chiang Mai area; generally it tended to be more austere in appearance and lacked such decorative touches as the carved *galae* at the ends of the top roof beam. Such classic houses, however, were already beginning to disappear by the end of the last century, when Lampang developed into a major center of the teak industry, as well as other trade from the region.

According to one source, Nakhon Lampang, as it was then known, had a population of over 20,000 by the turn of the century, as well as over 4,000 working elephants. Ten caravans from the Shan States, each consisting of more than 100 mules, visited the market annually, and an estimated 10,000 bullock carts also brought goods. This prosperity attracted Thai, Shan, and Western traders, who floated massive rafts of logs down the Wang River and eventually to Bangkok, along with a cosmopolitan mixture of traders who also settled in the provincial capital.

The houses built by these relative newcomers tended not to be traditional Thai but rather a melange of architectural styles—Western, Chinese, Burmese, and sometimes a combination of these. Victorian gingerbread adorned many of them, along with fanciful towers and multi-layered roofs, reflecting a taste for novelty as well as the influence of faraway Bangkok, where a passion for Western architecture was already strong. Most of these residences were originally situated on the Wang, but some are now a considerable distance away due to alterations in the river's course.

The Sinanond House was built around 1919 by Luang Kamchornvanich, a government official and grandfather of Khun Boonchalerm Thipyamonton, the present owner. A handsome, two-story structure in Italianate style, it was the work of a Chinese builder from Canton named Sung Lee, one of the many artisans who came to Lampang in its boom period. Sung Lee is recorded as having received two baht a day for his efforts.

Baan Mae Daeng is on Talad Chine (Chinese Market) Road, once on the bank of the Wang River. The house was named after Mae Daeng Panichphan, the mother of the current owner, Khun Tham Panichphan. The upper floor of the two-story house has a verandah running along the front decorated with long panels of pierced carvings.

Moung Ngwezin House is altogether more fanciful and formerly belonged to a Burmese

Left : *Moung Ngwezin House, built in the early years of this century by a Burmese merchant in Lampang; Burmese carpenters were probably used in the construction.*

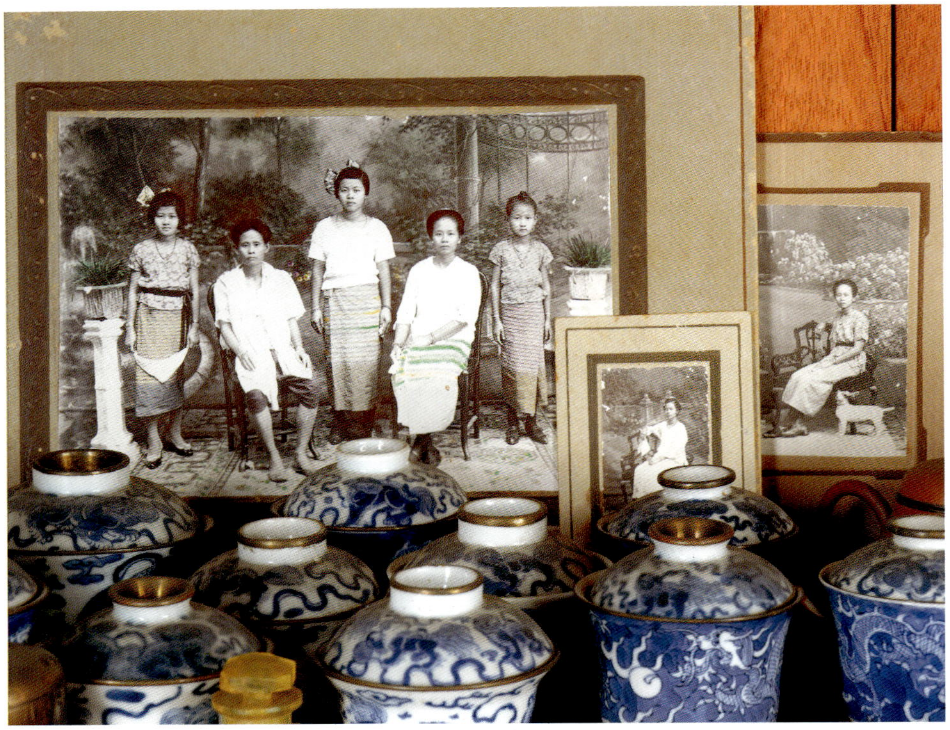

merchant, who probably utilized Burmese workers in its construction. A central tower, gables, and verandahs are adorned with ornate fretwork, as are the tops of the arched doorways on the lower level.

The present condition of the old Lampang houses varies. Some are being restored by their current owners, while others are in urgent need of preservation. All deserve attention as part of northern Thailand's architectural heritage.

Below : *Entrance hall of Sinanond House, showing the extensive use of teak then so plentiful in the region.*
Below left : *Sinanond House, built around 1919 by a government official.*
Left : *Family photograph in Sinanond House; on the far right in the group picture is Khun Boonchalerm Thipyamonton, the present owner and a granddaughter of the builder.*

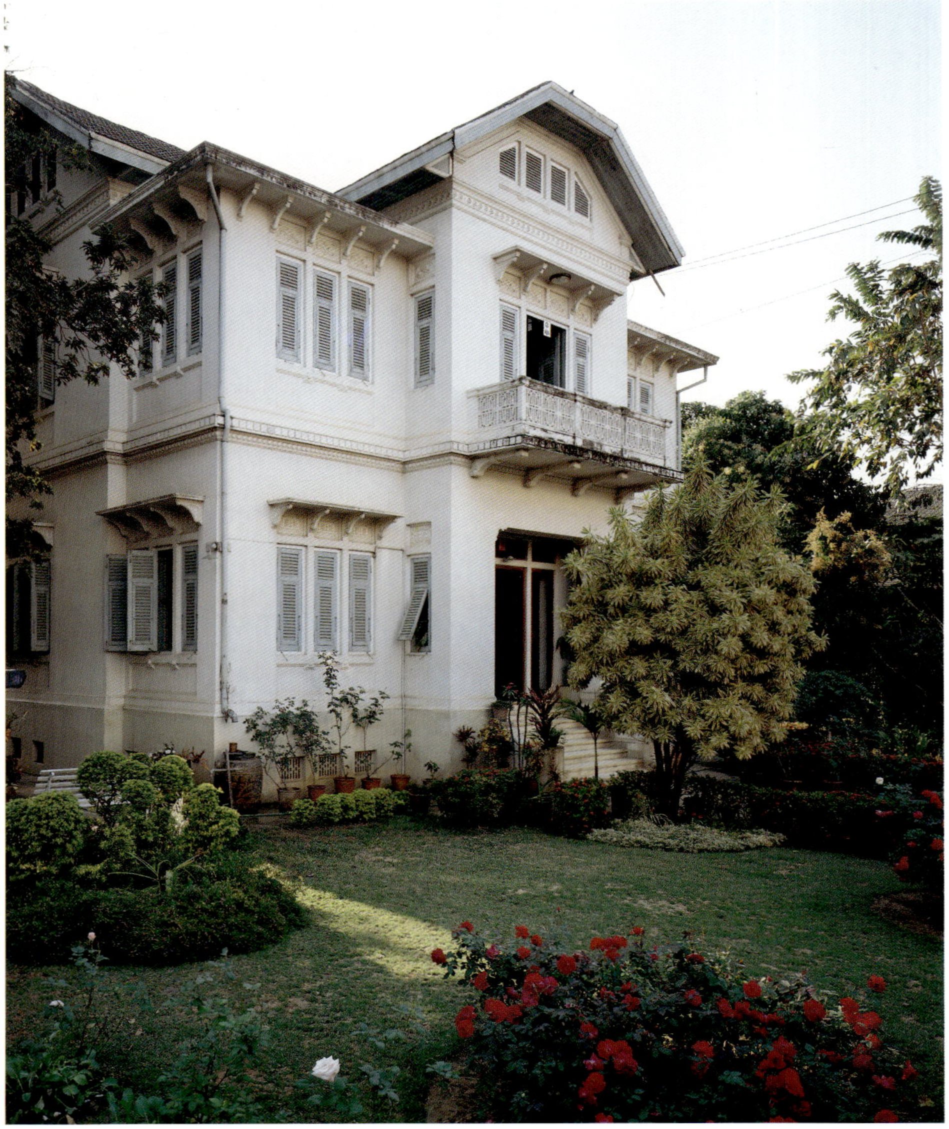

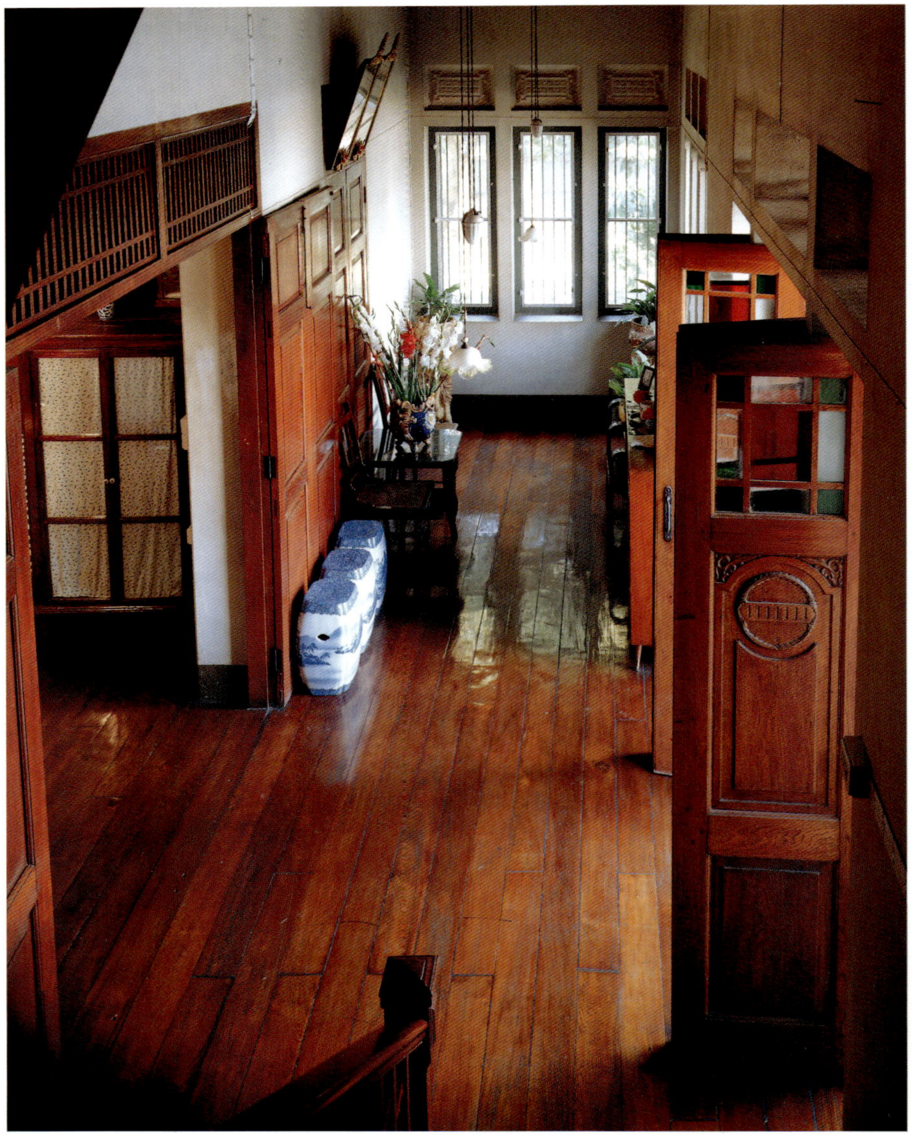

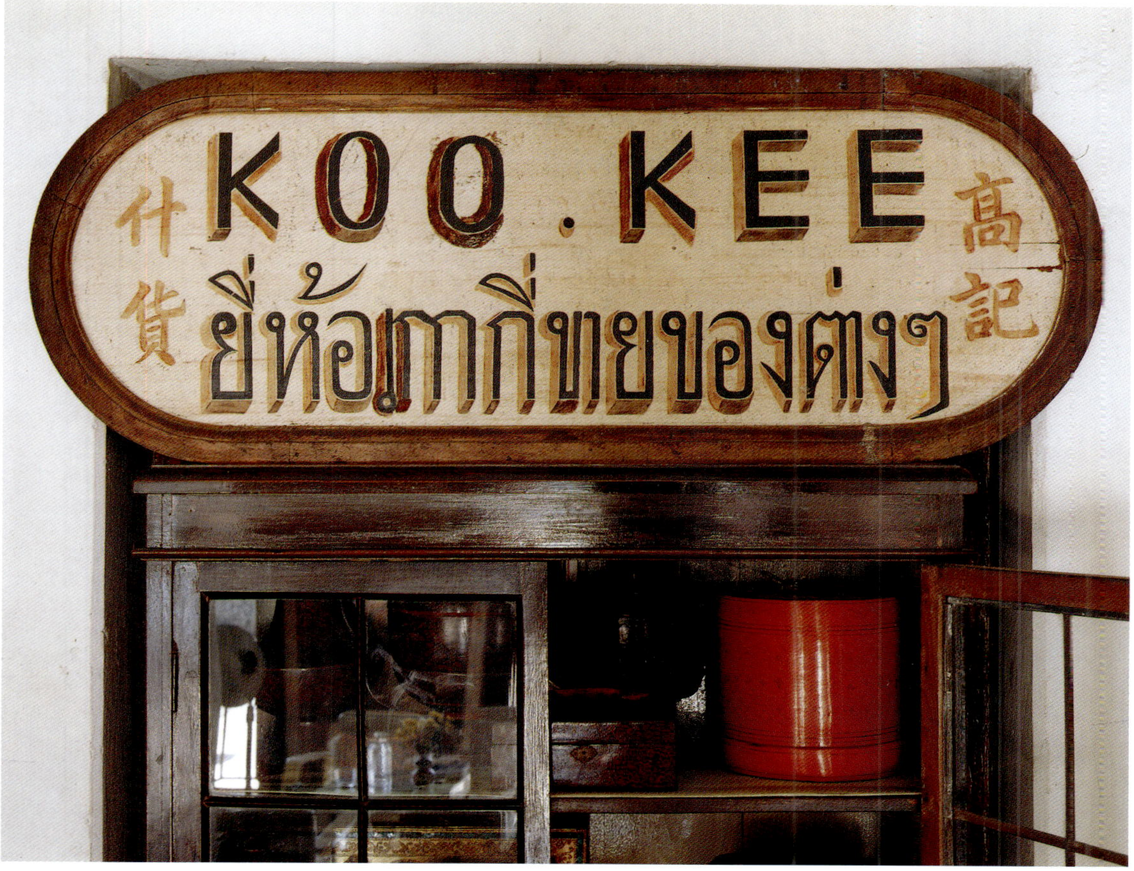

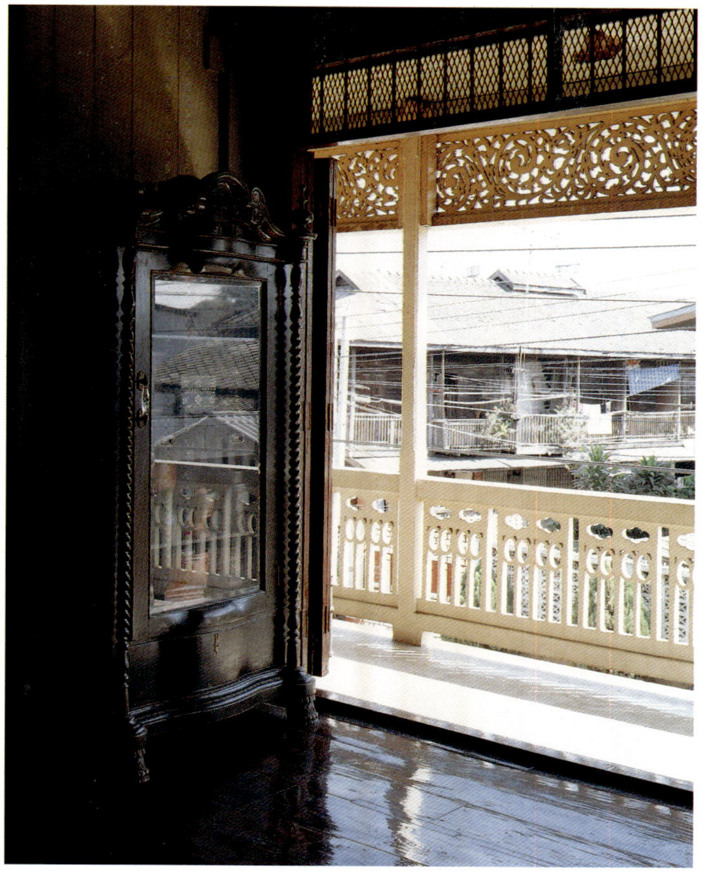

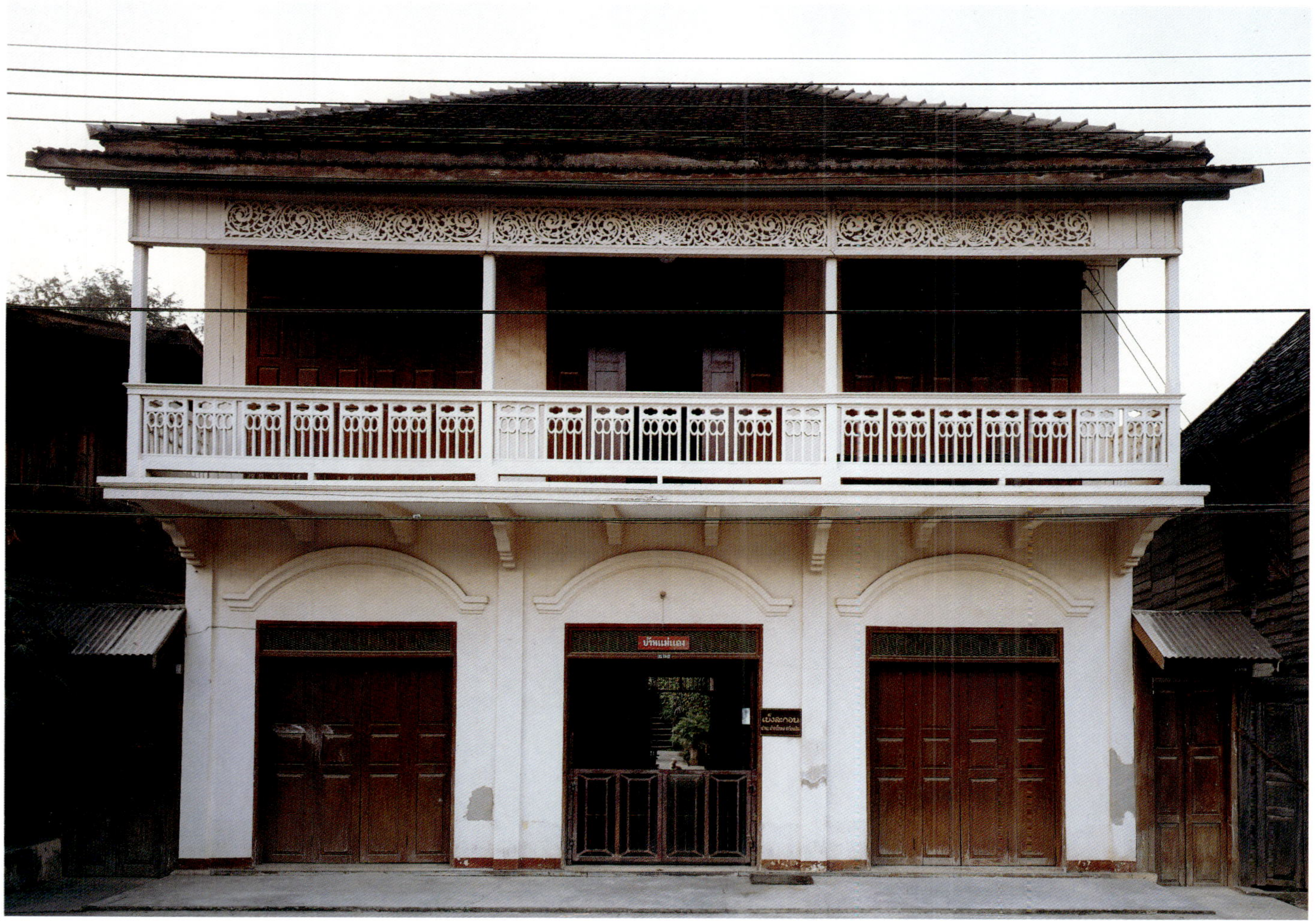

Left : *Baan Mae Daeng; a shop was on the lower floor, with residential quarters above.*
Above left : *Shop sign of the father of the present owner.*
Above : *Upstairs verandah of Baan Mae Daeng.*

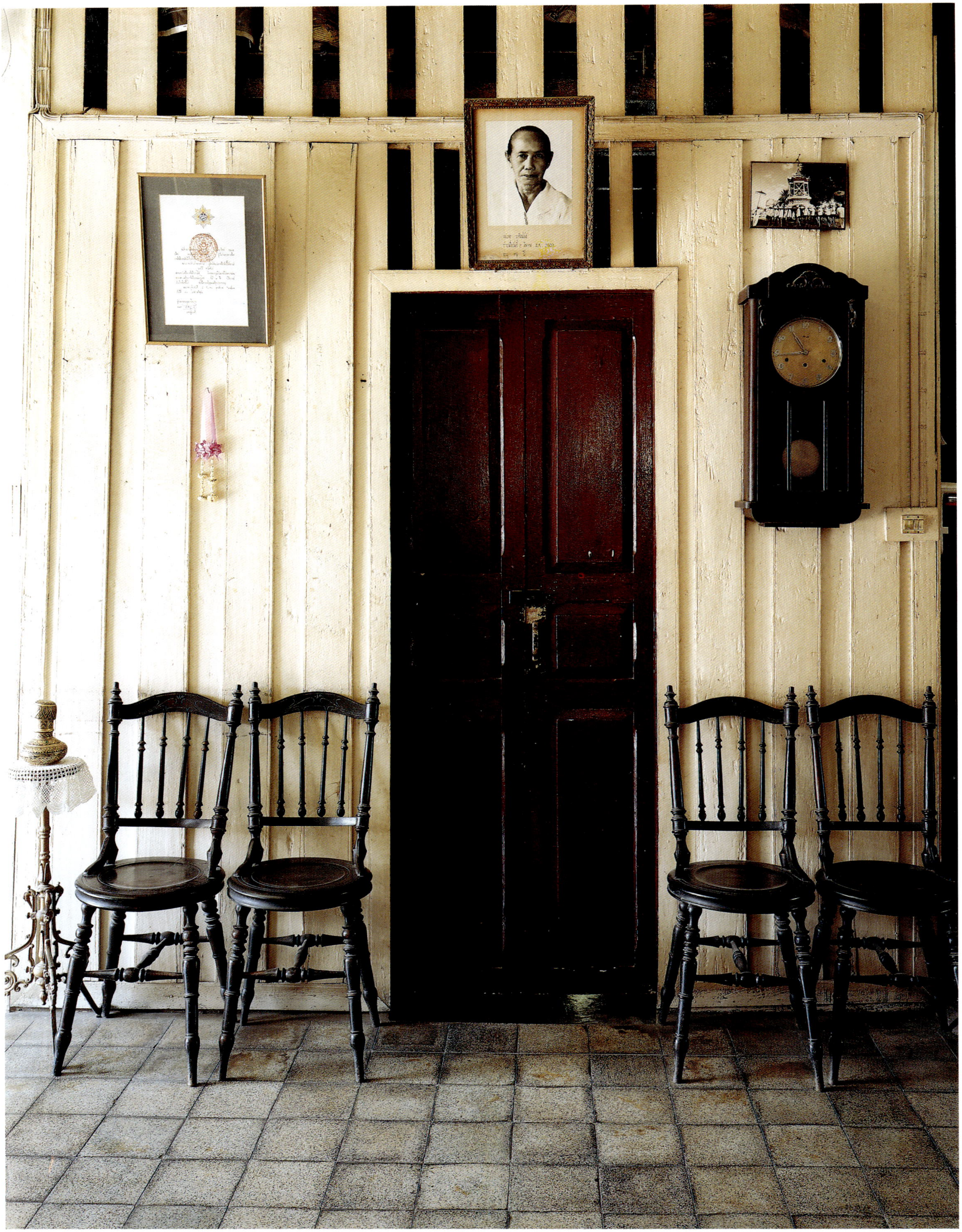

Left : *Baan Mae Daeng; above the doorway hangs a photograph of Mae Daeng Panichphan, mother of the current owner.*
Opposite page : *miscellaneous residences and shophouses, well maintained and otherwise; shown top left is Komsan House.*

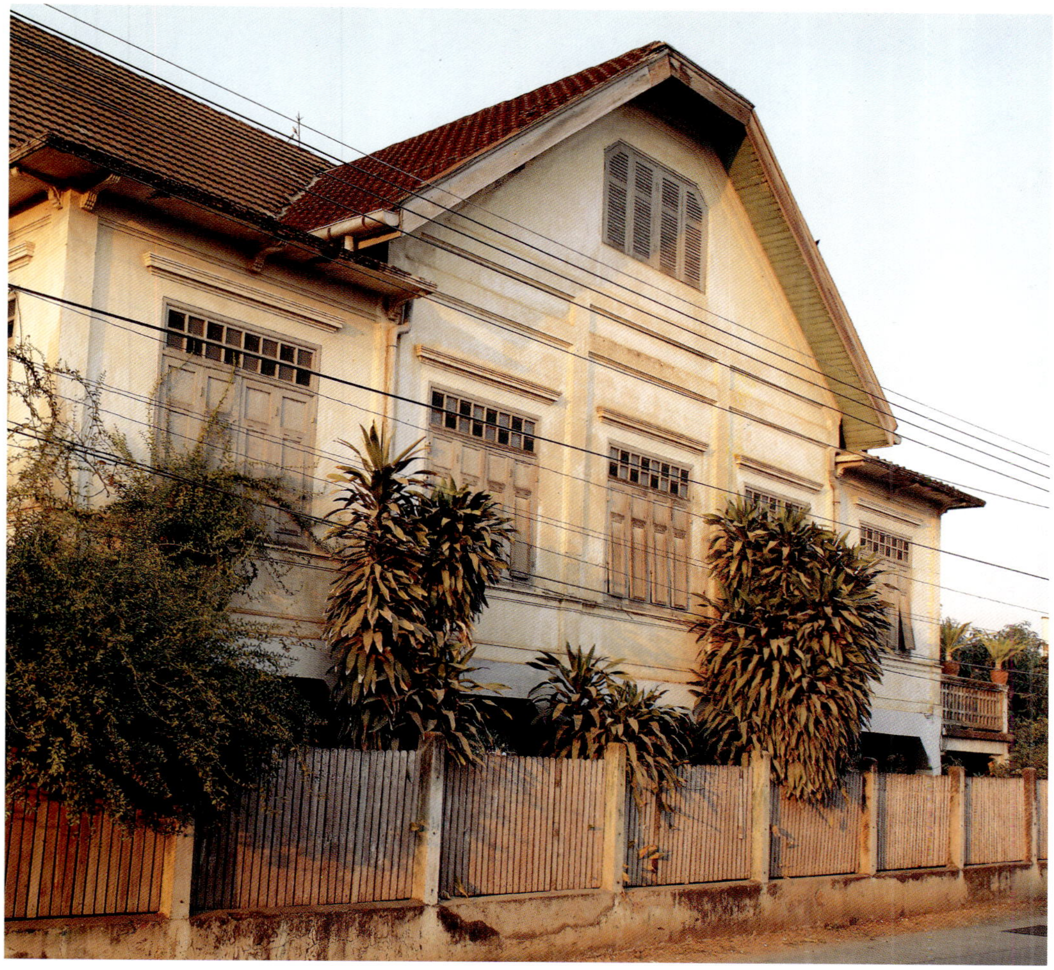

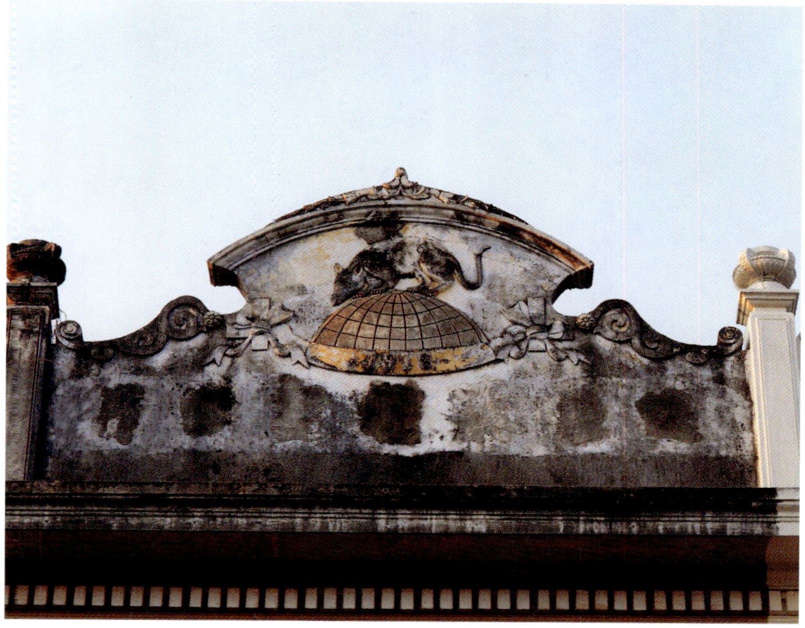

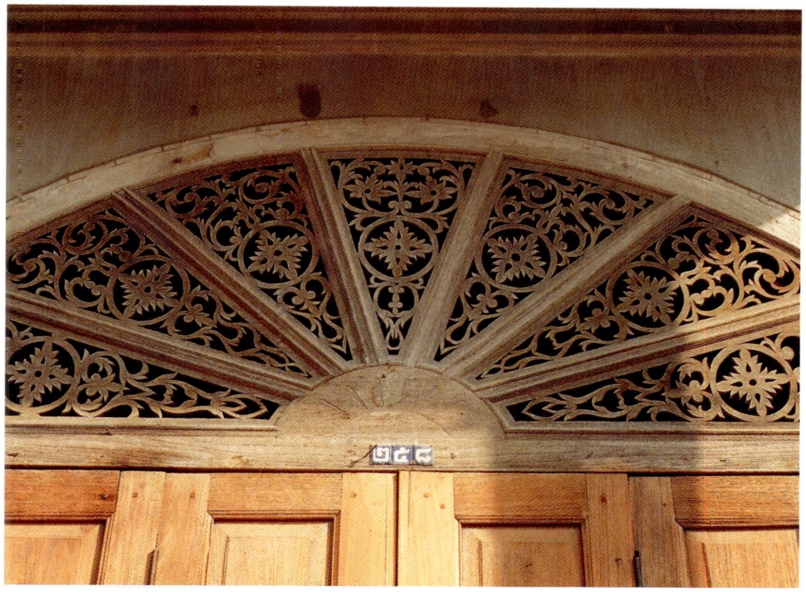
๒๔๘

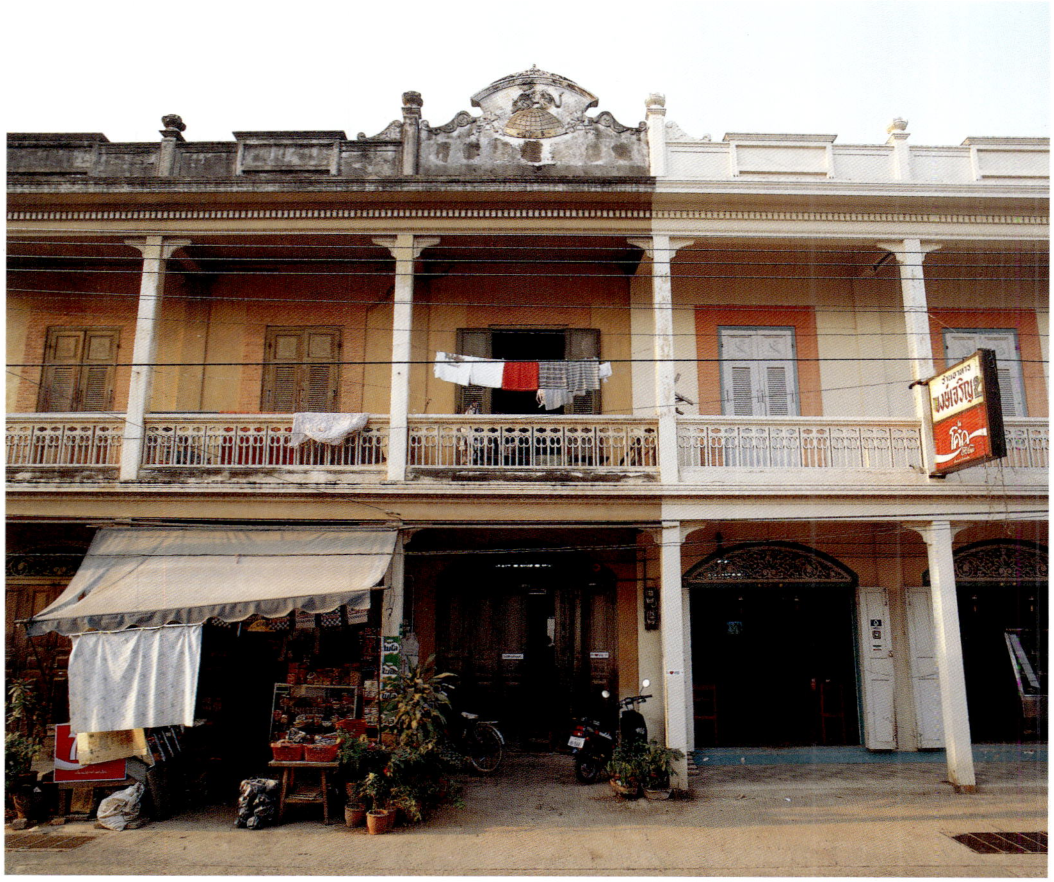

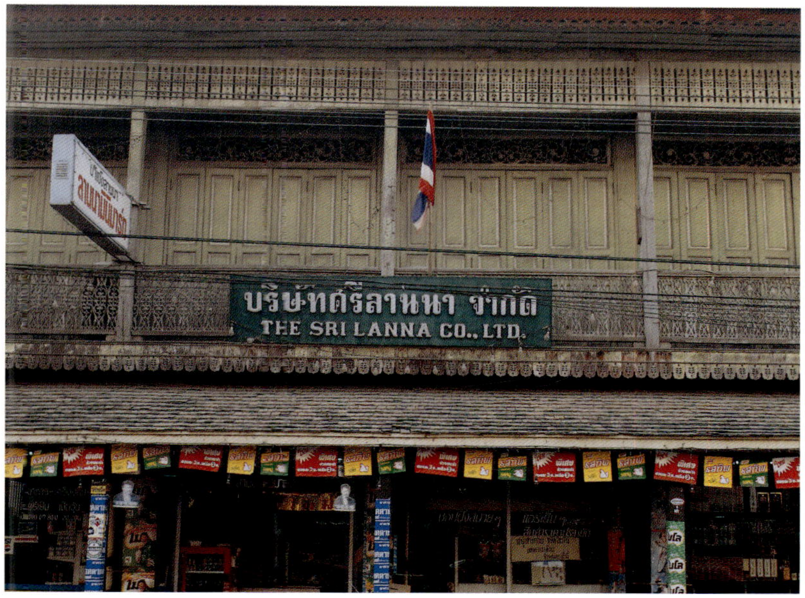
บริษัทศรีลานนา จำกัด
THE SRI LANNA CO., LTD.

Baan Phya Kham
Chiang Mai

Little is known about the history of this house, though it is clearly a fine example of the traditional Lanna style of domestic architecture developed in northern Thailand. While this displays certain characteristics of the central Thai style—for example, the use of prefabricated wall sections—it differs in other ways. The walls lean outward rather than inward, giving the structure a more solid appearance, the windows are generally smaller, and, particularly in the Chiang Mai area, the ends of the roof supports are adorned with a distinctive V-shaped ornament called a *galae*, the precise symbolism of which remains a subject of debate among scholars.

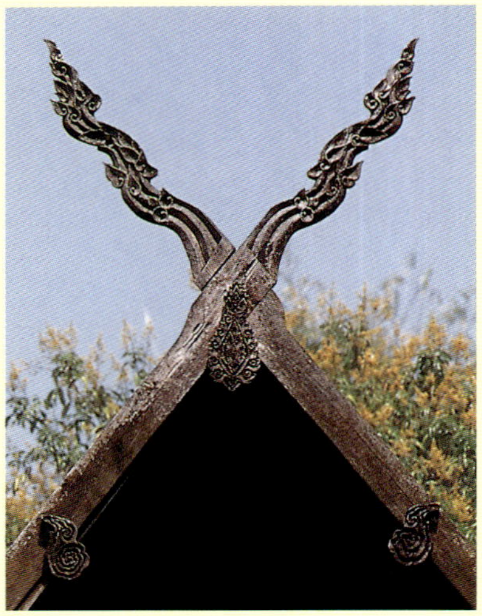

Though its exact age is uncertain, Baan Phya Kham was moved to its present location in a large lychee orchard called Suan Mae Keow, near Chiang Mai University, around 30 years ago by a former governor of the province. It was later acquired by Khun Chatri Sophonpanich, who now uses it as a northern retreat.

The house consists of two adjoining units which share a common verandah. The units have now been converted into air-conditioned bedrooms with modern bathrooms. Some renovation work was also necessary on the classic thatched roof as well as on the flooring and wall panels, but the basic structure remains as it was originally. An unusual feature is that the supporting columns are octagonal rather than round, while the verandah extends over a picturesque lake that reflects the structure's elegant lines.

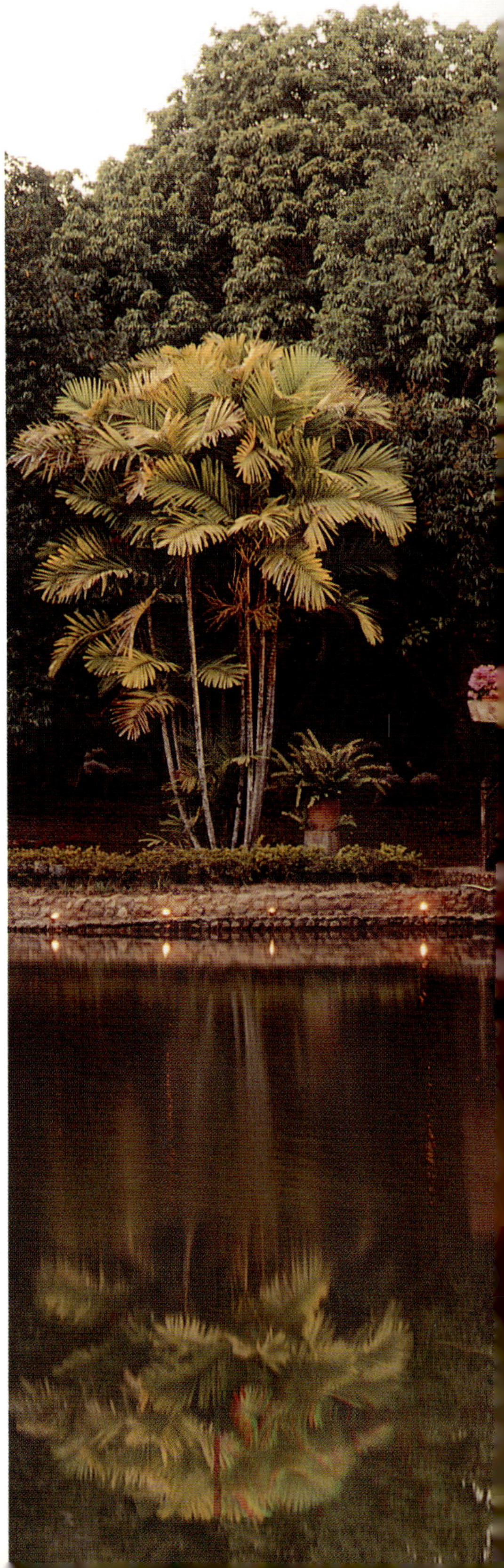

Right : *Baan Phya Kham built partially over a lake.*
Above : Galae, *an architectural decoration typical of Chiang Mai houses.*

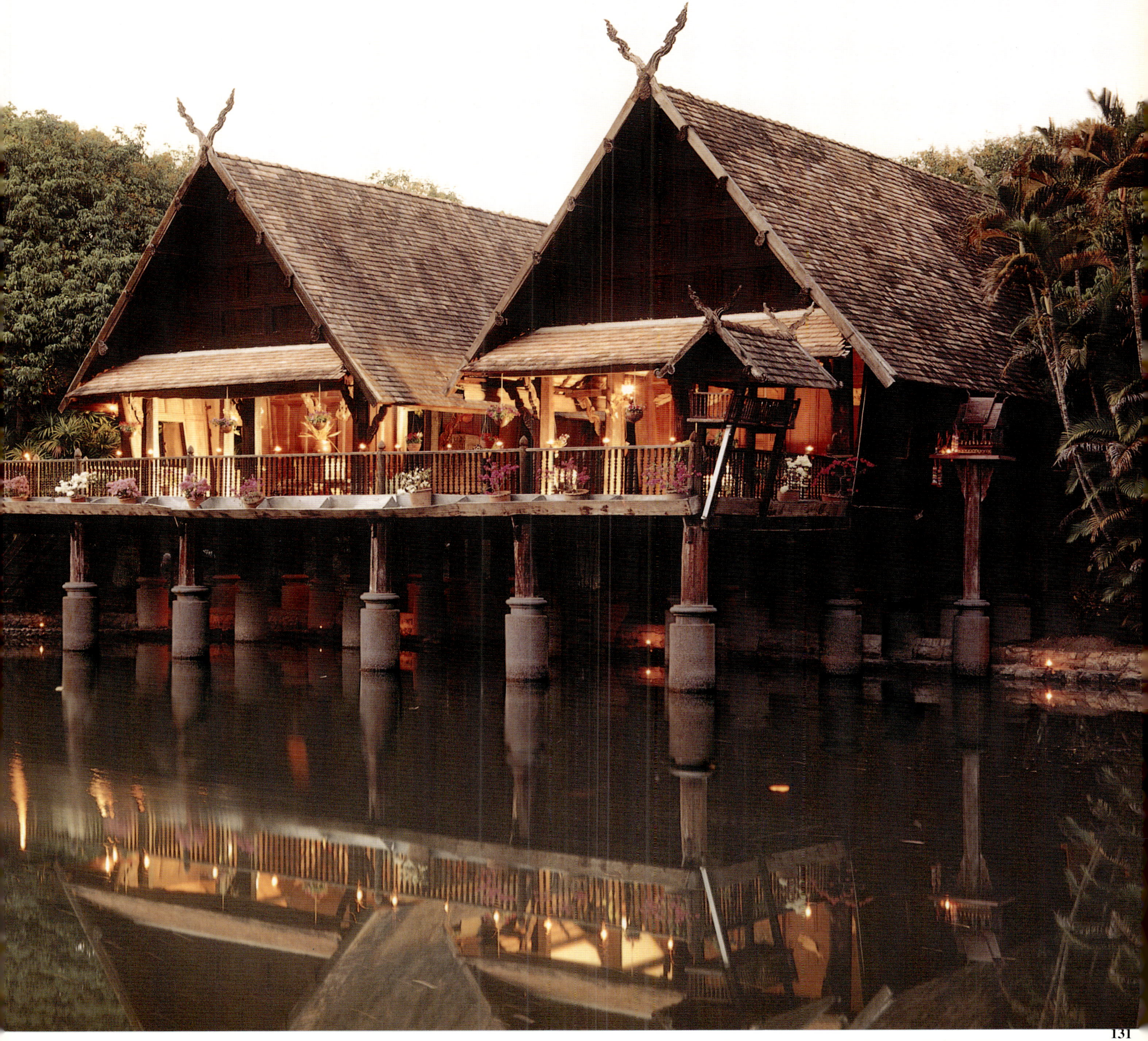

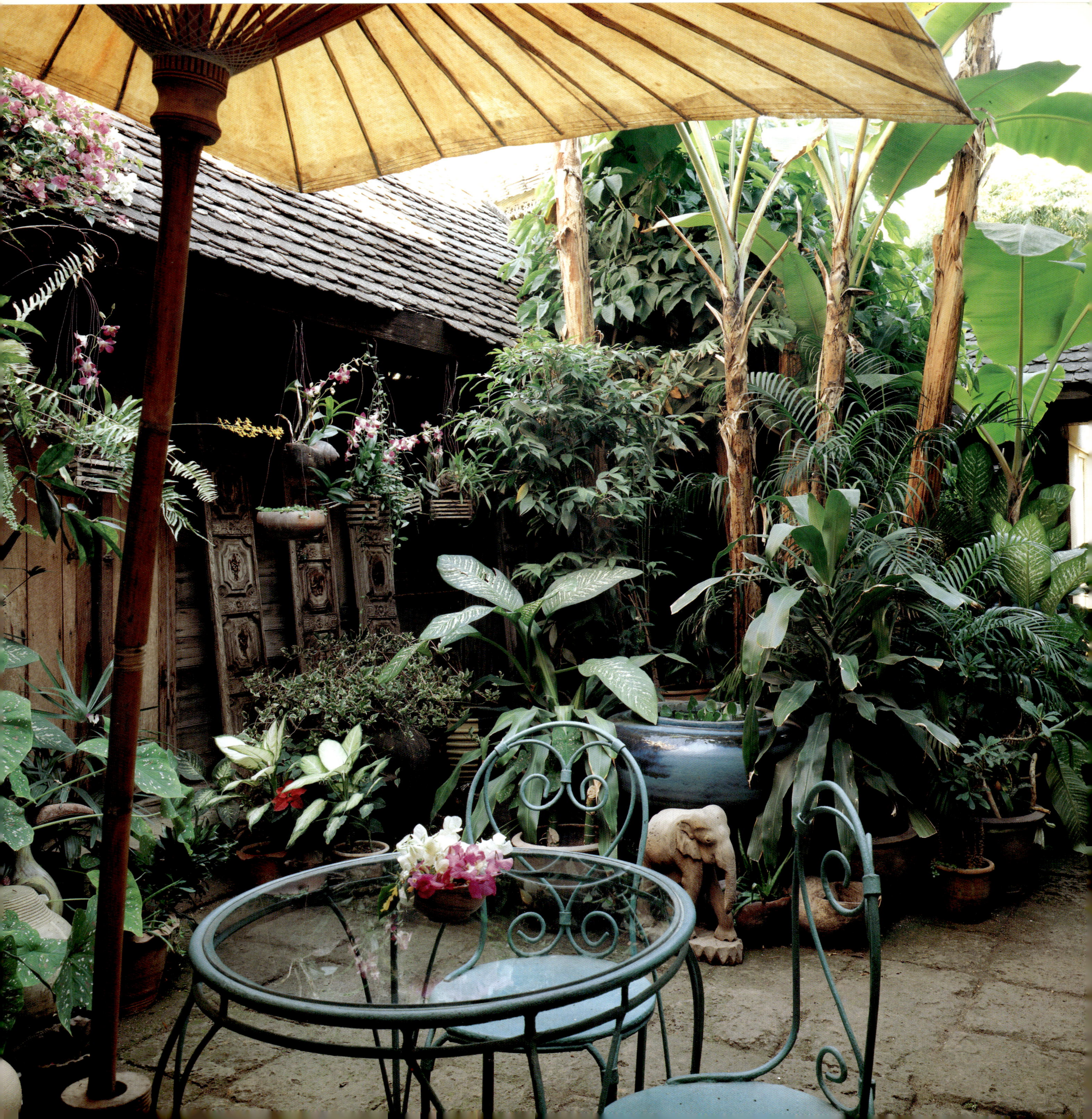

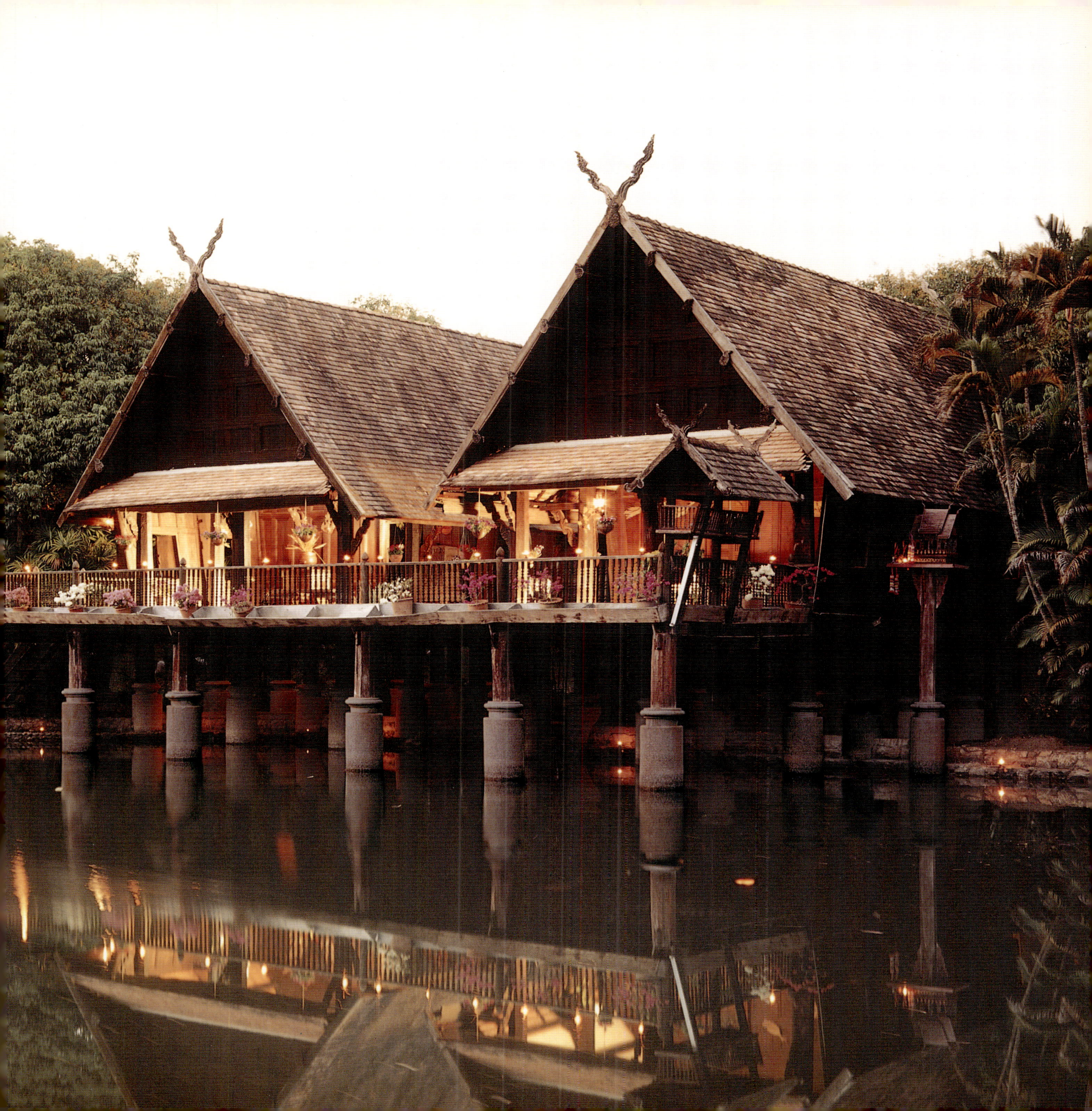

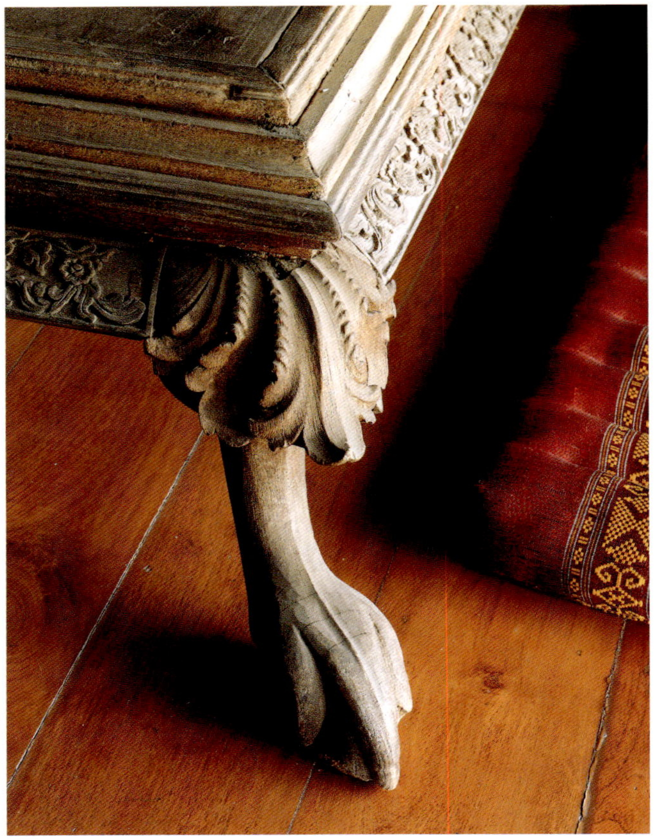

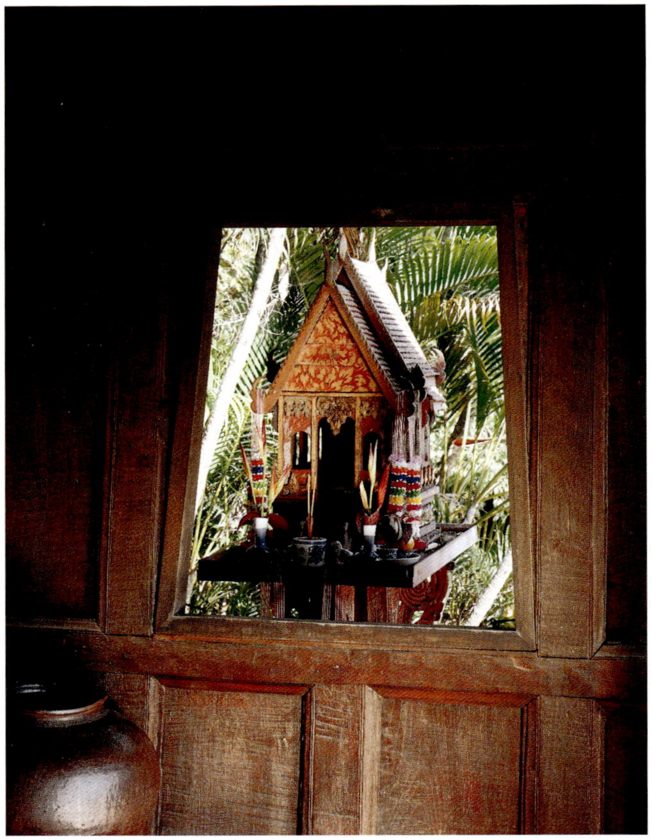

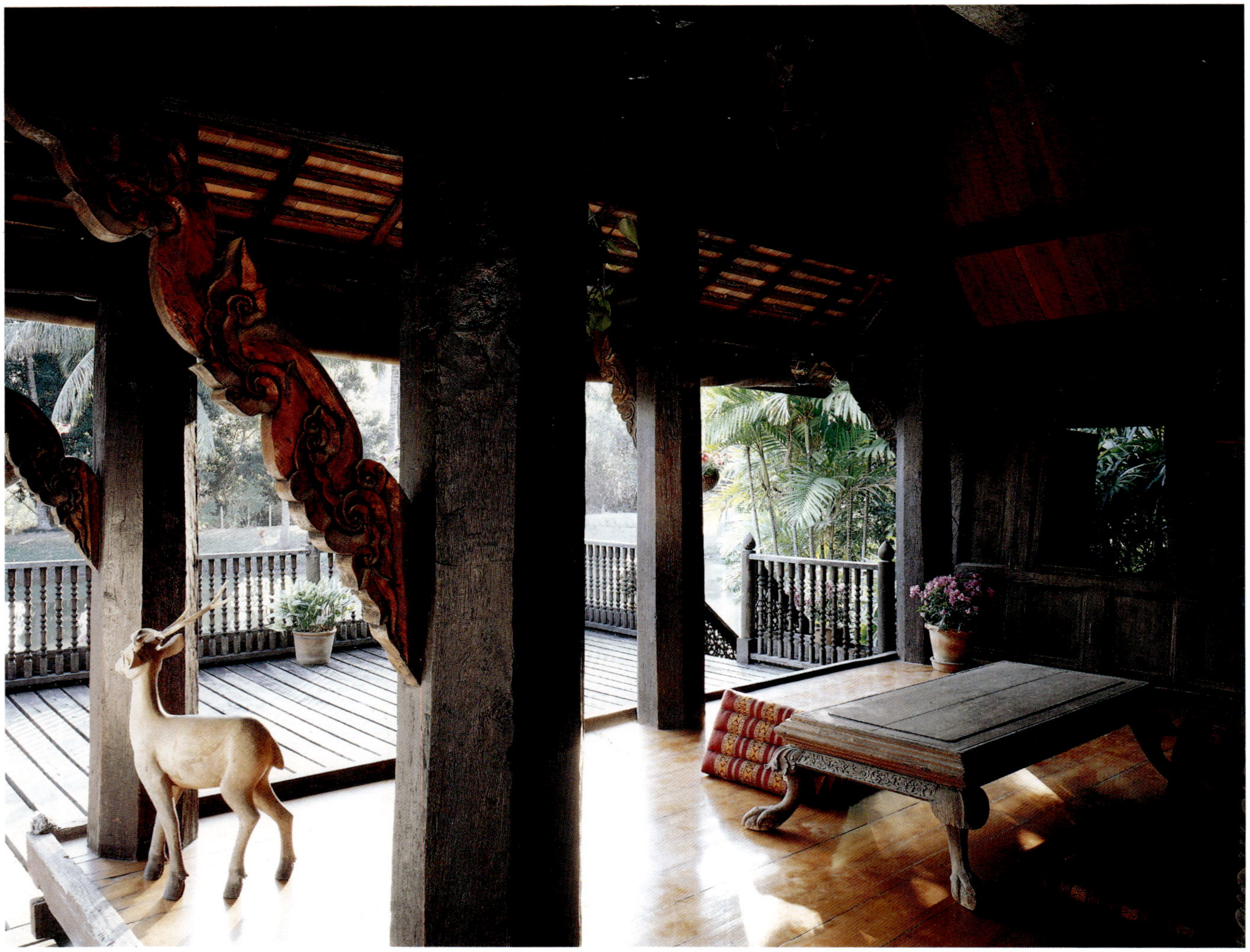

Right : *Sitting area, the carved vents encourage air circulation, while the bamboo poles facilitate repair work.*
Left : *The sitting area, opening to the verandah.*
Above far left : *Detail of a leg on an antique table.*
Above left : *The spirit house.*

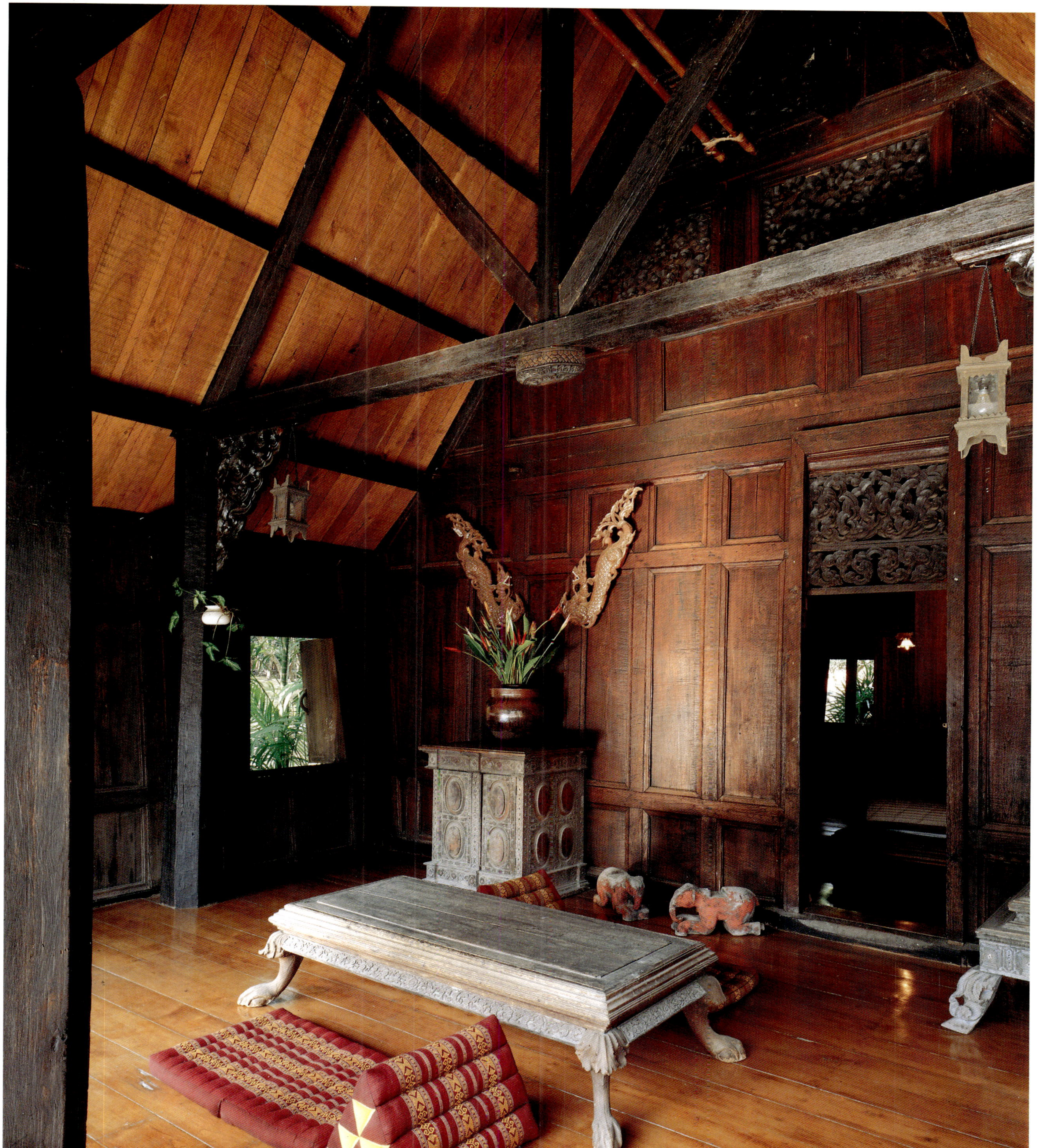

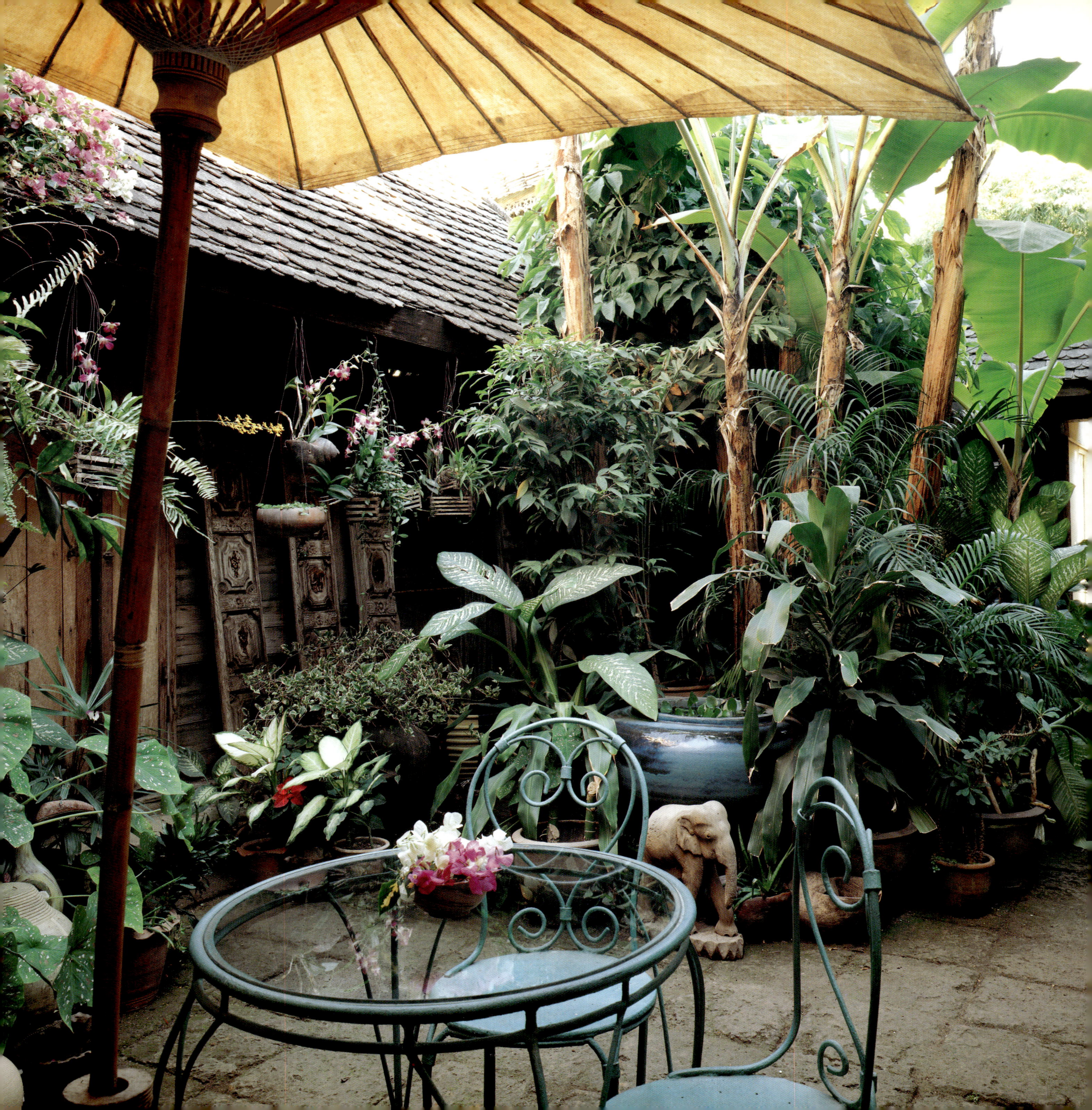

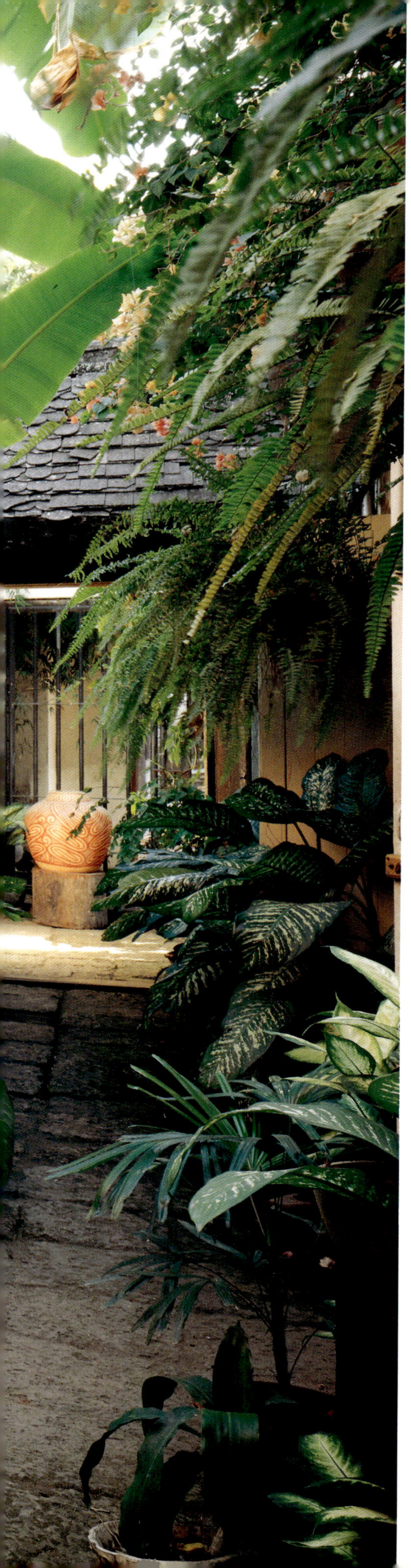

The Six Pole House

Chiang Mai

This shophouse was constructed during the reign of King Rama VI (1910-25) and is located on Charoen Rath Road, which runs along the east bank of the Ping River in Chiang Mai. At the time this was a predominantly Chinese trading area known as Tha Chang, or Elephant Landing, due to the fact that elephants once dragged logs to the river bank here to be floated downstream. The building originally served as a home as well as a shop and, at one time, a warehouse for rice; its survival is probably due to the fact that Chiang Mai's center of trade later shifted across to the west bank, where newer shops and markets replaced many older ones.

A two-story structure built of wood and masonry, it has a wooden colonade on the front supported by six columns, thus leading to its popular local name of the Six Pole House. An open courtyard at the rear is characteristic of Chinese houses, while above both doors and windows are intricately carved air vents. Between the ground and first floor is a trapdoor through which rice was moved in the days when the building was used as a warehouse.

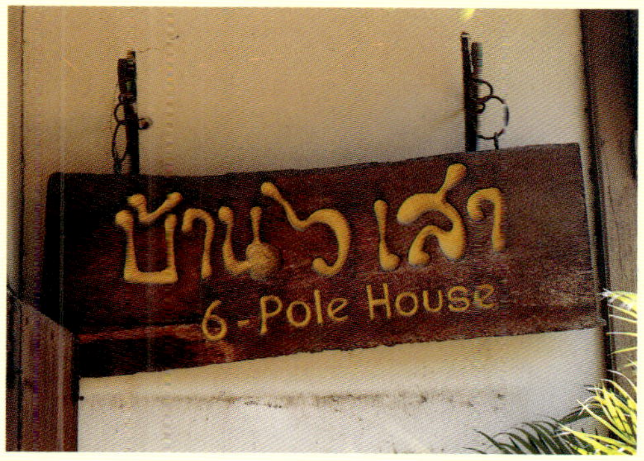

Long neglected, in 1991 the Six Pole House became a show room for Oriental Style, a company formed by a group of Thais and foreigners to provide quality items to interior decorators. The basic character of the old building was carefully preserved during the necessary renovations and, with its high ceilings, decorative carvings, and lush tropical courtyard, provides an evocative setting for the assorted antiques and locally-made items on display.

Left : *Interior courtyard of the Six Pole House, with bananas, Bougainvillea and other tropical plants.*
Above : *A wooden sign bearing the popular name for the house hangs above the entrance.*

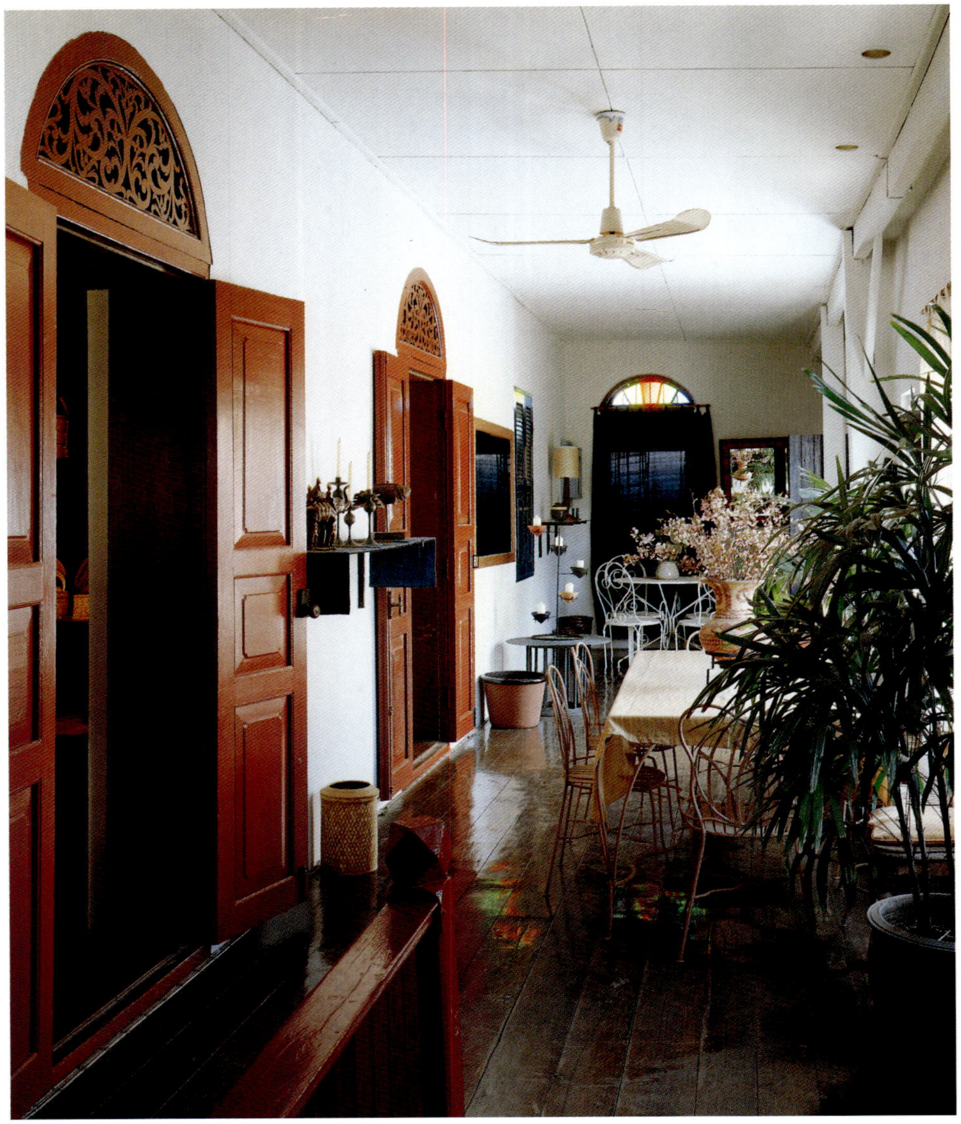

Below : *Exterior of the Six Pole House on Charoen Rath Road; the name derives from the six columns that support the colonade of the shophouse.*
Right : *The upstairs landing.*
Below right : *The courtyard.*
Opposite page : *Second-floor sitting room.*

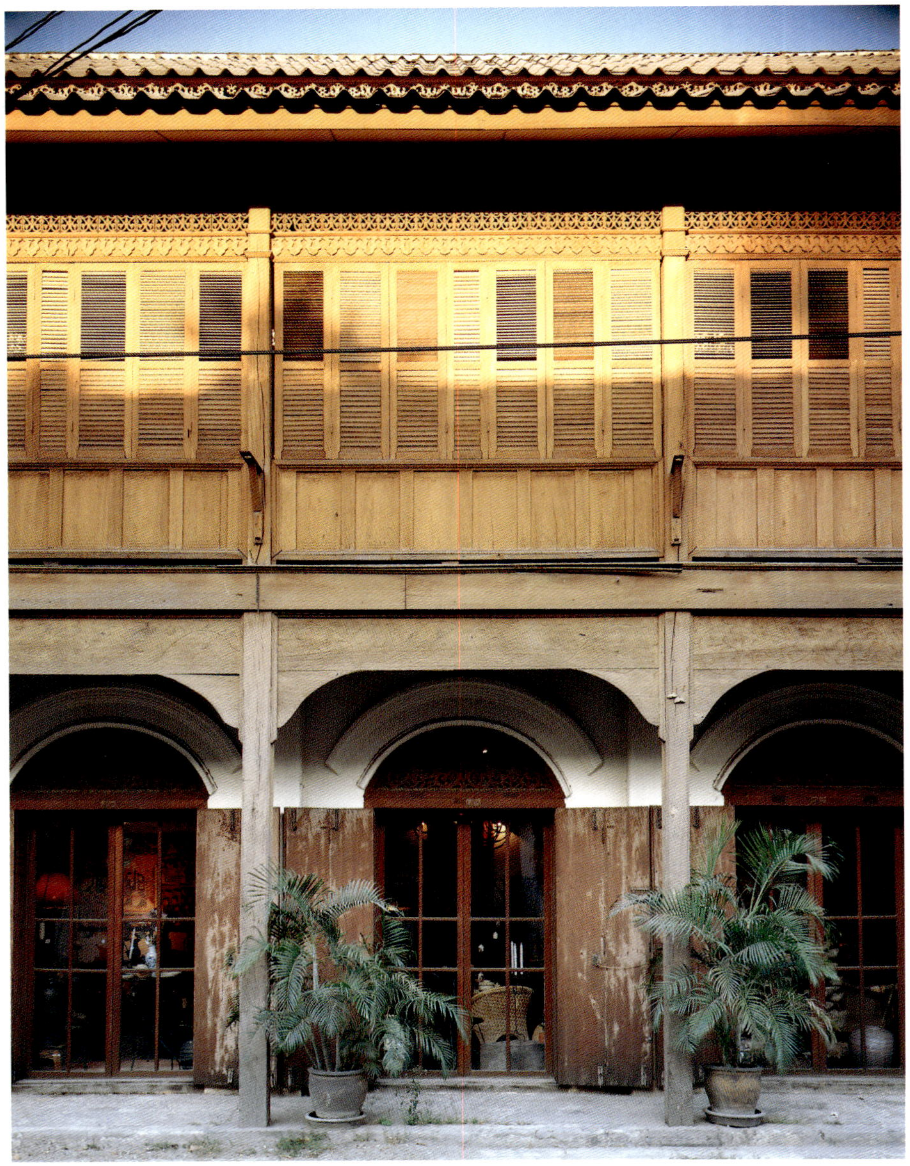

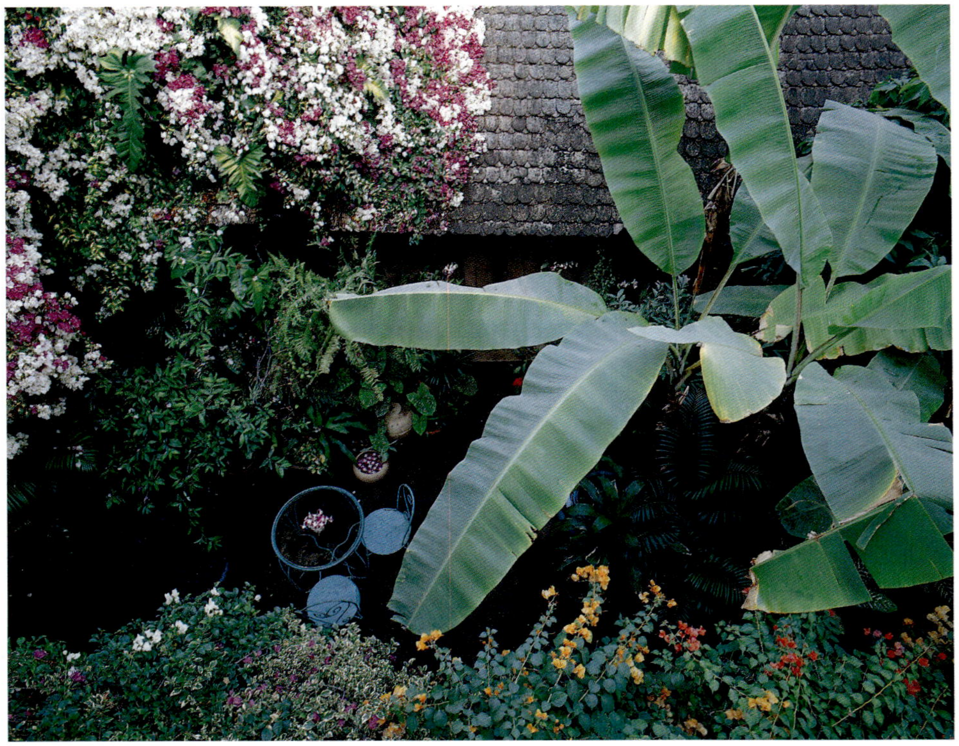

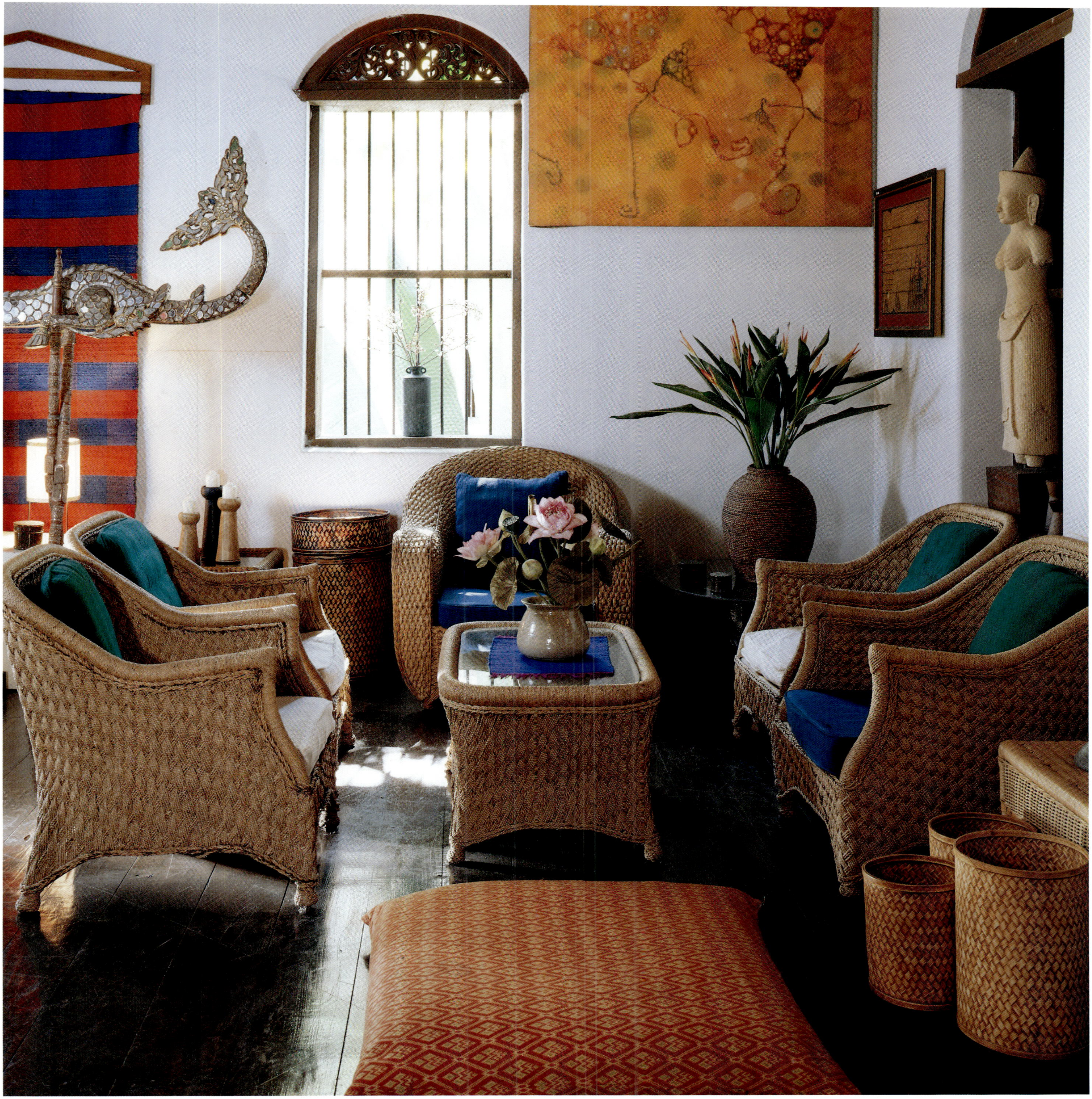

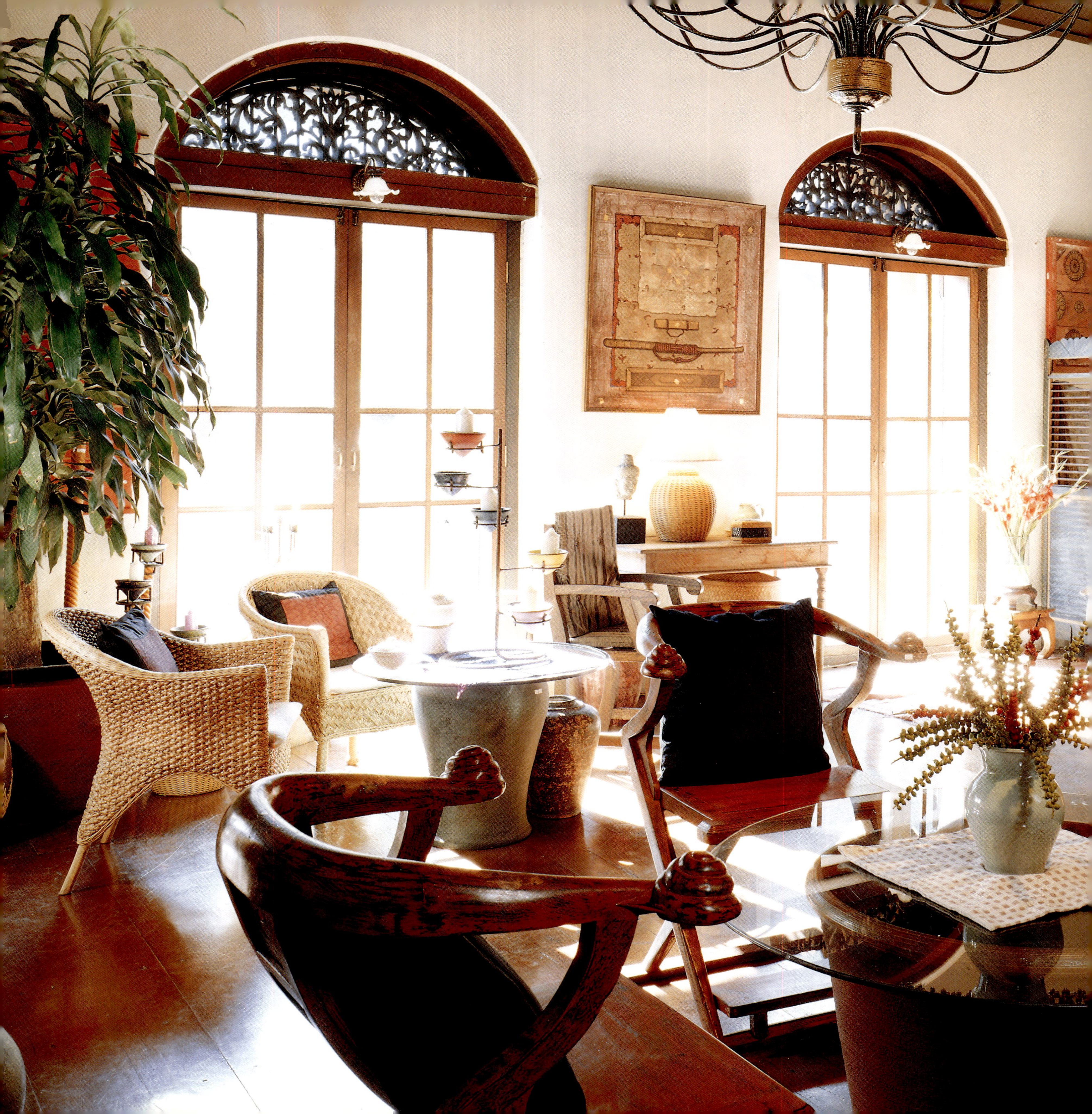

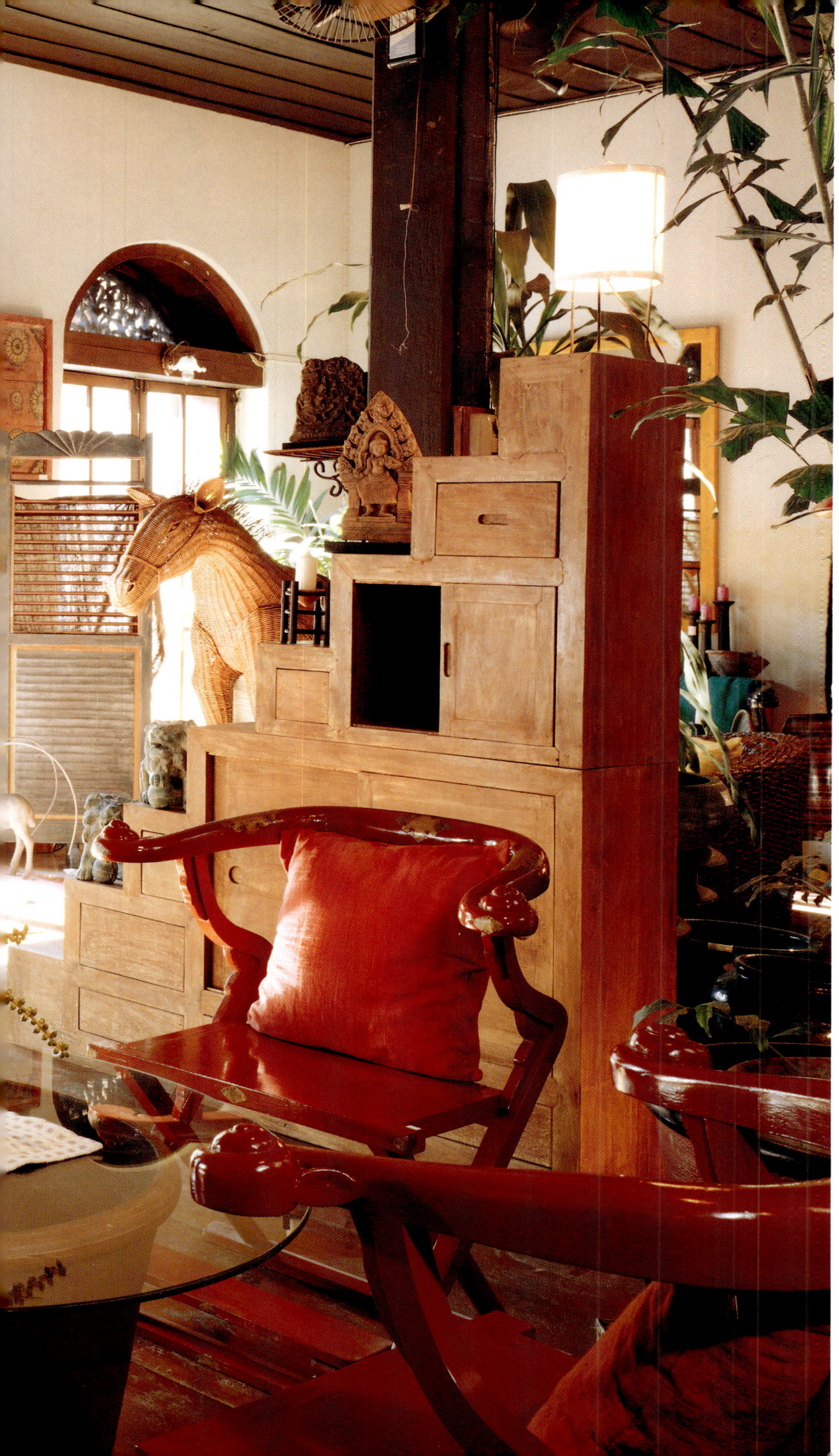

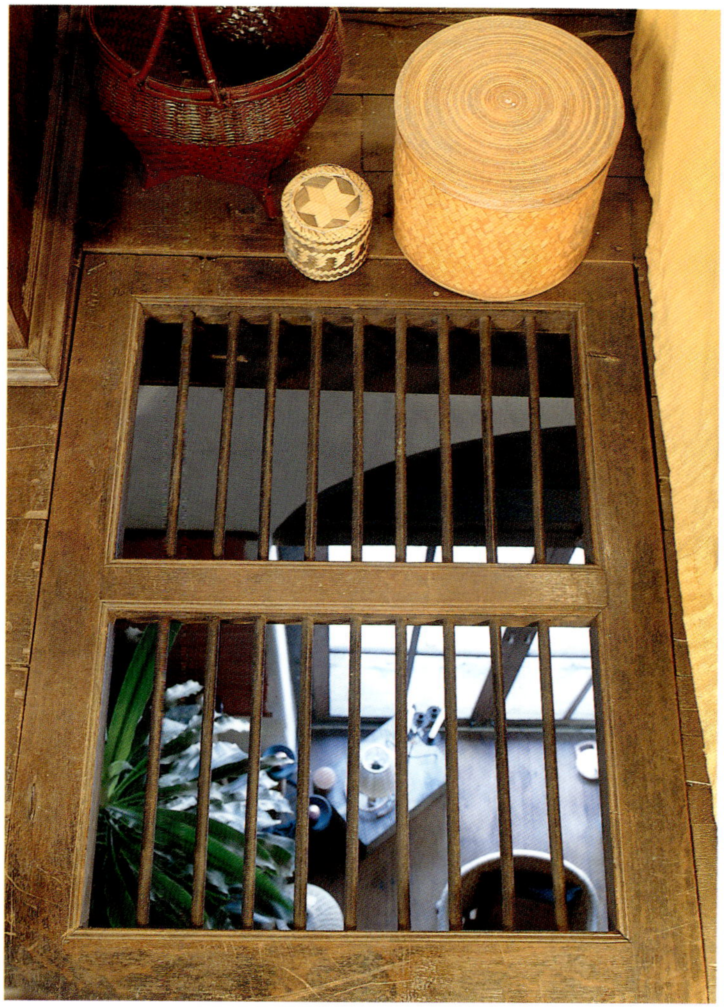

Left : *Ground floor of the shophouse, now an antique and furniture gallery, called Oriental Style.*
Above : *Trap-door, once used for conveying rice when the building was used for storing the grain.*

L'École Française D'Extrême-Orient
Chiang Mai

Though it has existed in its present form for a relatively short time, L'École Française d'Extrême-Orient is in fact composed of a number of old northern Thai houses and rice barns. Since all these were in danger of being destroyed and, moreover, since a conscious effort has been made to retain as much of the old feeling as possible, the complex deserves inclusion as an example of how buildings of architectural significance can be preserved even when moved from their original locations.

The center is located on Charoen Prathet Road, in the middle of Chiang Mai, on a large site granted to the French Government by King Rama V toward the end of the 19th century for the use of the French Consul. The property overlooks the Ping River and has many venerable trees from various parts of Thailand and neighboring countries. A plot on the opposite side of the road, formerly occupied by the Consulate, is now the Alliance Française.

Some 20 years ago, François Bizot, a member of L'École Française d'Extrême-Orient, a noted Buddhist scholar, and an admirer of Lanna-style architecture, conceived the idea of gathering several old teak houses and rice barns from Chambon, a village outside Chiang Mai. Like all traditional Thai residences, the structures consisted of prefabricated sections joined with wooden pegs and raised off the ground on a framework of stout columns. They were thus easily dismantled and moved to a new site, as indeed they may have been at earlier points in their long history. Mr. Bizot personally oversaw the process and drew up plans for the reconstruction; local carpenters were used for the job, under the leadership of a foreman named Sla-chai.

The present building was constructed in three phases at different times, demonstrating the practical nature of Thai houses which can be enlarged as the family expands. According to Dr. Louis Gabaude, also a Buddhist scholar presently stationed at the center, the French Government is allowing L'École Française d'Extrême-Orient to use the building as a place for research into the history, archaeology, and religion of the region. One of the important tasks in this work, for example, is the collection and repair of old Buddhist scriptures written in northern Thai dialect on rice paper, a task in which French experts on restoration and preservation are called upon for consultation.

Various parts of the center are used for an air-conditioned library and restoration room, offices, and living quarters for the staff.

Right : *East side of the house facing the Ping River.*

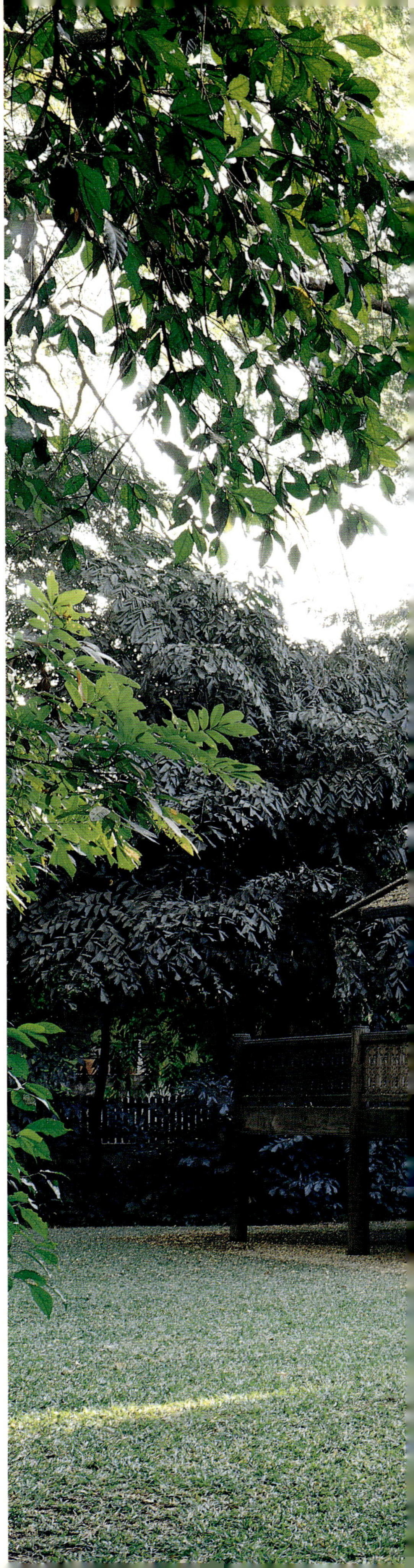

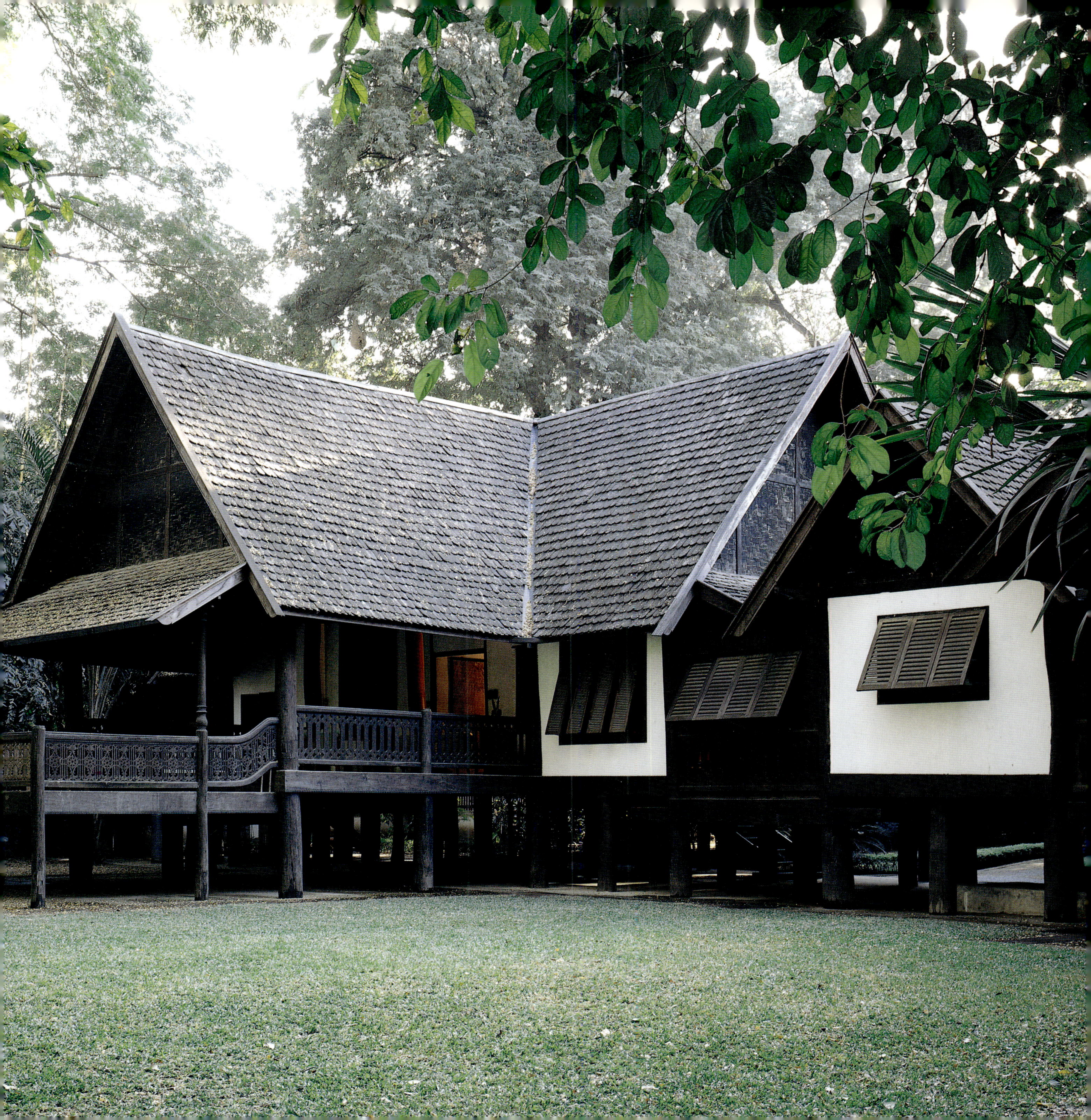

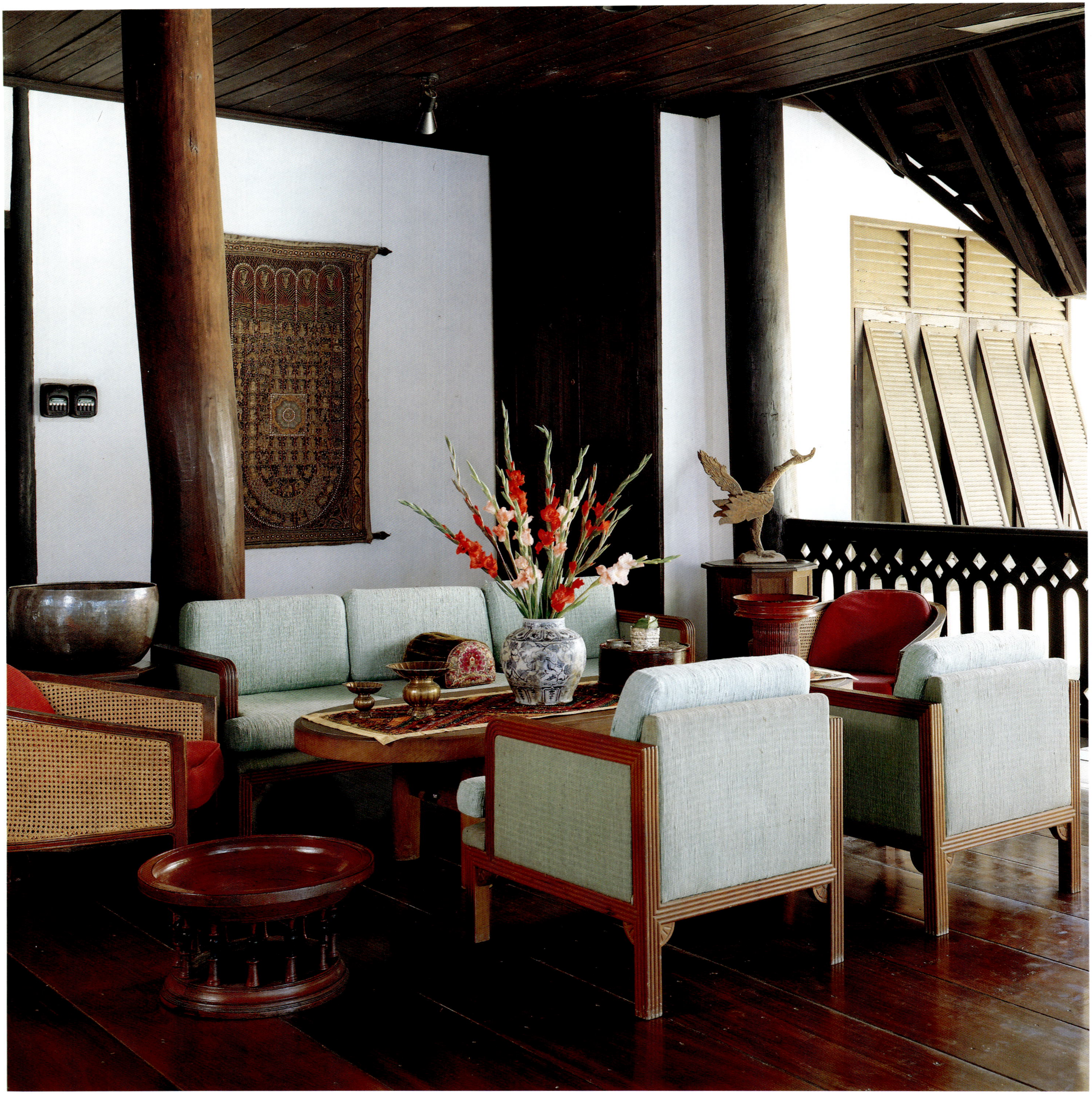

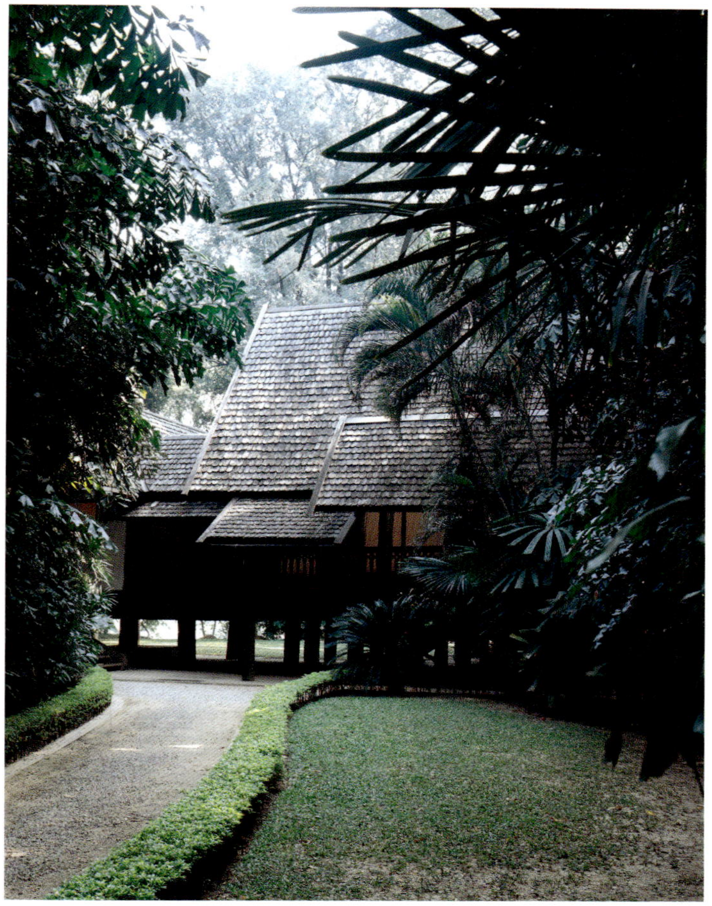

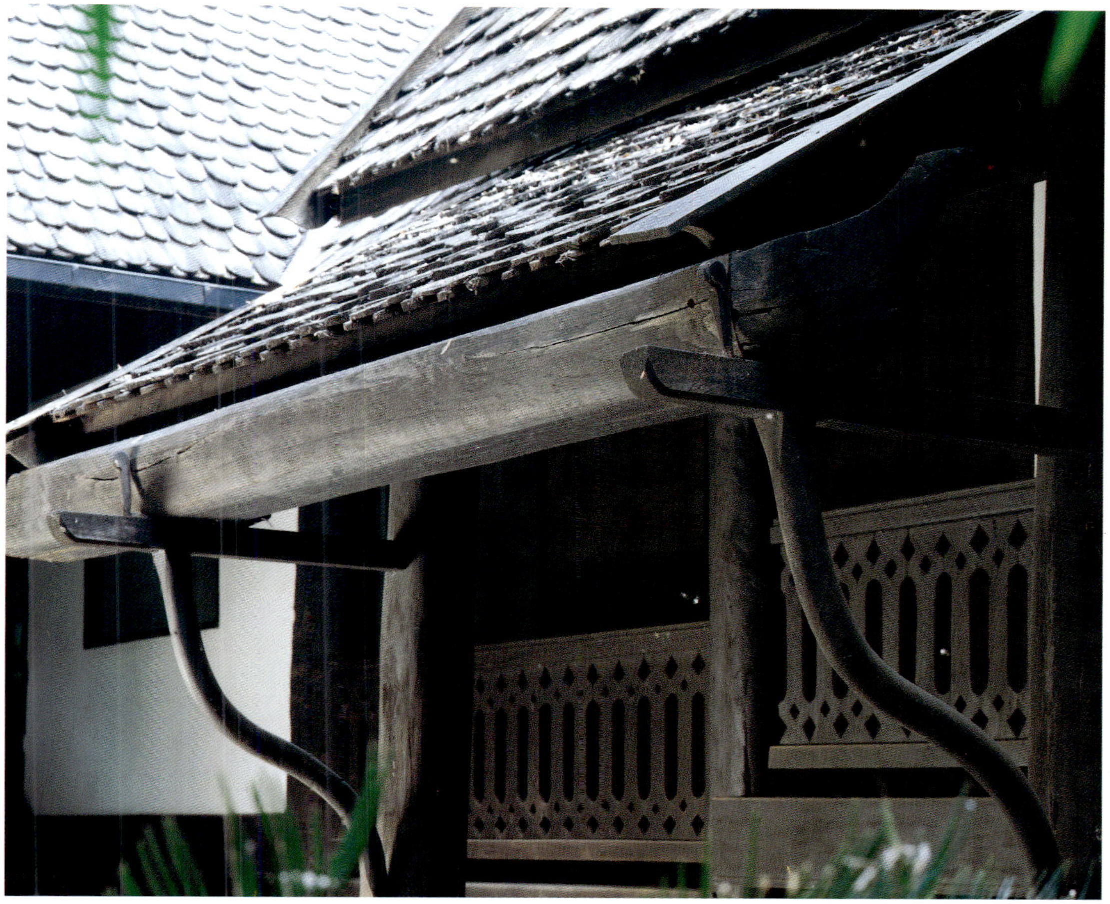

Opposite page : *Verandah which serves as a sitting area.*
Above : *Approach to the house, which is set in a grove of old trees gathered from all over the country.*
Above right : *Teakwood rain gutter.*
Right : *A Rain Tree beside the river towers over the house.*

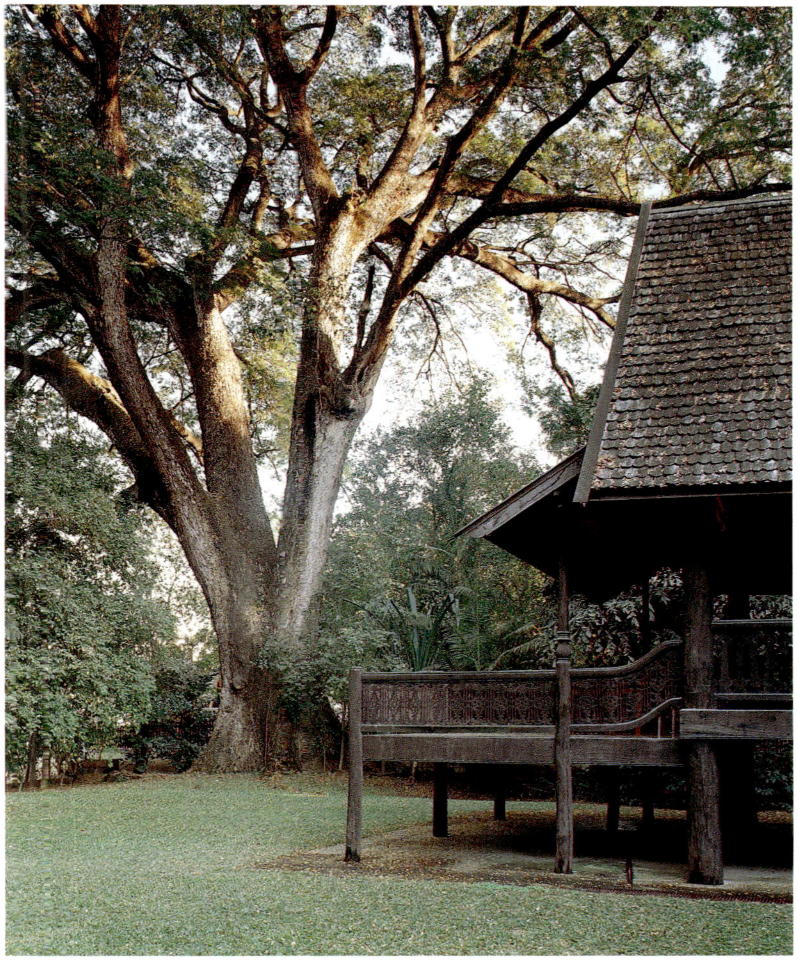

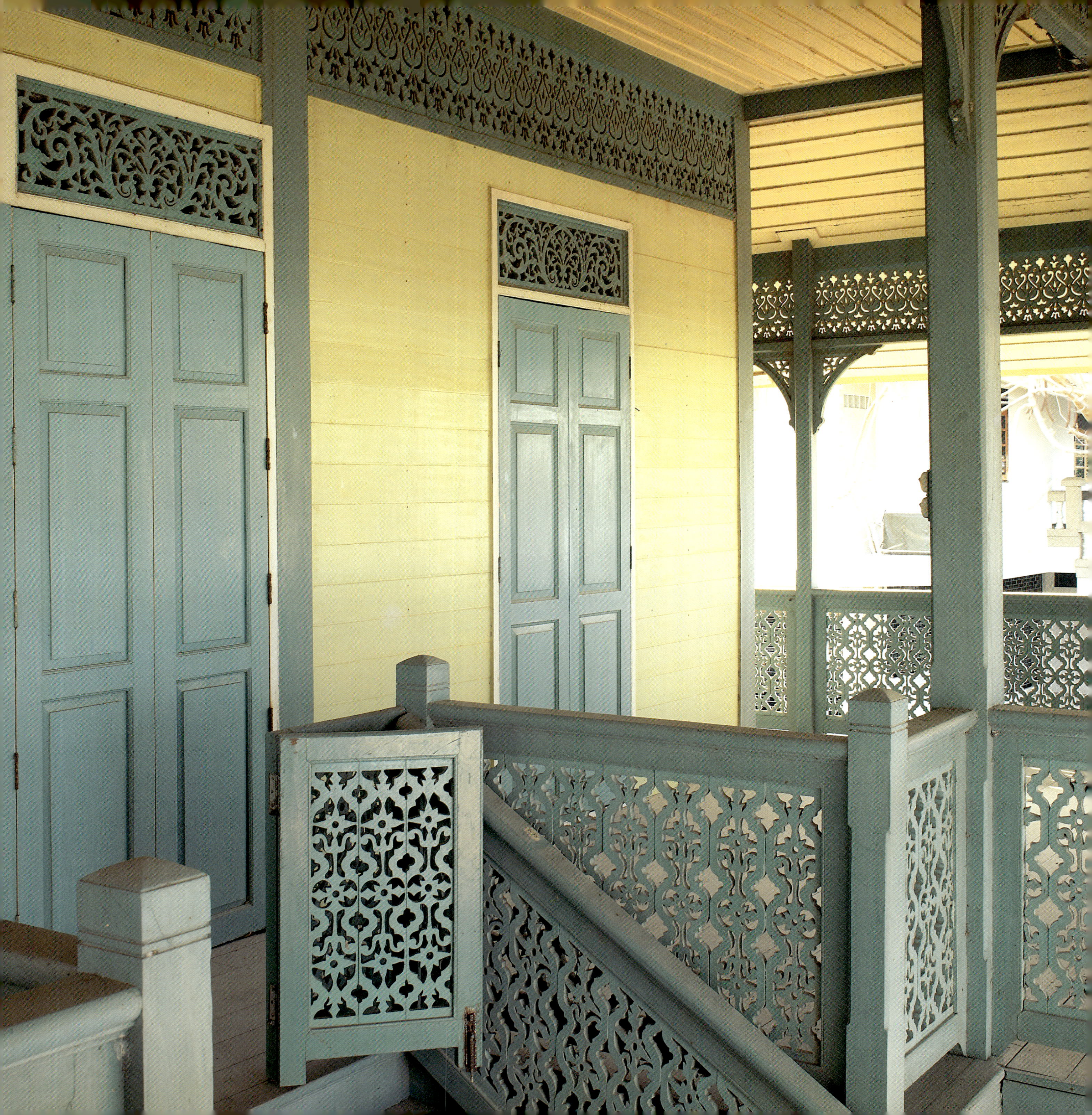

The South

Culturally and economically, the south has played a prominent role in Thai history. Early Chinese and Indian traders began coming to the lower parts of the century at least a thousand years ago in search of such valuable local products as gold, tin, spices, scented woods, rhinoceros horn, and edible birds' nests harvested from lofty limestone caves. They brought with them new ideas both social and religious, which eventually, in one form or another, spread far beyond the original point of contact and had a profound influence on the country's later development.

In terms of domestic architecture, scarcely anything remains of these significant cultural influences. The oldest residences date only from the late 19th and early 20th century, especially in such centers as Phuket and Songkhla.

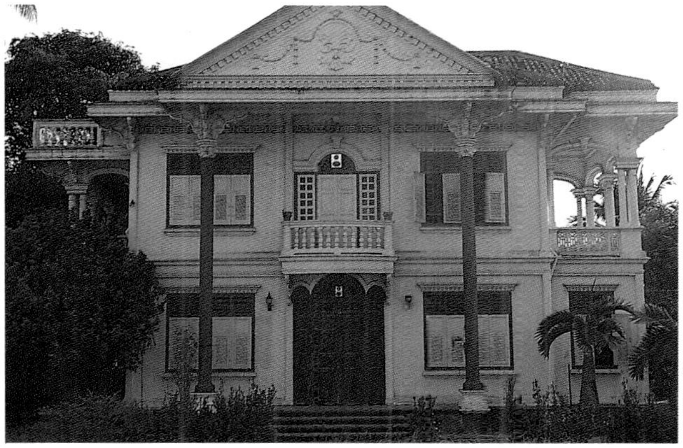

Phuket was already a prosperous island when Bangkok became the Thai capital, its economy based on seemingly endless deposits of tin ore, a commodity for which Thailand was virtually the only Asian source until the British opened mines in Malaysia. During the 19th century, thousands of Chinese immigrants came to work in the industry and some who achieved success built splendid mansions in the provincial capital. In style, these were mostly inspired by houses in Malacca and Singapore, a blend of Western and Chinese features and designed to accommodate large extended families. Many still survive, thanks to the fact that they are far from the areas of tourist development that has transformed so much of Phuket, and are still owned by descendants of the original builders.

Songkhla, once known as Singhora, was also an important port in the past, the only natural shelter in the lower part of the Gulf of Thailand. It, too, was mainly settled by Chinese traders, some of whom, like the Na Songkhla family, became important officials in the Thai government; the Na Songkhla mansion, which once served as the town hall, has been preserved and is now a branch of the National Museum.

A later scene of development, further up the western coast of the gulf, was Hua Hin. The first small holiday home on this scenic beach was built in 1913 by Prince Chakrabongse, a son of King Rama V, and his Russian-born wife. This was later replaced by a much larger one designed by an English architect, of which Prince Chakrabongse wrote, "Being in the new house is like being in a ship...the balcony resembles a deck and the various rooms are like cabins, and one hears all the time the sounds of the waves and the wind..." With the opening of the southern railway line a decade or so later, Hua Hin became a popular retreat for Bangkok aristocrats, many of whom also built bungalows there.

Prince Chakrabongse's house was taken down some years ago and moved to another picturesque setting. Other, less fortunate old residences in the area have vanished to make way for modern condominiums and hotels, though a few still survive to recall the leisurely past of Thailand's first seaside resort.

Left : *Tropical colors on Kitikong Villa in Hua Hin.*
Above : *An abandoned house in Phuket town, displaying Sino-Portuguese architecture.*

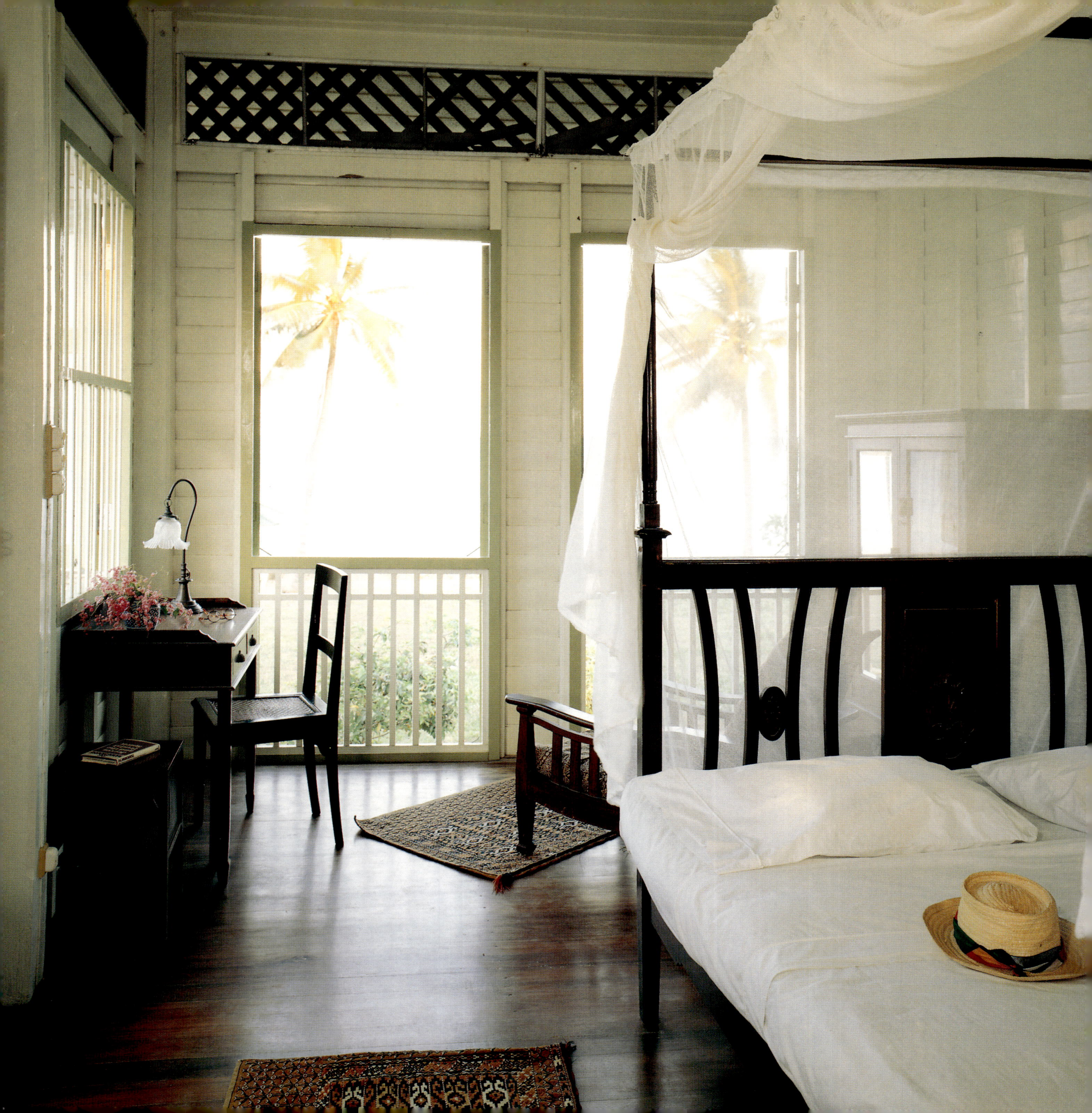

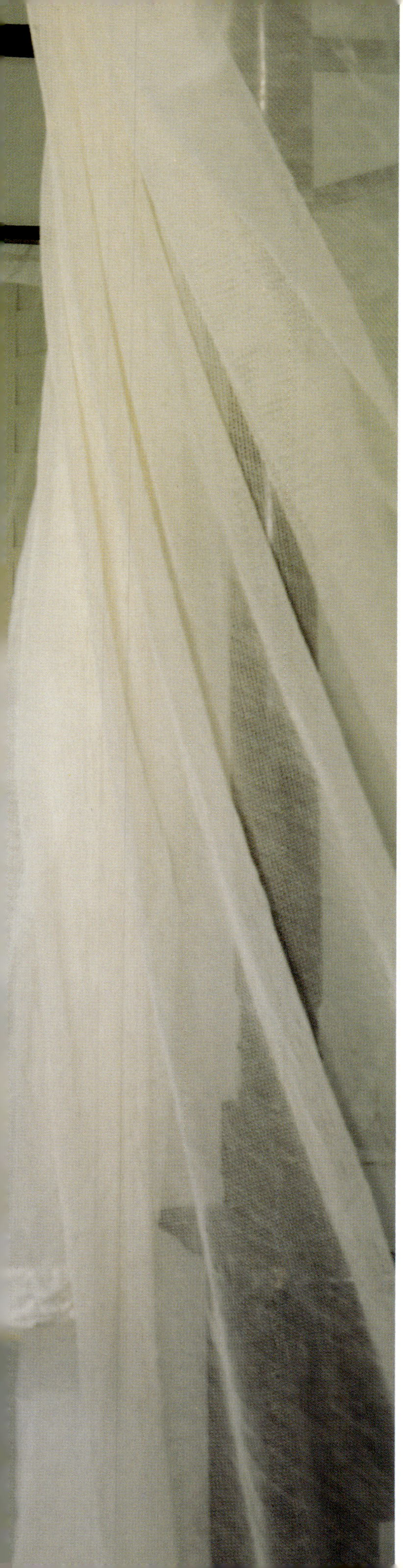

Sawang A-rom Villa
Hua Hin

Overlooking the beach at Hua Hin, Sawang A-Rom Villa was designed and built in 1935 by the current owner's parents, Phya and Thanpuying Manavarajsevi. The name they selected, meaning "bright mood," seemed suitable for a place in which they planned to relax and recover their energies before coming back to work in the city.

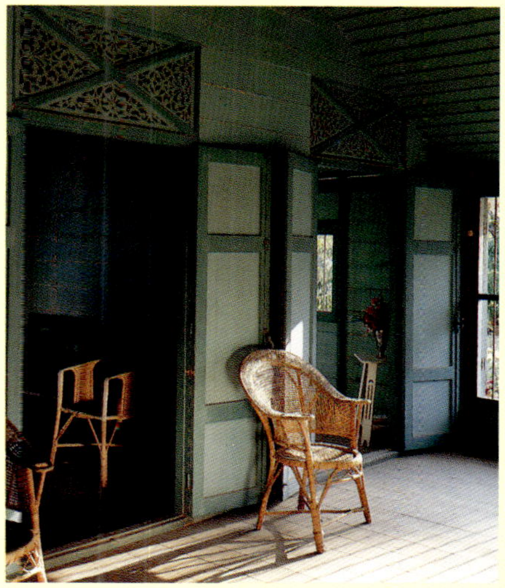

The main house, an all teak structure, has a sitting room, four bedrooms, a dining room, a bath, and a storage room; the dining room is located in the center, with the other rooms leading off from it, all open to sea breezes during the day and those from the hills behind at night. In addition, there is an annex with a kitchen, bath, and two additional bedrooms.

By 1989, when Phya Manavarajsevi's grandson, Khun Dechapiwat Na Songkhla and his wife, M.L. Rojanatorn, decided to restore the house, it had fallen into a state of considerable disrepair. Termites had eaten away much of the wood, and the stairs were collapsing. In making repairs, the couple used old wood from a supply they had at their Bangkok home and also managed to find diamond-shaped "kite" roof tiles to replace the original ones, which they considered crucial to maintaining the appearance of the residence.

The result is typical of many villas at Hua Hin, which became Thailand's principal seaside resort when the southern railway line made it easily accessible to the capital during the 1920s. Like their ancestors, Khun Dechapiwat and M.L. Rojanatorn close up their Bangkok residence and take the whole household with them for an annual holiday. A further link with the past is the caretaker of the property, whose father and grandfather also served in the same capacity.

Left : *One of the bedrooms of Sawang A-rom Villa overlooking the sea.*
Above : *Carved vents above the doors of an adjacent house in the family compound.*

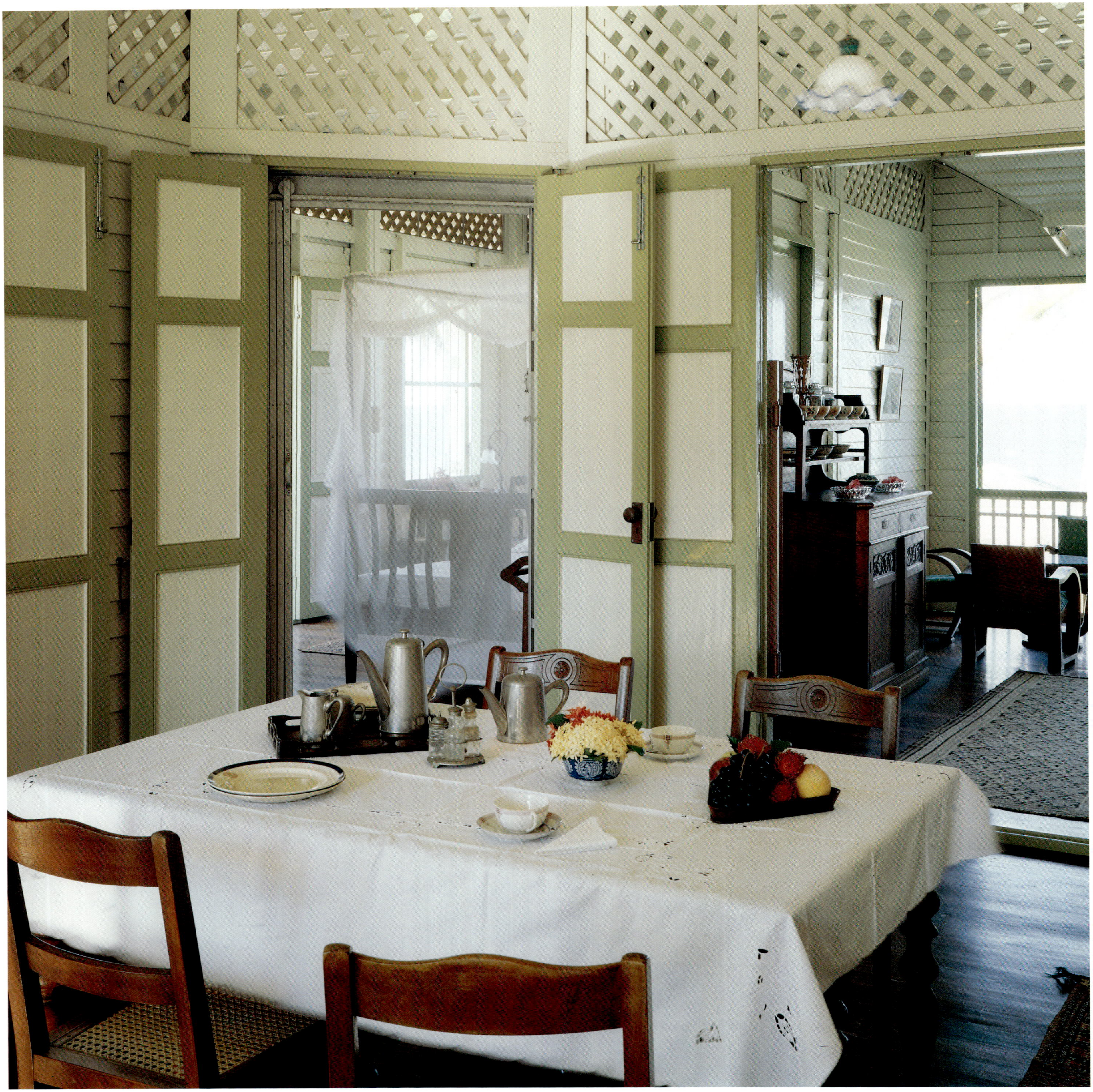

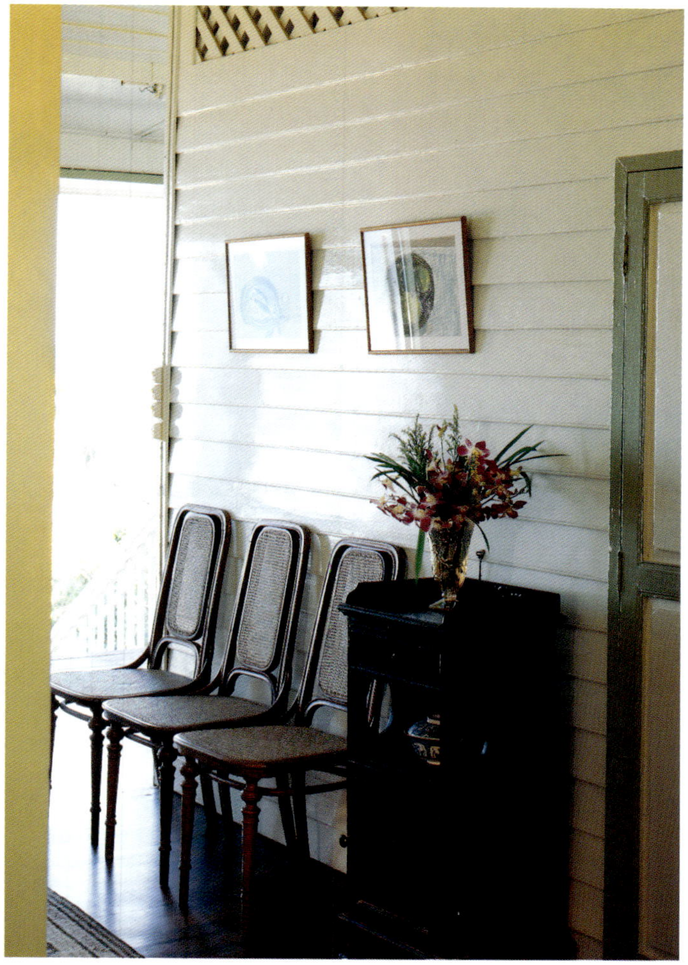

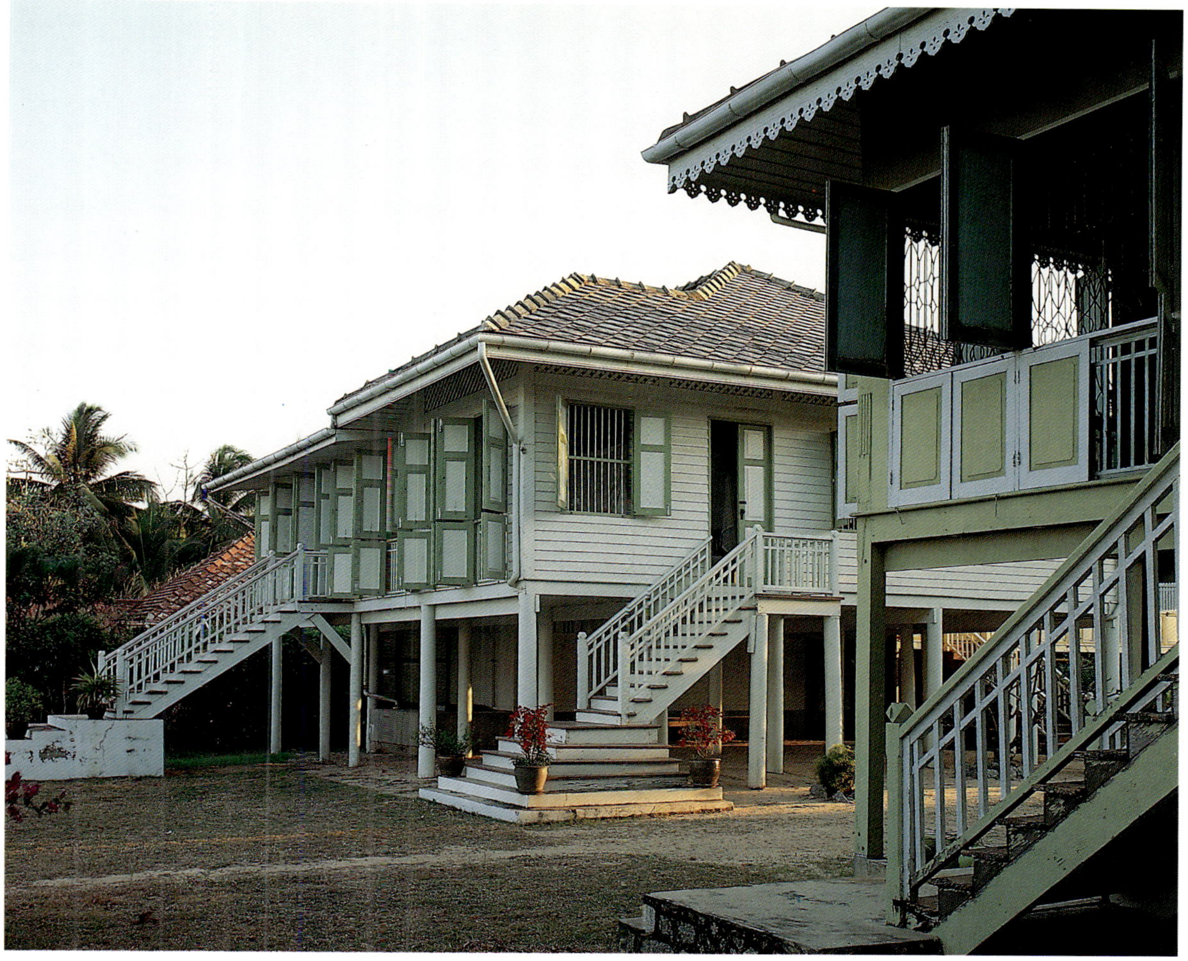

Opposite page: *Dining room, located in the center of the house with the bedrooms and sitting verandahs on either side.*
Above left : *part of a sitting area.*
Above right : *Exterior of one of the two houses in the compound.*
Right : *An old sideboard in one of the sitting areas.*

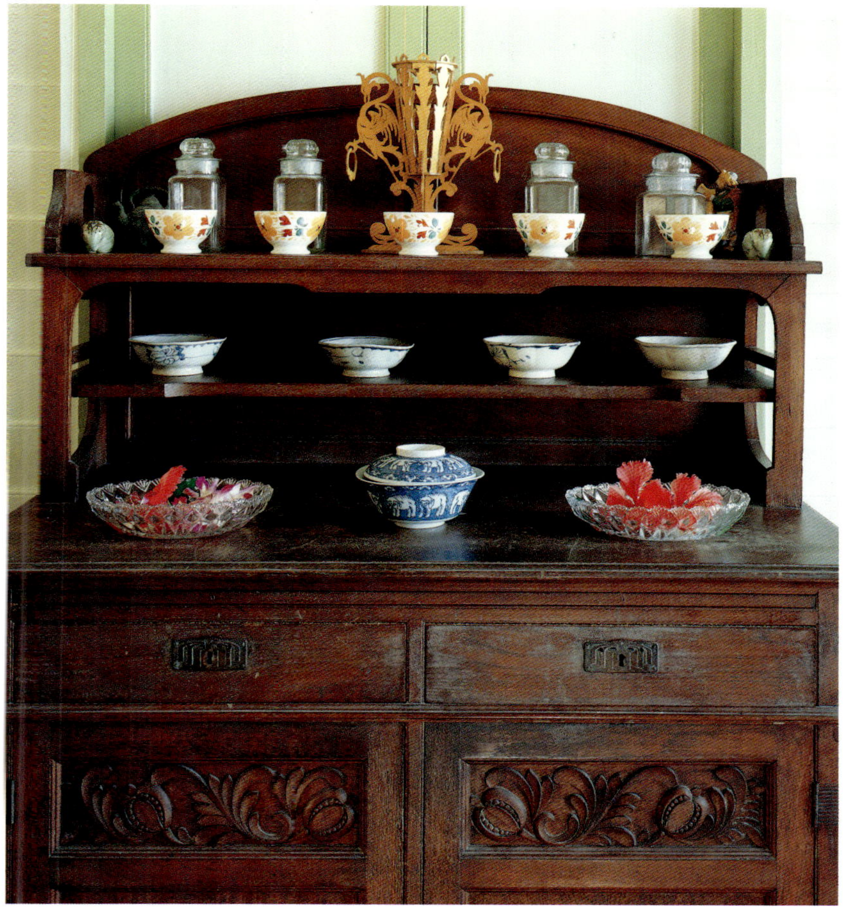

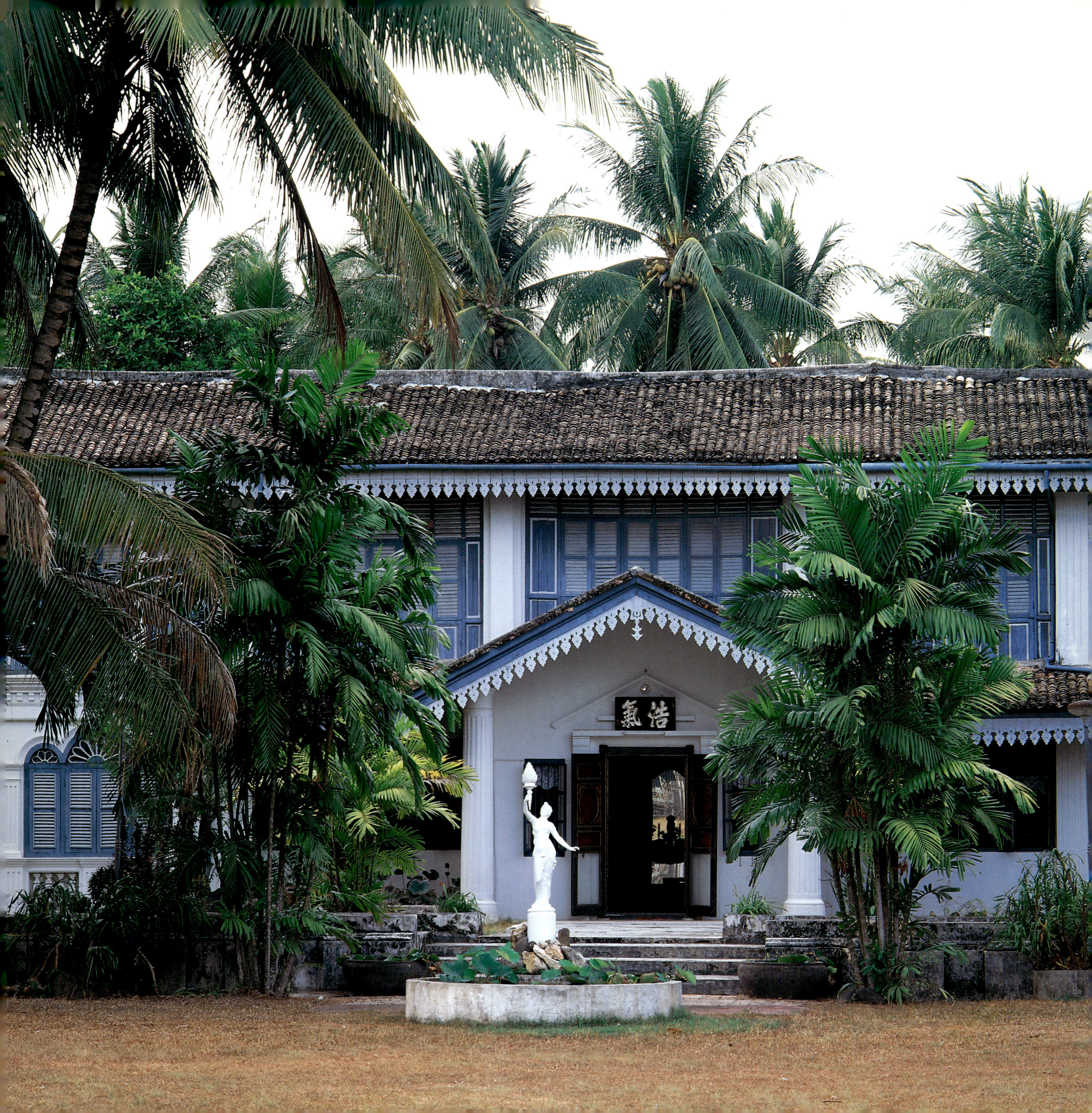
浩氣

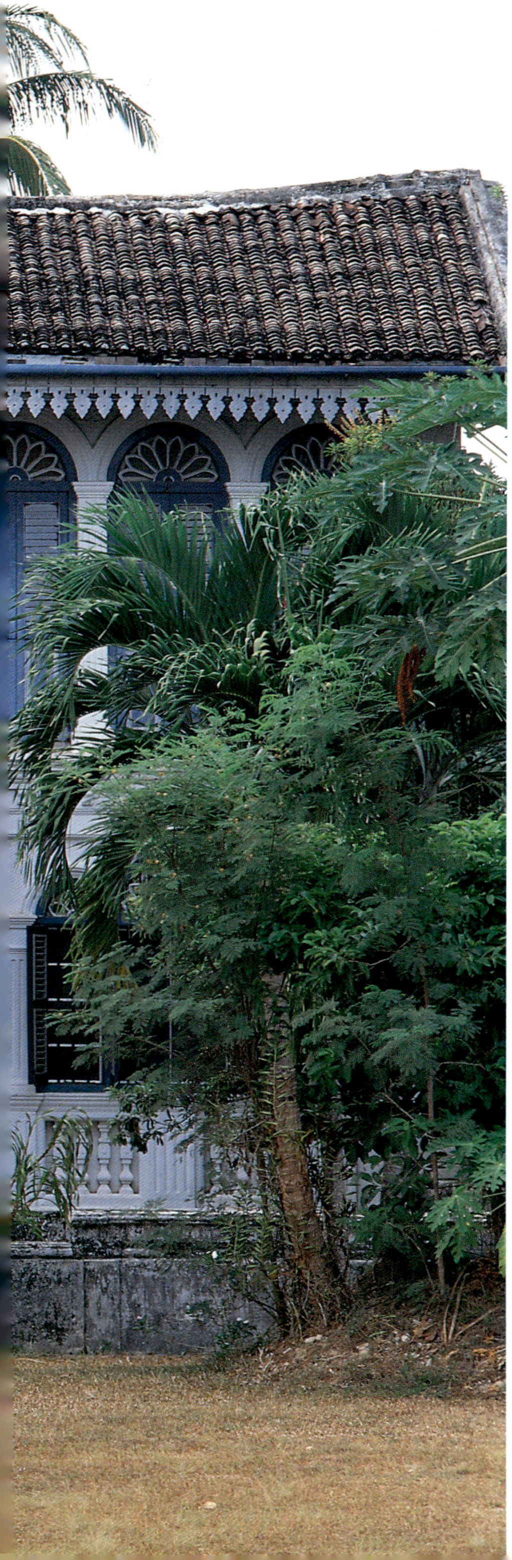

Chyn Pracha Mansion

Phuket

Chyn Pracha Mansion was built in 1907 by Phra Phitak Chyn Pracha, a Phuket-born Chinese who operated a number of the island's prosperous tin mines. His father in turn had been a general in the Chinese army who had emigrated to Phuket during the Ch'ing period and married a local girl, with whom he had eight sons and five daughters. Penang in those days was more easily accessible than distant Bangkok, which was why Phra Phitak Chyn Pracha was sent there for his education. It was in Penang that he became familiar with the Sino-Portuguese style of architecture; later, in fact, he used a building contractor from the British-held island when he came to build his residence.

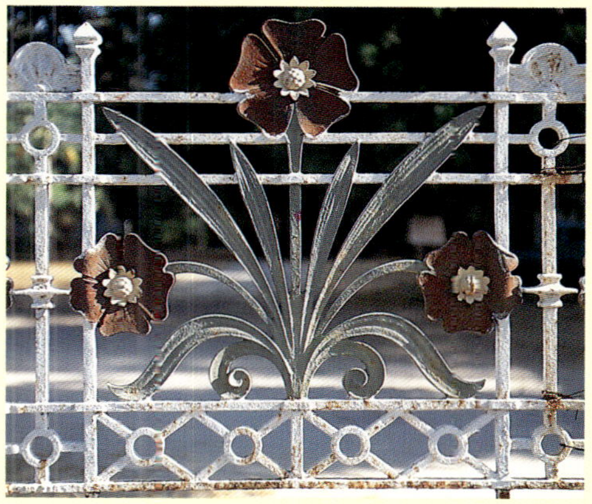

The house stands on a 3-rai site, facing south to catch any available breeze. Like others of its type in Penang and Malacca, it has an open courtyard in the center for further air circulation. The floor tiles were imported from Italy, while the wrought-iron fence came from Holland, evidence of both the affluence and cosmopolitan nature of Phuket during the early years of the present century.

According to the present owner, Khun Pracha Tandavanitj, grandson of the builder, the front section of the house was removed by his father, apparently because he considered the house too large, with the result that only 30-40 per cent of the original residence remains. Khun Pracha, however, has endeavored to preserve the existing structure, even to the extent of retaining the old roof tiles, which by now are brittle and leak during rains.

The classic style of the house has led to its use as a setting in a number of films, most recently Oliver Stone's "Heaven and Earth".

Left : *The front of Chyn Pracha Mansion, facing south onto Krabi Road in old town Phuket.*
Above : *Detail of wrought-iron fence from Holland.*

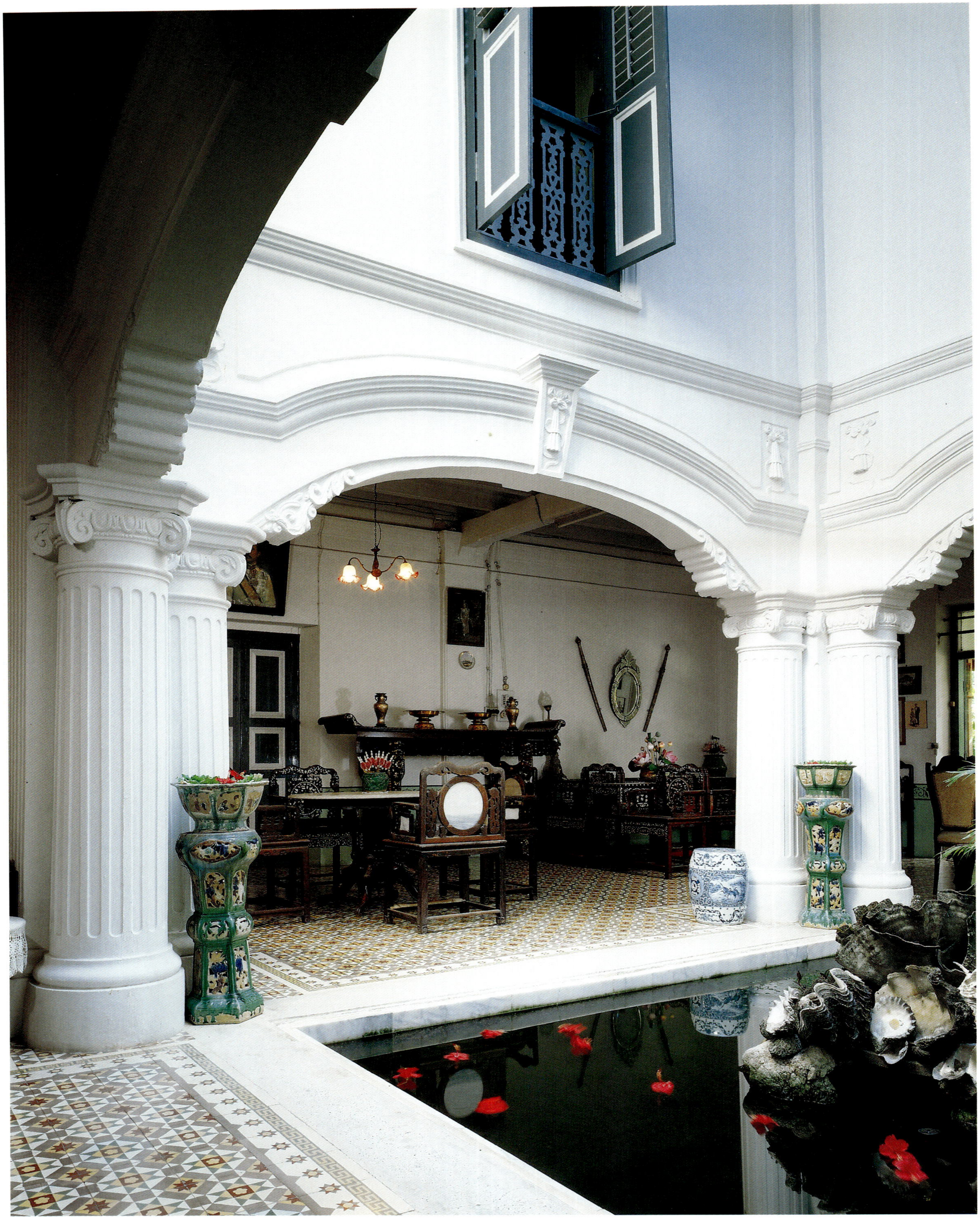

Left : *Interior courtyard, open to the sky.*
Right : *Old photograph, dated 1920, showing Chyn Pracha Mansion before the front part of the house was removed.*
Below : *Detail of window and eave decorations.*
Below right : *East facade of the house, showing stucco decorations and carved wooden fretwork.*

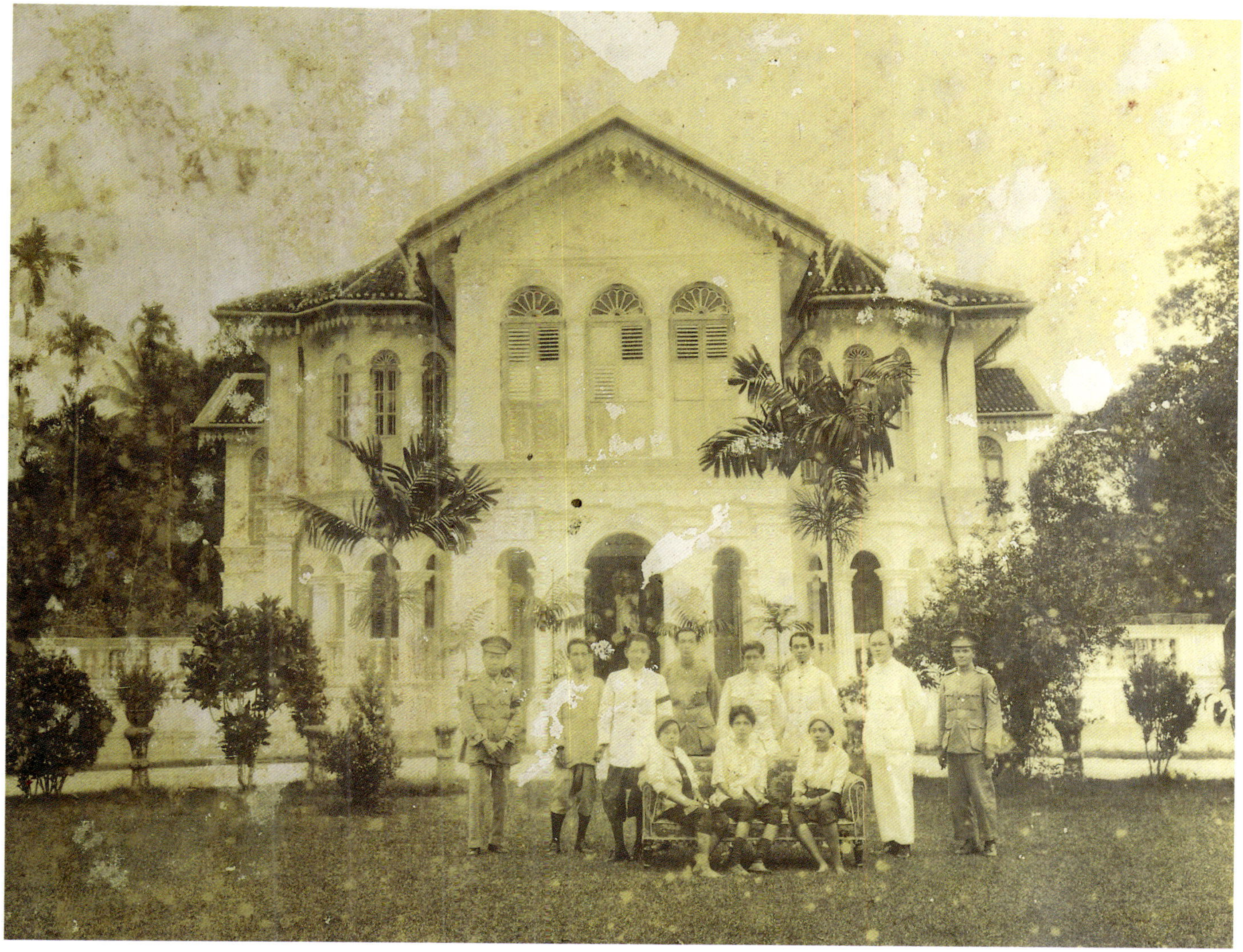

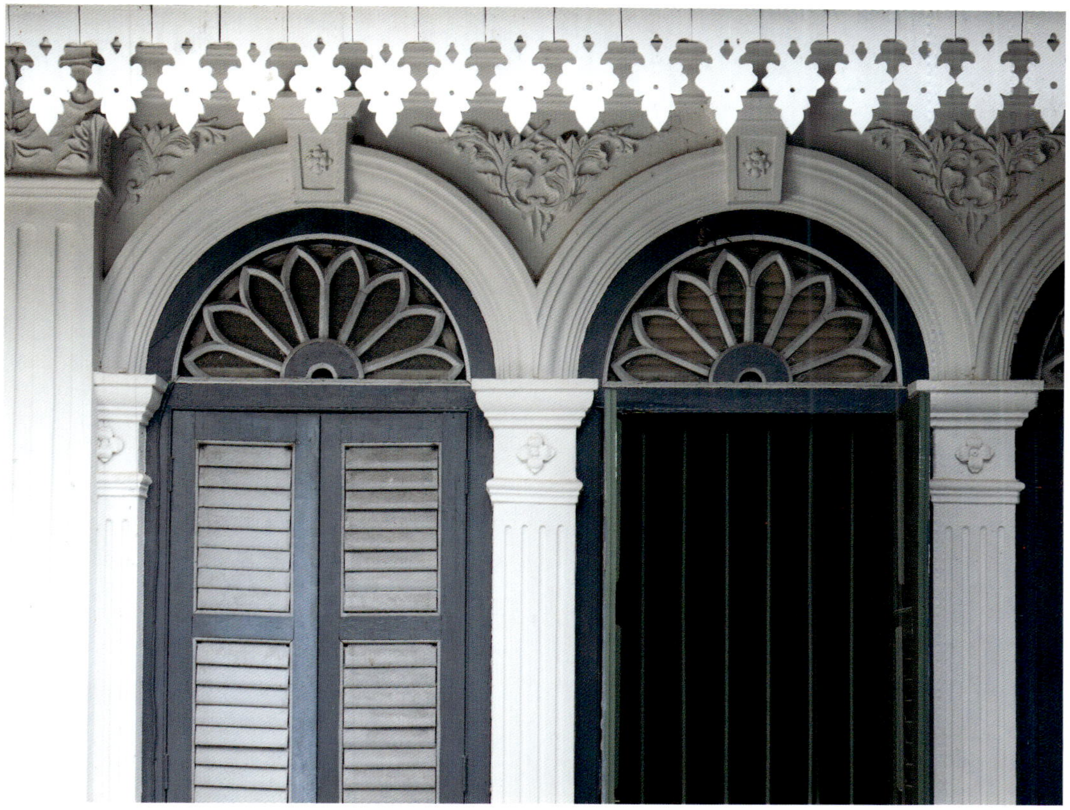

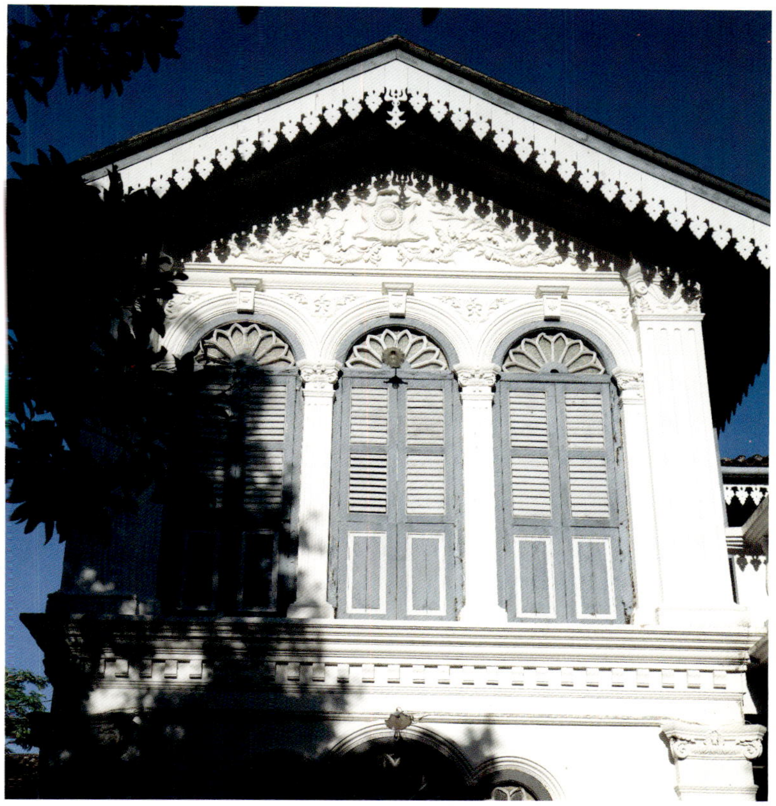

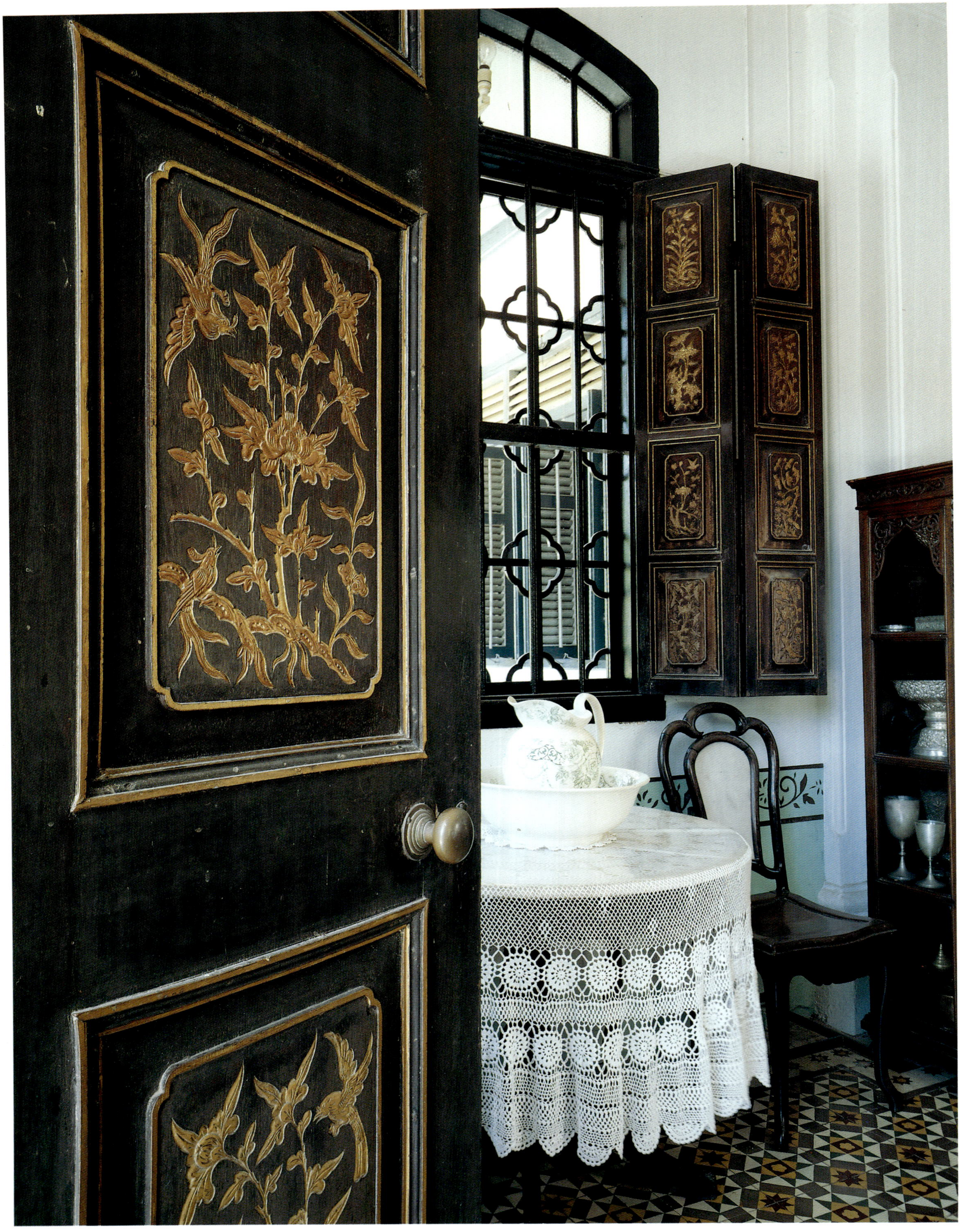

Right : *Elaborate carved wooden decorations adorn the underside of the staircase.*
Left : *Front door with Chinese decorations; the window shutters in the hallway are also carved.*

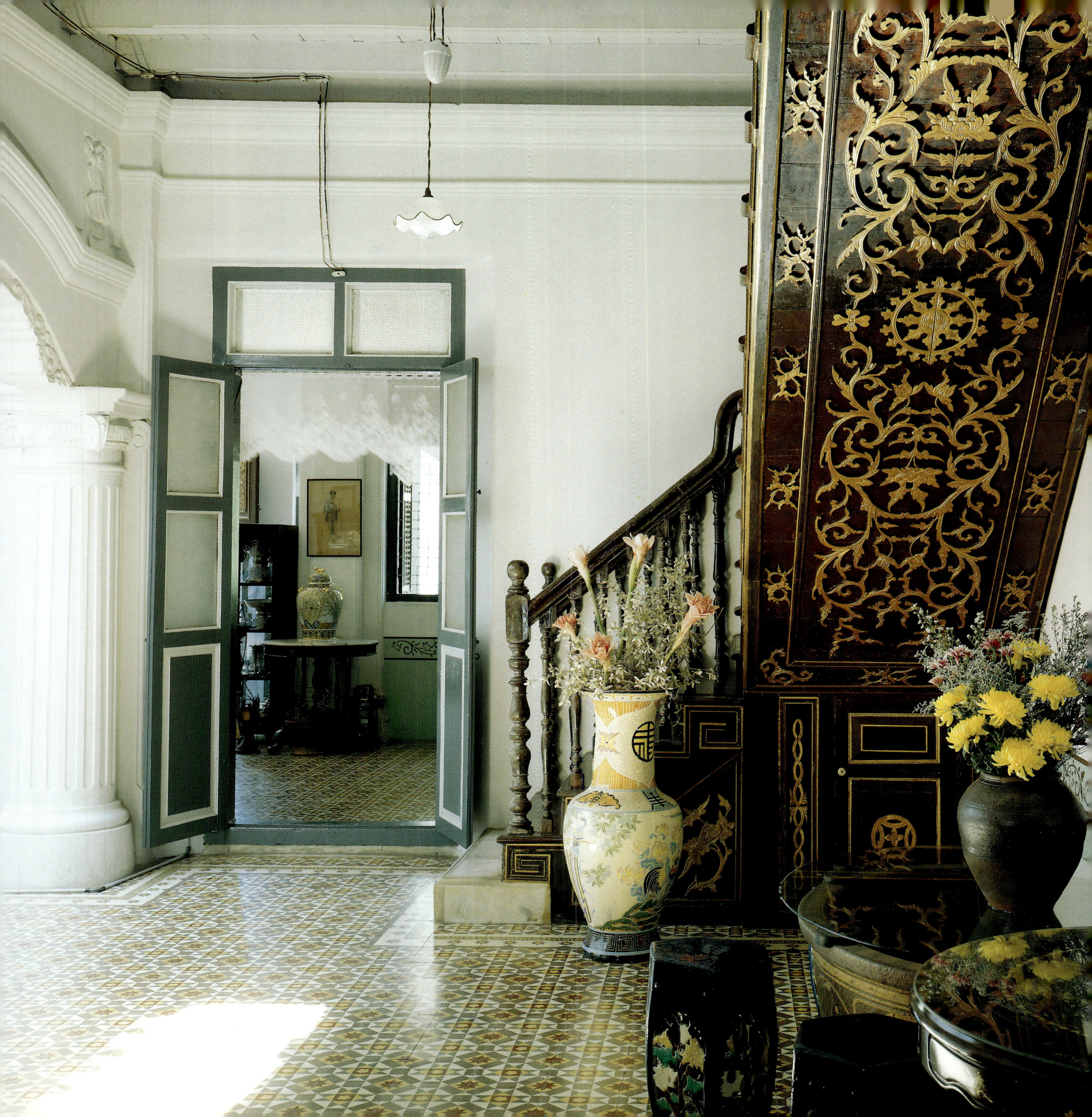

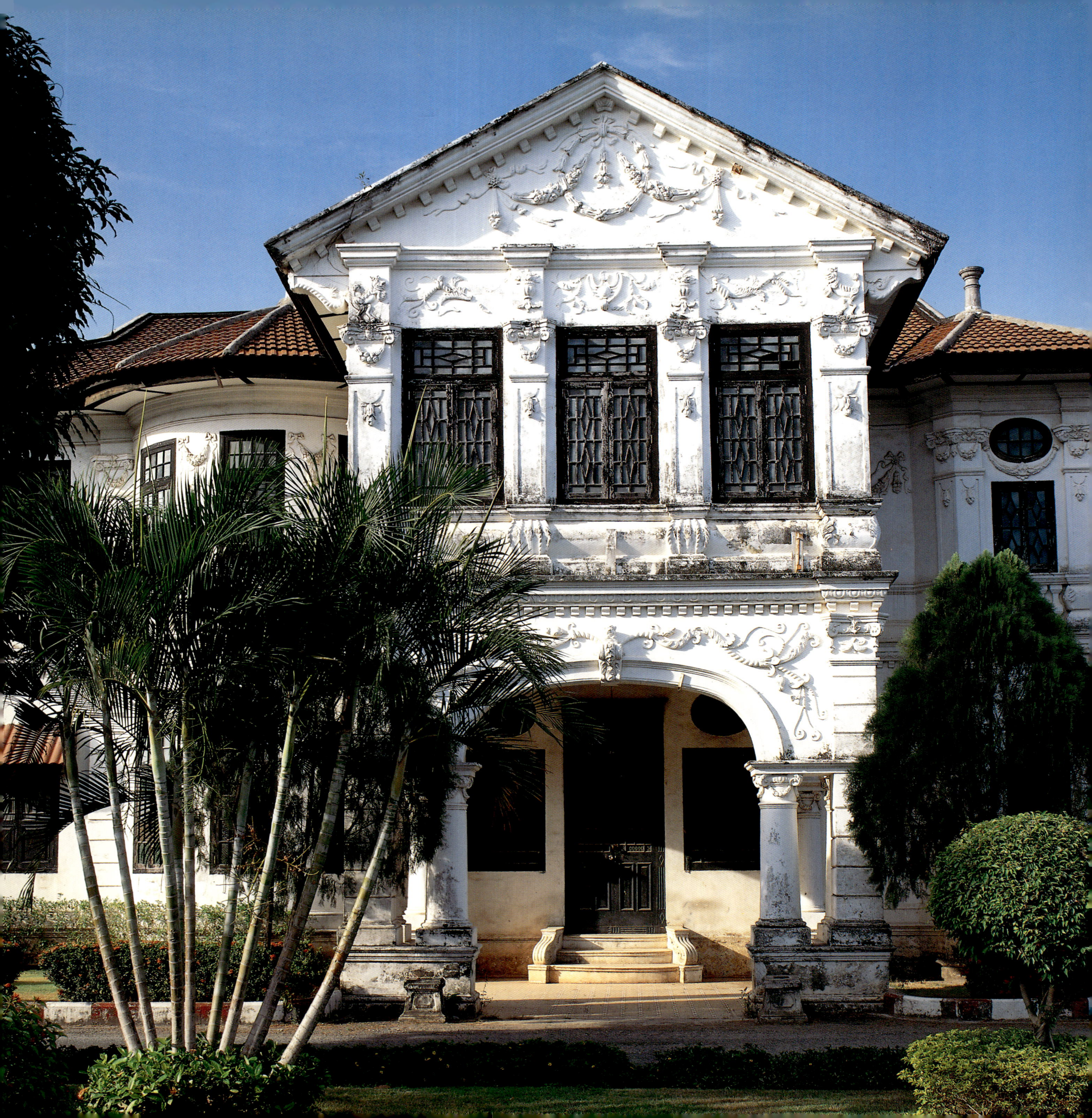

This & opposite pages : *Miscellaneous architecture in Phuket Town.*
Left : *House of Phra Aramsakornkhet, built about 80 years ago and now in the compound of Thai Airways; it has been registered with the Fine Arts Department as a National Historic Building.*
Top right : *House on Krabi Road.*
Middle right : *Detail of decorations on a shophouse.*
Bottom right : *A well-restored residence.*
Below : *The former Chartered Bank building, built during the reign of King Rama V with a colonade similar to those on buildings in Vienna.*

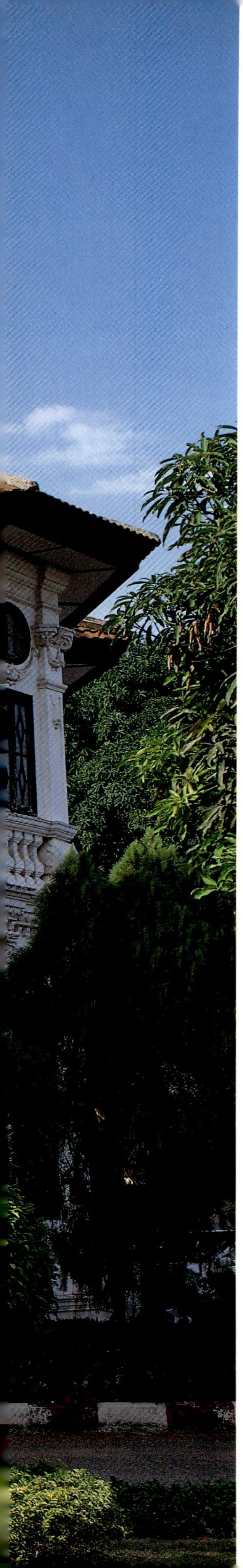

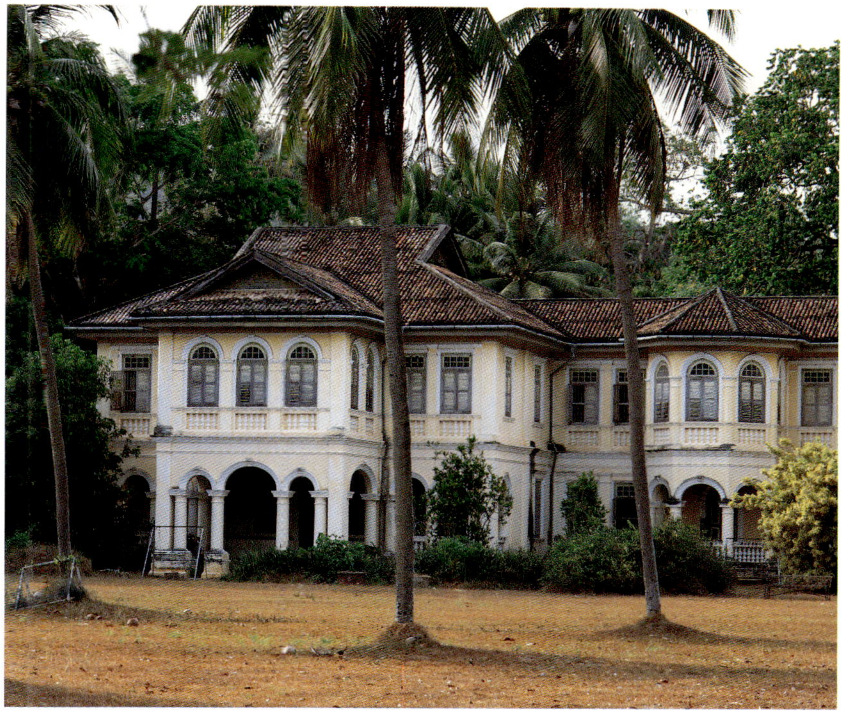

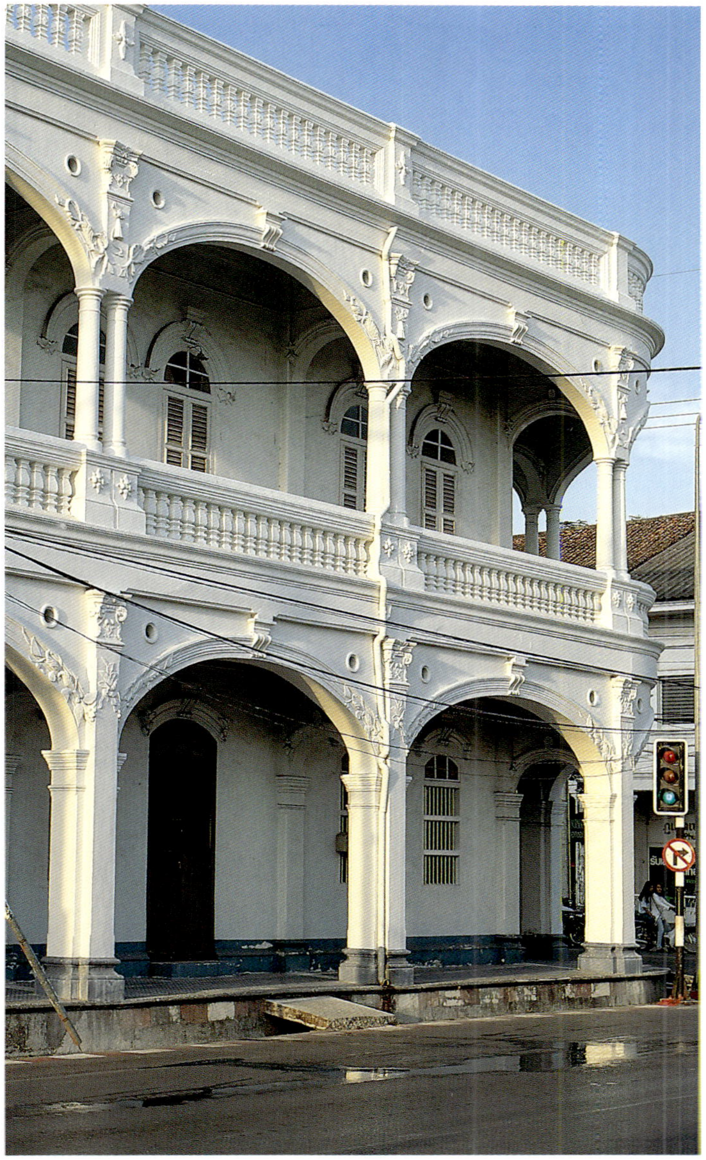

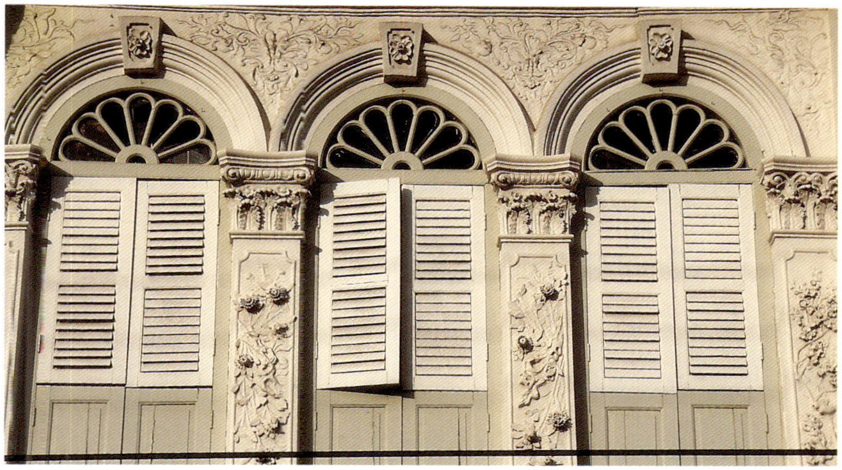

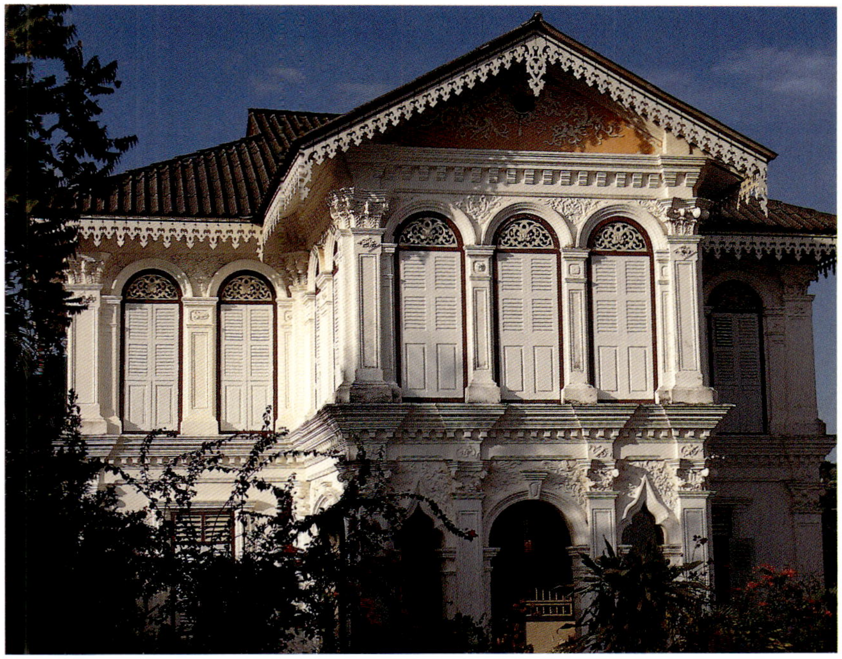

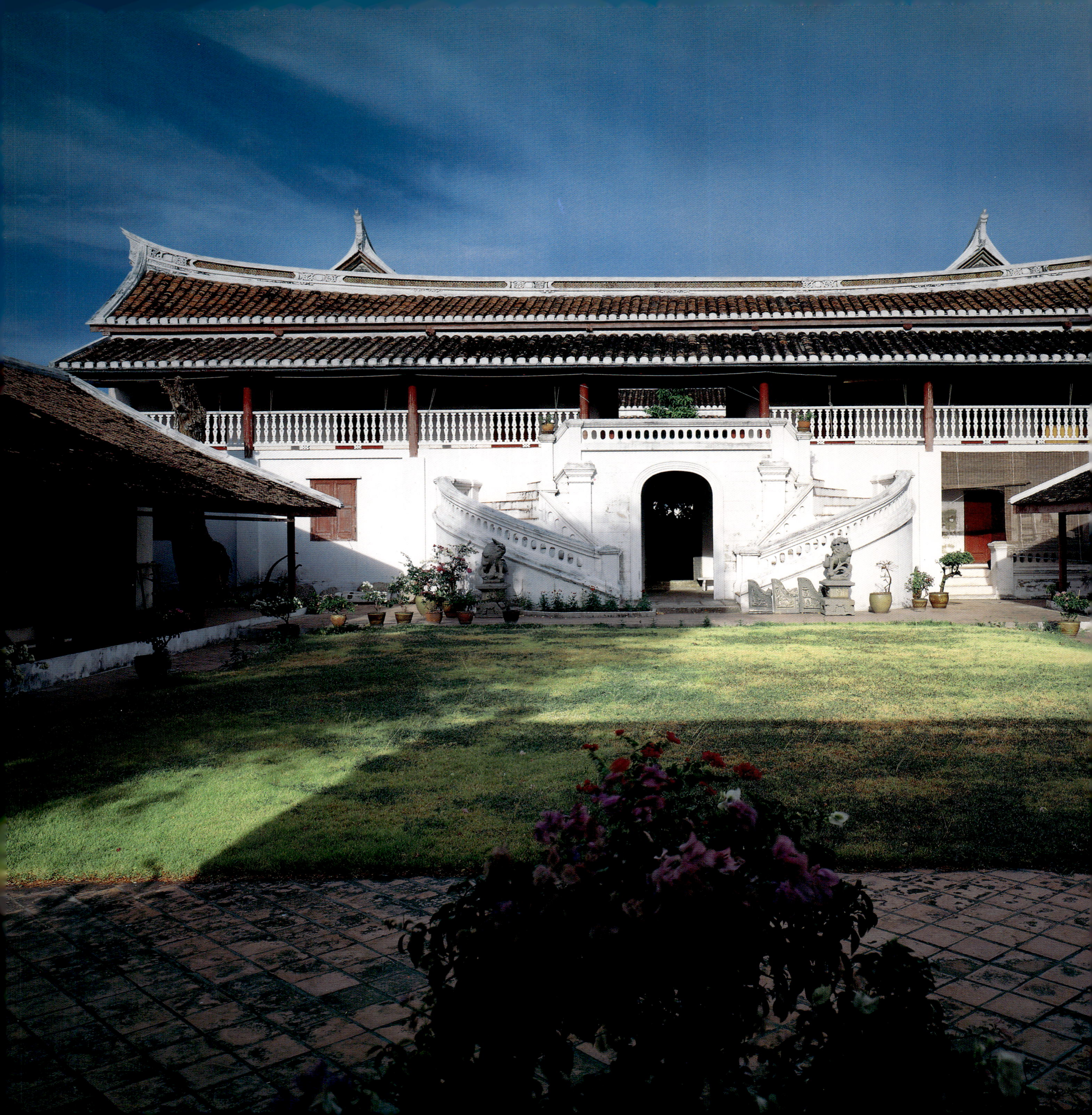

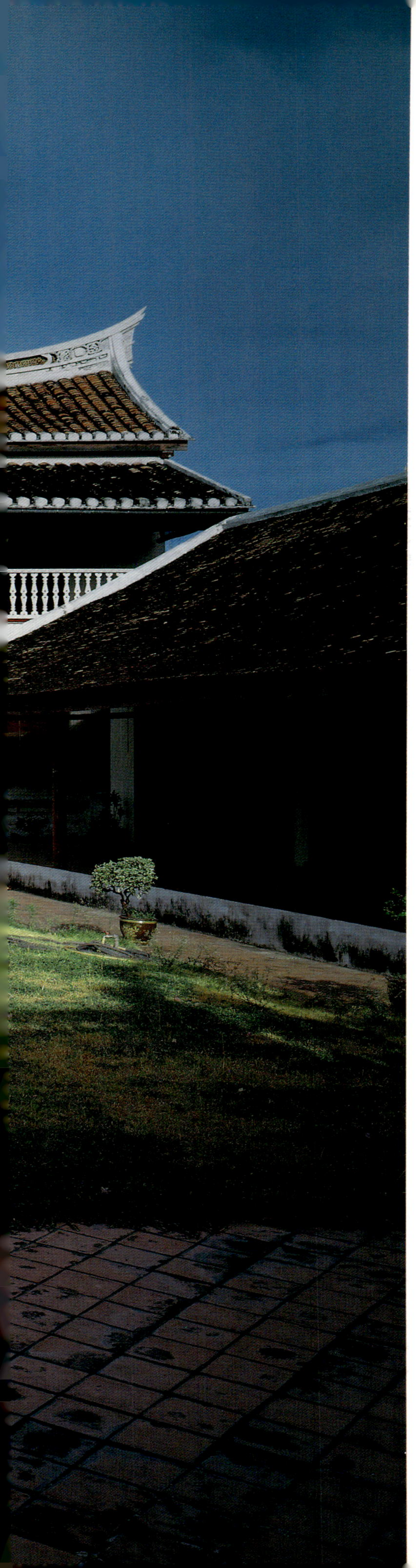

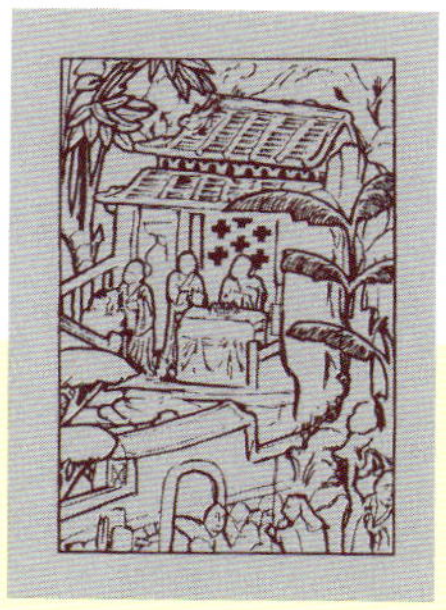

Songkhla National Museum

Now designated a National Historic Building by the Fine Arts Department, the Songkhla National Museum was built as a private residence in 1878 by Phya Sunthranuraksa (Netra na Songkhla), who for 16 years was Deputy Governor of the southern city. Songkhla was then one of the most important ports on the Gulf of Thailand, as it had been for centuries before under the name of Singhora; the Na Songkhla family played an important role in the city's history and have also been prominent in national events as well. Much of Songkhla's commercial significance declined with the rise of Hat Yai as the region's main railway junction, though as a result it also suffered less from the effects of rapid development.

The building is in an architectural style inspired partly by southern China, from which most of the early settlers came, and partly by Western adaptations as seen in Malacca and Penang. It consists of four two-story units joined around a rectangular courtyard and originally faced Songkhla's inland sea, or Thale Sap, though at present the view is blocked by more recently constructed buildings.

Phya Sunthranuraksa lived in the house for 16 years, after which from 1894 to 1896 it was used by Phra Vichitravarasasn (Chao Phya Yomaraj), Governor of Songkhla and Nakhon Si Thammarat. Later, until 1917, it served as the State Hall of Nakhon Si Thammarat Province (then a much larger administrative area than today), and from 1917-53 as the City Hall of Songkhla Province. Thereafter the building was neglected for nearly 20 years before it was registered as a National Historic Building by the Fine Arts Department and underwent extensive renovation. Today, as a branch of the National Museum, its elegant teak-beamed interior displays a large collection of Chinese porcelains, statuary, and various objects found in regional archaeological excavations.

Left : *Exterior of the Songkhla National Museum, this side once faced the inland sea.*

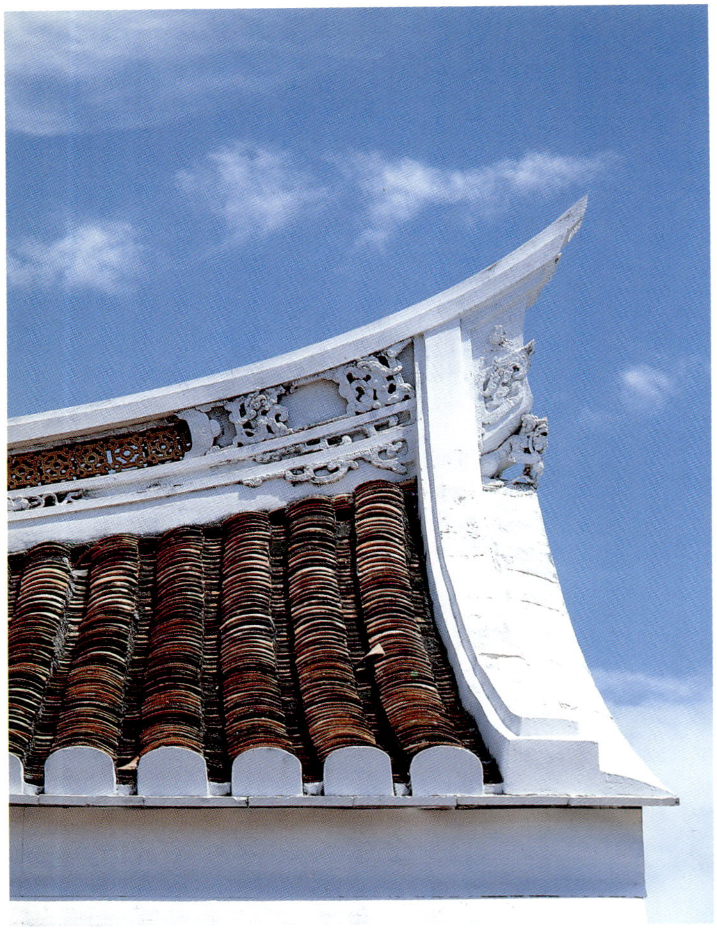

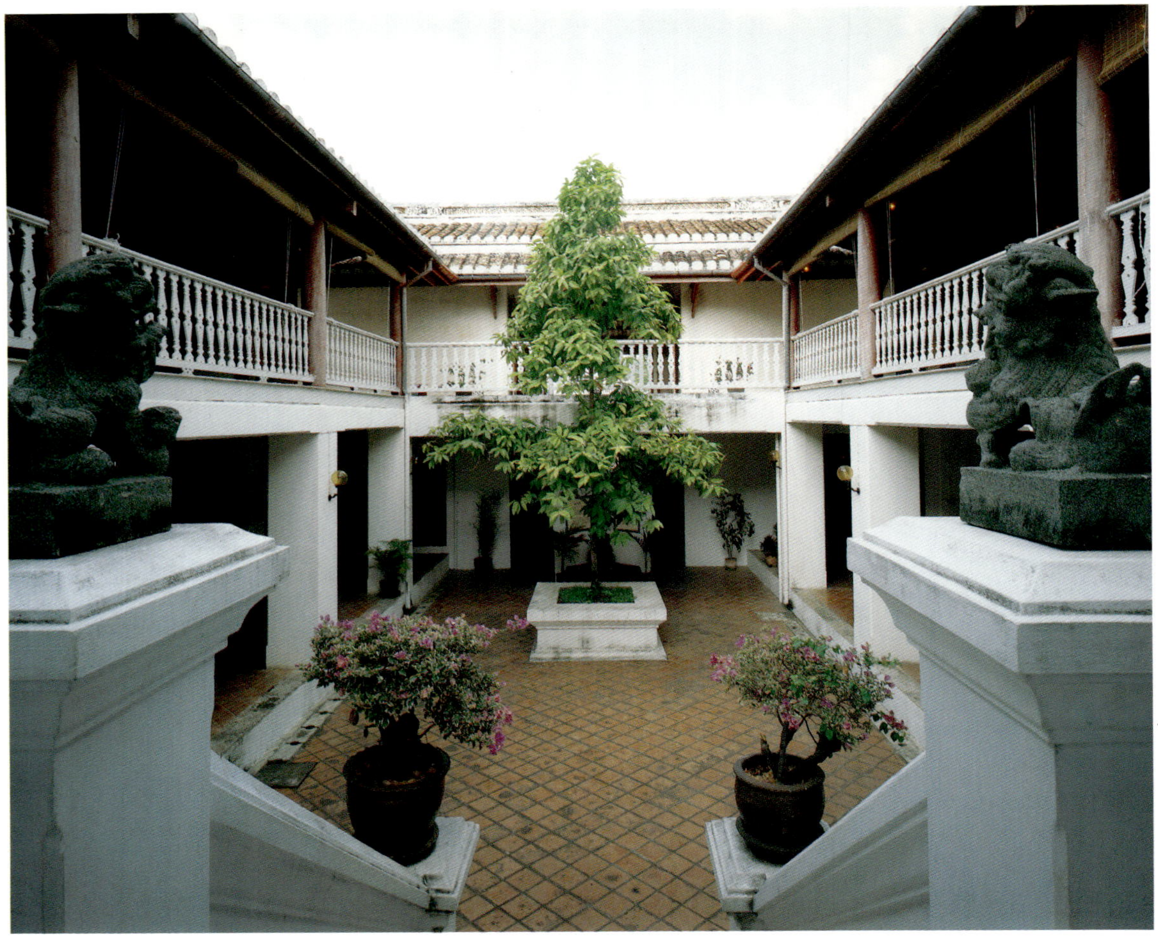

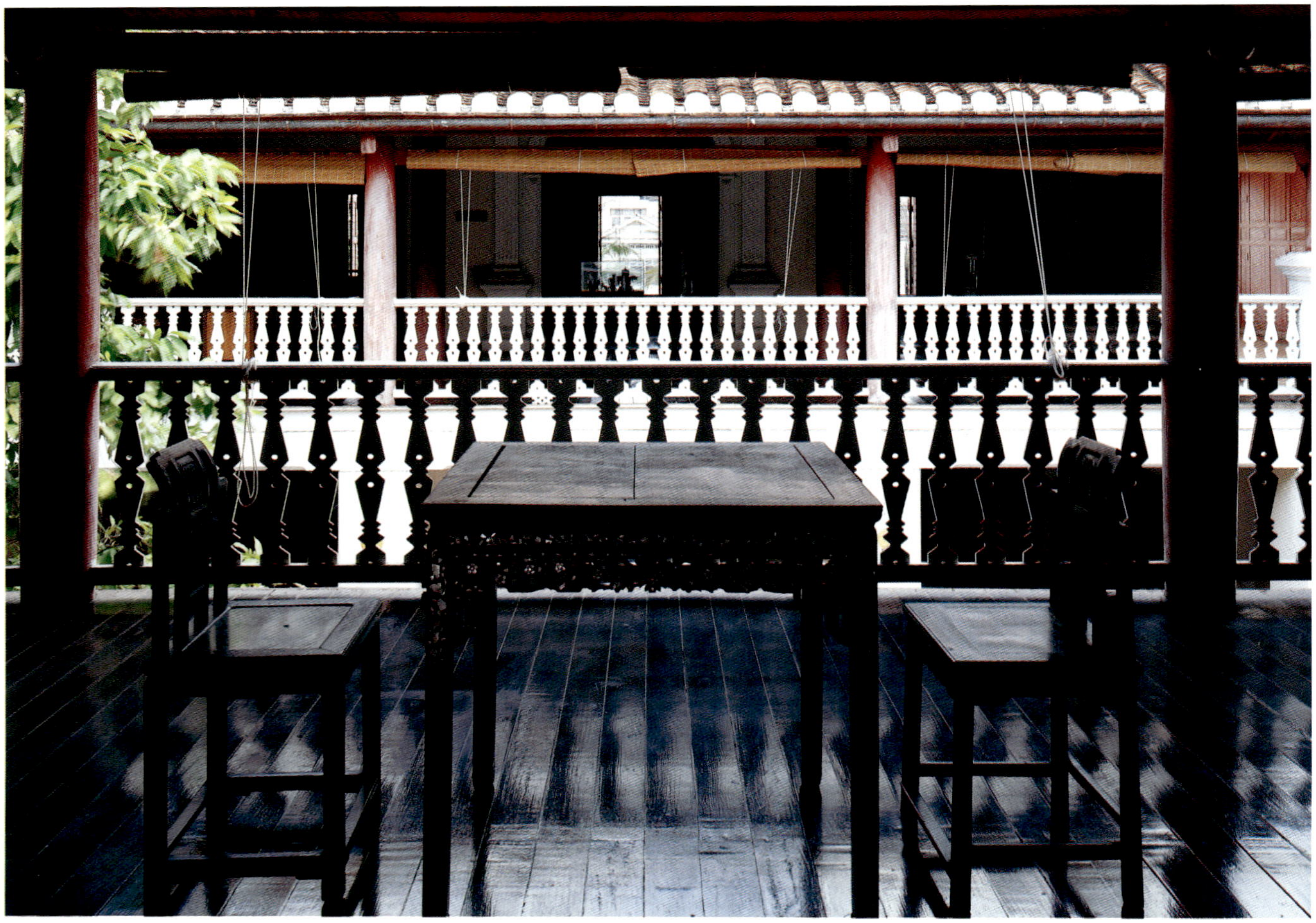

Above left : *Detail of roof decorations.*
Above : *The Chinese-style courtyard.*
Left : *Second floor verandah surrounding the courtyard.*

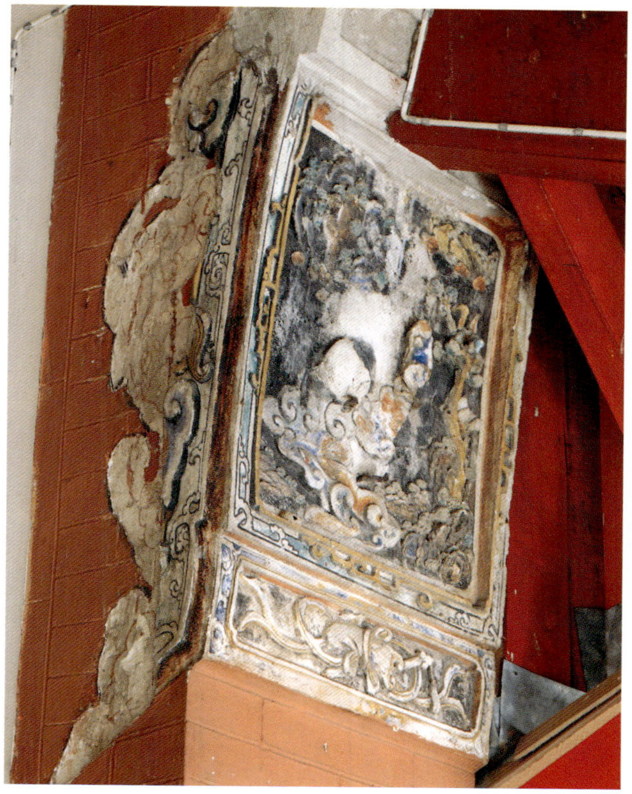

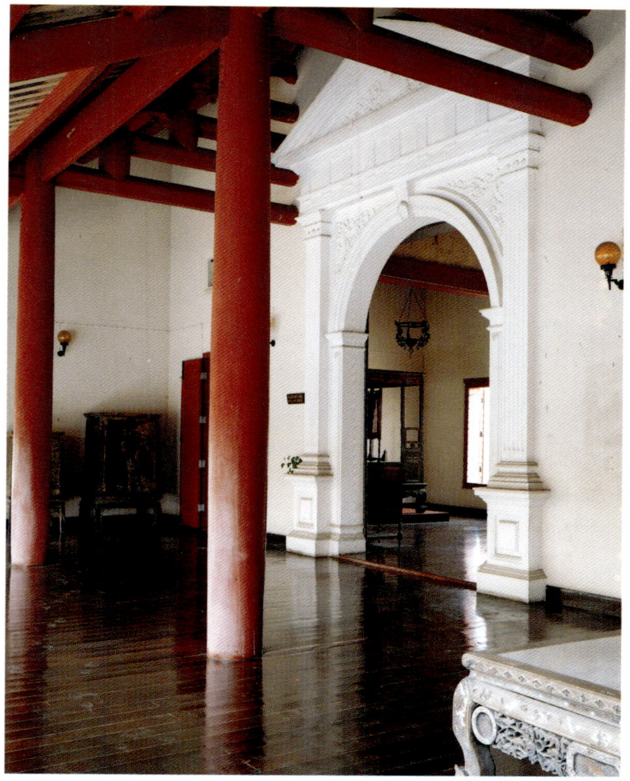

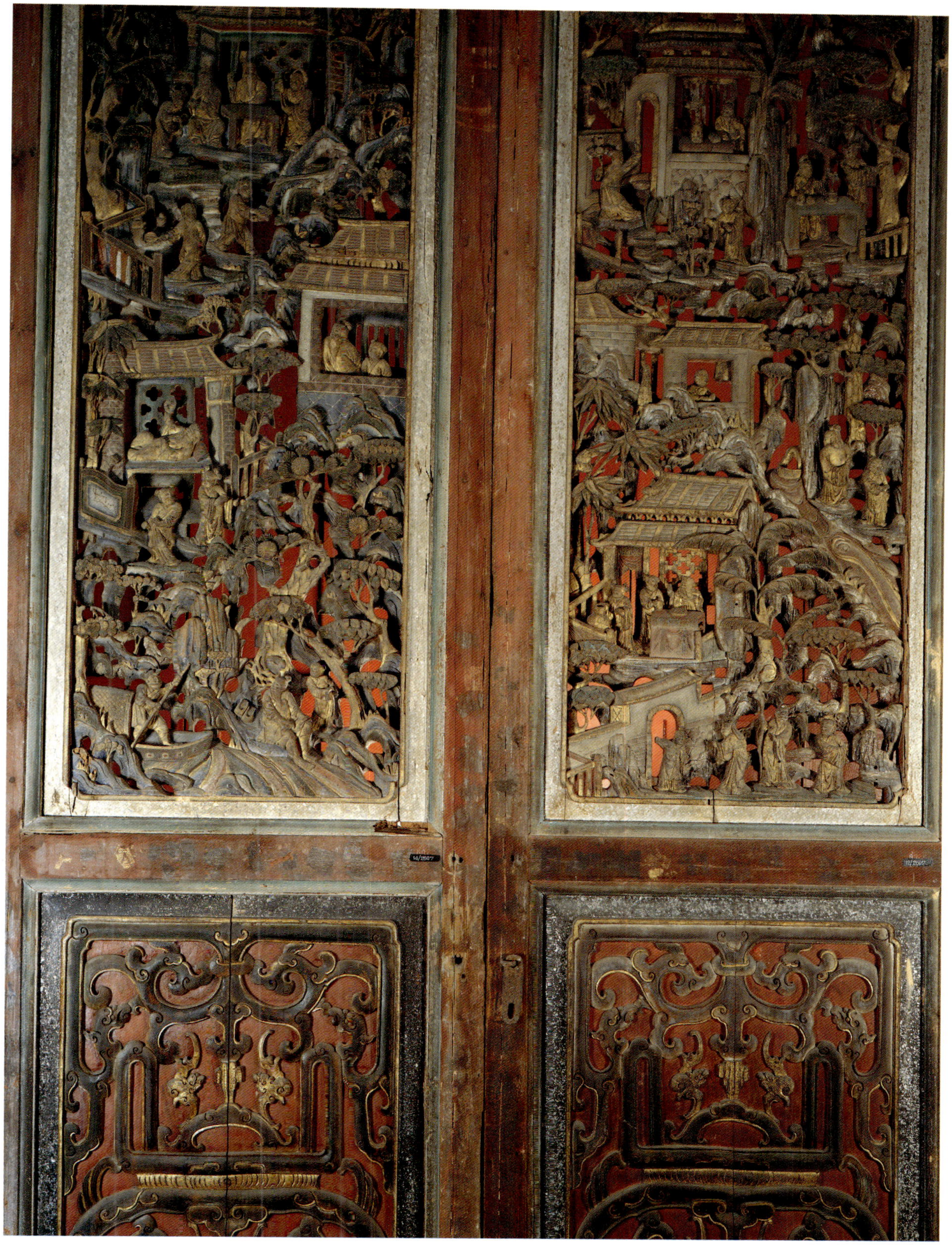

Top : *Original stucco decoration at the top of a column.*
Above : *Second floor interior, showing European styles that were probably added to the building after its original construction.*
Above right : *Detail of one of the original door panels now a display in the museum.*

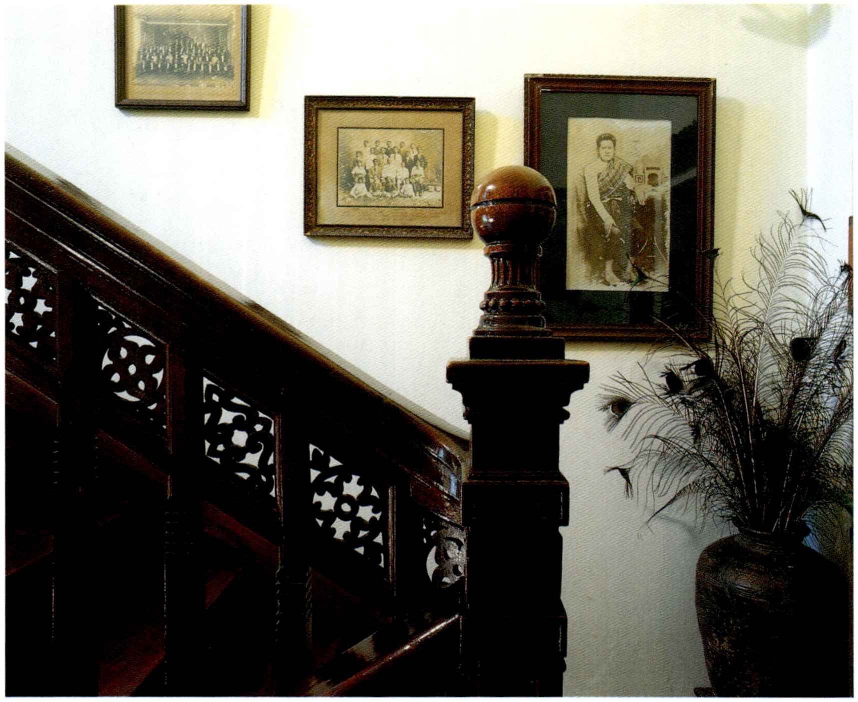

"Fragile Link"

Given the purpose of the present work, to instill an awareness of the value of Thailand's architectural heritage, it was thought fitting to offer a selection of photographs of once beautiful homes that no longer exist.

Most of these pictures were taken by Barry Broman and published in a book entitled "Old Homes of Bangkok" just over a decade ago, in 1984; it was subtitled "Fragile Link." The truth of the last phrase becomes all too apparent as one looks through the book today and discovers that several of the residences have either vanished completely or been dismantled and moved to new locations - a reminder of how fragile indeed are these links with our past.

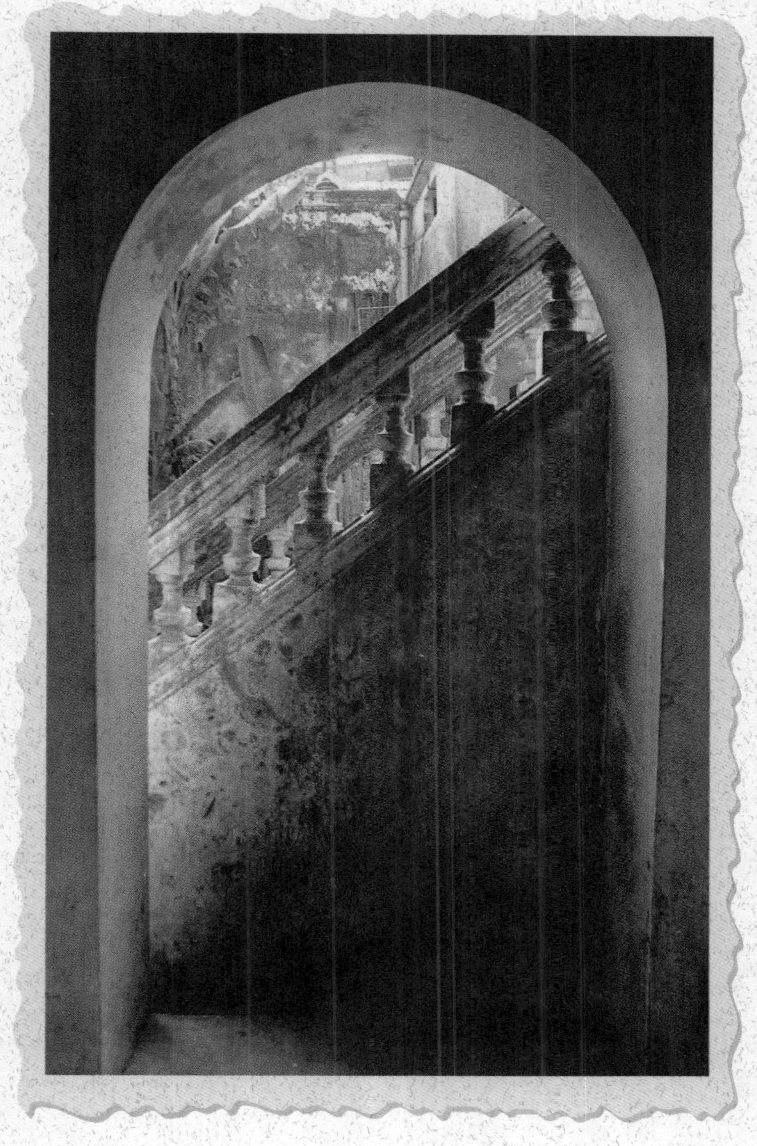

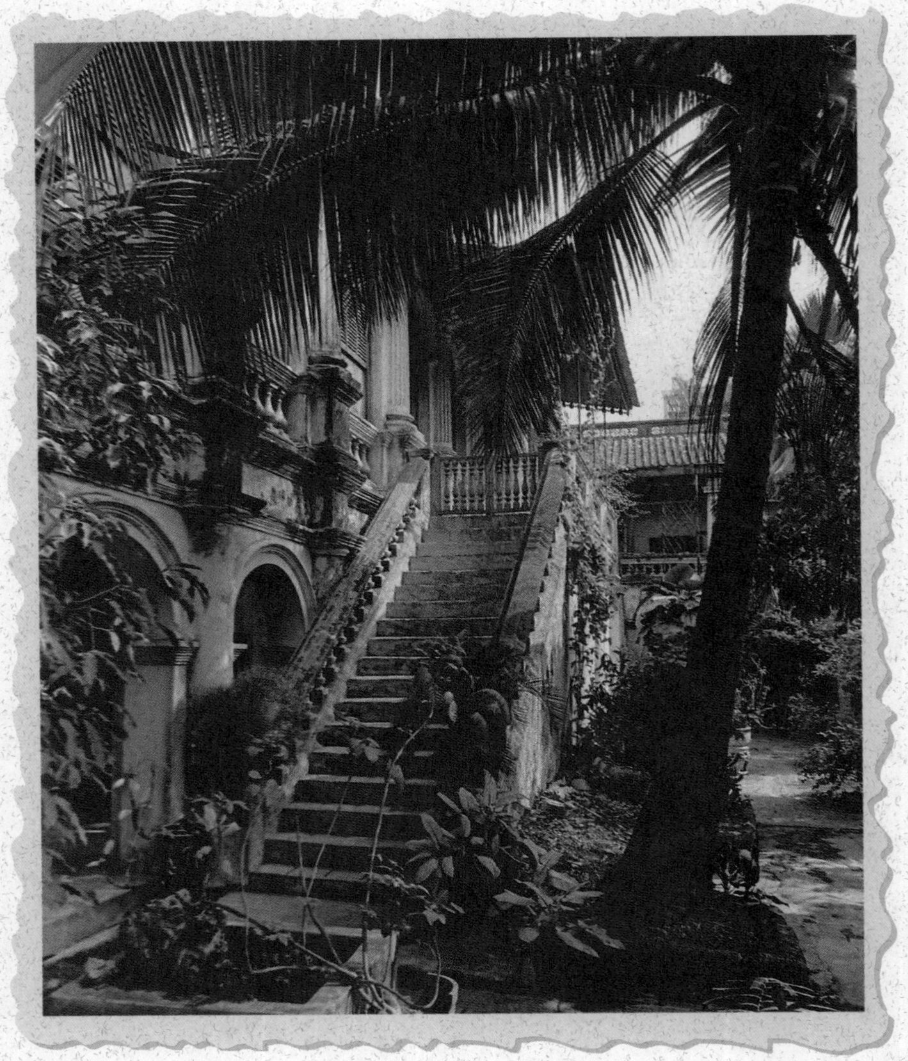

The Chinese-style house of Khun Vichai Posayachinda, formerly on Phya Krai Lane.
(Above and preceding page)

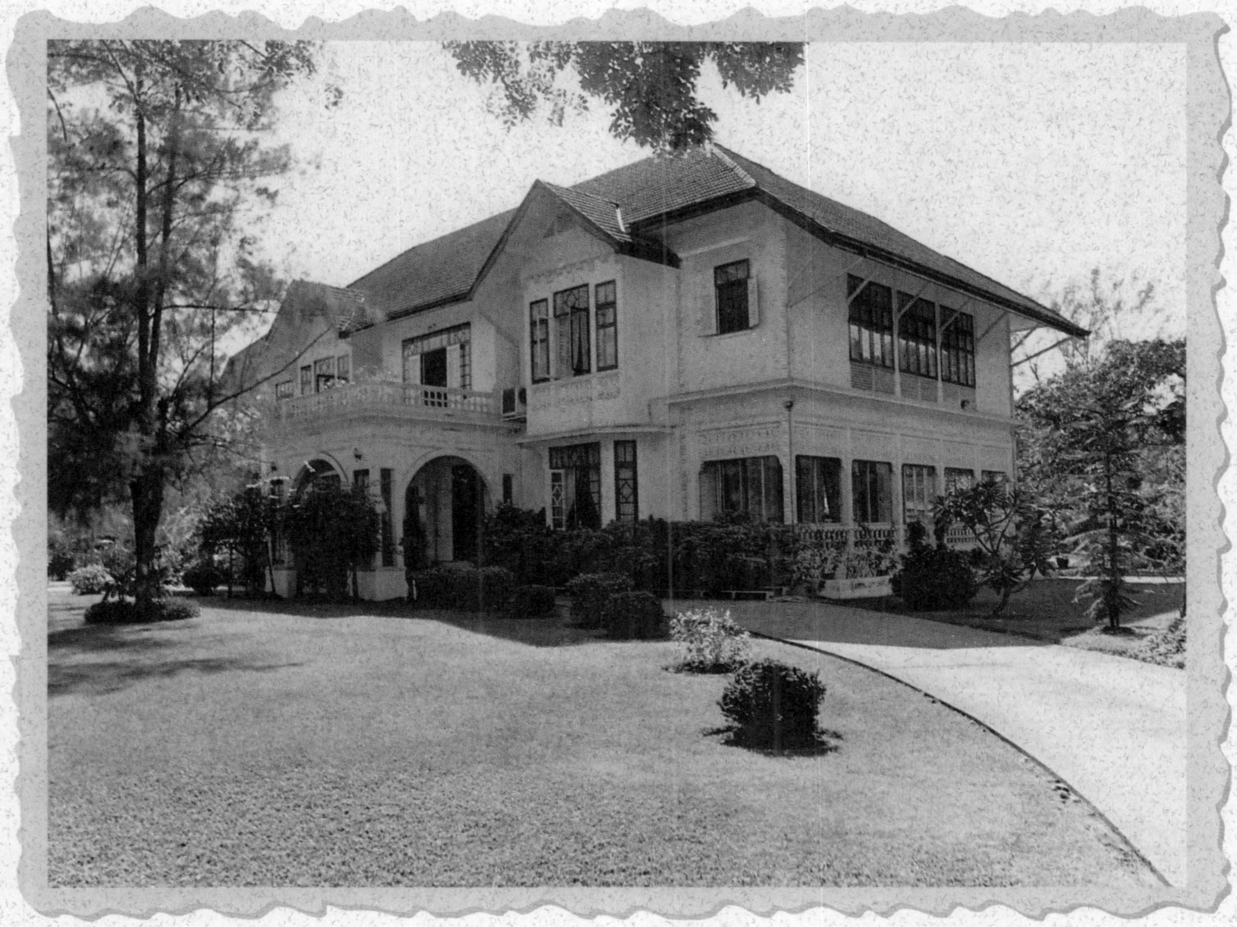

The Chartered Bank House on Wireless Road, now the site of the All Seasons Place.

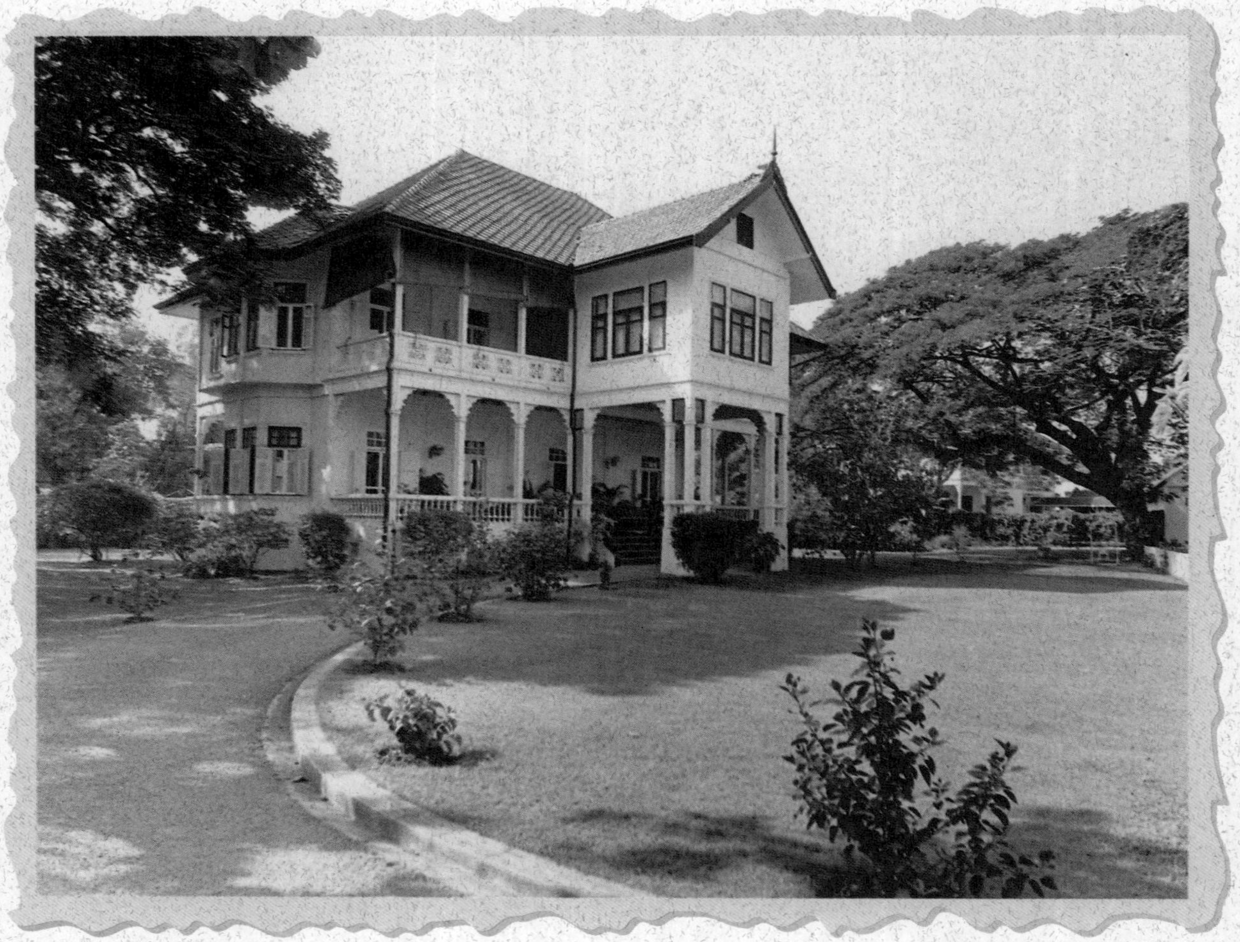

The Hong Kong and Shanghai Bank, formerly on Sathorn Road.

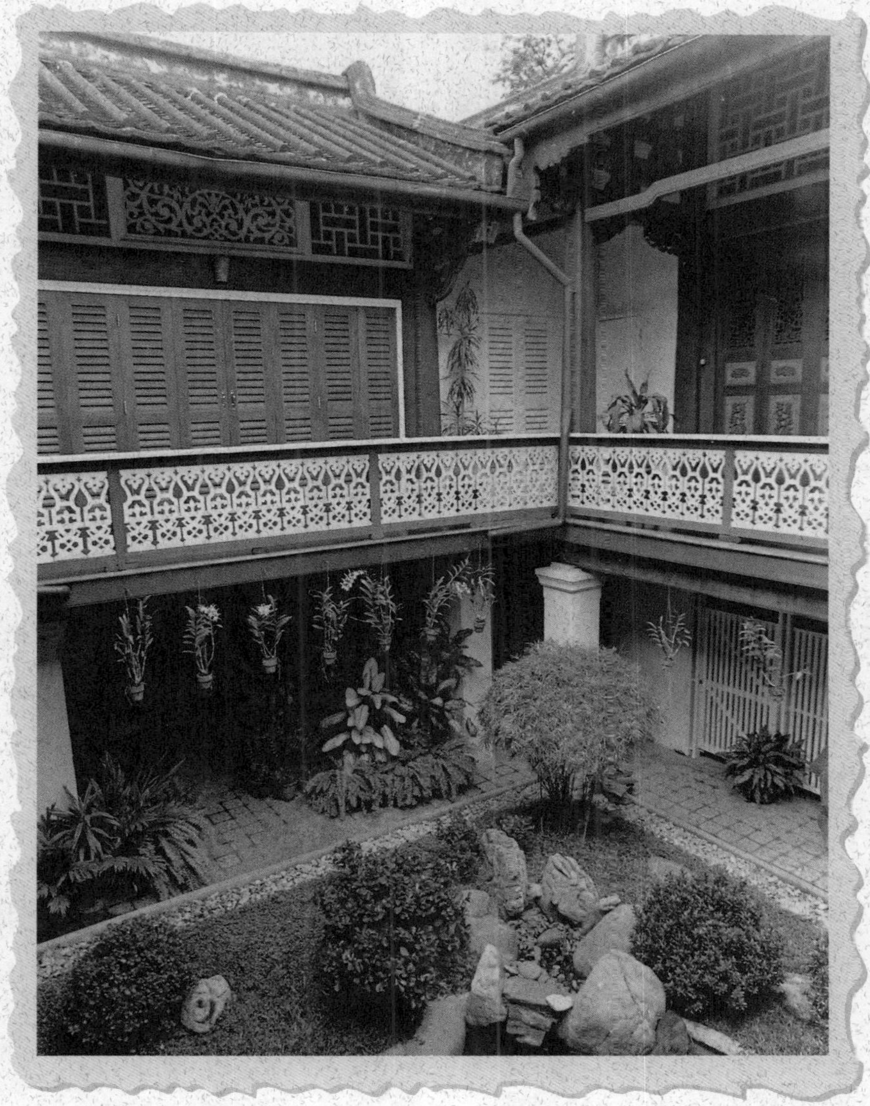

The Hok Lok Siew House, formerly on Sathorn Road.

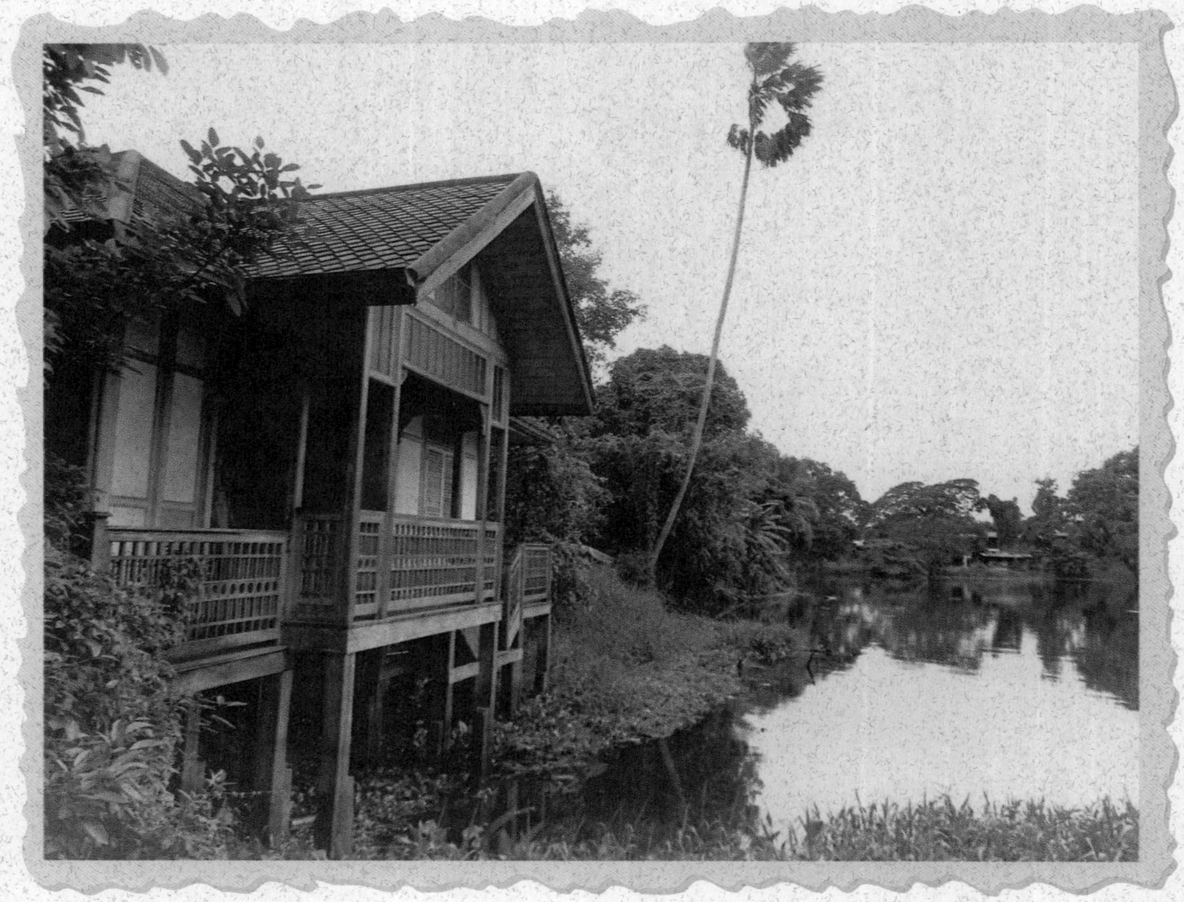

House of the Prince of Petchabun, now the site of the World Trade Centre.

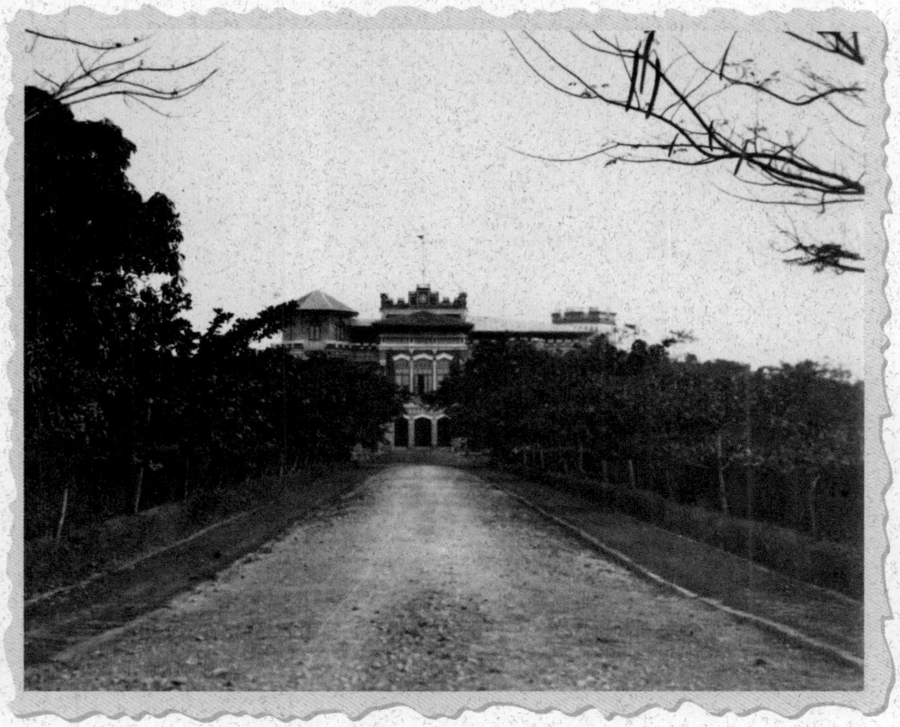

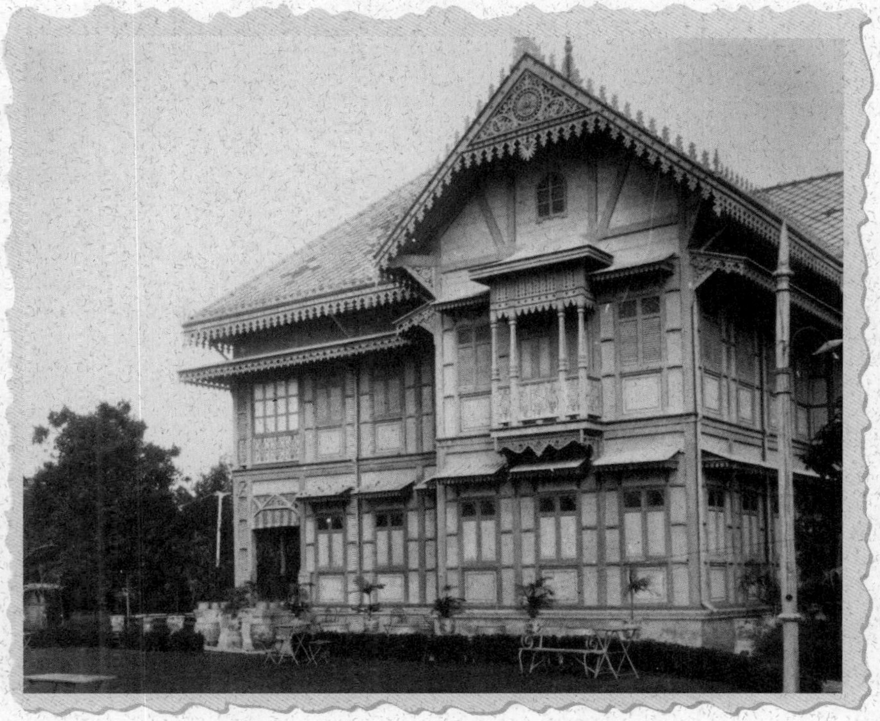

Above : *Wang Khlang Tung, built by King Rama V and inspired by Windsor Castle; now the site of the National Stadium.*
Right and above right : *European-inspired buildings on the grounds of Dusit Palace.*
(Pictures on this page supplied by the National Archives).

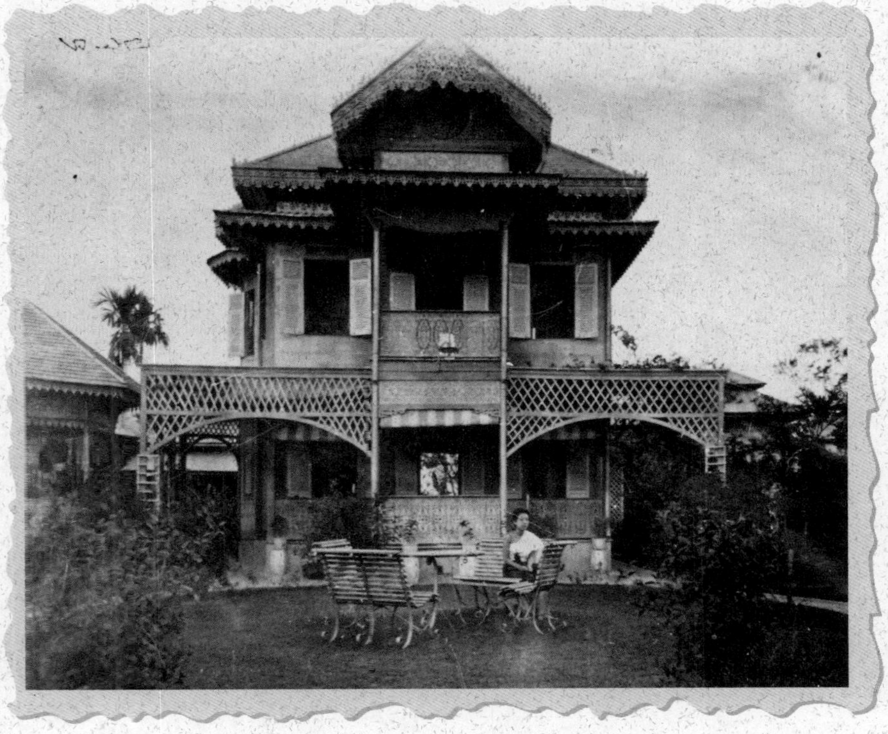

Acknowledgements

The author and photographer wish to express our gratitude to the following people and organizations for their help and cooperation without which this book would not have been possible : Khun Prachoom Abdulrahim, H.E. the British Ambassador & Mrs. Christian Adams, Dr. Piyasvasti and Khun Anik Amranand, Amway (Thailand) Ltd., The Bank of Thailand, Khun Churai Bencharit, Khun Pimpa Bencharit, M.R. Muanchit Bhirombhakdi, Mr. François Bizot , Mr. & Mrs. Ralph Boyce, M.R. Narisa Chakrabongse, H.E. the French Ambassador and Madame Gerard Coste, Mr. Jacques Deen, L'École Française d'Extrême-Orient, Dr. Louis Gabaude, Hollywood E-6, Khun Suwanee Jenpanichkarn, Mae Fah Luang Foundation, H.E. the Portuguese Ambassador & Madame Gabriel Mesquita de Brito, Khun Dechapiwat and M.L. Rojanatorn Na Songkhla, The National Economic & Social Development Board, The Oriental Hotel, Oriental Style gallery, Khun Sa-ngiem Palawatvichai, Khun Tham Phanichphan, Khun Vithi Phanichphan, Khun Boonma Phanvivattana, Ms. Pia Pierre, Khun Nakorn Pongnoi, The Royal Thai Navy, Thanpuying Lursakdi Sampatisiri, Khun Bilaibhan Sampatisiri, Khun Pongkwan Sukwattana, Khun Preecha Prakobkit, Songkhla National Museum, the Sophanodorn family in Tak, Khun Chatri Sophonpanich, Khun Chanchai & Khun Orawan Supanichvoraparch, Khun Pracha Tandavanitj, Thanpuying Petchara & Dr. Sidhi Techakampuch, Khun Boonchalerm Thipyamonton, Dr. Khanchai & Khun Watcharaporn Vongburi, Mrs. Patricia Young.

And a special thank you to Khun Boonyavan Chandrviroj, Khun Hasan Basar, Mr. Barry Broman, Khun Vimala Siripongse, Khun Duangjitt Thawisri, and the staff of The Siam Society and Siam Araya Magazine for their invaluable assistance and support.

THE SIAM SOCIETY
Under Royal Patronage

The Siam Society is Thailand's longest-established learned society. Founded in 1904 under Royal Patronage, the society is dedicated to the preservation and promotion of Thailand's cultural and artistic heritage. Membership is open to everyone who shares in these interests.

The HERITAGE HOMES of Thailand

Initiated by The Siam Society and supported by Amway (Thailand) Ltd., the objective of The Heritage Homes of Thailand program is to encourage the preservation of Thailand's secular architectural heritage through increased public awareness of the homes and their recognition as national treasures.

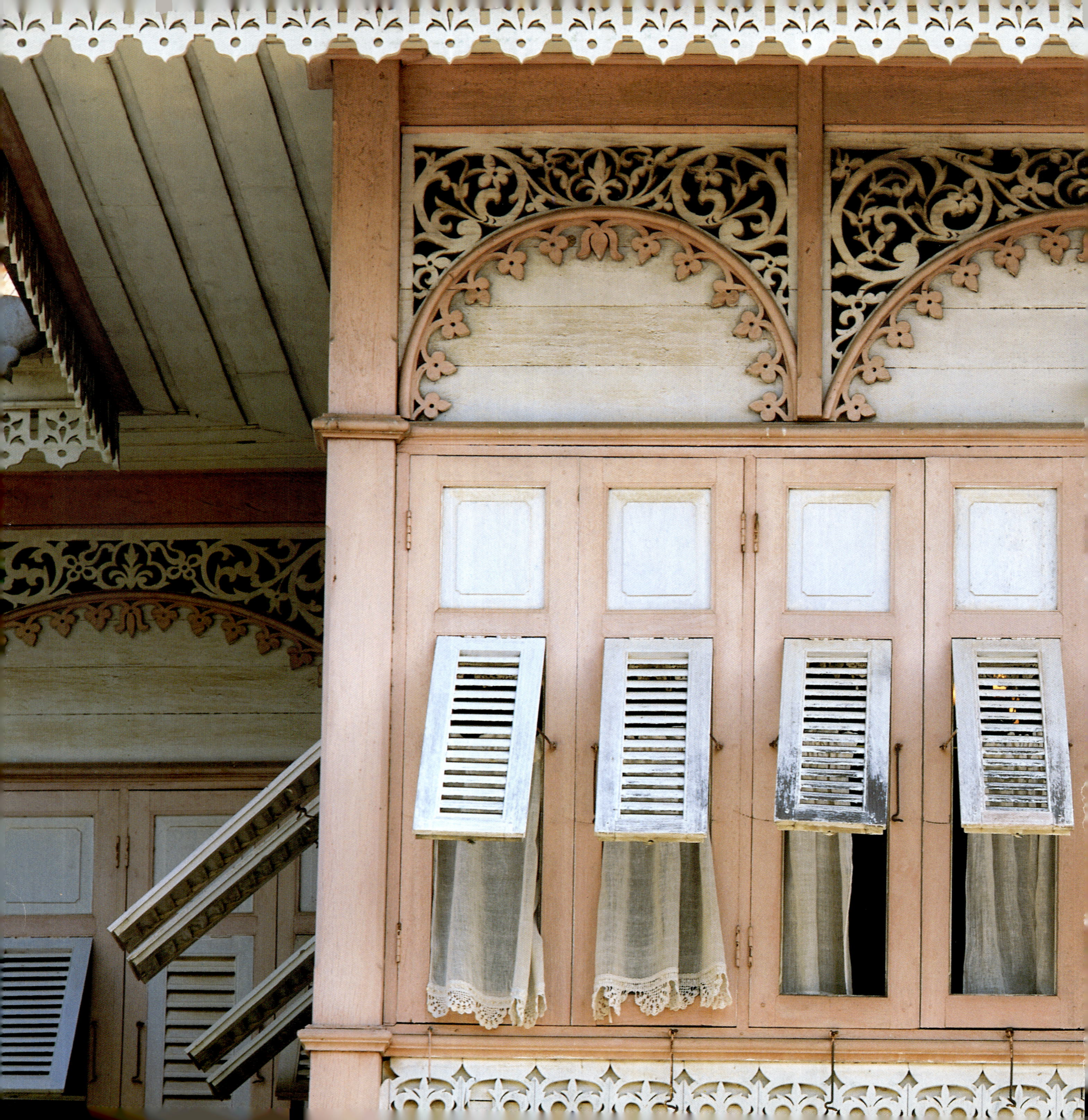